THE CONSTITUTION OF THE LEGAL RELATION

This book defends the relational approach to law.

It begins by exploring how law is constituted in the context of either rational or reasonable conduct. Having identified reasonableness as the unifying theme of natural law theories, it argues that the form and authority of law originate in the practical resolution of a moral antinomy that these theories leave unaddressed.

The reasonableness of law lies in the structure and principles of relations in which rights are correlated with obligations and powers with liabilities. Rather than descending upon us from above in the form of directives, law emerges from our interactive efforts to cope with persistent moral disagreements.

Ultimately, the relational approach views the legal rules governing our interactions as expressions of a common will. The book concludes that, unsurprisingly, modern constitutionalism represents a thoroughly pragmatic and most defensible conception of the authority of law.

The Constitution of the Legal Relation

A Pragmatist Philosophy of Law

Alexander Somek

•HART•
OXFORD • LONDON • NEW YORK • NEW DELHI • SYDNEY

HART PUBLISHING

Bloomsbury Publishing Plc

Kemp House, Chawley Park, Cumnor Hill, Oxford, OX2 9PH, UK

1385 Broadway, New York, NY 10018, USA

Bloomsbury Publishing Ireland Limited, 29 Earlsfort Terrace, Dublin 2, D02 AY28, Ireland

HART PUBLISHING, the Hart/Stag logo, BLOOMSBURY and the Diana logo are trademarks of Bloomsbury Publishing Plc

First published in Great Britain 2026

A catalogue record for this book is available from the British Library.

A catalogue record for this book is available from the Library of Congress.

ISBN: HB: 978-1-50997-922-6
ePDF: 978-1-50997-924-0
ePub: 978-1-50997-923-3

Typeset by Compuscript Ltd, Shannon

For product safety related questions contact productsafety@bloomsbury.com

To find out more about our authors and books visit www.hartpublishing.co.uk. Here you will find extracts, author information, details of forthcoming events and the option to sign up for our newsletters.

Preface

In previous works I suggested that with the demise of legal positivism the relational approach is the way forward. With this book, I am attempting to explain how the relational approach differs from natural law theory and is, indeed, the most plausible alternative to this venerable tradition. While, concededly, both natural law theory and the relational approach endorse reasonableness as the proper perspective on law, the former has uncritically concerned itself with substance at the expense of form. The relational approach is about form and the structure of correlated positions. The book attempts to demonstrate that this structure – the form of law – results from a self-critique of practical reasons. Form embodies reasonableness.

Most importantly, this structure emerges from processes of practical problem-solving and is therefore prefigured in quotidian interactions long before we encounter it embodied in full-blown legal systems. The critique of practical reason is an activity that cannot be carried out in advance as part of a theory. It is set into historical time. Structures correlating rights and duties, or powers and liabilities, are built up in the course of human problem-solving.

The emphasis on time and actual happenings explains why the relational approach rediscovers and breathes new life into themes familiar from the historical school of jurisprudence. Not by accident, this school, represented by Savigny, Puchta and Jhering, has always represented the only plausible alternative to the mind-numbing exclusivism inherent in the 'Either/Or' between legal positivism and natural law. There is an alternative.

The relational approach is not a variety of legal positivism, for it believes unwaveringly in the notorious 'necessary connection' between law and morality. It does, however, not join forces with natural law either, owing to its insistence on the relevance of sources of law and its liberal admission of facticity. While this may, at least to the uninitiated, appear like a contrived hybrid position, I wish to assure readers, that, on the contrary, legal positivism and natural law theory are misrepresentations – reifying and moralizing, respectively – of the truth articulated by the relational approach.

I would like to avail myself of this opportunity to express my debt to two philosophers who are entirely ignorant of the immense influence that their work has had on my thinking: Christine Korsgaard and Robert Brandom. While I briefly shook hands with Brandom and, as the occasion presented itself, uttered with an appropriate attitude of humility my childlike admiration, I never ever met Korsgaard in person. The clandestine one-sided relationship I have with her as her devoted student is entirely due to the influence of my dear friend Herlinde Pauer-Studer. She introduced me to Korsgaard's work several decades ago. This was eye-opening for me.

Be that as it may, what I admire about both authors is how easily they straddle the divide between Anglo-American and German philosophy. Korsgaard, possibly inadvertently and due to her circumspect attempts to make sense of Kant's moral theory, developed a philosophical theory of her own that is not by accident somewhat reminiscent of the work of Johann Gottlieb Fichte. Brandom, by contrast, quite self-consciously undertook to reenact the pilgrimage from Kant to Hegel, however, employing a vocabulary that no German scholar, not even in their wildest dreams, would have imagined of using. While I may have, invariably, gotten some of their ideas wrong, my intellectual debt to these outstanding philosophers is immeasurable.

I would like to thank the many kind people who have in one way or another contributed to making this book possible, above all Kate Whetter, Linda Goss, Sasha Jawed, Verity Steward, Rosamund Jubber and Tom Adams from Hart Publishing. I have the good fortune that Hanna Mosler has returned to working with me. The manuscript benefitted from her diligence as much as its condition was improved by Dawid Biegaj's reading of the proofs. Again, my dear wife Sabine and Vadim Arko took it upon themselves to read various draft chapters. My regular conversations with Fabio Wolkenstein had no direct impact on this work, but I consider them nonetheless indispensable for sustaining my intellectual sanity. Finally, but not lastly, I would like to mention that it was a distinct pleasure to have had the opportunity to benefit from the expertise and patience of such an experienced editor as Catherine Minahan. Repeatedly and with inexhaustible erudition, she explained 'higher points' of English grammar to me. The exchanges with her were some of the happiest moments in the gestation of the book.

Alexander Somek
Vienna, November 2025

Contents

1

Scepticism and Agreement

What This Book Is about

When Jean-Jacques Rousseau placed the general will at the centre of his legal and political philosophy,[1] he appropriated for his own project the essence of natural law.[2] Human laws ought to sweep evenly, without conferring undeserved privileges on some and shoving iniquitous burdens on others. Roughly a century before, Thomas Hobbes comforted the readers experiencing strain in remembering his 19 laws of nature by claiming that all they needed to remember was the Golden Rule: Don't do to others what you do not want to have done by others to yourself.[3] He did not, however, thereby announce breaking news for the natural law tradition. The recognition of a principle of this type had already been one if its core commitments.[4]

The law is thus taken to revolve around some understanding of reciprocity, generalisation or universalisation.[5] It accounts for its reasonableness. Possibly, this is the legacy of natural law in most condensed form. The book accepts this legacy and argues that, nonetheless, the natural law tradition is flawed. The law is not an expression of practical reason; rather, it is the enactment of its self-critique.

Practical reason is that part of our intellectual capacities that allows us to determine what we ought to do. For the purpose of these introductory

[1] See J-J Rousseau, *The Social Contract* (trans C Betts, Oxford, Oxford University Press, 1994) II.1, 63.

[2] See AM Melzer, 'Rousseau's Moral Realism: Replacing Natural Law with the General Will' (1983) 77 *American Political Science Review* 633–51. The history of the use of the concept before Rousseau is more complex and replete with theological connotations. See the magisterial study by P Riley, *The General Will before Rousseau: The Transformation of the Divine into the Civic* (Princeton, NJ, Princeton University Press, 1986).

[3] See T Hobbes, *Leviathan* (ed I Shapiro, New Haven, CT, Yale University Press, 2010) 96, 151 [79, 138].

[4] See O du Roy, 'The Golden Rule as the Law of Nature from Origen to Martin Luther' in J Neusner and B Chilton (eds), *The Golden Rule: The Ethics of Reciprocity in World Religions* (London, Continuum, 2008) 88–98.

[5] For a classical enquiry in the context of moral theory, see MG Singer, *Generalization in Ethics: An Essay on the Logic of Ethics, with Rudiments of a System of Moral Philosophy* (New York, Alfred A Knopf, 1961).

remarks, we can take it for granted that practical reason is manifest in both rationality and morality (or 'reasonableness' as it will be called in this book, echoing terminological choices made by Rawls, who in turn seems to have intended to echo Kant).[6] Rationality is about taking the means requisite for the pursuit of one's own good. Reasonableness ('morality') is about treating other persons as equally real[7] and, hence, about also taking their interests into account in the planning of our conduct just as if these were our own.

Both rationality and reasonableness, ably exercised, are the repositories of 'good' reasons and decisive for spotting reasons we are likely to dismiss as 'bad'. I am not acting rationally if I am systematically harming myself by ingesting large quantities of junk food: I had better not. I should also not feed such food to my children, for it would be bad for their health. More specifically, saving money by administering junk food to my children while reserving a diet of greater nutritional value for myself is vile, for my conduct is based on a rule that does not pass the test of universalisation. If I adopted this rule, I would attribute greater importance to my life than to the lives of my children and would, in a sense, regard mine as more real than theirs. This would be a clear instance of conduct that we consider to be unreasonable.

For reasons to be good, universalisation is a necessary condition.[8] It can happen, however, that people universalise and still end up disagreeing with each other. Some may find paying for accelerated ('fast-track') airport security checks unobjectionable. They take it to be a service offered, and services are available for booking on markets. Some others may find a privilege granted to those who can easily afford it repugnant to the principle of equality, on the grounds that no one should be able to buy his way out of burdens that should be borne equally, not least because they result from the confluence of uncoordinated behaviour. A burden brought about jointly and unintentionally ought to be carried by all.

Presumably, none of those defending these contending views claim an exception. None refuse to have the rule they support applied to

[6] See J Rawls, *Political Liberalism* (New York, Columbia University Press, 1991) 48–49, fn 1, where Rawls aligns his vocabulary with the empirical practical reason of the hypothetical imperative ('rationality') and the pure practical reason of the categorical imperative ('reasonableness').

[7] See T Nagel, *The Possibility of Altruism* (Princeton, NJ, Princeton University Press, 1970) 88.

[8] See, for example, RM Hare, *Moral Thinking: Its Method and its Point* (Oxford, Oxford University Press, 1981) 108: 'It follows from universalizability that if I now say that I ought to do a certain thing to a certain person, I am committed to the view that the very same thing ought to be done to me, were I in exactly his situation, including having the same personal characteristics and in particular the same motivational states.'

themselves. Both, if asked, would say that they have taken the interests of all affected people into account. In such a situation we are inclined to find that reasonable people may legitimately disagree over an issue. Supporting one or the other position depends very much on personal evaluative outlooks, and it does not seem very likely that opponents can be persuaded to change their minds, for it is the overall outlook that, while also facilitating individual conviction, presents the obstacle thereto. The buy-out is an innocent way of enjoying a slim advantage, and it is available to those who are willing to pay for it. Equal burden sharing is a harmless way of recognising the equal responsibility of all who create congestion by showing up simultaneously at the same place. Whether one finds one or the other preferable depends on the strength of one's liberal or egalitarian dispositions, but neither alternative must strike one as clearly mistaken.

In recognising a reasonable agreement,[9] we implicitly commit an attribution to which we have to stay committed for as long as we sustain this recognition. We attribute an equal ability to persons to arrive at some sound judgement.[10] Indeed, as Rawls' account of reasonable disagreement suggests, we concede that we might share the opinion of those with whom we disagree had we had different upbringings, experiences or biographies.[11]

[9] It is, of course, a persistent fact about reasonable disagreements that those being caught up within them may first consider the persons with whom they disagree unreasonable. Detecting the reasonable disagreement may require, therefore, a more extended process of deliberation. See C McMahon, *Reasonable Disagreement: A Theory of Political Morality* (Cambridge, Cambridge University Press, 2009) 2, 110–11, 120.

[10] Christiano arrives at this result in reverse gear. In his view, the equality of citizens is the normative reason for taking the relativity of claims to objectivity objectively for granted. As democratic citizens, we need mutually to accept that people can assert their interests only if they are allowed to put their views forward, regardless of how capable they are to judge well. See T Christiano, 'Disagreement and the justification of democracy' in S Wall (ed), *The Cambridge Companion to Liberalism* (Cambridge, Cambridge University Press, 2015) 237–60, 248.

[11] See Rawls' explanation of the 'burdens of judgment' in Rawls, n 6, 56–57. Note that Hegel recognised that such a sceptical admission involves the abdication of the privileged position of the first person. Hegel puts this point quite forcefully by saying that privileging one's insight over the insight of others would merely reverse credulity towards authority into credulity towards oneself, but credulity it would remain. See GWF Hegel, *Phänomenologie des Geistes* in *Werke in zwanzig Bänden* (ed E Moldenhauer and KM Michel, Frankfurt aM, Suhrkamp 1969–71) vol 3, 73: 'Der eigenen Überzeugung folgen ist allerdings mehr, als sich der Autorität ergeben; aber durch die Verkehrung des Dafürhaltens aus Autorität in Dafürhalten aus eigener Überzeugung ist nicht notwendig der Inhalt derselben geändert und an die Stelle des Irrtums Wahrheit getreten.' In English: 'To follow one's own conviction is, however, more than surrendering to authority; but by reversing the belief in authority into a belief in one's own conviction, the content of it is not necessarily changed and truth has not taken the place of error.' Hegel thus seems to have anticipated the problem inherent in Rorty's 'irony'. See R Rorty, *Contingency, Irony, and Solidarity* (Cambridge, Cambridge University Press, 1988) 73.

Tepid Relativism and Mighty Scepsis

Ascribing to dissenters the equal capacity of judgement imputes to them, by default, reasonableness in the sense that one does not suspect their opinions to be clouded by bias, ignorance, moral zeal, selfishness or in-group preference. The sources of reasonable agreements – what Rawls calls the 'burdens of judgment'[12] – do not 'impugn'[13] the reasonableness of those who happen to disagree.

The ordinary response growing out of this attribution is some pedestrian form of moral relativism. All are entitled to their views. Such relativism is a slovenly and timid response to the scepticism that the experience of disagreements must in fact invite in us. Rawls stole himself away from facing up to this challenge. The fact that people whom we regard as equally reasonable disagree – among themselves and with us – indicates that practical reason may not be able to deliver on the promise of objectivity that the practice of raising and defending moral claims suggests. Run-of-the-mill relativism is a convenient and affable panacea; but it shies away from asking the question whether a disagreement that is grounded in reasonable judgements does not call the objectivity of practical reason into question.

The critique of practical reason commences with sceptical anxiety. Lest we forget, the matter is dead serious. Scepticism is the view that ultimately there is nothing to underpin our beliefs.[14] It is the born enemy of – and the antidote to – the quest for foundations.[15] Sceptics think that we cannot know whether our beliefs are true.[16] The ancient Pyrrhonian sceptics,

[12] For Rawls, n 6, 56–57 they are manifest, for example, in the difficulty to assess evidence, doubts concerning the relevance of considerations to an issue, misgivings concerning the weight that these considerations are to be accorded, the indeterminacy of normative language and how our overall moral outlook is shaped by our total experience.

[13] ibid 55.

[14] Admittedly, this is a rather ancient way of stating the point of scepticism. It is different from the modern scepticism that is tenaciously haunted by the question of whether we are dreaming or in touch with a world that is real. See B Stroud, *The Significance of Philosophical Scepticism* (Oxford, Clarendon Press, 1984) 105–11. A more recent sceptical problem of this type is posed by Hilary Putnam's 'brains in a vat'. See his *Reason, Truth and History* (Cambridge, Cambridge University Press, 1981) 1–21.

[15] See DH Heidemann, *Der Begriff des Skeptizismus: Seine systematischen Formen, die pyrrhonische Skepsis und Hegels Herausforderung* (Berlin & New York, de Gruyter, 2007) 174. Foundationalism is, if anything, the quest to ground all knowledge in a hierarchically structured sequence of reasons at the end of which stands a first indubitable principle. Foundationalism can be usefully contrasted with coherentism, according to which there is no first principle but merely a network of mutually supporting considerations. See ibid 221, 231.

[16] See Heidemann, ibid 1, 8, 199. Whoever cast the justification of knowledge into doubt also doubts the possibility of any genuine knowledge.

named after Pyrrho of Elis, were extremely cautious at this point. They disavowed even any *belief* in our ignorance of the alethic status of our beliefs and merely reported to be under the impression of ignorance.[17] Any profession of belief would, in their eyes, have raised the spectre of 'dogmatism'.[18]

Sceptical challenges – from a Kantian perspective, which is quite congenial to Pyrrhonianism[19] – involve antinomies.[20] Two claims appear to be supported by good arguments, but they remain irreconcilable. In his discussion in *Critique of Pure Reason* of the claims made in the context of rational cosmology, Kant juxtaposes, within a set of four antinomies, the rationalistic quest for the unconditional with empiricist counterclaims.[21] From the rationalist's perspective, for example, the chain of natural events has to begin at some point of time, to which the empiricist rejoins that an event's not coming after another contradicts the principle of succession. From the rationalist perspective, a cause is possible that is itself not caused but rather an act of freedom, while empiricists dismiss this idea as humbug. Rationalists contend that there is a being the existence of which is necessary, while empiricists reject this claim.

According to Kant, antinomic claims not only contradict one another, but each of them is also contradictory in itself. This explains why, in his view, each advocate of one element of an antinomic pair cannot offer more than a mere 'apagogical' proof of its correctness, for all that they can do is to expose the internal contradiction of its contradictory opposite.[22] In this context, Kant not only emulates ancient Pyrrhonian scepsis in his attempt to demonstrate the *isosthenia* (equipollence) of antinomies,[23] he also, in a

[17] See K Vogt, 'Ancient Skepticism' in *Stanford Encyclopedia of Philosophy* at https://leibniz.stanford.edu/friends/members/view/skepticism-ancient/a4/, 29–30, 53–62. On the difficulty of reporting without using assertive speech, see her *Skepsis und Lebenspraxis: Das pyrrhonische Leben ohne Meinungen*, 2nd edn (Freiburg, Karl Alber Verlag, 2015) 72–86; *Belief and Truth: A Skeptic Reading of Plato* (Oxford, Oxford University Press, 2012) 140–57.

[18] See M Gabriel, *Antike und moderne Skepsis zur Einführung* (Hamburg, Junius, 2008) 74, 80–81.

[19] On the latter, see K Vogt, *Law, Reason, and the Cosmic City: Political Philosophy in the Early Stoa* (Oxford, Oxford University Press, 2008) 46–51.

[20] For a highly illuminating introduction, see P Guyer, *Knowledge, Reason, and Taste: Kant's Response to Hume* (Princeton, NJ, Princeton University Press, 2008) 23–70.

[21] See I Kant, *Critique of Pure Reason* (trans P Guyer and A Wood, Cambridge, Cambridge University Press, 1998) 530–32 (A 556–60).

[22] See O Höffe, *Kants Kritik der reinen Vernunft: Die Grundlegung der modernen Philosophie* (Munich, CH Beck, 2003) 241.

[23] See Vogt, *Belief and Truth*, n 17, 129–31. On Kant's transcendental dialectic as an application of Pyrrhonian scepticism, see M Gabriel, *Transcendental Ontology: Essays on German Idealism* (New York and London, Continuum, 2011) 5; see also PW Franks, *All or Nothing: Systematicity, Transcendental Arguments, and Skepticism in German Idealism* (Cambridge, MA, Harvard University Press, 2005) 154–55.

Pyrrhonian spirit, casts the underlying foundational ambition into doubt.[24] This is one of the most important lessons to be learned from Kant's so-called 'transcendental dialectics'.[25]

We need not dwell long on the history of philosophy. What bears emphasis, nonetheless, is that, if anything, scepticism – the 'closer look' we take at beliefs that we suspect to be immodest[26] – turns out to be the medium for the self-determination of reason.[27] If the critique of reason is to be carried out by reason itself, the most straightforward way of delivering the task consists of interrogating its potency. The project of self-examination, however, is only then brought to full fruition if the examiner, scepsis, is not exempt from her own scrutiny.[28] This final move, however, must not result in a restoration of foundationalism, but rather an altered conception of knowledge. The conflicting claims are not cancelled but merely suspended and assigned a function different from stating the truth. Truth itself is no longer supposedly vested in a foundational principle but in the relation among beliefs in which reason has instilled the propensity to claim too much than any warrant can support. Kant's recalibration of so-called transcendental ideas provides a good example for how scepticism, as it reaches out beyond itself, can assign former beliefs in foundations and grounds a different function. Unprovable truth claims can survive in more modest form, namely either as practical postulates (eg, about the immortality of the soul)[29] or as guidelines (ie 'regulative ideas')[30] that do not track actual

[24] On foundationalism, see n 15. Foundational reasoning seeks to reconstruct an inferential chain of reasons leading to a final point. The chain is supposed to be irreversibly asymmetrical. These desiderata imply that all reasons are supposed to be derivative of others. The noteworthy exception is a final ground. The chain of reasons is supposed to be asymmetrical so that, in contrast to coherentist accounts of reasonableness, the reasons do not merely amount to a set of 'mutually supportive' considerations. See Heidemann, n 15, 220–21. A reason cannot have its place, in particular, at the beginning of the chain if it appears only later as the consequence of other reasons (ibid 48–53). The derived reason must not be the same as the reason of which it is derivative (ibid 51–54). For the Pyrrhonians, such as Sextus Empiricus, the quest for foundations can never be successful and results in anxiety and the constant worry about being wrong. But any such quest is futile and does not attain the goal of *ataraxia*, the tranquility of the soul that can be compared to the stillness of the sea (see Heidemann, n 15, 29–30). The practical scepticism of the Pyrrhonians aspired to living an unopinionated life – actually, abstaining from having any opinions – that involved only moderate suffering (see ibid 33, 109). See also Vogt, 'Ancient Skepticism' n 17, 32.

[25] See Kant, n 21, 673–74 (B 825–27).

[26] See Gabriel, n 18, 12, 55.

[27] See R Pippin, *Hegel's Idealism: The Satisfactions of Self-Consciousness* (Cambridge, Cambridge University Press, 1989) 94–95.

[28] Unsurprisingly, it was Hegel who emphasised this idea. See Hegel, n 11, 72. Heidemann, n 15, 200.

[29] See Kant, n 21, 414, 673 (A 349–50, A 798).

[30] See ibid 522, 590 (B 544–45, 670–71).

facts but are nonetheless indispensable for conducting research (eg, the idea that the world is a systematically organised whole).[31] The sceptical self-determination of reason does not simply destroy convictions. It suspends them and rearticulates them in a non-constative mood (eg, subjunctive rather than indicative, prescriptive rather than descriptive).[32]

The Antinomy of Morality

While the section on dialectics in Kant's *Critique of Practical Reason* is unexciting from our perspective,[33] what should interest us is the relevance of Kant's findings in the first critique to the schizophrenia inherent in sustaining and suspending belief in the face of reasonable disagreements. They also seem to confront us with an antinomy. The dissenters, not unlike the advocates of antinomic positions, purport to know more than they should and fail to convince their opponents. They assert what they believe to be right. But if they attribute to their opponents equal judgement capability and do not believe them to be mistaken on the facts, the views of these others cannot be wrong either. The question must arise, hence, how the respect owed to another person's judgement can be sustained without allowing it to be fully transitive and to invest that judgement with moral objectivity. Were this the case, there would be no discharge from the antinomy.

Equal judgement capacity is the vehicle originally supposed to carry persuasion. Only if we possess equal judgement are we not just contingently or accidentally but independently of one another and, should the matter be truth-apt, necessarily persuaded of the same. Should we, albeit convinced of the veracity of our own judgement, fail to persuade others, we can attribute this failure either to a potentially still undetected weakness in our view or to their lack of education, ill-will, bias or any other factor impinging

[31] See ibid 525–28 (B 546–51).

[32] See H Vaihinger, *Die Philosophie des Als Ob: System der theoretischen, praktischen und religiösen Fiktionen der Menschheit auf Grund eines idealistischen Positivismus*, 9th edn (Leipzig, Felix Meiner, 1927) 620–21, who championed this idea.

[33] Since the *Critique of Practical Reason* is not about the conditions that make knowledge possible, it would only have space for moral scepticism. But the problem does not arise, since Kant regards the categorical imperative as a fact of reason. The antinomy discussed by Kant concerns the problem of motivation, namely the question whether happiness is the motive for being virtuous or virtue the effective cause of happiness. Kant resolves the antinomy in favour of the latter. See I Kant, *Kritik der praktischen Vernunft* (ed HD Brandt and H Klemme, Hamburg, Meiner, 2003) 153–54 (A 204–05). For a commentary, see O Höffe, *Kants Kritik der praktischen Vernunft: Eine Philosophie der Freiheit* (Munich, Beck, 2012) 168–70.

temporarily or permanently on their judgement.[34] If we resort to grounds of the latter kind to explain a disagreement, we can, however, no longer speak of a *reasonable* disagreement. Only if we concede that unavoidable factors – Rawls' 'burdens of judgment'[35] – explain the divergence, can the attribution of equal judgement capacity be sustained. But since the substantive reasons underpinning a judgement are affected by these factors, they have to be held in abeyance. Metaphorically stated, the reasons do not travel along the road of persuasion.[36]

Sceptical Solutions

The antinomy of morality is manifest in the obligation to respect as true the wrong judgements of others. It consists of a conflict between the substantive and the social dimension of moral judgement. The first exclaims 'no', while the second replies 'yes'. Indeed, the difference between these dimensions would not be thrown into relief if it were not for demands pulling in opposite directions.

The simple sceptical solution[37] to the problem is to suspend judgement *tout court*. We simply do not know who or what is right. Objectivity drops

[34] On 'reasonableness-as-competence', see McMahon, n 9, 38–39, 41, 82. See also C McMahon, *Reasonableness and Fairness: A Historical Theory* (Cambridge, Cambridge University Press, 2016) 136–42.

[35] One of these factors sweeps particularly broadly. According to Rawls, n 6, 56–57, how 'we assess evidence and weigh moral and political values is shaped by our total experience, our whole course of life up to now'. To which Rawls adds (ibid 57) 'and our total experiences must always differ'. This is a very bold claim, which is buttressed, in Rawls' case, by a sociological observation. A modern society is marked by a great variety of positions and offices that are occupied by people of different ethnic and cultural backgrounds. It is to be expected, hence, that the experiences of citizens are at variance with each other enough to give rise to divergent judgements. This sociological explanation seems insufficient to account for the synthesising force of 'total experience'. McMahon attempts to draw out its meaning by translating the 'difference of total experience' with the 'difference in judgment history'. See McMahon, n 9, 78, 81. But this explication equally leaves open what the synthesising force might be. It does not pinpoint what it is that puts a sequence of judgements together in order to give rise to a particular individual's view. The 'total experience' that gives rise to disagreement is not any of these particular factors mentioned by Rawls, but rather what makes them come together. Their confluence requires a synthesising moment, namely, a reasoner whose thoughts are moving in a certain direction. See IH Fichte, *Die Idee der Persönlichkeit und der individuellen Fortdauer*, 2nd edn (Leipzig, Dyk'sche Buchhandlung, 1855) 101: 'Die Persönlichkeit als das in sich verschlossene Selbst, ist die geheimnisvolle, dem Anderen unergründliche.' In English: 'The personality as the self enclosed in itself, is the mysterious one, unfathomable to the other.' Reason is possible only if it is embodied in individuals. This embodiment is the source of its struggle with disunity.

[36] Evidently, regarding an agreement as reasonable or unreasonable depends on a meta-judgement. This need not detain us here.

[37] On the notion of a 'sceptical solution' that begins by conceding that the sceptic's negative assertions are unanswerable and adds that the ordinary practice in question does not require the type of justification the sceptic has demonstrated to be untenable, see SA Kripke, *Wittgenstein on Rules and Privat Language: An Elementary Exposition* (Cambridge, MA, Harvard University Press, 1982) 66.

out of the picture. But it would be difficult to make sense of the world of action if it did not include a shared commitment to normative standards. There would be too many instances in which we lacked rules and capacities for cooperation.[38] The simple solution hence turns out to be unconvincing, for it fails to account for reason-based practices.

A sceptical solution that, by contrast, savours its own tartness suggests that we stay together and part company at the same time. We sever our connection by no longer extending the substantive debate, without deprecating its seriousness, and cease to regard each other, as far as the issue is concerned, as interlocutors. All the same, we stay together by yielding to the determinations made by someone in whom we invest authority.

That the institution of authority is apt to resolve the antinomy is indicated by the antinomy itself (see 'The Antinomy of Morality' above). Authoritative directives are binding even if we regard them as wrong. The root of bindingness, however, cannot be tantamount to moral objectivity, for otherwise the antinomy would persist. Substance no longer matters. Authoritative determinations are rendered as choices. Their relevance shows that cooperation bases itself on an agreement to disagree. Choices are reasons for a practical reason moderated by self-critique. They are reasons detaching themselves from their substance.[39]

The truly sceptical resolution of the antinomy reverses the thrust of moral arguments. The original idea is that good reasons constrain people to agree without their being coerced thereto.[40] The persuasive force acts from the substantive towards the social dimension of judgement. Good reasons motivate an agreement.[41] By contrast, the self-critique of practical reason shifts to giving priority to the social dimension (see Figure 1.1).[42] It transmutes substantive reasons into choices and anchors their relevance in an

[38] On the 'circumstances of politics', see J Waldron, *Law and Disagreement* (Oxford, Oxford University Press, 1999) 101, 160.

[39] It is important to note the relational element inherent in this detachment. It reflects a second-personal perspective on the first person making the choice.

[40] See J Habermas, 'Was heißt Universalpragmatik?' in K-O Apel (ed), *Sprachpragmatik und Philosophie* (Frankfurt aM, Suhrkamp, 1976) 174–273, 176: 'Ziel der Verständigung ist die Herbeiführung eines *Einverständnisses*, welches in der intersubjektiven Gemeinsamkeit des wechselseitigen Verstehens, des geteilten Wissens, des gegenseitigen Vertrauens und des miteinander Übereinstimmens terminiert.' In English: 'The goal of understanding is to achieve an agreement, which terminates in the intersubjective commonality of mutual understanding, shared knowledge, mutual trust and mutual agreement.'

[41] Admittedly, the conception of moral reasoning that is presupposed here obviously has a Habermasian slant. See J Habermas, 'Wahrheitstheorien' in his *Vorstudien und Ergänzungen zur Theorie des kommunikativen Handelns* (Frankfurt aM, Suhrkamp, 1984) 127–86.

[42] As will be seen below, this priority is not simple and cannot easily be taken for granted.

agreement to accept these. In a sense, this amounts to the socialisation of reason. Someone concedes to someone else the right to choose a course of action for both. The concession and its acceptance come first; the choice, which supplants substantive reasons, follows in its wake.

Figure 1.1 Self-critique of practical reason

Pre-critical	*Post-critical*
moral objectivity	legal validity
↑	↑
reason	choice
↑	↑
warrant	power
↑	↑
morality	agreement

From Persuasion to Acquiescence

Owing to the reversal, the force mediating the relation between the social and substantive dimension is not persuasion: it is, rather, acquiescence. The social bond is knit of the deference inherent in yielding to choices. Again, just as equal judgement capacity has already been presupposed within the substantive dimension to explain what makes persuasion possible, the deference inherent in letting someone go forward has already been implicitly anticipated in the complement to the uncoercive force of persuasion. Those who are persuaded give in to the power of reasons by yielding to their force.

Now that the tables have turned, the social dimension is taking the lead. Against the backdrop of the revealed difference between the two dimensions of judgement, persuasion and acquiescence come to appear ever more dissimilar. With an eye to their function, they are reminiscent of the two virtues necessary to facilitate voluntary or 'political' rule according to Aristotle. These are the abilities to rule and to be ruled.[43] Whereas the former ('persuasion') must involve, as part of the skills of a leader, the capacity to instill belief in the followers, the latter ('acquiescence') requires the quality of good team players to do what they are expected to do in extant situations. Stating the matter again, differently, there is a variance between

[43] See Aristotle, *The Politics*, 2nd edn (trans C Lord, Chicago, IL, University of Chicago Press, 2013) 1277b12–17 (at 69).

following a suggestion while shouting out 'That's right!' and muttering shruggingly 'Why not?'. Acquiescence is more like the readiness to abstain from raising issues out of awareness that arguments would be of no avail or merely inflame discord (see Figure 1.2). It opens the gate for the acceptance of choices on the path along which reasons cannot travel owing to the obstacle posed by persistent dissent.

Figure 1.2 Different propositional attitudes

persuasion	acquiescence
A → B	A ← B
That's right!	Why not?

Perhaps it helps to clarify the matter even more by stating it once again in terms congenial to the Kantian project. At least in the case of reasonable disagreements, moral objectivity can be viewed as a 'regulative ideal'. Even if it is unavailable, we have to stay guided by it, lest we sacrifice the respect that we owe to others as reasonable beings. Our shared commitment to objectivity gives rise to disagreements to which we respond by constructing legal relations. The legal validity that supports them replaces moral objectivity. With substance neutralised, the former is both less serious and more powerful than the latter.

Relations of this type are arrangements that allocate rights or powers and the duties or liabilities that go with them. Of course, the conditions under which people are ready to concede rights to others reflect their moral intuitions. The reversal, lest it should not occur, remains incomplete in practice. Not merely initially, but most definitely already at its outset, the legal relation remains steeped in morality. At the same time, since its basis must also be consistent with the freedom of choice that it constitutes, the power to make choices that are binding on others must be voluntarily endorsed. The foundation blinks and comes to rest uneasily between being a manifestation of the quasi-natural force of moral background knowledge[44] ('Of course, I'll get to decide, I am much older than you are') and being quite simply the expression of a common will ('But we have agreed that I would get to decide'). See Figure 1.3.

[44] See J Habermas, 'Handlungen, Sprechakte, sprachlich vermittelte Interaktionen und Lebenswelt' in his *Nachmetaphysisches Denken: Philosophische Aufsätze* (Frankfurt aM, Suhrkamp 1988) 63–104, 96.

Figure 1.3 Archetype of the legal relation

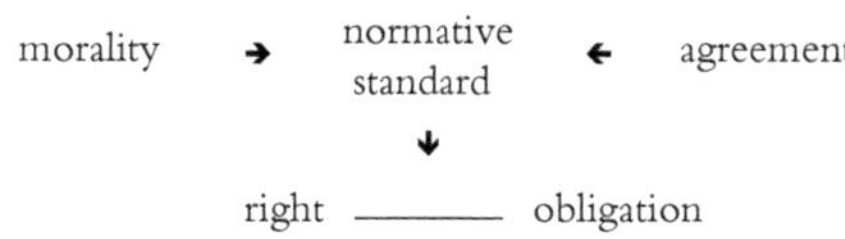

Critique as a Social Practice

The antinomy sketched above concerns two different bases of moral correctness. One was supposed to originate from good reasons themselves, the other from the equal capacity of others to believe themselves to have such reasons. The antinomy disappears to the extent that the ground of obligation shifts to a common will. The antinomic positions thereby become sustained in modified form. Persons get to decide, but their moral judgement capacity is no more relevant to the determination of the scope of their power. The *de facto* voluntary institution of authority matters. Complying with its decisions is a strictly 'external' affair – 'detached',[45] content-independent[46] and merely an expression of the 'legality of behavior'.[47] Legal validity brackets moral objectivity. This is how we part company while staying tied to each other within a legal relation.

Resolving the antinomy is not the work of a theorist. Critiquing practical reason does not need to be executed first in a philosophical treatise and then put into practice. It is a social practice set into historical time. As a quotidian affair, we engage in it long before a legal system with bailiffs and judges is even remotely of relevance. It comes to the fore already in these tender moments in which we abstain from engaging critically with others out of a sense that doing so might embarrass an interlocutor or be doomed from the outset in anticipation of obdurate tenacity of opinions. We suspend moral belief in our dealings. Not infrequently, however, an incipient legal relation is subject to immediate decay when we return eagerly to moral harangue.[48]

[45] See J Raz, 'The Purity of the Pure Theory' in SL Paulson and BL Paulson (eds), *Normativity and Norms: Critical Perspectives on Kelsenian Themes* (Oxford, Clarendon Press, 1998) 237–52, 247–48.

[46] See J Raz, *Practical Reasons and Norms*, 2nd edn (Princeton, NJ, Princeton University Press, 1990) 100–01.

[47] See I Kant, 'Die Metaphysik der Sitten' in *Werkausgabe*, vol 8 (ed W Weischedel, Frankfurt aM, Insel, 1968) 324 (A 15).

[48] Legal philosophy is about reconstructing how the legal relation is constituted from the practice of moral judgement. Hence, the book intends to shed the false expectation that legal philosophers are – or should be – capable of removing seemingly reasonable disagreements by demonstrating what the

Reasonableness without Natural Law

The idea that moral ideas provide external standards to which positive law must conform is also at odds with the relational approach defended here. The natural law tradition, for all it is worth, is easily mistaken for the sustained attempt to identify and support such external yardsticks.[49] As the book's chapters devoted to natural law theory try to demonstrate, this tradition viewed law as an integral component of the moral domain, even if it distinguished, for example, law from morality by the type of duty[50] and accorded a special place to positive law.[51] Nevertheless, even in modernity, and hence ever since Grotius,[52] law and other moral ideas are firmly associated with a problem that Kant would come to summarise as 'unsocial sociability',[53] namely the fact that our desire to live among others is so difficult to reconcile with our self-love.[54] The contrast, if not separation, of law and morality is a modern phenomenon and can come to the fore only after our external relations are conceptually breaking away from morality and embracing the common will on which they are built.

Owing to its emphasis on practical reason, the relational approach expounded in this book seems to be aligned with the natural law tradition. But in fact, it departs sharply from the latter. The natural law tradition remained 'uncritical'. It failed to recognise that the form of law is achieved by the self-critique of practical reason. Putting this into focus is the major advance made by the relational approach. From the natural law tradition, it retains, indeed, the idea that both law and morality belong to the domain of

right answer is. See R Dworkin, *A Matter of Principle* (Cambridge, MA, Harvard University Press, 1985). Philosophers are not better than non-philosophers at resolving moral questions. See J Habermas, *Theorie und Praxis: Sozialphilosophische Studien*, 2nd edn (Frankfurt aM, Suhrkamp, 1980) 42–45.

[49] For a critique, see already J Ritter, '"Naturrecht" bei Aristoteles' in his *Metaphysik und Politik: Studien zu Aristoteles und Hegel* (Frankfurt aM, Suhrkamp, 1969) 133–81, 160, 162.

[50] See S Darwall, *Modern Moral Philosophy: From Grotius to Kant* (Cambridge, Cambridge University Press, 2023) 21, 62–63.

[51] See, for example, Augustine, *On Free Choice of the Will* (trans T Williams, Indianapolis, IN, Hackett, 1993) I.6. 8.

[52] See H Grotius, *On the Law of War and Peace* (Student edition, ed SC Neff, Cambridge, Cambridge University Press, 2012) 4.

[53] See I Kant, 'Idea for a Universal History from a Cosmopolitan Perspective' in *Toward Perpetual Peace and Other Writings on Politics, Peace, and History* (trans DL Colclasure, ed P Kleingeld, New Haven, CT, Yale University Press 2006) 3–16, 6.

[54] Quite amazingly, this characterisation of the human condition has survived to this day and can be encountered, for example, in the work of Roberto Mangabeira Unger. See his *Passion: An Essay on Personality* (New York, Free Press, 1984) 21, where it is recast as the conflict between enabling conditions of self-assertion: social interaction and aloofness. Self-assertion can fail owing to our lack of participation in group life or owing to its inherent oppressiveness.

practical reason. But it emphasises, strongly, that moral reasoning – expressing the matter in Hegelian parlance – differentiates itself from itself in the constitution of the legal relation. In relation to reasons, choices advance to the mute avatars of a practical reason that has shifted from the uncoercive force of the better argument to accepting arrangements in which we yield to choices.

Sham Law and the Enigma of Authority

The reasonableness of law is first and foremost manifest in the *form* that confers on one person the right to determine the obligations of another. By virtue of this form, legal relations are embodiments of practical reason. Readers may suspect that this is reminiscent of Fuller's famous attempt to formulate an internal morality of law.[55] And, as in Fuller's case, one would expect from this book an answer to the question at which point the form of law becomes so degenerate that there is no more reason to give credence to what presents itself as its specimen. How do we identify sham law?

The form of law – the legal relation – comprises fewer principles than Fuller's morality of law. The principles are, nonetheless, substantive. People constitute a legal relation by implicitly recognising their equal freedom and placing their dealings in a context that they expect to be governed based on reciprocity.[56] Arguably, these principles suggest that arrangements can fail to be compatible with the form of law, such as those involving repugnant differences of status, vast inequalities of wealth or economic exploitation. All the same, incompatibilities of substance with the form of law are not self-authenticating. On the contrary, they tend to be veiled with lusters of idealisation, from which follows that even law that is a sham must be identified authoritatively. Chapter 9 offers a discussion of the enigma of authority, even though the problem is not limited to the challenges posed by insufferable borderline cases.[57] The point of authority is to pre-empt the relevance of independent judgements on the merits. Right or wrong, authority has spoken. At the same time, the ability to arrive at good decisions is a condition for seeing someone or some institution invested with

[55] See, notably, LL Fuller, *The Morality of Law*, 2nd edn (New Haven, CT, Yale University Press, 1969).

[56] For a short introduction, see my 'Legality and the Legal Relation' (2020) 33 *Ratio Iuris* 307–16.

[57] Strangely enough, it has occurred to theorists that 'torturing babies' could be such an insufferable case. See R Dworkin, *Justice for Hedgehogs* (Cambridge, MA, Harvard University Press, 2011) 24.

authority as a status.[58] The wavering between pre-emption and dependence on substance is the enigma of authority. The natural law perspective makes one inclined to attribute the power to say what is and what is not law to anyone who identifies grave substantive flaws.[59] Yielding to this temptation would clearly amount to according the substantive dimension precedence vis-à-vis its social counterpart. It follows from this that the protection of the form of law would invariably also undo this form. The root of this problem is that authority's dependence on substantively correct decisions translates into, and encourages, self-authorisations to say what is and what is not law.

Is there a way out of this predicament? The book suggests there is. Self-authorisations can be constrained if they have to be funnelled into allocated powers and end up being monitored and checked by others required to do the same. There is no other way of rescuing the form than by letting ambition counteract ambition.[60] And if there were a mutually shared permissive attitude among players that are set against each other within the system, this fact would be a reliable expression of what they jointly want and, hence, an act of collective self-determination. This explains why the integrity of the form can only be sustained within a system of checks and balances.

Blinking and Indeterminacy

This is the first explanation of why the legal relation requires a constitutional system. The second is, of course, that if law only fully comes to itself by credibly basing itself on a common will, then any such system needs to constitute the process of 'will formation' (as German constitutional parlance would have it). Any such regulation will, under the auspices of the principles of the legal relation, also lay down limits as to what democratic majorities may permissibly adopt. These are tantamount to the limits drawn to reasonable disagreements. Consistent with the legal relation, they are not simply considered to be natural law but, by virtue of imputing their adoption to

[58] See J Raz, *The Morality of Freedom* (Oxford, Clarendon Press, 1986) 47, 53.

[59] See J Locke, *Two Treatises of Government* (ed P Laslett, Cambridge, Cambridge University Press, 1960) II § 241, 427.

[60] See A Hamilton, J Madison and J Jay, *The Federalist* (ed C Sunstein, Cambridge, MA, Harvard University Press, 2009) No 51, 341; and my 'Real Constitutional Law: A Revised Madisonian Perspective' in C Bezemek, M Potacs and A Somek (eds), *Vienna Lectures in Legal Philosophy*, vol 2 (Oxford, Hart Publishing, 2020) 161–83.

the constituent power of the people, an expression of what at certain times and places a people have *taken* to be such.

Of course, at the level of fundamental constitutional principles the aforementioned 'blinking' between demands of political morality and expressions of the people's collective will is unavoidable. Even generally, the legal relation cannot prevent the moral 'reappropriation' of the terms under which people enjoy rights or are burdened with obligations. The origin of the legal relation is present in each and every one of its instances. The predicament that arises, and for which the author does not perceive a solution, is that, while methods of interpretation seeking to moor legal meanings firmly to the intentions of the law-giving institutions remain rather unconvincing, the morally informed idealisation of legal materials reproduces the problem from which the legal relation originates, namely the existence of reasonable disagreements. This does not raise any greater concerns. First, the idealisation of a constitutional system from different 'reasonable' perspectives is consistent with political liberalism. Any account of the legitimacy of a liberal and democratic regime must be formulated with an awareness that it concurs with others. Second, invariably, at the end of the day, the social dimension prevails. Moral readings of the law are authoritative only if they are adopted in the form of decisions. See Figure 1.4.

Figure 1.4 'Blinking'

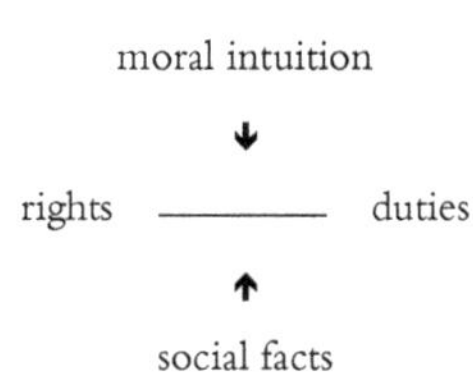

What needs to be recognised, ultimately, is that, aside from 'blinking' between moral insights and social facts, another original feature of the legal relation does not disappear either. The moral indeterminacy, which is indirectly taken for granted in the recognition of reasonable disagreements, is an enduring feature of law. The substantive indeterminacy persists, even if it is given different guises through the lens of the social dimension. On the level of the legal relation the law springs from sources,[61] that is law-creating or law-repealing

[61] See J Raz, 'Legal Positivism and the Sources of Law' in his *The Authority of Law*, 2nd edn (Oxford, Oxford University Press, 2009) 37–52, 47.

social facts. While the moral indeterminacy is absorbed owing to the exchange of reasons with choices, the choices *qua* sources are also encumbered by an indeterminacy that is inherent in their form. This can be easily shown for customary law and legislation. As a source, custom does not specify how many instances of practices one must have seen, and by whom, for there to be a legal standard. Legislation does not apply itself to cases. The rule-choice remains indeterminate. The indeterminacy is, however, particularly obvious in the final medium through which the law is given its most elaborate appearance. Legal scholarship inadvertently renders fluid and subject to unending controversies the law that is claimed to be settled. See Figure 1.5.

Figure 1.5 Legal indeterminacy

substantive indeterminacy	*customary law*	*decisions*	*scholarship*
social indeterminacy	how much practice by whom?	which rule for which case?	whose opinion on these issues?

It would be erroneous to conclude that nothing is gained from creating a legal system. The structure of a legal system constitutes constrained conversations[62] over issues that prevent debates from running out into the maelstrom of dissolute moral controversy.

Three Models of Reasonableness

Most of the above is laid out in the final two chapters of this book. In chapter 2, the book reflects on the difficult position that philosophical theory occupies in a world in which legal expertise is invariably drawn to be ancillary to economic interests or political agendas. It defends the idea that the philosophical pursuit of truth liberates the mind from the intellectual enslavement that it suffers at the hands of money and power. Unsurprisingly, the work thereby locates the relevant perspective on law in the world of human action. It does so with the confidence that doing so is most helpful when it comes to clarifying ideas. Since the strand of philosophical theory that has exhibited such confidence is called 'pragmatism', the book gladly and proudly aligns itself with this tradition of philosophical thought.

[62] See B Ackerman, *Social Justice in the Liberal State* (New Haven, CT, Yale University Press, 1980).

Chapters 3 and 4 explore the significance of the pragmatist outlook from the perspective of both rationality and reasonableness. Chapter 3 tries to show that the explanatory part of American legal realism, as well as raw and rough legal positivism, can be viewed as an account of law that adopts the perspective of rationality. The law becomes reified into a potentially overpowering force that needs to be reckoned with. The final sections of this same chapter prepare the exposition of the elementary conception of reasonableness relevant to this book.

These sections and chapter 4 are heavily indebted to the work of Thomas Nagel and Christine Korsgaard. One idea, however, developed in this chapter it inherits from Rousseau, namely the 'total alienation' of citizens from the sovereign body. The moral core of this idea is reconstructed in the book as the individual submission of person-relative reasons to an assessment from a person-neutral point of view. This idea – the kernel of the general will – prepares the ground for the discussion of three different models of actualising reasonableness in practice. These are: (i) arriving at a sustainable balance between reasonable and not reasonable parts of the soul; (ii) the further determination or implementation of a natural law; and (iii) processes of collective self-determination. In each of these models, reason is supposed to guide human action and law to provide its medium.

The ancient model reconstructed in chapters 5 and 6 – which, I hasten to disclaim, do not at all offer an exhaustive account of ancient political philosophy – revolves, bluntly speaking, around governance, be it the self-government of individuals or the government of the polis. The brief chapter 5 attempts to elucidate the matter with an eye to Plato's *Republic*. Chapter 6 turns to Aristotle. Both towering thinkers rely on a model of the human soul that is intended to explain how its reasonable component can be put in charge of governing the unreasonable part(s). Much is being said, in this context, about education and habituation. The law is of secondary and supplementary importance only. In the case of Aristotle, the dearth of normative orientation is particularly pronounced. At the end of the day, he ends up recommending that we rely on the good judgement of the people that happen to possess it.

Chapter 7 tries to explain how the model changes slowly, beginning with the Stoics and the subsequent evolution of medieval natural law theory. Reasonableness, according to this second model, is about following the 'cosmic' or 'common' law (*koinon nomos*). But this law is not manifest in some howsoever philosophically discovered book of rules. It is manifest in the practical wisdom of the sage and, thus, another name for practical reason that has attained its highest level of complexity. Medieval natural law theory, by contrast, views practical reasonableness as part of the ontotheological framework of God's creation. God, however, is, putting it mildly, an unruly factor for that type of natural law theory, for it is difficult to imagine how the Almighty could be bound by his commands, let alone not be free to repeal them. Voluntarist metaphysics struggled with this issue and seems to have failed to find a satisfactory solution. At the same time, the original edifice is subject to two noteworthy amendments in late scholastic doctrine. There is increasing attention paid to rights and to collective agreements in which is conceptually anticipated what would subsequently become the social contract.

The wavering between rationalism and voluntarism that one encounters in the scholastic context is carried over into the modern rationalist tradition, which is the subject of chapter 8. It also examines how modern natural law theory begins to bracket God and attempts to conceive of the law of nature as placed within the persistent tension between the natural sociality and self-love of human beings. Finding 'secular' sources is not an easy task, and not infrequently is rational insight complemented with God's command. It will be seen that modern natural law theory shifts emphasis between and among voluntarism, the utility of social cooperation and the protection of rights. With the focus on rights, the ground not only seems to be prepared for the absorption of natural law by modern constitutionalism, it also becomes possible to distinguish between law and morality as separate domains. The difference between perfect and imperfect duties plays a key role here. Nevertheless, a major shift in the orientation of natural law theory occurs once legal positivism enters the picture. Natural law ceases to be an integral part of a theory of practical reason and becomes engaged in the heroic struggle to wrest from legal positivism the concession that morality has to have at least some place in law. This ambition would have seemed rather strange to earlier natural law theorists. Surprisingly, however, in the course of this intellectual battle, contemporary natural law theory also seems to return to a format in which it is more congenial to its Stoic origins than before.

Unavoidably, however, natural law theory, despite its noble ambition, needs to confront the problem of authority. Who is to determine with binding effect for all what the law of nature demands (or permits)? Chapter 9 examines more closely the relation between the dependence of legitimate authority on its capacity to deliver right solutions and its power to pre-empt the relevance of concurrent or dissenting views of its choices. The matter can be most fruitfully studied in the case of Hobbes, not least because Hobbes views the sovereign as both dependent on and independent of the laws of nature. Superficially, of course, it may seem as if Hobbes, not least owing to the preponderance of peace as the most important objective, fully supports sovereign pre-emption. Yet there are instances when the laws of nature seep into the operation of the political body. The inconclusiveness with which Hobbes signs off from the enigma of authority marks the transition to the final model of reasonableness that declares it to be a matter of collective self-determination. It renounces all 'attitude-independent' authority and moves our way of thinking from natural law to constitutionally confined authority. Constitutionalism is the most straightforward consequence of the relational approach.

After chapter 10 seeks to provide a quick survey of more recent and prominent Anglo-American accounts of the legal relation, chapters 11 and 12 expound the third model of reasonableness and examine more carefully how the legal relation arises from the self-correction of the structure of moral judgement. The themes comprising the previous parts of this introduction are more fully elaborated there.

2

The Point of Legal Philosophy

Scientia juris

The Continental tradition of legal science harbours the belief that the meaning of authoritative legal materials, such as statutes or regulations, is to be elicited by means of interpretation.[1] After interpretations have done their work, legal analysis is supposed to disaggregate the meaning of laws into various elements of legal institutions.[2] The isolation and designation of these elements in concepts are geared towards establishing intelligible connections between descriptions of facts and their classification in legal terms. Legal science, charged with the pursuit of these objectives, counts as a scientific discipline of its own.

There is an objective and a subjective element to the belief in the respectability of legal science. The objective element is manifest in the claim that legal science is capable of providing us with an accurate perspective on the law. We need this type of science to know what the law is.

The subjective element suggests that this way of knowing the law is also congenial to what the law aspires to be. It facilitates the law's agency, as it were. We expect the law to be clear and predictable. Legal science provides us with the wherewithal to make the law approximate this ideal in the process of adjudication.[3] Hence, legal science is not only essential for attaining a clearer perspective on the law; it also guarantees the accuracy of the

[1] See J Schröder, 'Entwicklungstendenzen der juristischen Interpretationstheorie von 1500–1850' in J Schönert and F Vollhardt (eds), *Geschichte der Hermeneutik und die Methodik der textinterpretierenden Disziplinen* (Berlin, de Gryuter, 2005) 203–19; A milestone in the development of 'legal hermeneutics' was undoubtedly AFJ Thibaut, *Theorie der logischen Auslegung des Römischen Rechts*, 2nd edn (Altona, Johann Friedrich Hammerich, 1806).

[2] Jhering, not particularly fond of hermeneutics, considered the interpretation of rules the task of 'lower jurisprudence' and assigned the 'higher' level of jurisprudential reasoning to elevate elements of legal norms to the level of jural concepts. See R von Jhering, *Geist des römischen Rechts auf den verschiedenen Stufen seiner Entwicklung*, vol 1, 6th edn (Leipzig, Breitkopf und Härtel, 1907) 37.

[3] I tried to make this link between the rule of law and the task of legal scholarship explicit in *Knowing What the Law Is: Legal Theory in a New Key* (Oxford, Hart Publishing, 2021) 37–39.

production of more law based on already existing law. Legal science is the law's congenial way of recognising itself.

As adumbrated above, legal science uses concepts in order to classify legal materials and to link them to relevant social facts. For example, the basic scheme of fault-based tort liability involves elements such as 'harm', 'causality' in the relation between the tortfeasor's acts and the damage done, the 'violation' of some norm and some sort of 'fault'. The grid used to analyse tort claims involves various concepts that are arranged in a certain analytical sequence. At each step in the process, an intelligible connection is to be established between authoritative legal materials (eg, statutes, precedents) and a set of facts.

Basic Concepts and Theory

Occasionally, it is necessary to calibrate concepts and to fine-tune their meaning. This is the case whenever routine operations of legal thought become challenged (for example, when controversies arise over methods of interpretation) or when certain phenomena defy ready classification because they do not fit into an already established framework of analysis.

Some of the concepts used by legal science are more 'basic' than others.[4] When engaging in a debate over the meaning of these concepts, legal scholars ('scientists') speak of debating 'theory' or straying into 'theoretical reflection'.

Some of the basic concepts of legal thought are taken from the legal materials of various jurisdictions and raised to a higher level of abstraction. 'Freedom of speech' or 'property' are examples of such concepts. Their meaning is soon severed from the legal orders from which they have been taken, in particular when scholars engage in an attempt to arrive at their most appealing interpretation. Such interpretations (Dworkin: 'conceptions'[5]) of these concepts attempt to draw out the point justifying the existence of the

[4] On the role of basic concepts for disciplines, see the memorable remark by M Heidegger, *Sein und Zeit*, 14th edn (Tübingen, Max Niemeyer, 1977) 9: 'Die eigentliche Bewegung der Wissenschaften spielt sich ab in der mehr oder minder radikalen und ihr selbst nicht durchsichtigen Revision der Grundbegriffe. Das Niveau einer Wissenschaft bestimmt sich daraus, wieweit sie zu einer Krisis ihrer Grundbegriffe *fähig* ist.' In my English translation this reads as follows: 'The real movement of the disciplines takes place in the more or less radical revision of basic concepts, which is not transparent to itself. The level of a discipline is determined by the extent to which it is *capable* of a crisis of its basic concepts.'

[5] See R Dworkin, *Law's Empire* (Cambridge, MA, Harvard University Press, 1986) 90–96.

institutions that they designate. It is in this context that legal scholarship establishes the connection with philosophy.

Other concepts, which are possibly even more 'basic',[6] are not derivative of the authoritative legal materials at all. Rather, their function is to facilitate their most adequate comprehension. For example, the concept of a 'norm'[7] represents the form by virtue of which we apprehend the normative significance of law (its claim to create obligations, for example); or, taking another example, concepts such as 'order'[8] or 'system'[9] that are integral to legal scholarship are not derived from positive law itself.

Legal philosophy and theory are in the business of exploring basic legal concepts. What is more, a whole array of such concepts is regularly assembled into larger theoretical edifices. These edifices are generally taken to belong to two different schools of legal thought: legal positivism, on the one hand, and natural law theory, on the other. The former used to draw a sharp line between law and morality.[10] According to classical legal positivism, the law must be taken as it is, regardless of what one believes it ought to be.[11] Natural law theory, by contrast, sustains a stronger or weaker connection between law and morality.

What legal positivism and natural law theory have in common is that they are theoretical accounts of law. They aim to establish what the law *truly* is and what it takes to arrive at adequate accounts of its substance.

Hence, legal positivism and natural law theory are the most general expressions of the self-reflection of legal science. This type of reflection asks what it is that validates its claims.

[6] See Heidegger, n 4, 10.

[7] Kelsen's darling notion. See H Kelsen, *Introduction to the Problems of Legal Theory* (trans B Litschewski Paulson and SL Paulson, Oxford, Clarendon Press, 1992) 22–28.

[8] See C Schmitt, *Über die drei Arten des Rechtswissenschaftlichen Denkens* (Hamburg, Hanseatische Verlagsanstalt, 1934). There is an English translation of Schmitt's pamphlet, but it shows that it was not prepared by a legal scholar. C Schmitt, *On the Three Types of Juristic Thought* (trans J Bendersky, Westport, CT, Praeger, 2004).

[9] See, for example, J Raz, *The Concept of a Legal System: An Introduction to the Theory of the Legal System*, 2nd edn (Oxford, Clarendon Press, 1980).

[10] With the rise of 'inclusive' legal positivism, the 'social thesis', according to which the law is based on social facts, tends to eclipse the 'separability thesis'. See, for example J Coleman, 'Negative and Positive Positivism' (1982) *Journal of Legal Studies* 139–64.

[11] See HLA Hart, 'Positivism and the Separation of Law and Morals' (1958) 71 *Harvard Law Review* 593–621.

Socially Prevalent Forms of Self-reflection

There are, however, alternative forms of self-reflection.[12] They are not tied to the value of truth but rather to the values of wealth and power.

You can validate your knowledge of the law by asking whether it is useful to earn you a decent income (this is what I expected my future legal expertise to do for me when I enrolled as a student in a legal studies programme). If this is the point of the self-reflection of legal expertise, it is carried out in the medium of money.

You do not have to have any regard for theory in order to be a successful legal expert. All you need to do is to be successful in court and to generate sizable amounts of 'billable hours'.

In the setting of a university, the requisite training that you have to undergo is – the acquisition of basic analytical skills aside – imparted by more senior fellow students. It does not take a scientist to do that. The sites of training are various moot court programmes and advocacy competitions.

The analytical skills, by the way, are best taught by legal research and writing instructors.[13] Their function is, alas, largely unknown in the Continental legal tradition.

Alternatively, you can validate your knowledge of the law by asking whether it helps you in attaining noble (or merely your own) political objectives. You thus use existing types of legal arguments as instruments to push your agenda. You consider yourself and the law you draw upon as part of a movement heading in a direction that you have to be sure to characterise as 'forward'.

It is an amazing fact that legal academia has since the late twentieth century opened its door to agenda-driven scholarship. It used to be, noteworthy historical exceptions aside, unheard of in a setting that was self-consciously committed to the pursuit of truth.[14] Major instances of agenda-driven scholarship are normative law and economics, human rights

[12] For a more elaborate exposition of the following ideas, see my 'Die Macht der juristischen Expertise: Rechtliches Wissen als Steuerungsmedium' in K Lerch (ed), *Sprache und Recht*, vol.3 (Berlin, de Gruyter, 2005) 399–438. The following distinction among monetary, political and philosophical self-reflection very roughly matches Habermas' distinction between theoretical, practical and emancipatory epistemological interests. See J Habermas, 'Erkenntnis und Interesse' in J Habermas, *Technik und Wissenschaft als 'Ideologie'* (Frankfurt aM, Suhrkamp, 1968) 146–68, 162.

[13] See, for example, T Pollman and JM Stinson, *Legal Writing*, 4th edn (Burlington, MA, Aspen, 2023).

[14] For a salutary reminder, see J Komárek, 'Freedom and Power of European Constitutional Law Scholarship' (2021) 17 *European Constitutional Law Review* 422–41.

law, gender studies and, to a certain extent, European Union law. Their aims are straightforward: efficiency, deregulation, protection of marginalised groups, such as migrants and racial minorities, the recognition of proliferating sexual orientations and genders, and, of course, 'more Europe'. Interestingly, the pursuit of agenda scholarship rests much of its faith in courts, possibly even international courts, as the institutions in charge of precipitating social change.[15] The purpose of agenda-driven scholarship is to prepare the ground for path-breaking innovations by the judicial branch (or to draw out the meanings of innovations that have been handed down before). Human rights law, for example, is quite adventurous by traditional methodological standards. Any possible form of legal argument is convenient for the pursuit of the good agenda.[16] Chicago-style law and economics[17] is decidedly different from traditional scholarship, not least because it openly and single-mindedly pursues the overarching goal of wealth maximisation.[18] Given that agenda-driven scholarship nonetheless scarcely ever openly advocates the redistribution of wealth by the state, it is fully compatible with the world of economic liberalism.

The major sites of agenda-driven legal science are the international conference, where one meets like-minded people, or the conspirative workshop, in which participants mutually reassure one another of the righteousness of their cause.

The pursuit of truth is the defining feature of legal positivism and natural law theory. No such ambition is to be found in skills training and agenda scholarship. The former is just 'instrumentalist' and entirely unconcerned with legal ideas. The latter can sustain its blind devotion to certain ideas only by abstaining from any critique of practical reason, however moderate it might be. Since both refuse to engage with the basic conceptual level, it makes sense to view them as 'degenerate'[19] forms of the purportedly value-free or value-recognising pursuit of legal knowledge.

[15] For an account of international adjudication, see Armin von Bogdandy & Ingo Venzke, *In Whose Name? A Public Law Theory of International Adjudication* (Oxford, Oxford University Press, 2014).

[16] For an account, see David Robertson, *The Judge as a Political Theorist: Contemporary Constitutional Review* (Princeton, Princeton University Press, 2010).

[17] See, for example, RA Posner, *Economic Analysis of Law*, 3rd edn (Boston, MA, Little Brown, 1986).

[18] For a critique, see RM Dworkin, *A Matter of Principle* (Cambridge, MA, Harvard University Press, 1985) 237–66.

[19] I am borrowing the predicate 'degenerate' from Charles S Peirce, who used it to characterise the reduction of essentially triadic relations to dyads or immediacy. See CS Peirce, 'Harvard Lectures on Pragmatism (1903)' in Peirce Edition Project (ed), *The Essential Peirce: Selected Philosophical Writings*, vol 2 (Bloomington, IN, Indiana University Press, 1998) 133–256, 160–61. See also K-O Apel, *Der Denkweg*

Unfortunately, the site that is left to the original form of juridical self-reflection is the sparsely attended lecture and the forlorn seminar in which a few oddballs discuss complex analytical issues with their master.

If you happen to belong to this group, your job prospects are slim.

Form and Function of the Foundational Discipline

The intellectual situation of legal philosophy is further aggravated by the fact that its existence as a 'foundational' discipline systematically severs it from the type of self-refection that grows out organically, as it were, of legal scholarship.[20]

In fact, the existence of the foundational discipline facilitates and encourages an engagement with theory that treats it as a repository of answers for which doctrinal scholars do not have to take any responsibility. Since those who engage in theory also engage in theoretical controversy, the existence of the foundational discipline gives rise to a number of positions that 'doctrinalists' can draw on to rationalise their actions. The foundational discipline becomes a grab-bag of 'views' from which one can pick and choose without exploring the reasons for choices. They can always point out that there are endless controversies at the foundational level, but that, at the end of the day, they need to settle for something.

The situation is not mitigated by the fact that the engagement with grand theoretical edifices is surrounded with an aura of boredom. Kelsen's *Pure Theory* is a case in point.[21] Its first edition is an assemblage of a variety of critical engagements with basic concepts taken from the contemporary discipline of public law (eg, the concept of the state or the distinction between private and public law). Once Kelsen had put the outcomes of controversies together under one theoretical roof, they were studied as elements of a grander theory. The connection to the controversies receded into the background. As a grand theory, it became stale and drained of its lifeblood. It was turned into a 'contribution to legal theory' (ie, the

des Charles S Peirce: Eine Einführung in den amerikanischen Pragmatismus (Frankfurt aM, Suhrkamp, 1975) 236–37. Skills training and agenda scholarship link subjects with practice, but they skip theoretical reflection.

[20] For succinct observations, see H Castorp, 'Wittgensteinsche Einleitung in das Grundlagenfach Rechtsphilosophie' (2021) 76 *Zeitschrift für öffentliches Recht* 467–76.

[21] See n 7.

foundational discipline), and people grew fond of exploring metaphysical questions, such as the nature of the basic norm.

The Task Ahead

Philosophy of law should avoid being a graveyard of critical engagements. It may be objected that the author has just explained that this fate can scarcely be averted. The point of the project pursued here is, nonetheless, straightforward. Neither the cool but costly dispensation of legal expertise nor the fervent pursuit of an agenda takes seriously how the law presents itself. The law does not claim to be a mere resource available to produce services, nor does it present itself as a movement towards a more or less discernible destination. The law claims to possess authority over us.[22] While, as will be explained in chapter 3, it is in principle unobjectionable to conceive of law from the perspective of human action, the perspectives of both profitable expertise and the obedient pursuit of an agenda fail to focus on this elementary matter.

If theoretical self-reflection concerns what the law 'truly' is, its primary task is to explore seriously what legal norms and orders claim to be. Whenever legal enactments conflict with what we take to be the right thing to do, they purport to be of overriding significance and assert their force, regardless of whether we believe them to be morally right or wrong. The question that is raised by the existence of legal institutions is, therefore, whether such authority is legitimate. The most elementary condition of legitimacy is, however, the reasonableness of authoritative enactments.

The question is, in other words, whether it is reasonable to accept the law's claim to authority and, if so, how to accept it. If this question is answered at all, and legal positivists famously refuse to give an answer to it, it is suggested that obeying the law is reasonable only if the law is reasonable itself. Hence, legal philosophy ordinarily examines the conditions of reasonableness that the law has to meet in order to possess authority. These conditions are not infrequently spelled out in negative terms, for example in the form of the precept that positive law ought not be 'gravely unjust'.[23] Philosophy, thus understood, applies a yardstick to law that is somehow

[22] See J Raz, *The Authority of Law: Essays on Law and Morality* (Oxford, Clarendon Press, 1979) 30.
[23] See, famously, G Radbruch, 'Legislative Injustice and Supra-Statutory Law' (1946), trans B Litschewski-Paulson and SL Paulson, (2006) 26 *Oxford Journal of Legal Studies* 1–11.

external to it, as if its task was to sift out arrogations of authority that fail to meet a pre-established norm of justice or human decency.

This is not the path taken here. The relational approach developed in this book proceeds differently. Instead of submitting the authority of law to some external moral demand, it attempts to demonstrate how the form of law emerges from within the structure of moral justification. It claims that the law is the institutional manifestation of the self-critique of practical reason, which gives rise to 'legality' as a more demoted form of normative force resting content with 'outward' compliance with norms. It infuses our dealings with law with a modicum of irony and reconciles rational adaptation to the demands of law with behaving reasonably towards others.

Since the legitimacy of authority is the focus of legal philosophy, the academic seminar as the site of reflection entertains an invisible connection with those taking occasional walks on the wild side of democracy.

3

The Rational Perspective on Overpowering Force

Pragmatism

The most straightforward point for entering legal philosophy is human action. That is to say that encounters with anyone or anything claiming to represent 'the' law are a good place to begin, for such encounters raise the questions what a claim of this type entails and how we are to respond to it. The law affects us in our agency, for it may – for the most part, at any rate – create obstacles in the way of attaining our objectives. It is our agency that accounts for how we conceive of the law, and it is from this perspective that we attempt to answer the question of what the law truly is.

If anything, the precept that clarifying our ideas and conceiving of the world is most adequately done by examining how our concepts matter to human action is a characteristic feature of 'pragmatism' as a philosophical persuasion.[1] While authors differ over the figure that might best represent this philosophical movement[2] or what its true mission[3] is, I am taking the question of what difference an idea makes to human action to be essential.

Hence, what is offered on these pages is a pragmatist approach to law.

[1] This, at any rate, reflects the spirit of the pragmatic maxim. See CS Peirce, 'How to Make Our Ideas Clear' (1878) in N Houser and C Kloesel (eds), *The Essential Peirce*, vol 1 (Bloomington, IN, Indiana University Press 1992) 124–41, 132. For a useful introduction, see C Misak, *The American Pragmatists* (Oxford, Oxford University Press, 2013) 29–32. This is not to concede that I favour what Brandom calls 'instrumental' (concerned with what works) over 'fundamental' (concerned with knowing how) pragmatism. See RB Brandom, *Perspectives on Pragmatism: Classical, Recent & Contemporary* (Cambridge, MA, Harvard University Press, 2011) 13–21.

[2] For example, while Germans notoriously pick Charles S Peirce, Richard Rorty, an American pragmatist himself, has always favoured John Dewey. See R Rorty, *Pragmatism as Anti-Authoritarianism* (ed E Mendieta, Cambridge, MA, Harvard University Press, 2021) 4–6. For a different perspective, see D Anderson, 'Peirce and Pragmatism: American Connections' in C Misak (ed), *The Oxford Handbook of Pragmatism* (Oxford, Oxford University Press, 2008) 38–59.

[3] On pragmatism's deep roots in probabilism and Darwinism, see M Bacon, *Pragmatism: An Introduction* (Cambridge, Polity Press, 2012) 2–7; RB Brandom, *Pragmatism and Idealism: Rorty and Hegel on Reason and Representation* (Oxford, Oxford University Press, 2022) 20–22. Pragmatism has also always seen knowledge as a social practice. See C West, *The American Evasion of Philosophy: A Genealogy of Pragmatism* (Madison, WI, University of Wisconsin Press, 1989) 203–04.

As acting beings, we are also thinking beings. We deliberate about our conduct and weigh our options. What is more, thinking is an activity.[4] When we are adding numbers, we are performing a calculation. By drawing a conclusion from two premises we are arriving at a new belief.[5] When we are doing this, we are determining ourselves, that is our state of mind and our actions. Reasoning is an activity of self-determination.

There are two different structures of human reasoning underlying our determination of conduct. As agents, we can be either rational or reasonable.[6] It is possible, therefore, to account for the law from the perspective of either rationality or reasonableness. Each perspective, as we shall see, provides us with different accounts of what the law truly is.

The 'Self-ish' Nature of Rationality

Rational action is about agents' pursuit of their own ends. They want to live their life as well as possible, and the satisfaction of desires is at least prima facie conducive to this end.[7] The aims pursued, or desires had, by a self are referred to as that person's self-interest. This locution does not imply that the relevant interests are necessarily egoistic and self-centered. They are 'self-ish' in the sense that they are of concern for the self who has them.[8] But it is entirely possible that the self whose interests they are is utterly absorbed in promoting the well-being of others. From the perspective of rational action, even altruism is in the self-interest of an altruist.

Rational action is not without anything further about the choice of ends. If the concept is narrowly understood as an instrumental principle, it is about choosing the most effective and efficient means to attain these. In this form it cannot provide us with guidance as to what our ends should be, not even whether we ought to choose satisfaction of one desire rather than the maximisation of all.[9]

[4] This central contention of German idealistic philosophy has been reformulated in a quite mundane manner by CM Korsgaard, *The Constitution of Agency: Essays on Practical Reason and Moral Psychology* (Oxford, Oxford University Press, 2008) 2, 83.

[5] See CS Peirce, 'The Fixation of Belief' in Houser and Kloesel (eds), n 1, 109–23.

[6] For a seminal contribution, see WM Sibley, 'The Rational Versus the Reasonable' (1953) 62 *Philosophical Review* 554–60.

[7] See D Parfit, *Reasons and Persons* (Oxford, Clarendon Press, 1986) 8.

[8] For the related idea of 'subjective values', see T Nagel, *The Possibility of Altruism* (Princeton, NJ, Princeton University Press, 1970) 88.

[9] See Korsgaard, n 4, 70.

Among those who adhere to rational choice theory, rational action is understood to be about the most effective way of satisfying 'preferences'.[10] In this case, rational action is no longer entirely unconcerned about ends because the desires themselves are, in a sense, concerned about staying ahead of their competitors. Rational agents are expected to rank their ends according to their weight or urgency and to choose means in light of the feasibility of making them real. If an end were entirely out of reach, it would be irrational to pursue it. No boy should pursue a pretty girl that does not care about him. Rather, he should be looking out for other, possibly less attractive females who might make themselves available for mating. Apparently, this is what it takes to behave rationally. Nevertheless, from the perspective of rational choice, preferences simply afflict us, while, strangely enough, they also seem to say something about the rank they ought to occupy in a schedule of desires.[11] But even if preferences as longings that are imprinted onto the desiring part of the human soul would of themselves reveal their relative importance, the instrumental principle could not tell us which one we ought to satisfy first. We would have to add a normative principle according to which the relative urgency matters. Preferences in and of themselves do not supply this principle.[12]

One might want to reply that unless we harbour mistaken beliefs about what is good for us, satisfying preferences comes naturally to us. 'Rational' is a predicate for describing what we simply do. The problem that arises, then, is that even people who mistakenly believe that taking drugs is good for them would still have to pass as rational. The concept is then dangerously all-inclusive. Even people jumping from a skyscraper in a frenzy, believing themselves to have wings, would count as rational. They must have believed the wrong thing, but had the belief been correct, their action would have passed muster. Thus understood, however, the concept of rationality would lose its critical bite. Any critique of the actions of others would not involve a recommendation to act differently but merely hint at the fact that they would perceive matters in the same way were they, through some obscure circumstance, thrown into our state of belief.[13]

[10] See J Elster, *Nuts and Bolts for the Social Sciences* (Cambridge, Cambridge University Press, 1989) 22–29; DM Hausman and MS McPherson, *Economic Analysis and Moral Philosophy* (Cambridge, Cambridge University Press, 1996) 41–45.

[11] See also Korsgaard, n 4, 75.

[12] ibid 72.

[13] ibid 77.

A more promising understanding of rational action explains it in terms of prudence. Prudence dictates that we maximise our happiness.[14] Apparently, each satisfaction of a desire is rewarded with a bit of happiness, and more of these bits is better than less, while most is best. Yet our desires often conflict; some must be sacrificed to facilitate the satisfaction of others. Maximisation must involve some kind of balancing procedure[15] to weed out those that turn out to have lesser standing. But this does not alter the fact that desires clamour to be satisfied. How are we to explain to a desire that it is less important than others and must therefore step back? The problem may appear trivial, but it loses its apparent triviality when we transpose it to the collective level and examine it through the lens of the utilitarian calculus. Individual happiness is self-authenticating – just as desires are. Both do not come with a self-denying ordinance attached saying under which condition they are ready to cede ground to others. The principle that makes them yield is invariably external to them.[16] The principle of maximisation is such a principle, which is often dogmatically posited in the utilitarian tradition.[17] As a substantive theory of the good, however, it already exceeds the purview of instrumental rationality.[18]

Austin's Legal Positivism

The most straightforwardly rational conception of law from such a rational perspective is John Austin's legal positivism.[19] The ideas developed in *The Province of Jurisprudence Determined* are meant to reveal what the law really is.

Austin begins by explaining that the law consists of 'commands'.[20] A command is a special type of wish. It is a wish that is backed up with a sanction. A sanction is an evil that can be inflicted by commanders on the addressees of their commands if they fail to comply:

> A command, then, is a signification of desire. But a command is distinguished from other significations of desire by this peculiarity: that the party

[14] ibid 15, 78–79.

[15] ibid 75, 97.

[16] See CM Korsgaard, *Self-Constitution: Agency, Identity, Integrity* (Oxford, Oxford University Press, 2009) 56–57; Korsgaard, n 4, 90.

[17] A noteworthy exception is Parfit's 'critical present-aim theory'. See Parfit, n 7, 94.

[18] See Korsgaard, n 4, 15.

[19] See J Austin, *The Province of Jurisprudence Determined* (ed W Rumble, Cambridge, Cambridge University Press, 1995). The book was first published in 1832.

[20] ibid 21.

> to whom it is directed is liable to evil from the other, in case he comply not with the desire.[21]

Austin goes on to explain that, by virtue of the commander's issuing of a command, the addressees are obligated to comply:

> Being liable to evil from you if I comply not with a wish which you signify, I am *bound* or *obliged* by your command, or I lie under a *duty* to obey it.[22]

But that statement, of course, begs the question. It presupposes the normative bindingness of threats. Kelsen would have objected to Austin that his reasoning amounts to a flawed inference from 'is' to 'ought'.[23]

Yet the matter becomes more plausible once we view the avoidance of sanctions as an obligation that arises from the structure of rational action. Provided that steering clear of sanctions is one of my aims – and empirically it is plausible to suppose that most people share this aim – I have an obligation towards myself as a rational agent to avoid sanctions. Indeed, as Korsgaard would most likely put it, what is at stake in this case is my identity as a rational agent.[24] What is more, I could not even be called an agent if I did not take into account the means necessary to pursue my own good. I would be a rather odd creature.

The Normativity of Rationality

Rationality is a norm. It tells us what we ought to do.[25] The validity of the law is, therefore, a refraction of the internal normativity of rational action. The law derives its normativity from the perspective of individual rational action. This inherited validity is not, however, universal. For people who enjoy suffering or crave enduring humiliation, it would be rational to expose themselves to sanctions.[26] Only a few people, if any, come down with such a strange affliction.

How much normativity is inherent in rationality becomes clear in Thomas Nagel's account of prudence.[27] We are all likely to pay less attention to the

[21] ibid 21–22.
[22] ibid 22.
[23] See H Kelsen, *Introduction to the Problems of Legal Theory* (trans B Litschewski Paulson and SL Paulson, Oxford, Clarendon Press, 1992) 14–15.
[24] See Korsgaard, n 4, 83.
[25] ibid 144.
[26] Korsgaard, however, would object to such a 'descriptive' use of rationality. See ibid 76, 144.
[27] On the following, see Nagel, n 8.

future states we are going to be in than to the exciting thing we expect to happen next. We care very little about the distant future because we are much more interested in fulfilling our present desires and attaining our next objectives. We engage in what is called 'discounting' the future. This is not, however, a rational thing to do; not, in particular, given that in the future we are likely to find ourselves in the position in which we are no longer able to improve or to alter our circumstances (think of situations of assisted living, for example, or a chronic illness). We should not expose ourselves to the adverse consequences owing to a lack of foresight. Rationality, that is, requires that we treat each phase of our lives equally and accord an equal weight to the interest at stake at any time. Rationality thus involves an intertemporal equal treatment obligation. Nagel speaks of timeless reasons and suggests that only if we orient our conduct on these are we able to tie ourselves together as persons having an identity over time. Plainly and simply put, timelessness is what facilitates impartiality within one person over time, for the person regards each stage of their life as equally real.[28] Timelessness bridges the distance between the present and the future self. Nevertheless, this intrapersonal equal treatment obligation anticipates the possibility of altruism. The latter is, however, according to Nagel, not mediated by timeless reasons that constitute the identity of the person over time. Rather, it is mediated by objective or agent-neutral values.[29] They are the equivalent of timelessness in the interpersonal domain. Objective values make it possible to view every person as equally real from a point of view that transcends the individual self. A similar transcendence is, however, built into being prudently guided by timeless reasons.

Legal Realism *avant la lettre*

An alternative – and most famous – account of what the law amounts to from the perspective of rational action is presented by Oliver Wendell Holmes, Jr in his famous lecture 'The Path of the Law'.[30]

The business of legal scholarship, according to Holmes, is the prediction of court decisions. This is the case because doing so is in the interest of clients. Since clients may well be good or bad people, we have no reason to prefer a good person's perspective of the law to that of a bad person. It is the same for all, good or bad. Since whoever is really interested only in the

[28] ibid 59.
[29] ibid 87–88.
[30] See O Wendell Holmes, 'The Path of the Law' (1897) 10 *Harvard Law Review* 457–78.

consequences of court behaviour adopts the right perspective on the law and since consequences are all that the 'bad man' cares about, the bad man's view is also the universally rational view. It perceives the law as stripped of all unnecessary idealisations. The law comprises, as American legal realists would later explain, patterns of judicial behaviour.[31]

The consequence of this perspective is that we need to regard all legal scholarship and everything that we learn in law school as the intellectual means to anticipate court decisions. But is that plausible? Assuming that the story is correct according to which political scientists, by taking the political views of Supreme Court Justices into account, are better at predicting decisions of this Court than doctrinal lawyers,[32] it would make sense to say that ideology and political morality are the truly determining factors of American law. This matches indeed the conclusion that was reached by some American realists. In their view, it is the moral convictions and political ideology of judges that explain what they posit to be law. All legal doctrine is mere window-dressing distracting us from the true reasons underlying a decision.[33]

But this view attributes to doctrine possibly too little significance. It is far more plausible to assume that doctrine – and what we study when we study law – provides us with the semantics and grammar of the language game that is played inside a court of law. Against this background, it can be seen why Holmes and the realists give us only one half of the rational dimension of scholarship. Legal scholars, owing to their familiarity with what matters in the context of legal opinions, are moderately capable of anticipating decisions. But they are also in the business of influencing court behaviour based on their reconstruction of how courts have reasoned in the past and of the mindset animating their decisions.

Master and Servant, High Court and Scholars

An interesting asymmetry must not elude us, though. Courts are the masters of legal reasoning, scholars are the servants.[34] The servant's task is to satisfy

[31] See, notably, FS Cohen, 'Transcendental Nonsense and the Functional Approach' (1935) 35 *Columbia Law Review* 809–49.

[32] See TW Ruger et al, 'The Supreme Court Forecasting Project: Legal and Political Science Approaches to Predicting Supreme Court Decisionmaking' (2004) 104 *Columbia Law Review* 1150–1209.

[33] See FS Cohen, 'Modern Ethics and the Law' reprinted in L Kramer Cohen (ed), *The Legal Conscience: Selected Papers of Felix S Cohen* (New Haven, CT, Yale University Press, 1966) 17–32; J Frank, *Law and the Modern Mind* (New York, Brentano's, 1930).

[34] The relation plays a major role in the constitution of spirit in Hegel's *Phenomenology*. See GWF Hegel, *Phänomenologie des Geistes* (ed H-F Wessels and H Clairmont, Hamburg, Meiner 1988) 127–36. For a

the expectations of the master. The masters reason in a 'masterly' way. They just put things to us. Often, they leave the premises unstated, and their reasoning is replete with mental leaps and gaping omissions. It is the task of the servants to fill in the gaps when they go about reconstructing the mindset of the masters. Yet the elaborate reconstructions of what potentially grounds the master's reasoning can never bind the master and can also easily be undone by him. This is the intellectual tragedy of legal scholarship. Its servility does not come with the guarantee of a reward.[35]

Reasonableness

Reasonableness is a way of reasoning that takes not only the viewpoint of an individual, the self, but also the viewpoint of other selves into account. More precisely, it concerns individuals perceiving themselves from a point of view beyond themselves by giving equal consideration to the interest of others, possibly all.[36]

Rawls claims that what is relevant in our context, which is ultimately the context of modern law, is the idea of reciprocity.[37] We are ready to commit ourselves to benefitting others only if we shall benefit from them in turn. We are also ready to share in the burdens.

As Rawls explains, reciprocity demands more than mutual advantage but less than altruism.[38] The condition of mutual advantage is met by exchanges that involve improvements on both sides. Each party benefits.[39] The relevant starting positions, however, remain out of account. The exploitation of wage labour is mutually advantageous. The capitalist can extract surplus value, and the wage-earner is spared starvation. The unequal bargaining power is irrelevant. By contrast, the starting positions matter for the purpose of realising reciprocity. They ought to be roughly equal. Yet each party may legitimately pursue their own interests. They do not take an interest in the well-being of others (or in investing them with resources). This explains why reciprocity is less demanding than altruism.

meticulous reconstruction, see RB Brandom, *A Spirit of Trust: A Reading of Hegel's* Phenomenology (Cambridge, MA, Harvard University Press, 2019) 314–44.

[35] See my 'Herrschaft und Knechtschaft im Staatsrecht' in R Hofmann et al (eds), *Festschrift für Franz Merli* (Baden-Baden, Nomos 2023) 851–63.

[36] See T Nagel, *The View from Nowhere* (New York, Oxford University Press, 1986) 160; T Nagel, *What Does it All Mean? A Very Short Introduction to Philosophy* (New York, Oxford University Press, 1987) 70.

[37] See J Rawls, *Political Liberalism* (New York, Columbia University Press, 1991) 16, 94.

[38] ibid 16–17.

[39] See B Barry, *Justice as Impartiality* (Oxford, Oxford University Press, 1995) 31–38.

Reasonable people are interested in their own benefit subject to conditions of fair play. When it comes to law, this means that reasonable people will play by the rules so long as they can be reasonably assured that others will do so as well. Since fairness extends beyond the question of whether one has reason to obey the law, it also concerns the legitimacy of the legal system itself. Roughly speaking, reasonable people expect the legal system to exhibit impartial concern for all.

It is a major question of philosophical interest to explore the relation between reasonableness and rationality. The question can be asked, that is, whether one is derivative of the other. Is rationality derivative of reasonableness? Nagel's account of altruism seems to suggest this.[40] Rationality qua prudence appears to be an adaptation of the significance that objective values possess in the interpersonal relation to the intrapersonal relation over time. Nevertheless, the question whether reasonableness is rooted in rationality has attracted far more interest. One author, in particular, tried to bite the bullet and to derive the precepts of morality from hypothetical bargains among people whose interest is to reap the long-term benefits of cooperation. According to Gauthier, they would accept rules of fair play from their primarily self-concerned perspective.[41] David Hume,[42] by contrast, seemed to regard our moral point of view as some supervenient feature of arrangements that may initially have come about as a consequence of our self-interested behaviour. Once they are in place, the self-interested perspective becomes eclipsed by our celebration of artificial virtues, such as justice and public benevolence, and the adoption of an impartial perspective.

Since all attempts at deriving reasonableness from rationality remain doubtful, Rawls settles on a relation of complementarity.[43] Merely reasonable agents would have no personal aims to pursue; merely rational agents would lack a sense of justice and fail to recognise the independent validity of the claims of others.[44]

It is interesting that the rational is so easily taken as a given and the reasonable is considered to be in need of an explanation. One explanation

[40] See n 8.

[41] See D Gauthier, *Morals by Agreement* (Oxford, Clarendon Press, 1986). The two sentences in the text cannot do justice to a very complex and sophisticated argument.

[42] See D Hume, *A Treatise of Human Nature* (ed EG Mossner, London, Penguin, 1969) 551. So also B Barry, *Theories of Justice* (Berkeley, CA, University of California Press 1989) 163–65.

[43] See Rawls, n 37, 49.

[44] ibid 52. This shows that reasonableness and rationality work in tandem. Reasonableness provides you with choice-worthy and commendable objectives, rationality instructs you to take the means necessary to attain them.

of this asymmetry may be that we have more than merely one procedure to explain what reasonableness requires. The content of the reasonable is notoriously contested in a manner that rationality is not.

Reasonable Laws

If the focus of a conception of law rests entirely on how we are to deal rationally with intimations of coercive authority, then its basic maxim recommends the adaptations to institutions exercising overpowering force. Of course, it is always all right to escape their grip by cheating or, if possible, having them hoist with their own petard. From a rational perspective, however, there is no normative constraint that the coercive authority of law is supposed to satisfy. Rationality is interested in the 'law as it is', not as it ought to be.

Reasonableness, however, expects the law to live up to certain standards of fairness. The minimal standard demands to take into account that the addressees of legal directives are rational agents. The most minimalist position of natural law theory, which we encounter in the work of Lon Fuller, articulates this standard.[45] It arrives at a list of simple principles that the law is supposed to observe – such as clarity, absence of retroactivity, no conflicts between norms – so that we are able to plan our conduct in anticipation of the relevant reactions that might originate from the legal system. The law ought to behave like a machine: irresistibly, but predictably. Philosophers of German idealism, such as Johann Gottlieb Fichte[46] and Friedrich Wilhelm Joseph Schelling,[47] were also fond of this idea.

[45] See LL Fuller, *The Morality of Law* (New Haven, CT, Yale University Press, 1969).

[46] See JG Fichte, *Grundlage des Naturrechts nach Prinzipien der Wissenschaftslehre* (ed F Medicus, Hamburg, Meiner, 1979) 140–41.

[47] See FWJ Schelling, *System des transzendentalen Idealismus* (ed W Schulz, Hamburg, Meiner, 1957) 239–40.

4

A Modest Primer on Reasonableness

Law and Rational Action

Economic dealings are essentially, as Max Weber recognised, the field of rational conduct.[1] Contractual arrangements involve people availing themselves of the services or goods of others as means to their own ends. They do so in a mutually advantageous or possibly even reciprocal manner.[2] The engagement of their own rationality is embedded in constraints supposed to ensure that what they do is also not morally reprehensible.[3]

If one looks at contractual exchanges from the perspective of the parties involved, each of the parties, from their own point of view, believes that they will benefit from the bargain. Otherwise, rational actors would not entertain it in the first place. This means that resources end up in their most valued uses and that the welfare of a society is thereby enhanced. If one adopts a bird's-eye view on subjective gains, one can cast the good outcomes of rational interactions as 'Pareto improvements'.[4] An improvement of this type does not even require a mutual advantage. The condition for its existence is satisfied if, because of a transfer, at least one person ends up better off – and no one worse off – than before. Even if Pareto improvements do not reach the threshold level of 'mutual advantage', the idea demonstrates that we regard the single-minded pursuit of rational conduct as unobjectionable so

[1] See M Weber, *Economy and Society* (trans K Tribe, Cambridge, MA, Harvard University Press, 2019) 141–52; J Habermas, *Theorie des kommunikativen Handelns*, vol 1: *Handlungsrationalität und gesellschaftliche Rationalisierung* (Frankfurt aM, Suhrkamp, 1981) 346.

[2] They do not, therefore, violate the second formulation of Kant's categorical imperative, according to which one must not use others as mere means but always also regard them as ends in themselves. See I Kant, *Grundlegung zur Metaphysik der Sitten* (ed B Kraft and D Schönecker, Hamburg, Meiner, 1999) 53 (AA 428).

[3] Moreover, Weber also believed that the conceptual accuracy of a purely 'formal' mode of legal reasoning that abstains from evaluating the law from a moral point of view makes the operation of the legal system so calculable that it effectively serves the ends of rational conduct. Modern law, according to Weber, provides the conditions under which rational conduct can flourish and be successful. See M Weber, *Economy and Society*, vol 2 (trans E Fischoff et al, ed G Roth and C Wittich, Berkeley, CA, University of California Press, 1987) 875–76.

[4] See, for example, N Mercuro and SG Medema, *Economics and the Law: From Posner to Post-Modernism* (Princeton, NJ, Princeton University Press, 1997) 19.

long as it observes constraints. Pareto improvements, mutual advantage and reciprocity are different normative standards. They are not, however, on an equal footing. The unequal bargaining conditions that the concept of mutual advantage tolerates are objectionable from the perspective of reciprocity.[5]

Relative Reasons

According to the default position of 'naïve' accounts of rational human action,[6] reasons are reasons[7] only for the persons who happen to have them. Whether you have reason to do something depends on who you are and the condition you are in. If you are hungry, you have reason to eat, while I have none if I am not hungry. There is, undeniably, an 'objective' element inherent in the relation between hunger and getting food; nevertheless, it is the case that the condition that persons are in, in particular how they are affected by desires, accounts for whether they have reasons for action or not. You have reason to climb Kilimanjaro[8] because you have a desire to do so. But the fact of your having this desire does not imply that I also have reason to ascend to the top of this mountain, let alone to support you in your pursuit.[9] As self-interested agents we prima facie only have reason to do what is good for ourselves. Rationality demands that we pursue what we take to be our own good, possibly after examining how well-informed our preferences are. Reasons of this type are, as Thomas Nagel puts it, 'agent-relative' or, simply stated, 'relative' reasons.[10]

[5] See J Rawls, *Political Liberalism* (New York, Columbia University Press, 1991) 16–17, 50.

[6] They do not, however, amount to what Michael Thompson would call 'naïve action theory', which explains one action by redescribing it as another ('Why are you typing?' ''cause I'm writing a book'). See his *Life and Action: Elementary Structures of Practice and Practical Thought* (Cambridge, MA, Harvard University Press, 2008) 106.

[7] As Street explains, the concept of a reason is 'primitive' and its meaning can be rephrased exclusively by using other normative language or with an appeal to the experience of 'to-be-done-ness'. Nonetheless, there is nothing in the concept of a 'reason' that suggests that reasons are either attitude-independent or not. See S Street, 'Nothing "Really" Matters, but That's Not What Matters' in P Singer (ed), *Does Anything Really Matter? Essays on Parfit on Objectivity* (Oxford, Oxford University Press, 2017) 121–48, 127–28, 134.

[8] I am taking this example from T Nagel, *The View from Nowhere* (New York, Oxford University Press, 1986) 167.

[9] See CM Korsgaard, *Creating the Kingdom of Ends* (Cambridge, Cambridge University Press, 1996) 277.

[10] See Nagel, n 8, 152, 158–59. Originally, in *The Possibility of Altruism* (Princeton, NJ, Princeton University Press, 1970) 90 and 93, Nagel calls these reasons and related values 'subjective'. A shift in the terminology occurs in *The View from Nowhere*, n 8, 152, fn 4. 'Subjective' now refers to what *seem* to be reasons for the agent while they could turn out to be none. The former 'subjective' reasons are henceforth called 'agent-relative'. Nagel himself indicated that he followed Parfit's example. See D Parfit, *Reasons and Persons* (Oxford, Clarendon Press, 1986) 56, 143. See also the helpful commentary

Upon closer examination, however, the picture turns out to be somewhat more complex. Even the relative or 'private'[11] reasons informing our rational conduct can never be tantamount to mere sudden impulses. If people assert, even with regard to a very specific situation, that they have a reason for doing something, they are adopting some precept for themselves. By obtaining guidance from it, they make themselves into the cause of their actions.[12] They take charge and transcend the level of various, and possibly conflicting, impulses. What they thereby do is to rely on something 'over and above'[13] their inclinations or temptations. Their relation to this elevated level constitutes their capacity of choice.[14]

Practical Identities and Autonomy

Action is therefore possible only if it originates from reason-responsive beings rather than from the forces to which these beings are exposed. But how do we authenticate this 'over and above' of our actions?

At a most elementary level,[15] we rely on some 'precept'. If the will is to be a cause, as it is required for there to be action, it must observe some law or principle,[16] for it is a normative standard that permits us to do what *we* do as opposed to seeing something happening to us.[17] If such line-drawing were not possible, we would drown in various factors impinging upon our

by Korsgaard, n 9, 303. For a highly elaborate reconstruction of the various shifts in the vocabulary and the divergent uses of the distinction between relative and neutral reasons, see M Ridge, 'Reasons for Action: Agent-Neutral v. Agent-Relative' *Stanford Encyclopedia of Philosophy* at https://plato.stanford.edu/archives/spr2023/entries/reasons-agent/ (last visited 24 April 2025). In what follows, I will refer to 'person-relative' or 'agent-relative' and 'person-neutral' or 'agent-neutral' reasons simply as 'relative' or 'neutral' reasons.

[11] This is the term that Korsgaard has come to use instead of 'person-relative' reasons. See CM Korsgaard, *Self-Constitution: Agency, Identity, Integrity* (Oxford, Oxford University Press, 2009) 191.

[12] ibid 41.

[13] ibid 72, 75, 126, 134.

[14] Korsgaard occasionally speaks of the thinking and the acting self, with the former representing rational and reasonable volition and the latter the capacity of choice. CM Korsgaard, *The Sources of Normativity* (Cambridge, Cambridge University Press, 1996) 104, fn 15, 138.

[15] Ultimately, this is a question concerning our personal practical identity that is rooted in our moral identity as a rational being. See Korsgaard, n 11, 24–25, 45, 58–59. See also Korsgaard, n 14, 120–21.

[16] See Korsgaard, n 14, 97. This is an idea that she inherits from Kant.

[17] See Korsgaard, n 14, 93: '[O]ur capacity to turn our attention on to our mental activities is also a capacity to distance ourselves from them, and to call them into question. … I desire and I find myself with a powerful impulse to act. But I back up and bring the impulse into view and then I have a certain distance. … Shall I act? Is this desire really a *reason* to act? … We need reasons because our impulses must be able to withstand reflective scrutiny. We have reasons when they do.' See also RB Pippin, *Hegel's Practical Philosophy: Rational Agency as Ethical Life* (Cambridge, Cambridge University Press, 2008) 71.

conduct.[18] This explains why the reasons helping us to constitute ourselves as agents must be different from inscrutable impulses or opaque affections. Were they not, it would be impossible to distinguish agents from the emotional and vegetative forces intersecting – possibly at cross-purposes – within them.[19] Reason-responsiveness constitutes us as autonomous agents.[20] As Korsgaard explains, '[w]e are active to the extent that our movements are caused by a conception of what we ought to do'.[21] As beings with the capacity for willing an end – in contrast to merely wishing or contemplating it – we determine ourselves to bringing it about.[22]

More precisely, whatever presents itself as an incentive must be endorsed *as a reason* from a point of view that reveals something about what or whom I, as an agent, take myself to be. A student contacts me during my sabbatical leave, requesting a meeting to discuss questions concerning an upcoming exam. My spontaneous reaction is to delete her e-mail message, for I can confidently assume that she must have received the out-of-office reply explaining my unavailability. But next I wonder whether doing and saying nothing would not be inappropriate for a professor, and decide to send her a riposte, drawing, thereby, on my conception[23] of my 'practical identity' as a professor.

An identity of this kind is what guides me in my conduct. It is a source of reasons for me.[24] We all live with a jumble of various overlapping and occasionally conflicting practical identities (they are the 'roles' that we play in contexts of social interaction).

[18] See, on the 'wanton', HG Frankfurt, *The Importance of What We Care About: Philosophical Essays* (Cambridge, Cambridge University Press, 1988) 16–17.

[19] See Korsgaard, n 11, 75–76.

[20] ibid 83.

[21] Korsgaard, n 33, 11. She puts the matter as follows, and we can, in this context, read what she refers to as a principle as a 'reason': 'You regard the choice as yours, as the product of your own activity, because you regard the principle of choice as expressive, or representative, of yourself. You must do so, for the only alternative to identifying with the principle of choice is regarding the principle of choice as some third thing in you, another force on a par with the incentives to do A and to do B, which happened to throw in its weight in favor of A, in a battle at which you were, after all, a mere passive spectator. But then you are not the cause of the action. Self-conscious or rational agency, then, requires identification with the principle of choice on which you act.' Korsgaard, n 14, 123.

[22] See Korsgaard, n 11, 69, 125. This is how Korsgaard explains the concept of 'willing' and concludes that Kant's hypothetical imperative is a constitutive principle of willing. In contrast to mere wishing or contemplating options, willing an end means to determine oneself to bring the end about, that is, to cause it. We become active.

[23] Korsgaard, n 14, 114, explains the Rawlsian distinction between concepts and conceptions in the following way, 'The concept names the problem, the conception proposes a solution'.

[24] Korsgaard, ibid 117, puts this dryly as follows, 'A view of what you ought to do is a view of who you are.'

According to Korsgaard's transcendental argument,[25] such identities are necessary conditions of the possibility of our actions. The idea is straightforward. Various conceptions of who we are or aspire to be serve as sources of reasons for actions.[26] We could not be reason-responsive beings were it not for these.[27] For something to serve as a medium for the recognition of what is valuable or good or right requires that the evaluators be of value to themselves. If they were not, nothing else could be of value to them; indeed, nothing would matter to persons attributing nil importance to their lives and existence.[28] Since being reason-responsive is what makes us human, we could not identify anything as valuable based on various practical identities if we did not value our humanity first.[29] If we did not treat our ultimate practical identity as human beings as normative, no other and more particular practical identity could guide us either.[30] Since our identity as moral agents[31] not only stays in the background of more specific practical identities but also facilitates the resolution of collisions between and among them, any incentive that might potentially be a reason engages our reasonableness as such. The capacity in which we matter eventually for action is that of reasonable agents *tout court* (*überhaupt*, in German philosophical parlance), over and above particular practical identities, contingent desires and occasional resources of action.

[25] ibid 117, 123.

[26] A transcendental argument usually hinges on there being no alternative to these conditions. I do not want to dispute this. What is in question, however, is what accounts for the possibility of practical identities. They are, after all, not conjured from thin air but part of the normative fabric of social life. Korsgaard might therefore be closer to Hegel than she herself may be ready to acknowledge. She teases this proximity out a bit when discussing the basic communitarian claim that we can only be agents if we are members of a moral community (see ibid 119). She emphasises correctly that communitarians can only claim that some or any community is necessary but never one in particular. But this is not different from Hegel's claim about *Sittlichkeit*.

[27] Korsgaard, n 14, 122.

[28] ibid 117, 122.

[29] See ibid 117, 123: 'You must value your humanity if you are to value anything at all.'

[30] See S Street, 'Coming to Terms with Contingency: Humean Constructivism about Practical Reason' in J Leuman and Y Shemmer (eds), *Constructivism in Practical Philosophy* (Oxford, Oxford University Press, 2012) 40–59, 46–47. Street (ibid 50) puts Korsgaard's argument into question. When one asks what the conditions are to regard anything as a reason, one asks a normative question: Should we? At the same time, by suspending the sphere of reasons, one brackets everything that would make answering the question possible. The value of humanity is hence asserted from nowhere and there is no way of warranting its correctness. Street (ibid 52–55) also challenges the idea that we as sources of values have to be valuable in ourselves. Worker-bees see reason to do their work, but they consider themselves only to be of instrumental value.

[31] Korsgaard then quickly concludes that owing to our membership to humanity, it behoves us to act as part of humanity and therefore as a member of the 'Kingdom of Ends' (*Reich der Zwecke*). See Korsgaard, n 14, 129. But this is not what the transcendental argument has demonstrated. It has merely demonstrated that we have to be a law unto ourselves. Using Korsgaard's distinction between the 'categorical imperative' and the 'moral law', it has demonstrated only the former and not the latter. See n 14, 98–99. For a critique, see also Pippin, n 17, 88.

Universality and Happiness

Since any action engages us as reason-responsive beings as such, even relative reasons that engage merely our rationality have to be universal.[32] This means that for them to be reasons in the full-blown sense, they have to claim that *any* person invested with a certain set of desires, an evolving sense of their practical identities, and finding themselves in the selfsame situation has reason to perform the action required or at least suggested – subject to further deliberation – by an appropriate incentive.[33] This is the one reason for universality; the other is the unification of the agent over time. If agents haphazardly changed their minds from one situation to the next, they would cease to be agents unless they had, indeed, adopted wantonness as their reason of action.[34] Of course, only if universality is combined with judging impartially vis-à-vis others does it represent the form that is relevant for reasonableness as moral universalisation.

Universality is what makes relative reasons comprehensible.[35] We can ask others for their advice ('If you were in my place, what would you do?') or discuss intractable personal issues. From this it follows that, as both rational and reasonable agents, we never occupy only the 'subjective' standpoint, but also some 'objective' correlative from which each of us is cast as one person among others, moved to act by reasons they might have.[36]

The universality of reasons is not undermined by the fact that they are relative to the type of person one would like to be or to the variety of satisfaction one seeks. Indeed, 'happiness' is the concept that permits us to combine universality with most idiosyncratic relativity.[37] Agents can find themselves ridden with a variety of and occasionally even queer strivings. For the constitution of a reason it matters, though, that agents yield to an incentive[38] because it is approved by something that accounts for who or

[32] See Korsgaard, n 11, 191.

[33] See CM Korsgaard, *The Constitution of Agency: Essays on Practical Reason and Moral Psychology* (Oxford, Oxford University Press, 2008) 121, 123.

[34] For a further, and more sophisticated elaboration of this point, see Korsgaard, n 11, 203–06.

[35] On intelligibility, see JD Velleman, *How We Get Along* (Cambridge, Cambridge University Press, 2009) 17, 32. Korsgaard draws a distinction between generality and universality: a principle or reason is general if we believe that it applies to a wide range of similar cases; it is universal if we believe that it applies to every case of a certain sort, unless there is a reason to make an exception. See Korsgaard, n 11, 73. Since I wish to establish the connection between reasons, universalisation and moral justification, I stick to the predicate 'universal'.

[36] See T Nagel, *What Does It All Mean? A Very Short Introduction to Philosophy* (Oxford, Oxford University Press, 1987) 66; Nagel, n 8, 135.

[37] See Korsgaard, n 11, 191.

[38] See Korsgaard, n 14, 117, 127.

how they would like to be. The striving for happiness qua satisfaction of desires is a relative reason that we recognise for ourselves and others. Each has reason to pursue their happiness, but this does not in and of itself suggest that all have reason to promote everyone else's happiness. Were that the case, we would have a neutral reason to do so – a reason, that is, regardless of who one is and the situation in which one finds oneself.[39]

Suppose some people enjoy watching operatic productions staged and directed by Calixto Bieito.[40] Even though I have no clue how anyone could ever develop such an aberrant predilection, I understand that these persons have reason to attend as many of the performances staged by him as possible, because doing so ostensibly gives them aesthetic pleasure. Relative reasons can be shared even if they are, using Brandom's parlance, in the cases under consideration, 'attitude-dependent'.[41] Their existence for agents depends on whether they believe themselves to have them based on what they take to be their projects or desires. And I hasten to add that there is no neutral reason to expose oneself to the fruitiness of Bieito's bumbling lack of ingenuity.

This universality of relative reasons to seek happiness comes in two forms. First, I can understand what makes you happy by imagining what it would be for me to be like you. Second, we can fully abstain from imagining whether it is also sound what others crave. We can focus, rather, on the *fact* that something is simply desired by agents. If the satisfaction of desires makes them – at any rate, prima facie – happy, they have reason to satisfy them. Happiness confers value on activity owing to its desire-fulfilling quality.[42] It is the relative reason *par excellence*, establishing the link between personal preference and universality (actually, it grants agents *authority* to establish that connection).

Leaving the determination of universality to the individual agent, of course, also suspends it. This explains why, as a reason, happiness must appear both shallow and paradoxical. It is shallow, for the experiences making people happy require – from the second-personal perspective – merely an authentication by the happy persons themselves ('I love it').[43] It is paradoxical, for the

[39] An easy way to make sense of the distinction between neutral and relative reasons is to think of the duty of parents to take care of children. The reason is relative with regard to one's own children. But it is not neutral. There is no reason to care for all children.

[40] For an introduction, see https://werktreue.com/calixto-bieito/?lang=en (last visited 25 April 2025).

[41] See RB Brandom, *A Spirit of Trust: A Reading of Hegel's* Phenomenology (Cambridge, MA, Harvard University Press, 2019) 263, 265–66.

[42] See Korsgaard, n 9, 284. The point can be stated simply as follows: something is good because it makes me happy, and it makes me happy because it satisfies one of my desires.

[43] Korsgaard regards this shallowness as following from people's building up a bulwark against incomprehension. See ibid 289.

connection between the relative reason and its trigger – that is, the anticipation of a happiness-inducing experience – is entirely left to the agent to establish. The universality of the relative reason is thereby emptied of substance. We may, for that reason, forever suspect the Bieito afficionados of being totally bonkers.

Neutral Reasons

If Bieito's managers had the power to constitute for all of us, even against our personal preferences, a reason to watch their client's productions, they would be invested with a power of 'moral' legislation.[44] They would lay down a neutral (Korsgaard: 'public'[45]) reason.[46] We would all be required to watch singers perform in grotesque costumes on messy stages.

This is one way of stating the neutrality of reasons. It highlights the generality of their addressees. This lends them a semblance of 'perfect duties', which are mostly duties of omission.[47] Nobody must harm other people. By contrast, what one is supposed to do to treat others with appropriate respect needs to be fleshed out at a greater level of detail for specific situations. The relevant determinations should reflect neutral concerns, but they may give rise to reasons relative to persons.

There is, however, an alternative way of characterising neutral reasons, which should not elude us. It invests the concept with another meaning. Neutral reasons are those we use to weigh and evaluate reasons for action from the perspective of no particular person. We thereby detach the person-relative reason from its relevance to the person's self-interest alone. We examine it from an impersonal point of view.

This, I submit, is what Rousseau had in mind when he spoke of the 'total alienation' of the person with all its rights to the community.[48] It stands for nothing else than the surrender of one's relative reasons to a judgement that is to be arrived at from an impersonal point of view, from which, in Rousseau's case, we articulate the general will. It is as though one submitted relative reasons for approbation.

[44] See ibid 285.

[45] See Korsgaard, n 11, 191, 196.

[46] See Nagel, n 8, 152–53, 158–59; Korsgaard, n 9, 276–77. See Korgaard, n 14, 133, 'public reasons are reasons that have normative force for everybody'.

[47] On the history of this concept, see S Darwall, *Modern Moral Philosophy: From Grotius to Kant* (Cambridge, Cambridge University Press, 2023) 21, 62–63.

[48] See J-J Rousseau, *Major Political Writings* (trans JT Scott, Chicago, IL, Chicago University Press, 2012) 173.

Rousseau, as is well known, believed in a necessary connection between impartiality and generality. In his view, the impersonal general will can only arrive at general laws without failing to be what it ought to be.[49] He did not contemplate that impersonality may occasionally require that we make an exception in order to lift burdens from someone who may find these too onerous to carry. This shows, however, that the first meaning of neutral reasons, their generality, is derivative of how they come to be conceived. Generality is, thus understood, inherited from approving reasons from the impersonal point of view. This explains why the matter is also a tad confusing. Acting on relative reasons passing muster from the impartial angle can be defended, with an eye to their conception, in neutral terms. I am vindicated in choosing my profession if acting on the relevant relative reasons is supported from an impersonal perspective.[50]

Shared Reasons

Relative reasons have force only for some agents, even though they are intelligible to others.[51] One has to be X to have X's reason for doing y. We have just seen, however, that they can be defended in neutral terms if they come to be shared.

As speakers of a natural language, we have learned to perceive ourselves not only from the first-, but also from a second- and third-personal perspective.[52] We can look at ourselves from the outside and view ourselves 'objectively' as one person among others who are 'equally real'.[53] Perceiving myself and others as having reason to avoid pain due to the intrinsic

[49] See ibid 181.

[50] In relation to relative reasons, neutral reasons are 'second-order' reasons. See J Raz, *Practical Reasons and Norms*, 2nd edn (Princeton, NJ, Princeton University Press, 1991) 39, '[a] second-order reason is any reason to act for a reason or to refrain from acting for a reason' (emphasis omitted).

[51] Korsgaard seems to suggest that reasons are 'public' or 'neutral' by default, for they are just as much a shared and a common possession as linguistic meanings (Korsgaard, n 14, 138). Just as there can be no private language, in the sense of meanings that exist only for a person considered in isolation, there can be no private reasons (ibid 137). While this idea is in fact intriguing, it is to be feared that Korsgaard is at this point guilty of conflating neutrality and intelligibility. As proficient speakers of an ordinary language and as people with a modicum of life experience, we are all able to understand the reasons people have. We can share (ibid 136) them with others, however, without thereby exposing ourselves immediately to their normative pull. Language makes it possible to share reasons in a proto-normative state before determining to treat them as either relative or neutral. We can recognise the normative force for others without being subject to it.

[52] See GH Mead, *Mind, Self, and Society from the Standpoint of a Social Behaviorist* (ed C Morris, Chicago, IL, Chicago University Press, 1934) 160–61.

[53] See Nagel, *Possibility of Altruism*, n 10, 88.

awfulness of the experience, I can arrive at a conception of its disvalue because it is disliked by whoever is affected by it. The value of being free from pain can thus be intersubjectively shared.

A joint reaction is not, however, a sufficient condition for sharing a reason, for it does not yet give me reason not to turn my back on suffering people by telling them that I can feel their pain while surreptitiously congratulating myself on having been luckily spared. Rather, shared reasons are possible only if I regard their condition as not different from my own. I have to cross the line separating me from others.[54] This is precisely what happens if we surrender ('alienate') our relative reasons and reconceive them jointly from an impersonal angle. Recasting relative reasons in neutral terms is the mirror-image of shifting from the personal to the impersonal perspective and adopting the having of relative reasons as a common concern. Obviously, with this shift we are then no longer individual selves responding to a common situation. We transcend our personal perspectives and look together 'from above' – vertically – at the relative reasons we have.

The most straightforward consequence for us as occupants of positions 'below' is that we must ask ourselves how we would evaluate, were we affected ourselves, the effects of our acts on others, for we are now, at the level 'above', rendered as no particular person and, hence, belong to all conceivably affected by our own actions (see Figure 4.1). The horizontal 'reversal of perspectives' follows from attributing equal standing to the reasons of all and from suspending the separateness of persons.[55] The reversal taking place 'below' also shows what is at stake. My reasons are returned to me nesting in the perspective of others taking my own perspective into account while I am adopting theirs. My reasons and interests are, in a sense, held hostage by others expecting me to take their own interests adequately into account. If I devalued theirs, they would have reason to devalue mine (and I would, indeed, do this to myself, for my devaluation would be immediately returned to me).

[54] See also T Nagel, *The Last Word* (New York, Oxford University Press, 1997) 120–21. Nagel concedes that there is no substitute for direct concern for other people as a basis of morality (or what we call 'reasonableness' here). See Nagel, n 36, 63–64. It would be ludicrous to claim, for example, that I am reasonable out of rational fear to be castigated with remorse. If I were, I would merely want to avoid the torments of conscience caused by my wrongdoing. But there is no simple causal connection between wrongness and guilt. Compunction or shame are reactions inherent in understanding that one has done the wrong thing. They can arise only after one has felt the pull of moral reasons and realised that one has failed to live up to them.

[55] See Korsgaard, n 14, 142–43.

Figure 4.1 Two perspectives on reason

above	No particular person's perspective on relative reasons
below	Taking into account of relative reasons of others taking our relative reasons into account

Conceiving of the interaction as a 'bargaining' situation is congenial to the 'view from below'. But we can only be really reconciled with one another, not by bargaining from below but by legislating from above. At this point, what the shared standpoint amounts to can be sketched as follows:

> One is constituted out of his own interests; and when those interests are frustrated, what is called for then is in some sense a sacrifice of this narrow self. This should lead to the development of a larger self which can be identified with the interests of others. I think all of us feel that one must be ready to recognize the interests of others even when they run counter to our own, but that the person who does that does not really sacrifice himself, but becomes a larger self.[56]

Arriving at the perspective of the larger self is experienced as a discovery as well as formation. The concrete terms of commitment have to be determined against a background of rather vague intuitions. We shall return to this below (see below pp 52–53).

Strategic Action and Mastery

The picture remains incomplete. It does not reveal clearly enough the understanding of who we come to be to one another in constituting this intersubjective type of reasonableness.

More often than not we treat the having of reasons by others as a mere factor to be taken into account in explaining their behaviour. Reasons make agents calculable. We can determine under which conditions their actions might pose obstacles in the path of our own.[57] Viewing their conduct from an angle that treats reasons as possible causes and the effect of such causes

[56] Mead, n 52, 386.
[57] See Korsgaard, n 11, 193–94.

as potentially affecting adversely one's own projects prepares the ground for strategic action. The point of such action is then to manipulate the conditions of action, as perceived by others, in order to make them do what best serves our own interest.[58]

From the perspective of strategic action, however, one does not treat other persons as equally real. On the contrary, their interests count for nothing. The matter becomes even clearer when contrasting strategic with communicative action.[59] This type of action takes place when we coordinate behaviour or cooperate based on the premise that the participants mutually take their interests into account and attempt to arrive at a jointly agreed course of conduct. For example, when we engage, as I frequently have to do, in scheduling a meeting with others,[60] we ideally take cognisance of their routines and other commitments, and attribute to these the same importance and urgency that we accord to our own. Should we fail to do so, we would end up belittling the agenda of others as trifling and consequently try to extract cumbersome rescheduling concessions from them while remaining unwilling to undertake like efforts ourselves. If others seem to benefit more from meeting us than we from meeting them, we have better bargaining chips and may easily succeed at communicating an inflated sense of the prominence of our doings. Others, in attempts to ingratiate themselves with us, may resign themselves to putting items on their agenda on the back-burner. We can, simply put, in such a situation exercise 'mastery',[61] which is, nonetheless, different from strategic interaction where we do not enter a common reasoning process at all.

In any event, if people abstain from exercising mastery, every participant's reasons that are relevant to scheduling a meeting are on an equal footing. Then it is the case that each participant in a deliberation adopts the perspective of another person and thus shifts to the impartial perspective.

But what happens after each person has put herself into the shoes of others and is then perceived by these others as also viewing matters from their point of view? It is, indeed, at this point that we arrive at a very significant fork in the road. Since the constitution of neutral reasons involves suspending the boundaries between and among persons, the dividing lines

[58] See Habermas, n 1, 385.
[59] See ibid 385–86.
[60] This is Korsgaard's very illuminating example, n 11, 189–90.
[61] See Brandom, n 41, 314.

can either fall by the wayside – even though 'identity' recurs invariably, as we shall see – or be redrawn in the process of communication.

Aggregative Egoism

In the former case, when boundaries become irrelevant, relative reasons end up simply being depersonalised. They are anyone's and nobody's. They float freely. Apparently, when viewing the matter from such an impersonal angle, we are inclined to treat any person's interests as if they were preferences that are prima facie equally entitled to satisfaction: They lend themselves to a comparative assessment of their intensity and urgency only within some *haphazardly* bounded unit. The necessity of such a unit for the purpose of the application of the utilitarian calculus is all there is to the utilitarian conception of individual persons and groups. The calculus can only be applied to a closed set. If, when it comes to defining this set, the focus rests on groups, the lines drawn between and among persons are irrelevant. Small wonder that utilitarianism rides roughshod over the 'separateness of persons'.[62] All that matters is the maximum satisfaction of desires.[63] Consequently, hardship suffered by some persons can be outweighed by the satisfactions enjoyed by others. The reward for sacrifice does not have to be realised in the individual person that has incurred it.

It is quite puzzling that such aggregative neutrality appears even remotely plausible to us, for it fails to have a plausible equivalent in an institutional stetting. There is no reason to limit the application of the utilitarian calculus to a nation state. Indeed, the calculus looks to utility wherever it may be calculable. Paradoxically, the nonchalance vis-à-vis boundaries is again owed to how utilitarianism perceives individuals.[64] There are no pre-established limits to our desires. An individual is the spokesperson of the passively

[62] See, famously, J Rawls, *A Theory of Justice* (Cambridge, MA, Harvard University Press, 1971) 26–27: 'The most natural way, then, of arriving at utilitarianism (although not, of course, the only way of doing so) is to adopt for society as a whole the principle of rational choice for one man. Once this is recognized, the place of the impartial spectator and the emphasis on sympathy in the history of utilitarian thought is readily understood. For it is by the conception of the impartial spectator and the use of sympathetic identification in guiding our imagination that the principle for one man is applied to society. It is this spectator who is conceived as carrying out the required organization of the desires of all persons into one coherent system of desire; it is by this construction that many persons are fused into one'.

[63] On the groundlessness of that principle, see Korsgaard, n 33, 89–90.

[64] See, however, on the number problem that will later be famously discussed by Parfit in R Nozick, *Anarchy, State, and Utopia* (New York, Basic Book, 1974) at 41, 'Maximizing the total happiness requires continuing to add persons so long as their net utility is positive and is sufficient to counterbalance the

carried desires that happen to affect it.[65] 'Universalistic hedonism'[66] is, as regards its form, not different from universalistic egoism; in fact, it is just as egoistic, with the ego defined as whoever calculates and maximises satisfaction across a range of relevant desires. This may even explain utilitarianism's strange allure. The calculus is administered by an anonymous impartial spectator acting as the guardian of preferences.

From I to We

A more plausible rendering of the impartial perspective merely suspends, without thereby abandoning, the separateness of persons. As already adumbrated above, it amounts to the anticipation of some inchoate community.

We have seen above (at p 49) that if people do more than merely mutually assure each other of their sympathy, the care of their own interests – that is the reasons they have – is returned to them as these interests are perceived and evaluated by others. Their own perspective is nested in those of the latter. This captivity, which is mutual, forces everyone to rid themselves of their partiality. Under this condition, all can arrive at a general will. This supervenient step gives rise to neutral reasons on the permissible relevance or irrelevance of relative reasons.

The separateness of persons can be preserved by remaining amenable to objections from individuals.[67] The formulation of the common will must not amount to a unilateral imposition. Returning to the scheduling example, if we stayed masters of our own reasons for action we could only interact strategically with one another or attempt to prevail with a masterly imposition. There would be, quoting from Rousseau, 'no common superior that could judge' between us and the others.[68] Such a 'superior' can supervene on our deliberations only if we relinquish exclusive control of our reasons and pool them with the reasons of others. As

> each gives himself to all, he gives himself to no one, and as there is no associate over whom he does not acquire the same right that he grants him over himself, he gains the equivalent of everything he loses ...[69]

loss in utility their presence in the world causes to others.' On the 'repugnant conclusion', see D Parfit, *Reasons and Persons* (Oxford, Oxford University Press, 1984) 381–91.

[65] See Rawls, n 5, 186.

[66] See H Sidgwick, *The Method of Ethics*, 7th edn (London, Hackett, 1987) 497.

[67] We will return to this matter in chapter 11.

[68] See Rousseau, n 48, 173 (*Social Contract* I.6.).

[69] ibid.

Once we surrender our reasons to an assessment by the general will, we act, even if only in the context of small joint projects, as members of one body, 'and as a body we receive each member as an indivisible part of the whole'.[70] Reasonableness necessarily involves transcending one's private existence and viewing oneself as part of some collective body. The only alternative thereto is the consequentialist path along which the reasons in the pool are aggregated with the aim to maximise satisfaction. The separateness of persons can then no longer be raised as an issue, for the lines of personal identity are being wiped out. If we are, by contrast, members of a common body, we can voice our dissatisfaction about how we are treated by objecting, for example, that we are expected to contribute more than we should.

The shared perspective from which emerges a common will is likely affected by Rawls' 'burdens of judgment' and for that very reason again irredeemably 'relative'. These burdens, it will be remembered from the introduction to this book, point to prerational factors synthesising our practical reasoning. They can be morally accounted for – and this is the argument of this book – by constructing a legal relation. This may also explain that, at the end of the day, political communities have to be built on particularity.

Objective Realism

Nagel has a different take on neutrality.[71] In his view, we perceive reasons that speak for or against the existence of something regardless of whether there is a particular person to whom the reason is related. Here is how Nagel introduces this idea:

> The desire to be rid of pain has only the pain as its object. This is shown by the fact that it doesn't even require the idea of oneself in order to make sense: if I lacked or lost the conception of myself as distinct from other possible or actual persons, I could still apprehend the badness of pain, immediately. So when I consider it from an objective standpoint, the ego doesn't get between the pain and the objective self. My objective attitude toward pain is rightly taken over of an evaluation of the pain itself, rather than merely a judgment of what would be reasonable for its victim to want: 'This experience ought not to go on, whoever is having it'.[72]

[70] ibid.
[71] See Nagel, *The Last Word*, n 54, 88.
[72] Nagel, n 8, 161.

Just as intentionality, according to phenomenological doctrine, intends to discover the object in the manner in which it presents itself,[73] our comprehension of the nature of agony seems to give us a reason to avoid it.[74] Possibly, our comprehension of pain confronts us immediately with the demand that *it* abate. The normativity springs from the 'overwhelming urge to battle'[75] pain. This seems continuous with the proto-normativity of natural desires.[76] The organism has 'authority', the desired object is 'responsible' for making itself available.

For objective realists, by contrast, the value resides not in the relation of the subject to the object but in the object itself.[77] Korsgaard explains such objective realism very aptly by comparing it to a world devoid of creatures perceiving the light. The sun would still shine, but it is possible that nobody existed to see it.

Parfit believes that reasons are provided by intrinsic features that account for a state or event to be good.[78] In his view, at the beginning of the chain of reasons there must be some fact that gives us a reason to want some possible event or situation.[79] Reasons are based in rational intuitions.[80] If, conversely, reasons were merely based on desires, our evaluative outlook would ultimately depend on desires we have no reason to have.[81] If that were the case, 'nothing' mattered.[82] Parfit claims that if only our choices accounted for

[73] See M Heidegger, *Grundprobleme der Phänomenologie* (1927) in *Gesamtausgabe* (ed FW v Herrmann, Frankfurt aM, Klostermann, 1975) 96–97.

[74] See D Parfit, *On What Matters*, vol 2 (ed S Scheffler, Oxford, Oxford University Press 2011) 551. Elsewhere (see D Parfit, *On What Matters*, vol 1 (ed S Scheffler, Oxford, Oxford University Press, 2011) 54), Parfit says that what is bad about pain is not our sensation 'but our conscious state of having a sensation that we dislike'. This is, as Street perceptively argues, a concession to the attitude-dependence of value, for it appears to be the 'dislike' of the sensation that confers value on being free of pain. See S Street, 'In Defense of Future Tuesday Indifference: Ideally Coherent Eccentrics and the Contingency of What Matters' (2009) 19 *Philosophical Issues* 273–98, 283, 288.

[75] Korsgaard, n 14, 148.

[76] See Brandom, n 41, 326.

[77] See Korsgaard, n 9, 279.

[78] See Parfit, *On What Matters*, vol 1, n 74, 91.

[79] In this respect he seems to argue like utilitarians, who claim that pleasure and pain are facts that are also values and, hence, phenomena where the natural and the normative are one. See Korsgaard, n 14, fn 146.

[80] On this notion, see SD Hales, *Relativism and the Foundations of Philosophy* (Cambridge, MA, MIT Press, 2006) 36.

[81] See Parfit, *On What Matters*, vol 1, n 74, 88.

[82] ibid 107. Mind that this appears to be a transcendental argument. Things matter. Since things could not matter if reasons were attitude-dependent or entirely subjective, reasons must originate from something attitude-independent.

what is good or bad on the ground of being or not being chosen, 'we must make our choices in the dark'.[83]

What is disturbing about this view is that pursuant to such strict agent-neutrality, taking the perspective of another becomes entirely ephemeral. What matters instead is that pain ought not be. The fact that it is experienced by someone is of peripheral importance. The reasoning becomes consequentialist[84] in a manner that again has difficulty to account for the separateness of our existence as persons. Possibly, therefore, Nagel's emphasis on the neutral value of avoiding pain is an attempt to correct depersonalisation and can therefore be regarded as shorthand for remembering that persons are equally real.

Internalism and Externalism

Contemporary practical philosophy widely accepts the distinction between 'externalism' and 'internalism'.[85]

According to externalism, a distance remains between the reasons perceived by persons and the motives actually causing their conduct. A person can still reply to a moral demand by saying 'I understand that what I am about to do is wrong, but I am confident to get away with it; in fact, I am pretty smart if I do not get caught doing the wrong thing.'

Internalism, by contrast, insists that reasons are only what they claim to be if they incline us towards action. After all, actions would be inexplicable if reasons did not motivate. Strategic interaction would be impossible too.

None of this implies, of course, that the demands of reasonableness must always trump self-interested rationality. It can still be the case that although I know that I should give money to charity, enjoying a family vacation is more important to me. Nonetheless, internalism invites our attention to the fact that the personal goal that I pursue ought to be of a certain moral significance to attain weight vis-à-vis competing considerations. The example therefore would look entirely different if I said that I don't give money to charity because I am greedy. Possibly, it is rational to be greedy,

[83] Parfit, *On What Matters*, vol 1, n 74, 46; 55: 'Though it is good to have sensations that we *like*, nothing is merely good because we want this thing'.

[84] See Korsgaard, n 9, 281.

[85] ibid 317. For an elaborate introduction to the debate, see JD Velleman, *The Possibility of Practical Reason*, 2nd edn (Ann Arbor, MI, Maize Books, 2015) 153–86; Velleman, n 35, 118–20.

but greediness is unreasonable. Externalists would shrug their shoulders and explain that this demonstrates that moral reasons do not motivate conduct. Internalists, by contrast, do not ignore the moral problem that is posed by the externalist's perspective. Internalists can therefore rightly object to externalism that it is merely another name for one's lack of concern for the equal reality of others.

Objections to Moral Relativism

The topic of relativism[86] is going to concern us more in a subsequent chapter, but it should at least be mentioned at the end of our brief consideration of reasonableness.

It is rather difficult to wrap our heads around relativism, not least because by default we all seem to be attracted to it. The explanation is that we tend to shy away from moral controversy. It is so heated and personal. We rationalise our lack of toughness with the belief that there are no universally valid moral ideas, that all that we regard as reasonable is in some way relative to a point of view, be this the point of view of a culture, a group or a person.

But professing moral relativism does not make sense.

First, relativism presupposes an imaginary focus, namely, 'the person' or 'the culture' as the organising centre of a totality of experience that is allegedly different from, and incommensurable with, any other. As Donald Davidson tried to explain, it is not clear how we might be able to identify such partial, yet closed totalities.[87] It makes more sense to doubt their existence. Davidson's idea is simple. If people reason from their conceptual scheme and use it to make sense of the content of their experience, we should be able to infer the existence of these schemes based on persistent failures of translation. How A reasons from scheme C cannot be made intelligible within the conceptual universe D occupied by B. They live in different worlds. Davidson's analysis shows that inability to translate is not a sound idea, for it is always possible, occasional failures notwithstanding, to arrive in processes of 'radical interpretation' at interpretations of the meanings of linguistic utterances based on attributing the value of truth to them. We should be able, he contends, to reconstruct at least part

[86] For an extremely helpful introduction, see S Lukes, *Moral Relativism* (New York, Picador, 2008).

[87] See D Davidson, 'On the Very Idea of a Conceptual Scheme' in his *Inquiries into Truth and Interpretation* (Oxford, Oxford University Press 1984) 183–98.

of the meaning of a foreign vocabulary based on the premise that the speaker says what we believe to be true. We need to be generous, though, as Davidson explains:

> Charity is forced on us; whether we like it or not, if we want to understand others, we must count them right in most matters. If we can produce a theory that reconciles charity and the formal conditions for a theory, we have done all that could be done to ensure communication. Nothing more is possible and nothing more is needed.[88]

The observation can be transferred, *ceteris paribus*, to the moral domain. By hypothetically accepting as true a claim that we reject, we can infer premises and commitments necessary to make it defensible. We may still disagree, but there is no reason to suspect that people reason differently from us. It is just the case that they arrive at conclusions that we find wrong, perhaps because they accord to the relevant values different weight and priority.

Second, if relativism is true and recognised, we would share some conceptual grid that explains how what we take to be right or wrong depends on the views each already has. We can mutually assure each other of our respective views or even criticise one another by adopting the point of view of another. We share an overarching meta-perspective. Owing to this fact, it is inexplicable why there even is controversy. This is *in nuce* Paul Boghossian's objection to relativism.[89]

Third, relativist arguments are often based on a faulty genealogical perspective that simply suggests that we harbour certain views because they have been inculcated into us. But this mistakes genealogy for validity.[90] The fact that I happen to have certain beliefs as a Western European does not show that they are for that reason alone not universally valid.

Three Models of Reasonableness

This brief introduction of the concept of reasonableness offers merely a very rough idea. Reasonableness involves regarding other people as 'equally real', taking their interests into account in determining our actions and judging impartially ('don't do unto others what you would not want to have done

[88] ibid 197.

[89] See PA Boghossian, *Fear of Knowledge: Against Relativism and Constructivism* (Oxford, Oxford University Press, 2006).

[90] See Nagel, *The Last Word*, n 54, 103–04.

to yourself'). What this requires at a level of greater detail remains largely to be determined within more copious accounts of reasonable conduct.

The history of legal and political philosophy provides us with three models of fleshing out further what reasonableness demands.

The first model locates reason within the broader context of other factors relevant to your conduct, such as instincts, drives, haphazard desires, the sense of pride and our loyalties. The point of this model is to imagine how reason can prevail in the face of adversarial forces (eg, sudden urges, strong longings or unbridled ambitious self-assertion) without, however, behaving despotically towards these other factors. Indeed, the idea is that reason must engage in efforts to befriend these other forces and to establish harmony within the human soul. The appealing idea implicit in this model is that the turmoil of factors impinging on individual agents is characteristic not only of the individual soul, but also of larger communities of people. In this context, it is possible to recognise the prevalence of certain motives in certain groups and to attempt for political communities to attain the same type of harmony that can be established within the individual soul. We encounter this model of reasonableness in most prominent versions of ancient political thought.

The second model takes very little interest in the human soul. It highlights, rather, the order and the norms that are purportedly amenable to reasonable insight. The second model is manifest in the natural law tradition, which is united in its belief that reason and the order to which it gives rise are independent of what we take them to be.

The third model breaks with this basic premise and suggests that order and norms emerge from processes of collective self-determination. This model unearths the most basic precepts of reasonableness – equal reality of persons, their freedom and reciprocity – and puts them to use in the context of social contract theory and constitutionalism.

We begin, as we ought to, in the next chapter with exploring the first model.

5

Soul and the City

The Conflicted Self

The concept of reasonableness that we encountered in the previous chapter involves two simple ideas. We behave reasonably towards others if we treat them – to repeat Nagel's already oft-repeated expression – as 'equally real'. We would fail to do so, if we did not attribute to their interests the same relevance that we attribute to ours.

A consequence of transcending our subjective take on situations is, therefore, to accord relative reasons of others standing in our practical deliberations and to treat those reasons as at least prima facie neutral. Presumably, they are reasons for everybody.

The other consequence is, indeed, a consequence of the first. Reasonable persons no longer approach the world from within their perspectival private outlook. Rather, they view it from a perspective that is 'ours', no matter how unspecified and indeterminate the presupposed 'we' may be. Reasonableness entails, therefore, viewing yourself as a member of the 'kingdom of ends', that is, of a community of beings who cooperate while respecting each other as ends in themselves.[1] Whatever is an end in itself is not meant to be subordinate to an end outside of itself. Hence, such a being must not be treated as a 'mere means', for doing so would deny it the status of being an end. Whatsoever ends those who are ends in themselves pursue, the ends must be chosen by them simply because they are ends in themselves.

From our membership of the moral community it follows that if one judges a matter of moral significance, one can do so only by speaking on behalf of this community. The question must arise, invariably, whether making oneself into its representative is supported by adequate authority. This question concerns the substantive dimension of moral judgement.

There is a further consequence, however, following from the elementary axiology of reasonableness. In our practical deliberations we encounter

[1] See I Kant, *Grundlegung zur Metaphysik der Sitten* (ed B Kraft and D Schönecker, Hamburg, Meiner, 1999) 59–60.

tensions and conflicts between impulses and their evaluations. Desire says 'please', usually with a twinkle in the eye, yet reason raises the index finger and replies by saying 'no'. This is the case for the prudent conduct concerning ourselves, but it is also the case for reasonable persons transcending themselves. In the latter case we are taking the reasons of others into account. We are doing the same thing when we reason together about what we have most reason to do. At the end of the day, such reasoning is also always about impulses or proposals and their evaluation. The reasoning within the larger group is not different from the reasoning of individuals. The same antagonists make their appearance in both.

In accounting for ourselves, we ordinarily attribute these potentially conflicting items to different sources. For example, we ascribe hunger and thirst to the vegetative part of our nature. When and how much we eat or drink is a matter to be determined by reason. Hence, we make sense of how we reason and what we do by viewing ourselves as invested with a vegetative and a reasonable component. Ancient philosophers believed both to be essential parts of the human soul.[2]

Such attributions, however, can also be made on a grander scale, depending on which part of our nature – or of our soul – is more salient in certain social groups, even if doing so involves a supple measure of haughtiness. We may believe that unskilled labourers are mostly motivated by their natural drives for survival, the enjoyment of simple pleasures and an indiscriminating longing for sexual pleasure. We would thereby implicitly suggest that the vegetative part of human nature is strong in them. By contrast, we may posit that the capacity of reasonableness is much more strongly articulated in the more learned classes. Doing so would suggest that the same problem of governance ('governmentality'[3]) that arises within the individual also arises within the larger group, the polity. From this it is only a small step to Plato's idea that we can study polities in order to elucidate the human soul and, conversely, the individual soul to improve our understanding of polities.[4] What makes the analogy possible, is the core idea that 'the desires

[2] For a brief introduction, see S Goetz and C Taliaferro, *A Brief History of the Soul* (Oxford, Wiley-Blackwell, 2011) 6–29. A more extensive discussion is offered by M Davis, *The Soul of the Greeks: An Inquiry* (Chicago, IL, University of Chicago Press, 2011).

[3] This is Foucault's infelicitous term.

[4] See *The Republic of Plato*, 2nd edn (trans A Bloom, New York, Basic Books, 1991) 368e–369a (at 45), 435b (at 113).

of the common many are mastered by the desires and the prudence in the more decent few'.[5]

Self-consciousness and the Unity of the Agent

Indeed, the self-awareness of us as thinking and acting beings implicates viewing the self as composed of different parts. Again, this is the case for entirely pragmatic reasons. To enhance our self-understanding, we simply want to come up with an account of our moral experience, which involves matters such as urges, burning desires, transgression, feelings of guilt, weakness of the will (*akrasia*) or inner conflict. In attempting to explain these phenomena, it makes sense to view our inner life as a battleground or, less dramatically put, as a playing field of various forces that differ in kind.

Plato already suggested that not only cities can be fundamentally divided by warring factions;[6] an individual can also be torn apart by internal division.[7] Taking her cue from both Plato and Hume, Korsgaard speaks in such cases of the 'combat model' of the soul.[8] The model suggests that 'reason' and 'passion' are at war with each other and engage in intermittent skirmishes.[9] The self is a place marked by an enduring propensity for conflict. While passion spews out desires, reason refuses to satisfy them (not always, but in the case of conflict it does). It is a contingent matter which of these parts of the soul happens to prevail over the other. Consequently, there is nothing to unify the self. The agent is indeed split apart into two different armies. The result is that the actions of the agent could never be based on a conception of what the self would like to be. The individual is just tossed around by hostile forces. One may be inclined to believe that if matters go well, reason will not be the slave of passion[10] but that the relation might as well be the reverse. Ideally, reason rules and passions comply. But even such an arrangement smacks of oppression.[11]

[5] ibid 431d (at 109).

[6] See, for example, ibid 462b (at 141), 423a (at 100), 547e (at 225), 551d (at 229).

[7] See, for example, ibid 554d–e (at 232–33).

[8] See CM Korsgaard, *The Constitution of Agency: Essays on Practical Reason and Moral Psychology* (Oxford, Oxford University Press, 2008) 100–01.

[9] It need not be necessarily the case that only reason and passion are at loggerheads. The soul can be also the battleground of different desires and appear to be stable as long as those that are necessary prevail over those that are frivolous and luxurious. See, on the oligarchic soul, *Plato*, n 4, 559d (at 237).

[10] But see D Hume, *A Treatise of Human Nature* (ed EG Mossner, London, Penguin, 1969) 460–65.

[11] See, correctly, Korsgaard, n 8, 156–57.

Korsgaard goes on to suggest that Plato introduced a different model of the soul, according to which the soul features a 'constitution'.[12] While this constitution accords reason the leading role, it also comprises other parts of the soul that are not considered to be alien or hostile forces but integrated into a larger whole.[13]

The constitution of the human agent (ie the self) is brought about in a piecemeal fashion and is in each instance of self-constitution based on conceptions of identity that the agents entertain of themselves. These conceptions are further specified or revised within the lifespan of the individual. They function, in a sense, like the constitutions of common law systems that are subject to elaboration and amendment from one case to the next.

The Basic Analogy

Plato's *Republic* begins with a famous discussion of the meaning of justice as an individual virtue.[14] After a famous 'sophist' and Plato's brothers (Thrasymachus on the one hand, and Adeimantus and Glaucon on the other) have had their turns at explaining that just is what is to the advantage of the stronger,[15] and raising issues such as that people would do unjust things if they got away with it with impunity and did not harm their reputation,[16] Socrates suggests that for the purpose of answering the question it is advisable to study the composition of a well-ordered political community.[17] Doing so would, he submits, cast light on the condition of the individual soul. Justice consists, according to Socrates, in the right composition of the human soul, that is, in each part of the soul doing its proper work.[18]

[12] ibid 101. This claim appears to say more than it in fact does. In Plato's case it is merely about the harmonious, ie just, interaction of the parts of the human soul. It is the form of common good constitutionalism that is characteristic of constitutions prior to the advent of written constitutions and modern constitutionalism. Also, there is no 'law' governing Plato's constitution, just the wise adjustment of its parts.

[13] In a faction state, according to Plato, the hostility that citizens have towards their external enemies is matched by the hatred of one's own. See *Plato*, n 4, 470b (at 150).

[14] ibid 331a (at 7).

[15] ibid 338c (at 15).

[16] ibid 365c (at 43).

[17] ibid 368d–e (at 45), 434d (at 113).

[18] ibid 434a (at 112), 441d (at 121), 453b (at 131).

The idea underlying the cross-reference in the relation of the soul and the city is that studying the composition of the city helps to elucidate the soul and studying the soul sheds light on the composition of a well-ordered city.[19] The simile is reversible. Plato does not suggest a necessary causal relation in the sense that a particular constitution of a city is composed of people whose souls have a like constitution. What matters is the likeness of the structure.[20]

The Structure

The human soul is composed of three parts.[21]

Reason is the calculating part and has access to real knowledge, which is wisdom.[22] It possesses foresight without being lost in specifics. It aims for the good, which is the good of the human being or of the city as a whole.

Thymos (spirit) involves resoluteness and the sense of self-respect or firm adherence to one's personal commitments.[23] The self can respect itself only if it sticks firmly to plans that it has adopted. The self can take pride in itself if it does not act like a weakling and proves capable of defending itself against attacks. *Thymos* is that part of the self that assists it in sustaining its identity against hostile forces, also when these forces originate from within itself (for example, seduction by frivolous enjoyments, anxiety, etc).[24] Remorse or self-loathing at one's shortcomings are articulations of *thymos*, as is the anger directed at opponents.[25] The fear of being either distracted or disrupted fuels its resolute determination.

Finally, the appetitive part of the soul provides the soul with desires and various cravings. Its presence indicates that we also belong to nature.[26]

[19] The original idea is that studying the larger entity facilitates the analysis of the smaller and invisible entity. See N Pappas, *The Routledge Guidebook to Plato's Republic*, 3rd edn (London, Routledge, 2013) 78.

[20] See GRF Ferrari, *City and Soul in Plato's* Republic (Chicago, IL, University of Chicago Press, 2003) 65–66.

[21] See *Plato*, n 4, 439d–e (at 119), 580d (at 261). Of course, upon closer inspection, matters are never as simple as they might seem. Plato ascribes to each part of the soul particular desires; hence, desires do not originate only from the appetitive part. See C Meinwald, *Plato* (London, Routledge, 2016) 146.

[22] See *Plato*, n 4, 428d (at 106).

[23] ibid 449d, 440a–e (at 119–20).

[24] ibid, 430a (at 108) on *thymos*' tacit association with courage.

[25] ibid 375c (at 52), the spirited people 'must be gentle to their own and cruel to enemies, if not, they'll not wait for others to destroy them, but they'll do it themselves beforehand'.

[26] ibid 439d–e (at 119).

By analogy, the city is composed of the rulers, the auxiliaries and ordinary working folk. The rulers and the auxiliaries together form the group of the guardians. The rulers are drawn from the auxiliaries.[27]

The rulers are charged with governing the place. They do what reason does in the individual soul. Both provide the whole to which they belong with guidelines and general maxims. Since the rulers cannot, presumably, attend to every detail, their major task must, for the most part, consist of laying down general rules. But rules are not in and of themselves effective. Their implementation requires motivating beliefs. Hence, the thymotic part of the auxiliaries needs to be 'dyed' with beliefs about what ought to be feared and averted to such an extent that 'the dye could not be washed out by those lyes so terribly effective at scouring, pleasure, so much more effective than soap and soda, and pain and fear and desire, the most effective of all'.[28] What the rulers thereby instill into the auxiliaries is the 'power of preservation … of the right and lawful opinion about what is terrible and what not'.[29] This power is then called 'courage'.

The auxiliaries occupy the executive branch and must make sure that the orders issued by the rulers are carried out.[30] Not only are they the equivalent of *thymos* in the human soul writ large, they also need to have the resolution and perseverance that *thymos* begets.[31]

Ordinary working folk take care of providing for the needs of the inhabitants of the city. They are concerned with appetites. What is more, the satisfaction of desires is all there is to their lives. They do not aspire to something greater and higher.[32]

Wisdom, Courage and Moderation

According to Plato, a city and the human soul are functioning well if each part of the city runs within its own channel.[33] Just as in the individual soul reason identifies with the person as a whole and is therefore not likely to repress unnecessarily the satisfaction of desires, the rulers of the city identify

[27] ibid 414b (at 93).

[28] ibid 430a (at 108). I have simplified the translation by adding wording from Lee's translation. See Plato, *The Republic*, 2nd edn (trans D Lee, London, Penguin Books, 2007) 133.

[29] *Plato*, n 4, 430b (at 108).

[30] ibid 414b (at 93).

[31] The auxiliaries are like dogs. See ibid 440d (at 120).

[32] ibid 580e (at 261).

[33] ibid 433a–b (at 121), 434a (at 112).

with the city as a whole and aim at realising the common good. Realising the common good, however, requires that each part is doing its bit and carries out its proper task faithfully. Justice is the realisation of such harmony,[34] but it can be brought about only if each part moderates its in-built tendency to assert itself vis-à-vis others.[35] Mutual encroachments are destructive of the harmony and happiness of the city. Rule by the ordinary folk ('democracy'[36] was clearly abhorred by Plato) would affect the city adversely, at least in the long term. Ordinary folk are myopic, concerned only with the satisfaction of immediate pleasures, given to idle passions and lacking in courage to defend their place.[37] By contrast, a city in which the thymotic energies of auxiliaries dominate would overemphasise military virtue, authorise excessive warfare and likely overindulge in inflicting cruelties on its foes.[38] Such a city may leave a track record of bloodshed and mindless destruction.[39] A city in which people with an unquenchable thirst for amassing wealth call the shots – an oligarchy, that is – will be marked by a stark inequality of wealth[40] and thrift or austerity.[41] The ruling class will sit on top of a 'boiling pool' of unsatisfied desires, in particular those of the exploited lower classes.[42]

Plato's idea is, however, not that the groups will keep each other in check. Rather, the citizens have to possess their proper virtues. A virtue is a capability to do good things. It has become part of the disposition of the person. A virtuous person is disposed to do what is right when the occasion thereto arises.

The rulers need to possess wisdom.[43] The auxiliaries must be courageous.[44] Courage not only makes them, in the event that they have to, ready

[34] See ibid 443d (at 123), for the following account of the just man: 'He doesn't let each part in him mind other people's business or the three classes in the soul meddle with each other, but really sets his house in good order and rules himself; he arranges himself, becomes his own friend, and harmonizes the three parts, exactly like three notes in a harmonic scale, lowest, highest and middle'.

[35] See ibid 430e–432a (at 109–10). Moderation permeates the whole city. Each part of the soul and the city confronts the other with its own conception of the good. The appetitive part is interested in gain, the spirited part in victory, the reasonable part in wisdom. Conflict is unavoidable. See ibid 581a–582a (at 262–63).

[36] See ibid 555b–562a (at 233–40).

[37] For some of democracy's ills, see ibid 557d–558d (at 236).

[38] Thymotic characters are definitely harsh with slaves. See ibid 549a (at 226).

[39] See Korsgaard, n 8, 115. See also CM Korsgaard, *Self-Constitution: Agency, Identity, Integrity* (Oxford, Oxford University Press, 2009) 165.

[40] See *Plato*, n 4, 551a (at 228).

[41] ibid 554a, 554d–e (at 232–33), 559d (at 237).

[42] ibid 554d (at 232).

[43] ibid 428d (at 106).

[44] ibid 430a–b (at 108).

to put their lives at risk and behave fearlessly in combat;[45] they also fear the right things and do not abandon their rightful fears when they are under the impression of another immediate danger. Indeed, courage should make them more afraid of an invasion by their enemies than of losing their own lives.

All that the ordinary working folk is expected to be is moderate[46] (a virtue which is supposed to pervade the whole).[47] Moderation creates in them the readiness not to enjoy simple pleasures excessively and to stay resilient and healthy.

A Puzzle

Interestingly, this psychological model of reasonableness is based on the premise that, if all goes well, no part of the human soul will be oppressed by another.[48] This suggests that there is a reasonable element present in the other parts too,[49] for what else would account for the fact that appetites occasionally agree to put up with a sacrifice and that *thymos* may be persuaded to waive revenge. Viewed from this angle, the model is not quite satisfactory. This may be the reason why Aristotle attributed to the unreasonable 'striving' part of the soul the ability to listen to reason and to adapt voluntarily and habitually to its demands.[50] In Plato's model, after all, reason also has to be capable of moderation and to allow simple pleasures to have their way. It seems that not only is moderation a virtue that is required of all parts, but all the other parts have to be able to develop an understanding of what their place is in the larger scheme of the soul and the city.

[45] ibid 429d (at 107), 442c (at 122).
[46] ibid 389e (at 67).
[47] ibid 432a (at110).
[48] Indeed, Plato seems to defend a 'harmony theory' of reasonableness. See Korsgaard, n 8, 155, 172.
[49] See *Plato*, n 4, 586e (at 269).
[50] See Aristotle, *Nicomachean Ethics* (trans RC Bartlett and SD Collins, Chicago, IL, University of Chicago Press, 2011) 1102b30 (at 24). For a very elaborate introduction to Aristotle's political psychology, see FD Miller, Jr, 'The rule of reason' in *The Cambridge Companion to Aristotle's Politics* (ed M Deslauries and P Destreé, Cambridge, Cambridge University Press, 2013) 38–66.

6

The Best and the Most Feasible

Catering to Our Unhappy Consciousness

What is it that makes ancient political thought so attractive to this day? I guess the reason is that it offers a combination of realism and utopianism that is congenial to our jaded attitude towards the political world. We take the ancients, in the case of Plato and Aristotle, to have explored the question of what the best constitution might be. Obliquely, however, they conceded the utopian nature of their quest. We won't find the best system in the real world. They may not have believed the best constitution to be unimaginable, for in that case it could not be what we expect it to be. An impossible constitution would be none at all. They merely concede that given how people ordinarily conduct themselves, the realisation of the best system of all seems extremely unlikely. Human beings notoriously disappoint. This conclusion is reached, therefore, based on a clear sense of the realities of political life. The bleaker outlook of the ancients is, however, an outgrowth of a somewhat snooty aristocratic attitude: 'With these people we cannot build a truly excellent political community.'

Our era is strongly affected by 'unhappy consciousness',[1] namely, an embarrassing commitment to a system of government the authority of which we have now come to defend only by pointing to worse and historically failed alternatives (such as fascism and communism). We have developed a lingering fatigue about liberal democracy and endure a longing for something we can neither sketch nor fathom, let alone set our minds to. Hence, we clutch faintheartedly to what we have. We readily pardon Plato and Aristotle for their utopianism and admire them for the realism

[1] This type of consciousness is to be encountered at the end of Hegel's discussion of Stoicism and ancient skepticism. See GWF Hegel, *Phänomenologie des Geistes* (ed H-F Wessels and H Clairmont, Hamburg, Meiner 1988) 144. I am following Pinkard's account. He summarises 'unhappy consciousness' thus: 'The "unhappy consciousness" *takes* certain things to be authoritative but cannot quite *believe* in their authoritativeness. … Thus, the participants in the "unhappy consciousness" find that they have a certain self-conception rooted in a set of social practices that for them is authoritative, but for which they can neither see any justification nor envision any concrete alternative.' T Pinkard, *Hegel's Phenomenology: The Sociality of Reason* (Cambridge, Cambridge University Press, 1994) 70. Judith Shklar used the concept to label a romantic mindset that had lost its faith in progress. See JN Shklar, *After Utopia: The Decline of Political Faith* (ed S Moyn, Princeton, NJ, Princeton University Press, 2020) 65–66.

with which they studied politics without drawing a distinction between the 'formal' constitution and its 'real' counterpart.[2] The ancients, indeed, study 'real constitutions', in particular the manner in which these blend and flow into each other, occasionally in quick succession.[3] The name that we use today for what they were after when they spoke of *politeia* is the 'regime'.[4] They also have a live sense that the real constitution is an arrangement of offices[5] that are staffed with whoever successfully claims to merit[6] investiture with political power. What is more – and this is possibly the most salutary contrast to our modern constitutionalism – the ancients do not turn a blind eye on how socio-economic circumstance influences the constitutional politics of groups.[7]

All of this is quite perceptive in contrast to the lifeless normativism of modern constitutional law. Indeed, our established legal scholarship adopts towards the constitution, which it takes to be a 'norm', a perspective reminiscent of what moral theorists would call 'externalism'.[8] It expounds the meaning of the constitution without regard to the distinct social perspectives and manifest or hidden motives of relevant actors. Political scientists, by contrast, regard the rational pursuit of one's self-interest as the default and supreme political motive.[9] Both perspectives can be aligned. Modern

[2] See my 'Real Constitutional Law: A Revised Madisonian Perspective' in C Bezemek, M Potacs and A Somek (eds), *Vienna Lectures in Legal Philosophy*, vol 2 (Oxford, Hart Publishing. 2020) 161–83.

[3] Most famously, Plato analysed how failed constitutions morph into their sequels. See *The Republic of Plato*, 2nd edn (trans A Bloom, New York, Basic Books, 1991) 545a–569c (at 223–49).

[4] See Aristotle, *The Politics*, 2nd edn (trans C Lord, Chicago, IL, University of Chicago Press, 2013) [hereinafter 'P'] 1278b10-11 (at 71): 'For what has authority in the city is everywhere the governing body, and the governing body *is* the regime.' This means that the *politeia*, the regime, is the group of people calling the shots and eligible for office. See ibid 1279a26, 1279b15-25 (at 73–74). Aristotle, however, also uses the term *politeia* for the regime that he believes to be the most feasible. It is the regime in which the *politeuma* – the governing body – is the multitude 'governing with a view to the common advantage' (ibid 1279a37 (at 73); see also ibid 1265b35 (at 37); 1289a36 (at 99); 1293a40 (at 109)).

[5] See P 1278b10 (at 71).

[6] See Aristotle, *Nicomachean Ethics* (trans RC Bartlett and SD Collins, Chicago, IL, University of Chicago Press, 2011) [hereinafter 'NE'] at 1131a26-27 (at 95).

[7] The politically most elementary division is that of social class, ie between the many poor and the wealthy few. See P 1291b7-12 (at 105). Hence, the two most important regimes are democracy and oligarchy. See ibid 1290a7-12 (at 101): 'Now a regime is an arrangement of offices, and all distribute these either on the basis of the power of those taking part in the regime or on the basis of some equality common to them – I mean, [the power] of the poor or the well off, or some [equality] common to both.' Aristotle also puts much emphasis on the role that is to be played by certain groups within certain regimes. For example, he believes that a democracy in which the farmers are the strongest group is to fare better than others for the reason that the farmers are busy with tilling their land and raising cattle and have only very little time for debates in political assemblies. The laws are going to do the work for them. See ibid 1318b7-22 (at 175–76). On the parts of the city see ibid 1299b27–1290a5 (at 100–01); 1261a21-24; 1274b27 (at 26, 62).

[8] See chapter 4, at 'Internalism and Externalism'.

[9] See, for example, W Riker, *Liberalism against Populism: A Confrontation Between the Theory of Democracy and the Theory of Social Choice* (San Francisco, CA, Waveland Press, 1982).

constitutional law has arisen from combining normativism with the hard-nosed attribution of self-interested motives to political actors. Not by accident, James Madison regarded a system of checks and balances as the chief mechanism for sustaining the constitution as law.[10] The idea is that the constitution must be arranged in such a manner that no branch can break the law without being visited upon by the others. Ambition must be made to counteract ambition.[11] Madison was the first to combine the perspective of a legal scholar with that of a *modern* political scientist (the emphasis the ancients put on different groups of estates disappeared).

Ancient constitutionalism is more nuanced, even if it appears a bit naive in suggesting that a regime could empower agents that are indeed not merely interested in promoting their own good.[12] But don't we believe something very similar when we believe ourselves to be safe only if there is some reserve power (*subsidium*) to manage crises for the good of all should the need arise?[13] The ancient constitutionalists were confronting this issue head-on and asking the question whether it is better to have laws[14] or to let the good officeholders do what they think is right.[15] The latter is a live possibility if leaders are virtuous and public-spirited. The distinction between following laws and taking immediate action provides the background of the time-honoured distinction between ordinary and absolute prerogative powers in the context of the common law.[16] According to doctrines

[10] See A Hamilton, J Madison and J Jay, *The Federalist* (ed C Sunstein, Cambridge, MA, Harvard University Press, 2009) 341.

[11] See Madison, n 10, 341.

[12] See, on aristocracy, P 1293b1-5 (at 109–10), 1284a1-2 (at 85), 1294a10-12 (at 111).

[13] See J Messner, *Das Naturrecht: Handbuch der Gesellschaftsethik, Staatsethik und Wirtschaftsethik*, 8th edn (Berlin, Duncker & Humblot, 2018) 294–301. Most recently, Vermeule adopted Messner's doctrine of subsidiarity in a manner that would strengthen the executive branch. See A Vermeule, *Common Good Constitutionalism: Recovering the Classical Legal Tradition* (Cambridge, Polity Press, 2022) 156–57.

[14] Aristotle is in favour of legality, however, it is clear to him that laws should be set aside if a situational judgement is required or when they appear inappropriate owing to their generality. See P 1286a20-25, 1287b19-17 (at 90, 94); NE 1137b6-23 (at 112). He also believes that coercive laws can bring about ethical virtue through a process of habituation. See NE 1180a1-5 (at 231). Aristotle is also aware that the best laws are to no avail unless they are supported by habituation. See P 1310a15-17 (at 153): 'For there is no benefit in the most beneficial laws, even when these have been approved by all those engaging in politics, if they are not going to be habituated and educated in the regime …' See also FD Miller, 'The Rule of Reason' in M Deslauriers and P Destrée (eds), *The Cambridge Companion to Aristotle's Politics* (Cambridge, Cambridge University Press, 2013) 38–66, 61 (emphasising that according to Aristotle, the law is needed to sustain reason in the face of political passion).

[15] The matter is most famously discussed in Plato's *Statesman* (trans R Waterfield, Cambridge, Cambridge University Press, 1995) 300d, 303b4 (at 68, 72), where it is suggested that the laws are merely imitations of truth and that superior to all constitutions is the rule of one god-like wise man. For a useful discussion, see FD Miller, 'The Rule of Reason in Plato's *Statesman* and the American *Federalist*' (2007) 24 *Social Philosophy and Policy* 90–129, 103–05.

[16] See, notably, G Burgess, *Absolute Monarchy and The Stuart Constitution* (New Haven, CT, Yale University Press, 1996) 72–74, 150; PD Halliday, *Habeas Corpus: From England to Empire* (Cambridge, MA, Harvard University Press, 2010) 68–69.

prevalent during the Stuart period, the latter may override the limits set to the former under exceptional circumstances. The existence of this distinction bespeaks that we are disposed to trust the application of laws only as long as we do not believe ourselves to be better off if a person with good judgement jumps in to straighten things out on the spur of the moment.[17]

Their seeming naivety aside, the ancients were clear about the fact that not all self-interests are alike, let alone on an equal footing, for they are too heterogeneous to be reduced to the maximisation of welfare. While some are after wealth, others just want to be free and lead modest lives without being kicked around by ambitious people. Machiavelli still had a very keen sense that these two different 'humours' matter to the emotional fabric of republics.[18]

Ruling and Being Ruled

While there is in Aristotle less of a straightforward analogy between components of the soul and parts of the city than the one taking pride of place in Plato's *Politeia*, it is nonetheless the case that the task of governing is basically the same for individuals as for relations among them.[19] Possibly, Aristotle considered it to arise in all living things, for he recognised that 'by nature' most things are ruling and ruled.[20] They contain, at any rate, a ruling and a ruled component.

Any rule, if correct, is by the 'better' part over the other.[21] Since within the human soul the deliberating part ('reason') is the better part than its non-reasonable components, reason ought to govern human conduct.[22] Reason is thereby engaging with the striving part of the soul that is, while itself not reasonable, able to listen to it and to adapt to its demands.[23] It is, nonetheless, the case that Aristotle regards ruling and being ruled as aspects of a common 'work' that belongs to the elements involved together and benefits them all.[24] Undoubtedly, the better or major part has to call the

[17] See P 1287a27-29 (at 93).

[18] See N Machiavelli, *The Prince* (trans HC Mansfield, Cambridge, MA, Harvard University Press, 1985) ch 9, 39. For commentaries, see JP McCormick, *Machiavellian Democracy* (Cambridge, Cambridge University Press, 2011) 5, 29, 92–93, 102; HC Mansfield, *Machiavelli's Virtue* (Chicago, IL, Chicago University Press, 1996) 93, 237.

[19] For an excellent introduction to these issues, see Miller, n 14, 45–47, 61, in particular the fine-grained analysis of psychological types and types of rule.

[20] See P 1260a8-9 (at 22).

[21] See P 1254a25 (at 7).

[22] See P 1254b5-8 (at 8).

[23] See NE 1102b29-32 (at 24).

[24] See P 1254a28-29 (at 7).

shots, but the minor or lesser part needs to do its bit by following the commands issued by the former. From the perspective of ruling, the distinction between the intra- and the interpersonal relations is not really a major issue. The rational component rules the less rational, and this is as true of the intrapersonal relation as it is for the relation between free person and slave, male and female, and parent and child.[25] Not surprisingly, Aristotle states that lack of self-control can exist in the case of an individual and also in the case of the city,[26] and that cities are made up of dissimilar persons, pointing by analogy to the heterogeneity of animals with their relation between the body and soul as well as to the different parts of the human soul.[27] The only difference of significance concerns the unit that is constituted and sustained by the activity of governing, that is, the person, the household of the family. Ruling is necessary for composite things to sustain themselves.[28] Animate things possess the ruling relation by nature, men need to use reason in order to determine what is right. It is possibly in this vein that Aristotle contends that 'reason is a master craftsman'.[29]

Ruling differs in kind, depending on the components involved and on the attitudes that these adopt toward one another. The rule of the master over the slave is just as despotic as the rule of the soul over the body.[30] The analogy is sound. The body yields to the pressure that we exert on it by means of either physical training or diets. We submit it to so much strain as we believe will keep it vigorous and strong. We force it out of its obstinate sluggishness. Appeals to good will are, of course, to no avail. We shape our physique (and with it the vegetative part of the soul)[31] essentially in a manner that is alike to how we domesticate an animal, even if animal nature comes in great variety. Ferocious animals like lions require harsher treatment than cattle, which are more disposed to becoming habitually obedient.[32]

[25] See P 1260a 7-11 (at 22). Aristotle continues as follows (ibid 1260a11-14): 'The parts of the soul are present in all, but they are present in a different way. The slave is wholly lacking in the deliberative element; the female has it but lacks authority; the child has it but is incomplete.' Miller, n 14, 46, 50 believes that Aristotle is of the opinion that women lack authority because they are less spirited than men.

[26] See P 1310a18-20 (at 153).

[27] See P 1277a5-10 (at 67–68).

[28] See P 1254a26-30 (at 7): 'For whatever is constituted out of a number of things – whether continuous or discrete – and becomes a single common thing always displays a ruling and a ruled element.'

[29] See P 1260a18 (at 23).

[30] There is more nuance in Aristotle's account of the soul of the slaves, who are after all able to listen to and to comprehend commands. See Miller, n 14, 48.

[31] See NE 1102a32-34 (at 23).

[32] See P 1254b10-12 (at 8).

The rule over free members of the family is either 'political', which is the case for the husband's rule over his wife, or 'kingly', which is the case for the relation between the father and his children.[33] Yet the rule over wives is 'political' only in the sense that the relation concerns people who are free, since Aristotle states that the rule of the husband over the wife is in fact aristocratic.[34] More truly political in the sense of some rotation among rulers and the ruled is the rule among brothers, at least if the age difference between them is not too large.[35] This is roughly equivalent to rule in the 'polity'.

Since unity is at stake in voluntary relations of ruling and being ruled, there is always an emotional component of friendship involved in it.[36] Whenever there is a community, there is friendship.[37]

The major difference between political and despotic rule is that the former is not like the rule of the soul over the body but a manifestation of the deliberating part of the soul, eliciting voluntary compliance from its longing or desiring counterpart.[38] Hence, the latter partakes of reason, but it lacks the authority to exercise it itself.[39] In the case of political rule in the polity, the authority is exercised by taking turns in ruling and being ruled. Good citizens know how to rule and to be ruled.[40] One becomes a good ruler by being ruled.[41]

Interestingly, Aristotle's analysis suggests that we pick up emotional dispositions towards rulers in the household first and then transpose them to the political domain.[42] Household affection makes people naturally obedient.[43]

[33] See P 1258a37–1259b7 (at 21).

[34] See NE 1160b32-36 (at 179): 'The community of husband and wife appears to be aristocratic: the man rules in accord with merit regarding the things over which a man ought to rule, whereas all things suited to a woman, he hands over to her.'

[35] See NE 1161a4-6 (at 179). See also Miller, n 14, 53.

[36] See NE 1161a10-29 (at 179–80).

[37] See NE 1159b26-27 (at 177).

[38] As we shall see, the 'deviant' regimes (tyranny, oligarchy, democracy) involve mastery. See P 1279a22-23 (at 73).

[39] See NE 1102b39–1103a3 (at 24–25).

[40] See P 1276a27-30 (at 68). See also P 1277b12-17 (at 69): 'Hence this too has been finely said – that it is not possible to rule well without having been ruled. Virtue in each of these cases is different, but the good citizen should know and have the capacity both to be ruled and to rule, and this very thing is the virtue of a citizen – knowledge of rule over free persons from both points of view.'

[41] See P 1277b10-11 (at 69): '[T]he ruler learns [ruling] by being ruled – just like the cavalry commander learns by being commanded …'.

[42] See P 1162a17-18 (at 182): 'For a human being is by nature more a coupling being than a political one, inasmuch as a household is earlier and more necessary than a city …'.

[43] See NE 1180b5-10 (at 232).

The Good Life

Human beings are by nature destined to live together.[44] Every human being feels the impulse thereto.[45] Aristotle notes that even if humans do not need assistance from one another, 'they no less yearn to live together'.[46] This indicates that a life is fully human only if it is somehow shared with others. People join together 'for the sake of living itself'.[47] According to one of the most famous sentences authored by Aristotle, someone who does not live in a community is either a brute or a god.[48] In a manner strangely anticipating Hobbesian social contract theory, he adds that a solitary human develops a desire for war, 'as if he were an isolated piece in a game of backgammon'.[49]

Ontologically, the city is prior to human beings, just as the whole is prior to its parts.[50] The city is, undoubtedly, an embodiment of reasonableness, for acting as a citizen involves recognising that one's own interests must be consistent with the larger whole to which one belongs.

Beings that in order to survive need to live together are 'political' animals. If that is the point of being 'political' (this is not the only sense in which the term is understood by Aristotle) then all animals that live in colonies, packs or herds (ants, wolves or cattle) are animals of this type.[51] The essence of any single specimen of the species is to be part of a larger whole. What distinguishes human beings from other beasts, however, and makes them even more into a species of their genus, is that they do not use their voice only to signal pain and pleasure by emitting grunts or neighs; they possess conceptual language and therefore articulate what they regard as just and unjust. The articulation of normative ideas is unique to human beings and relevant from the scale of the household to the full-blown city.[52] Whereas the conduct of animals is given direction through instincts and drives, the human political animals use reasoning and communication to make up their minds. Since being a political animal requires that one get along with others, being reasonable involves awareness of moral constraints.

[44] See P 1253a1–3 (at 4).
[45] See P 1253a30–37 (at 5).
[46] P 1278b20–21 (at 72).
[47] P 1278b25–26 (at 72).
[48] See P 1253a27–29 (at 4).
[49] P 1253a6–7 (at 4). Apparently, it is the boardgame that matters, not backgammon.
[50] See P 1253a20–24 (at 4).
[51] See P 1253a7–8 (at 4).
[52] See P 1253a14–15 (at 4).

Living and cooperating in a political community reaps as its reward not only a fair chance of survival, but also the prospect of living a good life.[53] This reward is not enjoyed privately and in isolation after one has fulfilled all duties towards others. Rather, individual life goes well by participating in community life.[54] If humans are aware that things are going well for them, they are happy.

Participation in community life requires that one do what is proper from the perspective of what George Herbert Mead called the 'generalized other', namely, the point of view from which we perceive what the community may legitimately expect its members to do.[55] Simply put, humans have to do what behoves members of a community to do. What it takes to act appropriately is articulated by Aristotle in terms of 'virtue' – a concept that may appear less old-fashioned if we translate it as 'social skill'. Aristotle undoubtedly believes that a life of virtue is good for us.[56]

Virtue

Given that life in a community involves sacrifices that may even go so far as to involve the loss of life in the field of honour,[57] we may find it difficult to believe that a life of virtue – at least for as long as we are spared ill luck and related adversities[58] – will makes us happy. Aristotle believes, however, that happiness is concomitant with engaging in the right activity. While, indeed, the right activity is, again, virtuous action, the explanation for its correctness is that any virtue is the characteristic or disposition that allows things to do their 'work' (*ergon*), that is, to fulfil their purpose.[59] Primarily, we are animals among others. Animals try to stay alive for as long as they can and to procreate. This is their proper 'work' (*ergon*). What makes us, as human beings, into a special species of animals is our capacity to reason. We can deliberate about our actions

[53] See P 1252b27-30 (at 3).

[54] An exception needs to be made for the life of contemplation. See NE 1174b20-23 (at 217).

[55] See GH Mead, *Mind, Self, and Society from the Standpoint of a Social Behaviorist* (ed C Morris, Chicago, IL, Chicago University Press, 1934) 154. Mead will later articulate our individual relation to the generalised other by using the concepts 'I' and 'Me'. See ibid 174–75.

[56] Happiness is an activity in accord with virtue. See NE 1177a12-18 (at 223–24).

[57] See the remarkable observations in NE 1115a25-36 (at 55). See NE 1115b4-5 (at 55–56): '[T]he courageous act like men in circumstances where prowess in battle is possible or dying is noble.' Drowning in a sinking ship in the course of a storm at sea, by contrast, is not a setting of noble action. See, however, also on the ability to endure suffering, when 'nobility shines through' as 'someone bears up calmly under many great misfortunes', NE 1100b30-33 (at 20).

[58] See the long discussion of always impending misfortune and the question at what point in life we can call a person happy in NE 1096a1-2 (at 7) and NE 1100a10-22 (at 18–19).

[59] See NE 1197b22-24 (at 12).

by considering their potential consequences and perceiving ourselves as one fellow citizen among others. The virtues are testament to how we embody reasonableness in our habitual conduct and thereby lend shape to attitudes and dispositions. It is our human *ergon* to activate and tame the shadier and more animalistic parts of our soul under the auspices of being good and dependable members of our community. Reasons are addressed to passionate impulses and meant to dispose the soul towards reacting with right action.[60] *Arete*, generally, is the ability to do one's proper work, that is, to accomplish one's objective. Just as it is the *arete* of a knife to cut things, it is the overall *arete* of humans to behave reasonably. Reasonable action is our good.[61] It is an end in itself.[62] If we attain it over the course of our life, we will be happy.[63]

Human virtues, however, come in different types: ethical[64] virtues, on the one hand, and intellectual (*dianoia*) virtues, on the other. Ethical virtues concern our character and hence our dispositions to do the right thing when the situation calls for it. Intellectual virtues are about our prudent judgement and our wisdom.[65] There is a whole variety of ethical virtues.[66] Chief among them is the virtue of justice, which is the ultimate focus of other virtues viewed through the lens of conduct that affects others (if you behave bravely, for example, you do not defend yourself in an excessive manner and hence do not act unjustly).[67] Given that virtues are, borrowing Amartya Sen's parlance, capabilities to do 'our work' properly, and assuming, with Aristotle, that doing what we can do makes us happy, then exercising what makes us human – ethical virtue and reasoning – is definitely good for us. Why would we want to be unhappy? Aristotle gives us the following example that appeals to our moral intuitions:

> No one would assert that a person is blessed who has no part of courage, moderation, justice, or prudence, but is afraid of the flies buzzing

[60] See 'Ruling and Being Ruled' above.

[61] See NE 1098a5-17 (at 13).

[62] Acting well is itself an action. See P 1325b20-23 (at 193); 1332a9-11 (at 209).

[63] See NE 1101a15-18 (at 20–21). On happiness qua complete practice of virtue, see NE 1098b29-31, 1099b28, 1129b31; P 1332a8-11 (at 15, 18, 92; 208).

[64] They are also translated as 'moral'.

[65] See NE 1103a151-20 (at 26) and 'Choices' below. On wisdom in contrast to prudence, see NE 1141a16–1141b3 (at 121–22).

[66] They are discussed from NE 1115a7 to 1138b18 (at 54–114).

[67] See NE 1129b30-35, 1130b23-25, 1130a9-11 (at 92–94). Aristotle differentiates justice qua totality of virtues as regards conduct towards others from two special forms of justice. First, corrective justice concerns those who grasp for more. See NE 1128a32-35, 1130a19-24 (at 91, 93). This partial form of justice is about evening out voluntary or involuntary maldistributions that have arisen in the horizontal relation among people. See NE 11311-3 (at 95). Second, distributive justice, by contrast, is introduced with regard to those who share in a regime, and concerns the criterion that is taken to merit access to office. See NE 1130b30-35 (at 94).

> around him, abstains from none of the extremes when he desires to eat or drink, kills his dearest friends for a trifle, and similarly regarding the things connected with the mind, is as senseless and as thoroughly deceived [by a false perception of things] as a child or madman.[68]

The Constitution: Ideal Theory

We usually translate the Greek term *politeia* as 'constitution'. This, however, creates the expectation that such a constitution is a written document. Yet it is not. Hence, it would be better to use the term 'regime', not least because it suggests that it is someone's. The political class, the *politeuma*,[69] and their mode of interaction comprise the regime. Occasionally, Aristotle also addresses the regime as a way of life of the city,[70] not least because it leaves its imprint on the character of the citizens. The regime of the 'good people' is an aristocracy; the regime of 'the most excellent person' is kingship.[71]

Aristotelian constitutionalism characterises the regime as an arrangement of offices,[72] yet the major point of studying regimes is to explore how officeholders are selected:[73] who gets to select whom and who is eligible for which office?[74]

Indeed, the centrality of virtue to leading a good life suggests that there must be a straightforward right answer to these questions. The virtuous persons should lead and select other leaders.[75] They get along well with others and do not undeservedly accord their own interests or those of their kin any unfair priority. It makes sense, therefore, to let the virtuous persons govern the city. The regime of the good people will pursue the common good and try to ensure that the next generation will also live together happily in the future. It will put great emphasis on education and hence pursue the objective to instil in its citizens the sense of virtue.[76]

[68] P 1323a28-34 (at 187–88).

[69] See P 1278b10-12 (at 71).

[70] See P 1295b1 (at 114).

[71] See, for example, P 1284a5-10 (at 87).

[72] See P 1278b8-10 (at 71).

[73] A citizen is whoever is entitled to share in an office, which involves deliberation. See P 1275b18-21 (at 64).

[74] More is associated with the 'regime', namely its 'authoritative element' (principle) and what the end of the community is. See P 1289a15-18 (at 98).

[75] The regime would then be an aristocracy. See P 1293a3-6 (at 110).

[76] The task of education is generally that of reproducing the character fitting the regime. See P 1337a17-20 (at 223).

Since good people are rare to find, the group leading the city is likely to be rather small. Possibly, if there is a person of superior excellence, it is even reduced to merely one.[77] Indeed, the whole conception of ruling and being ruled forces Aristotle to endorse kingship as the best form of rule,[78] for an outstanding person should be voluntarily and gladly obeyed.[79] Here is the idea:

> [W]hen another person is superior on the basis of virtue and of the capacity to achieve the best things, it is noble to follow this person and just to obey him.[80]

Aristotle is, however, aware that under conditions of politics – and this implies the prevalence of animosity, envy and spite – any attempt at identifying the most excellent person must elicit resistance. Candidates spotted by one party will be defamed and ostracised by the other.[81] He also recognises that under conditions of greater equality and sharply decreasing deference, monarchy is a regime that has had its day.[82]

The ideal regime is unattainable for us. Aristotle implicitly closes the book on ideal theory (in Rawlsian parlance).[83] It represents, indeed, the utopian element of his political thought. The rest is non-ideal theory, that is, political philosophy facing up to the sobering realities of ordinary politics.

From Ideal to Non-ideal

To understand why it is difficult to have aristocracy in the real world, one must merely ask the question how officeholders are supposedly chosen in

[77] Therefore, in aristocracies the same person is the good man and the good citizen. See P 1288a35-40, 1293b6-8 (at 96, 110). The good or 'fitting' citizens do not partake of the deficiencies of the regime. Outside of aristocracy, citizens are only 'good' in relation to their regime. See P 1276b33-36, 1283b40–1284a4, 1277a40–1278b5 (at 67, 85, 71).

[78] See, however, on the intellectual advantage of a greater number of rulers in an aristocracy, P 1286b2-7, 1287b12-14 (at 91, 94).

[79] See P 1284b28-35 (at 87). See also P 1310b3-15 (at 154).

[80] P 1325b10-13 (at 193).

[81] See P 1283b33-37, 1284b23-26 (at 86–87).

[82] See P 1313a7-10 (at 160).

[83] The distinction between ideal and non-ideal theory looms large in Rawls' theory of international relations. Ideal theory is basically about what ought to happen and disregards obstacles that might arise owing to adverse circumstances, such as animosity, ill-will or the prevalence of illiberal traditions. One should not make too much of this distinction; however, it is, even if only in rough outline, helpful to illuminate the basic set-up of Aristotle's political theory. See J Rawls, *The Law of Peoples* (Cambridge, MA, Harvard University Press, 1999) 89–90.

such a regime. All that we learn is that 'the best' are to rule.[84] If the best were free to identify themselves, all would raise their hands and claim membership of this group. If, conversely, all had a say on who, except oneself, belongs to the best, the selection would be infested with the poor judgement of myopic people. It follows that the best can be identified only from among the best by the best. This means, in practice, that well-established families control the political process and somehow determine who is to rule. This is why Aristotle includes the 'wellborn' into the group that notoriously claims to merit rule.[85] Being of good birth is a combination of wealth and good breeding that promises to be manifest in virtue.[86] Owing to the relevance of virtue, in addition to wealth, Aristotle includes a regime that combines both into the group of aristocracies, even if it is somewhat impure.[87] From the outside, however, such a regime will not look different from an oligarchy, since only sufficient resources will ensure that the offspring has access to good breeding (training in military skills or lessons with orators). The major difference between aristocracies and oligarchies is, then, that the aristocrats do what is good for all, while the oligarchs pursue their own interests. Aristocrats rule politically. Their government rests on consent. Oligarchs rule like masters.[88] They threaten ordinary people into obedience.

In the real world, however, ordinary folk will observe vigilantly and with envy what the ruling aristocrats do and how they allocate benefits and burdens. Notoriously, the people on whom the regime imposes burdens are not disposed to accept sacrifices. They are rather most likely disgruntled with what they take to be rude impositions from the ruling class. They will suspect that burdens are attributed unfairly and, yes, that everything is done to benefit the rich. They will listen to those saying that the game is rigged.[89] The pretension on the part of the ruling class to be superior to all others is therefore likely to be met with hostility.[90]

[84] See P 1293b3-5 (at 110).

[85] See P 1283b3-4 (at 84).

[86] See P 1294a20-24, 1301b1-4 (at 111, 130). This is my interpretation of Aristotle's juxtaposition of old wealth and virtue.

[87] See P 1293b10-12 (at 110).

[88] All deviant regimes rely on mastery. See P 1297a20-21 (at 79).

[89] The populist leaders using slander to demean the better off are on their way to becoming tyrants. See P 1310b15-17 (at 154).

[90] See P 1306b22-32 (at 144–45), where Aristotle states that aristocracies are often held to be oligarchies.

This may be the core of the explanation why Aristotle concedes that pure aristocracies and kingships are rarely to be found.[91] They are simply very difficult to accept for people, in particular if people believe themselves to be on an equal footing with others.[92] Aristocracies and monarchies may be feasible where the population feels inferior to their rulers. In fact, Aristotle may be right in believing that such a feeling of inferiority is indispensable for these regimes to exist. Ostentatious demonstration of wealth and glory, pomp and circumstance are the means to instil in ordinary folk a sense of being lowly members of society. Deference, after all, was the secret of British society in the nineteenth and early twentieth centuries.

The Republican Split

With that we arrive at the veritable predicament that Aristotle's *Politics* has possibly been designed to address. When the number of ordinary people in the city is growing and if there is contagion of the belief in natural equality, they no longer behave deferentially towards the upper class. The social perspectives become incongruent.

The better sort is cast from the perspective of the lesser sort as merely pretending to be 'better' on account of their wealth, whereas, conversely, the lesser sort is rendered as base by their opponents.[93] This is what one might call 'the republican split'. Those attributing virtue to themselves are debunked by their opponents as boorish oligarchs, while those believing themselves to be decent ordinary people are rendered by the better off as members of a fickle and stupid multitude.

According to Aristotle, this is the normal situation,[94] and he seems to take it for granted that we can realistically address it only if we bracket the group's self-idealisations and adopt the critical second-personal perspectives as our premise. This may explain why he claims that the major regimes, which can be found most often, are democracy and oligarchy.[95] What matters in these is the interest of the ruling class. Of all the various divisions

[91] See P 1288b5-28 (at 97), where Aristotle explains that the best regime may be unattainable for many cities and that one needs to inquire, therefore, what the best is that the circumstances allow.

[92] See P 1313a7-10 (at 160).

[93] See Aristotle's remarks in P 1306b23-27 (at 144–45).

[94] Indeed, the situation can easily bring societies to the brink of civil war, which is the worst political evil that both Plato and Aristotle want to avoid. See A MacIntyre, *After Virtue*, 2nd edn (Notre Dame, IN, Notre Dame University Press) 157.

[95] See P 1290a10-13, 1290b10-13, 17-20 (at 101–03).

in a city,[96] the one that is politically most relevant is the cleavage between the wealthy and the poor who are free:

> Democracy exists when the free and poor, being a majority, have authority to rule; oligarchy, when the wealthy and better born have authority and are few.[97]

Aristotle clarifies, however, that the number does not really matter. It is an accidental consequence of wealth and poverty, 'for many are free but few wealthy'.[98]

The Eclipse of Reason

The default situation of politics is that of 'factional conflict',[99] which occurs when one group happens to have the upper hand and the other is contending for power. Of the many and variegated analyses that can be found in the *Politics* of such conflicts,[100] the most impressive passages reveal the adverse effects that factional conflict has on reason.[101] This is not a minor issue, for the damage done to reason translates into a failure of governing that implicates the disintegration of the unit that ruling is supposed to sustain.

Popular leaders fight the well off and thereby split the city into two contending parts (what Socrates would have spoken of as a 'faction state').[102] The well off have a share of responsibility for this malaise, for they tend to behave arrogantly and to aggrandise themselves.[103] Their conduct breeds hostility towards them. Generally, those who, on account of their wealth, their strength or their good looks, feel superior to others are unlikely to be amenable to reason.[104] They become 'arrogant and base on a grand scale', while those who resent them behave maliciously and are 'base in petty ways'.[105]

[96] Aristotle distinguishes the component groups of the city by their profession: farmers, merchants, workers and labourers, who are all part of the multitude, and the warriors, who are divided into the horse-rearing, the heavy-armed, the light-armed and the seafaring. See P 1289b30-35, 1290b37-40, 1291b13-17, 1319a25-28, 1321a5-10 (at 100, 103, 105, 177, 181).

[97] See P 1290b17-20 (at 102–03).

[98] See P 1290b2-4 (at 102).

[99] See P 1301a40 (at 129).

[100] For example, Aristotle explains that two sorts of factional conflicts arise in oligarchies, namely the conflict between wealthy families and the people, on the one hand, and the conflicts among the families themselves, on the other. See P 1302b9-13 (at 131).

[101] The title of this section is borrowed from M Horkheimer, *Eclipse of Reason* (New York, Oxford University Press, 1947).

[102] Aristotle claims that these leaders had better demonstrate a readiness for compromise. See P 1310a2-12 (at 153).

[103] See P 1306a20 (at 146).

[104] See P 1295b8-9 (at 114).

[105] P 1295b8-910-11 (at 115).

Those who possess wealth and influence are neither willing to be ruled nor do they possess the requisite know-how. They refuse to obey whomever it is who attempts to exercise authority over them. The needy, by contrast, are by default too submissive and allow themselves to be ruled like slaves, which, as an attitude, is much welcomed by the wealthy, for all they know is to rule like masters. Political rule becomes thus perverted into mastery:

> What comes into being, then, is a city not of free persons but of slaves and masters, the ones consumed by envy, the others by contempt. Nothing is further removed from affection and from a political community; for community involves the element of affection – enemies do not wish to have even a journey in common.[106]

Economic inequality has a deleterious effect on human character.

Spheres of Justice

While the foregoing extract reveals that Aristotle also believes that 'common sympathies'[107] forge an indispensable emotional bond among the members of a city,[108] he also believes that democracy and oligarchy, qua deviant regimes, 'are in error'.[109] They are in error because they rest on mistaken conceptions of justice that are manifest in the entitlements that are taken to be derivative of either equality or inequality.[110] The wealthy people expect preferential treatment everywhere and in all respects simply because of their wealth. Their claim to superior standing extends, in particular, to the political domain. Contrariwise, the poor people who are born free claim to have rights to equal shares of everything on the ground of their free birth. In such a faction state, each class confronts the other with their factitious understanding of justice. 'Inequality, yeah!', 'Equality, aye!' There is no way of agreeing on a common good. Policies cannot but invariably serve the interests of either of the contending parties.

What these groups thereby override is what Michael Walzer would call, possibly even taking his cue from Aristotle,[111] the lines dividing different

[106] P 1295b21-23 (at 115).
[107] See JS Mill, *Considerations on Representative Government* (orig edn 1861, Amherst, NY, Prometheus Books, 1991) 308.
[108] See P 1280b38-40 ('affection as the intentional choice of living together'), P 1295b23-25 (at 77, 115). On 'dissimilarity of stock' and factional conflict, see P 1303a25-30 (at 135).
[109] See P 1301a37-38 (at 129).
[110] See P 1280a6-25, 1301b37-39 (at 75, 131).
[111] See P 1282b36-1283a-9 (at 82), which matches Walzer's core idea.

'spheres of justice'.[112] The idea is that each social good has its own and distinct criteria of distribution. Healthcare ought to be distributed according to need, commodities pursuant to private transactions, political offices depending on votes.[113] The world of justice would be entirely perverted if we voted on who is to obtain medical care or if political offices were for sale. Such transgressions happen, however, and the distributive standard governing the allocation of one particular good is systematically prone to override the criteria for other goods. The standard then becomes, according to Walzer, 'tyrannical'.[114] Thus understood, oligarchy is guilty of the tyranny of wealth and democracy of the tyranny of politics, since political clout rides roughshod over what might have been the relevant criteria of merit.

The tyrannical standard is inherent in the regimes that mistake skewed principles for the major standard of justice. Wealth is the principle of oligarchy, for in such a society the socially predominant meaning of life is the accumulation of private fortunes. Freedom is the principle of democracy. One may live as one pleases and do what one happens to want on the spur of the moment.[115] These principles also inform the exercise of political power[116] and govern eligibility for office.[117] These regimes that deviate from one built on virtue, even though always prone to conflict, can indeed be in an 'adequate condition';[118] not least, they each recognise an ideal type of citizen whose reproduction in the next generation they have to procure.[119] The 'good' citizen of an oligarchy is different from an archetypical democrat. Aristotle recognises, however, that oligarchies could not function if they only bred overambitious prigs. They also require submissive people to serve them.[120]

Non-ideal Theory

It is perhaps against this background that we can understand why Aristotle needs – again in Rawlsian parlance – a 'non-ideal theory', that is, a theory

[112] M Walzer, *Spheres of Justice: A Defense of Pluralism and Equality* (Oxford, Blackwell, 1989).
[113] This is the gist of Walzer's 'open distributive principle'. See ibid 20.
[114] ibid 19.
[115] See, for example, P 1310a28-30 (at 153); 1317a40 (at 172); 1317b12-14 (at 173).
[116] See P 1294a10-15 (at 111); 1283b15-21 (at 84).
[117] See P 1283a15-17, 1283b10-35 (at 83–84).
[118] P 1309b32 (at 152).
[119] See, for example, P 1276b33-36 (at 67); 1283b40–1284a4 (at 85).
[120] See P 1310a20-24 (at 153): 'But to be educated relative to a regime is not to do the things that oligarchs or those who want democracy enjoy, but rather the things by which the former will be able to run an oligarchy and the latter to have a regime that is run democratically.'

of good government that is workable where there is neither brightly shining virtue in the scions of old wealth nor deferential submissiveness in the lowly classes. Political philosophy is, after all, supposed to be relevant to human life. At first glance, such a theory seems to give us only the 'second-best'. Yet it should make us pause to contemplate that Aristotle uses the generic name of all regimes, namely *politeia*,[121] to designate the 'second-best'. Perhaps it is, after all, the only regime worthy of the high appellation of a constitution. Puzzlingly, Aristotle presents it as a mix – a blend – of the two constitutions of faction states, that is, of states that fail to attain the common good.[122]

What are we to make of this?

Polity (*politeia*)

Aristotle uses two distinctions for the classification of regimes.[123]

The first concerns whether the regime serves the common good. If it does not, the constitution has 'digressed' from its purpose and represents a *parekbasis* (which is the Greek term for anything, a train of thought in particular, that has gone off track).[124]

The second distinction examines the number of rulers: one, a few or 'the many'. Both distinctions in combination provide us with the simple classificatory grid seen in Figure 6.1.

Figure 6.1 Types of regimes

	one	few	many
for the common good 'correct' regime	monarchy	aristocracy	polity
for the good of the rulers 'deviant' regime	tyranny	oligarchy	democracy

[121] See P 1279a37-38 (at 73), 1289a36-29 (at 99), 1293b40 (at 109).
[122] See P 1265b26-29, 1279a37-39, 1289a35-38, 1294a40, 1293b32-34 (at 37, 73, 99, 109–110).
[123] On the following see 1159b31–1161a9 (at 178–79); 1288a32-49 (at 96).
[124] See P 1279a20-21 (at 73).

Aristotle goes on to explain that not all bad regimes are equally bad.[125] Tyranny is the worst of all, not least because it is falling far from the best. Democracy is the least corrupt, for it deviates only slightly from polity.[126] Aristotle even seems to concede that the mitigating factor speaking somewhat in favour of democracy is the 'wisdom of the crowds'.[127]

The straightforward explanation for this account is, of course, that monarchy is a risky regime. While in an aristocracy contending families are able to keep each other mutually in check, an unconstrained autocrat faces no obstacles to perpetrating horrid crimes. In oligarchies, the rich hideously defend their wealth against the poor. They are therefore worse than democracies, which are obviously simply relatively dysfunctional states.

The puzzle remains, however why polity – qua *politeia* obviously *the* candidate for the true constitution or regime – should be the commendable regime. Aristotle offers one pragmatic reason and a number of moral reasons for this.

The pragmatic reason is that regimes are practically possible only if they work with the human material at hand.[128] While it is the case, in the eyes of Aristotle, that the 'barbarians' are unfit to govern themselves and need to be ruled like slaves with despotic might,[129] a different solution is possible for most *poleis* that are split between the rich and the poor.[130] What needs to be found, hence, is an arrangement that promises to overcome the factitious state of city states.

One moral reason supporting polity is that a solid 'middle class' is most likely amenable to reason[131] and can act as an arbitrator vis-à-vis the rich and the poor.[132] The larger the middling part of society, the more wealth and extreme poverty are pushed to the fringes. The middling sort is neither self-aggrandising nor condescending, and also not obsessed with envy.[133] Their political judgement is not clouded with enmity.

[125] See P 1289a39-1289b5 (at 99).

[126] See NE 1160b20-21 (at 179). 'Polity' is also called 'timocracy' in the *Ethics*, for it involves property assessments. In the *Politics* Aristotle recommends that the assessments ought to be calibrated to ensure that the group meeting them is the majority of the population. This can also influence what is understood by the heavy arms carried by hoplites. See P 1265b26-29, 1297b1-7 (at 37, 119).

[127] See P 1281a42–1281b7, 1283b30-35, 1286a30-32 (at 78-79, 84, 90–91). See Miller, n 14, 59–60.

[128] See P 1288b10-40 (at 97–98).

[129] See P 1252b5-9, 1255a30 (at 2, 10).

[130] See P 1290b15-21 (at 102–03).

[131] See P 1294a35–1295b5 (at 114–15); 1296b35-49 (at 118).

[132] See P 1297a6-7 (at 118).

[133] See P 1295b30-34 (at 115).

There is, however, another moral reason that should not be ignored. The citizen body of the polity is composed of so-called 'hoplites'.[134] They are fit for military service and capable of affording their own heavy arms and armour. What is amazing about this criterion of citizenship is that it has two faces. It has an oligarchic side, for it says something about the resources that citizens can muster. But at the same time there is an important part of human virtue realised in them, namely military virtue. This is of no minor significance, as we already know from Plato. Good soldiers ('auxiliaries') fear the right things. They are brave, support their comrades and put the well-being of the city even above their interest in survival.

The polity is institutionally a mix of oligarchic and democratic elements.[135] The democratic element is most evident in some equal rotation of offices, the oligarchic in elections. The poorer citizens receive spoils for serving the city, even if only by attending meetings, while the wealthy are fined for non-attendance.[136] In any event, institutionally the polity is supposed to mix elements from both regimes so well that an external observer cannot tell whether it is either a democracy or an oligarchy.[137]

Finally, since the polity is a blend of democracy and oligarchy, it also involves a delicate equilibrium. As a result of political events, the polity can easily vacillate between resembling democracy more closely and resembling oligarchy (or even aristocracy).[138] From this angle it appears that the polity is the ideal regime, while democracy and oligarchy are one-sided deviations from a relatively indeterminate middle. If the solid combination of A and B represents the desired result, and A and B already exist, then one can only recommend the combination of both to create AB. Polities can therefore be understood in such a way that democracy and oligarchy represent inadequate realisations of an ideal. A is an AB lacking B, and B is an AB lacking A.

The polity is not the best constitution in a utopian sense. Offices are not allocated according to virtue and the aim of the polity is not to produce virtuous citizens. Yet the middle class of hoplites possesses some virtue and

[134] See P 1321a14–15 (at 181).

[135] See P 1294b22–39 (at 113). The better the mix, the greater the stability: P 1297a7–8 (at 118).

[136] See P 1294a38–1295b1 (at 112).

[137] See P 1294b14–19 (at 112): 'The defining principle of a good mixture of democracy and oligarchy is that it should be possible for the same polity to be spoken of as either a democracy or an oligarchy, and it is clear that it is because the mixture is a fine one that those who speak of it do so in this way.'

[138] See P 1293b34–38 (at 111).

may therefore be able to strike a balance between the interests of the rich and the poor. A polity can *realise* the common good.

Choices

The political world is the world of human action. What is supposed to guide people aside from seemingly nebulous notions such as 'the common good' or virtue? Given that Aristotle with some confidence speaks of better and worse regimes, we should expect to find in his work a natural law – a *lex naturalis* – providing guidance to the perplexed.

Aristotle's view of natural law is subject to controversial assessments.[139] The reason is that his statements in chapter seven of book five of the *Nicomachean Ethics* are far from coherent. While he states that the natural part of justice is unchangeable,[140] this statement is immediately contradicted by the claim that it may be subject to change.[141] If at all, he seems to believe in natural law for the best regime,[142] but one must wonder whether it can amount to more than the precept that the best person ought to rule. Whether he believes the principles of corrective justice to be part of the unchangeable natural law is just as unclear, as it is clearly the case that the distributive justice criterion concerning who merits political office is relative to regimes.[143] Arguably, when it comes to determining the reasonable, we have to look somewhere else.

Aristotle's theory of practical reason and action concerns the heart of our mindedness, for it presents us with habituation qua process by which we build, by means of choices, something that eventually functions like nature.[144] Such 'second nature'[145] is of human design.[146] Where we have managed to build it, however, it makes our conduct resemble reactions driven by instinct (or stimulus and response, as it were). Responses can be

[139] See, for example, J Ritter, '"Naturrecht" bei Aristoteles' in his *Metaphysik und Politik: Studien zu Aristoteles und Hegel* (Frankfurt aM, Suhrkamp, 1969) 133–81. For an overview and a highly nuanced perspective, see G Duke, 'Aristotle and Natural Law' (2020) 82 *Review of Politics* 1–23.

[140] See NE 1134b18-20 (at 104).

[141] See NE 1134b27-30 (at 105): '[A]mong us there is in fact something that is [just] by nature, though it is altogether changeable.'

[142] See NE 1135a3-5 (at 105).

[143] See NE 1131a25-20 (at 95–96).

[144] See NE 1103a30-1103b5, 1103b23-25, 1115a (at 26–27, 51).

[145] See GWF Hegel, *Enzyklopädie der philosophischen Wissenschaften im Grundrisse*, Part III: *Werke in zwanzig Bänden*, vol 10 (ed E Moldenhauer and KM Michel, Frankfurt aM, Suhrkamp 1969–71) § 410 at 164, 189.

[146] See C Menke, *Autonomie und Befreiung: Studien zu Hegel* (Berlin, Suhrkamp, 2018) 120–21.

viewed as the 'dynamic' apprehension of the significance of events by which they are triggered.[147] Searching for food demonstrates a sound understanding of what hunger means for an organism, namely, the need for nutrition.

An acquired automatism is not, in and of itself, a deficiency. Rather, habituation and the relatively mindless routine of custom invest us with various capacities to recognise situations and to get things done. Training and habituation are essential to being a competent person or a 'subject'. Subjects possess the capacity to do something and to pass judgement on certain matters.[148] Aristotle does not, however, address the danger inherent in habituation, which is the danger of mindless routine,[149] even though he recognises that routine without reflection can easily turn out to be numb and wrongheaded.[150]

While training and habituation are essential to Aristotle's account of moral goodness,[151] it is nonetheless the case that *proairesis*, choice – 'a longing marked by deliberation'[152] – is integral to doing the right thing.[153] Virtue is a disposition or a characteristic (*hexis*) that inclines us to doing the right thing in certain situations, but Aristotle makes clear that virtue in an 'authoritative sense' is a longing accompanied by prudent deliberation,[154] or at least awareness of the right course of action.[155] Only if persons grasp the

[147] See Mead, n 55, 72–73.

[148] See Menke, n 146, 62–65.

[149] According to Menke, Hegel had a keen sense that habituation is enslaving. See ibid 127–29. See Hegel, n 144, 185–87.

[150] See NE 1144b10-12 (at 133): '[J]ust as a strong body moving without eyesight will end up stumbling with considerable force because it is without sight, so it is also in this case [of having the natural virtues in the absence of intellect].'

[151] See NE 1103a14-120 (at 26).

[152] NE 1139a23-24 (at 116).

[153] See NE 1139a22-27 (at 116). On the distinction between ethical and intellectual virtues, see NE 1103a14-18; 1139a1-3 (at 26, 116). The major source of ethical virtue is habit in the sense that one becomes virtuous through repeated virtuous actions (which always also involve a choice). See NE 11033–1103b2 (at 26–27); 1105a18-20 (at 31). Intellectual virtue, which is also a disposition and not just a capability, arises from experience. See also NE 1142a13-16 (at 125). After noting that a young person does not seem to be prudent, Aristotle explains 'The cause is that prudence is … of particulars, which come to be known as a result of experience, but a young person is inexperienced: a long period of time creates experience.' Even though some may be born with the right temperament to display ethical virtue, the habitual responses are not sufficient to constitute full-blown virtuous action. See NE 1144b5-13 (at 127). On the distinctions between passions, capacities and characteristics (dispositions), see NE 1105b25-27 (at 32).

[154] Deliberation is not swift, it takes time. See NE 1142b1-5 (at 127). Choice is driven by neither desire nor spiritedness. Desire has to do with what is pleasant and painful, whereas choice has to do with what is noble or shameful (NE 1104a32, at 30). Spirited action 'seems least of all to stem from choice' (NE 1111b15-19, at 46).

[155] The relation between moral virtues and the intellectual virtue of prudence is characterised by Aristotle in different ways. Virtue selects the right target, prudence selects the means conducive to its attainment (NE 1144a7-9, at 131). The right choice is also characterised as practical thinking in

reasons explaining the appropriateness of their response do they demonstrate real virtue.[156] While habituation is primary, Aristotle also seems to believe that having desires that are coincident with reason makes the striving part of the soul susceptible to developing desires because of reason.[157]

Aristotle even claims that virtues are choices, or at least 'not without a choice'.[158] First, virtue itself is something that we have chosen to adopt.[159] Second, it is related to choices that we have to make.[160] Its mode of reproduction consists of repeated choosings, the substance of which is, however, always somewhat prepared by virtue, which, Aristotle states, 'becomes active in just those activities as a result of which it also came into being'.[161]

The evolution of the virtuous person is a process of choice-mediated self-constitution.[162] It begins, however, with education. We are constituting ourselves by steering the course towards which our educators have attempted to direct us.[163] This must raise the question whether we are responsible for our character. Aristotle answers it in the affirmative by offering the equivalent of a transcendental argument.[164] If our moral outlook were determined by the character that we acquired as a result of circumstance and education, we would never be responsible for the views that we have. The practice of judging others and judging ourselves would collapse. The world of the normative would disappear. Hence, we have to mutually shoulder responsibility for our character.[165] This argument is difficult to reconcile with other remarks made by Aristotle regarding the formative influence of education.[166]

agreement with the right longing. It is as though the non-reasonable part of the soul and reason found a position on which they converge (NE 1139a30, at 117). In the relation between the two parts, prudence is in charge of the final determination of conduct, for it issues a command (NE 1143a8-9, at 129).

[156] See CM Korsgaard, *The Constitution of Agency: Essays on Practical Reason and Moral Psychology* (Oxford, Oxford University Press, 2008) 154.

[157] ibid 163.

[158] NE 1106a2-3 (at 33).

[159] See NE 1112a25-30 (at 48).

[160] See NE 1106b37-38 (at 35).

[161] NE 1105b25-27 (at 32).

[162] See NE 1112a4-5 (at 47): 'For it is by choosing the good or bad things that we are of a certain sort, not by opining about them.'

[163] See NE 1103b2-4, 1103b20-1103b5, 1103b22-25 (at 26–27). Aristotle remarks that it normally makes a difference whether one is habituated in one way or another.

[164] See G Schönrich, *Kategorien und transzendentale Argumentation: Kant und die Idee einer transzendentalen Semiotik* (Frankfurt aM, Suhrkamp, 1981) 212.

[165] See NE 1114b1-5 (at 53).

[166] See NE 1105a2-8, 1114b8-11 (at 30, 53–54). See U Wolf, *Aristoteles' 'Nikomachische Ethik'* (Darmstadt, Wissenschaftliche Buchgesellschaft, 2002) 138.

For the Sake of the Noble

Good action is marked by several voluntary features:

> But whatever deeds arise in accord with the virtues are not done justly or moderately if they are merely in a certain state, but only if he who does those deeds is in a certain state as well: first, if he acts knowingly; second, if he acts by choosing and choosing the actions in question for their own sake; and, third, if he acts while being in a steady and unwavering state.[167]

The ethical virtues making us disposed to doing the right thing are located in that part of the soul which, without being reasonable itself,[168] is susceptible to reason,[169] while reason, inasmuch as it concerns particular actions,[170] appears in the form of prudence.[171] Both are necessary conditions of good human action that would, taken by themselves, remain insufficient. They have to work in tandem.[172] Most importantly, however, right action consists of doing the right thing for the sake of the noble, which means not for pleasure, even though education has to make sure that good people take pleasure in acting well for its own sake.[173] Action is not about making something else. Acting well – or nobly – is itself the end.[174] It is of intrinsic value and therefore recognisable in the functional arrangements of the means and the ends of action.[175] We shall see below that the 'mean' or the focus on 'the middle term' may well represent this type of arrangement.

[167] See NE 1105a29-34 (at 31).

[168] See, on the two non-rational parts of the soul, NE 1102b29-33 (at 24): 'It appears, therefore, that the nonrational part is twofold, for the vegetative part has nothing in common with reason; but that part characterized by desire, and by longing in general, shares somehow in reason inasmuch as it heeds it and is apt to be obedient to its commands.'

[169] See n 153 on the distinction between ethical and intellectual virtue.

[170] It is about things that come into existence through us. See NE 1112a25-30 (at 48). See also NE 1107a33 (at 36).

[171] Even though we do not choose the ends of action, we deliberately determine them. The ultimate end of all action, happiness, is not chosen. See NE 1111b26-28 (at 47). The other ends are also not 'chosen' but determined on the ground of one's 'practical identity'. See NE 1112b11-15 (at 49), 1113a4 (at 50).

[172] See n 155. So also Wolf, n 165, 159, who claims that virtue in the authoritative sense requires the combination of right dispositions and prudence.

[173] See NE 1140b5-10 (at 120), 1115b12 (at 56), 1116b3 (at 58), 1117b9 (at 61), 1119b116 (at 65), 1120a23 (at 68), 1122b6-7 (at 73).

[174] See NE 1140b 6-7 (at 120). Aristotle explains that something being done for the noble is most easily discernible in cases in which the actors do not obtain a benefit for themselves. This is clearly the case for sacrificing one's life for the good of the political community. See Aristotle, *The Art of Rhetoric* (trans RC Bartlett, Chicago, IL, Chicago University Press, 2019) 1367a1-5 (at 43).

[175] See Korsgaard, n 155, 191, 194.

Aristotle distinguishes what he calls 'three objects' of choice and pairs them with objects of avoidance.[176] Upon closer inspection, they turn out to be six different motives: pleasure or pain, advantage or disadvantage, and noble or shameful.[177] Aside from being noble, acting well is rare, not least because we – and definitely the fearful 'many'[178] – are easily distracted or deceived by pleasure and pain.[179] Pleasure may make things *seem* good even if they are not.[180] Our rootedness in nature constantly threatens to pull us back to the pre-human level of animality.[181] Given the overwhelming relevance of pleasure and pain to our life, it does not come as a surprise that the value of action is always connected to how we are dealing with these, not least because they provide the emotional fuel driving our conduct.[182] Virtue is concerned with connecting passions and actions.[183] Good action gives appropriate room – not too much, not too little – to the passions.

This leaves open whether there is a criterion for choosing the right action as soon as someone is motivated to act for the sake of the noble.

Indeterminacy

Aristotle provides us with such a criterion, even if he implicitly advises us to tread with caution. Acting for the right reason concerns the particulars of action.[184] One should not expect to arrive at much precision in this field,[185] and at the end of all deliberations the actors who possess judgement and are familiar with the relevant issue have to decide for themselves.[186] The criterion is, indeed, entirely formal. It says that in whatever you do, you should do neither too much nor too little of it.

This is Aristotle's categorical imperative, as it were, and it provides the focus of the so-called *mesotes* doctrine, according to which the standard of right action is determined by the 'middle term' between excess and

[176] See NE 1104b30-35 (at 30).
[177] Not doing the noble is tantamount to doing what is shameful. See NE 1117b9 (at 61).
[178] See NE 1116a30-33 (at 51).
[179] See NE 1109b5-9 (at 41).
[180] See NE 1113a38–1113b5 (at 51).
[181] See NE 1104b35 (at 30).
[182] See NE 1105a12-15 (at 31).
[183] See NE 1106b25 (at 34).
[184] See NE 1141b15-17 (at 124). Aristotle adds that navigating the terrain of action requires knowledge of both the universal and the particular, but more of the latter (NE 1141b22-24).
[185] See NE 1104a1-5 (at 28).
[186] See NE 1094a25-35 (at 4).

deficiency.[187] The disposition to aim for the middle term can be undone or be corrupted through engaging in too much excessive or deficient action.[188]

If we asked Aristotle what the middle term is, he would likely reply that it is what reason states it to be.[189] This response must appear disappointing, at least at the outset. Nevertheless, the formal doctrine makes a good deal of sense. The emphasis on obtaining guidance from the middle term is somewhat misleading, for the doctrine can assist us in the face of conceded epistemic indeterminacy. Bearing the latter in mind, we had better take heed of the wrong actions we ought to avoid.

A bad action is always either an overdone or underdone good action.[190] Staying clear of these, we are set towards the middle term. We should be kind towards others. Obsequiousness,[191] being as 'nice as pie', however, is not right. We do not want to come across as grovelling. But we also do not want to behave rudely either.

The limits marked by excess and deficiency still leave us with wide leeway. It can be further narrowed down by asking whether either excess or deficiency are closer to the mean.[192] Arguably, in the case of friendliness, our answer would be that obsequiousness is closer to the mean than rudeness (which shows, by the way, that the mean is not in the middle).[193] One extreme can be more in error than the other.[194] This indicates that our action would be less faulty if it erred on the side of that vice which is closer to the mean.

The final question to ask is where we ourselves stand with regard to our own virtue when we are judging the matter.[195] Can we confidently assume ourselves to occupy the mean, that is, with the sensibilities and attitudes we possess? Or are we, possibly, rude without being aware of it? If we were rude persons, any other person occupying the position of the mean would appear to us as overly pleasing and flattering. Should we have

[187] See NE 1106a29-30 (at 33); 1106b25-28 (at 34–35). At one point, Aristotle characterises virtue as a 'certain mean' that makes us skilful in aiming at the middle term. See NE 1106b29 (at 35).

[188] See NE 1104a15-20 (at 28).

[189] See NE 1138b20 (at 115).

[190] One may find this idea counterintuitive, nevertheless, even harm that is done to another is an excess of a just action. One has done too much of what one is permitted to do. See NE 1129a32-35 (at 91).

[191] See NE 1108a24-32 (at 38).

[192] See Aristotle, *Eudemian Ethics* (trans A Kenny, Oxford, Oxford University Press, 2011) 1220b23–1221b25 (at 18–20).

[193] See Aristotle's example of courage, for which he concludes that cowardice is in greater opposition to courage than recklessness. See NE 1109a1-3, 10 (at 39).

[194] See NE 1109a33-34 (at 40).

[195] See NE 1108b12-15, 23–26 (at 39).

reason to suspect that we tend to be uncouth, we have much reason to be as nice as pie, for then we can be reasonably confident of hitting the middle term. Ostentatious cordiality qua excess of politeness may thus even out our disposition to be harsh. Indeed, cognizant of these considerations an ideal equitable person hypothetically familiar with the mean would have to arrive at a sympathetic assessment[196] and conclude that we have done the right thing given circumstances, even if we had missed it.

The Social Dimension

The continuum on which the often unknown lines separating the mean from excess and deficiency are drawn gives rise to additional perplexity. Your character qua the total sum of virtues and vices determines your judgement.[197] This means that if you are excessively kind and friendly, you may find appallingly harsh people whose conduct is appropriately polite. The conduct that we end up choosing, however, depends on a dual determination. It is reflective of both our ethical virtue (or lack thereof) and on our prudent judgement (or, also in this case, lack thereof).[198]

As characteristic or disposition (*hexis*), virtue establishes for us a link between the passions aroused by our experiences and our incentives for action.[199] A virtuous person is able to control anger and frustration and will abstain from lashing out towards others. At the same time, virtuous persons are strongly inclined to let their anger grow against people who bully or threaten others into obedience and submissiveness. While virtuous action is not – at any rate, not when virtue is 'authoritative'[200] – about the unthinking translation of emotional impulses into action, the virtues or vices make us disposed to pursue certain aims. They also determine our moral outlook of the world. It is for that reason that Aristotle asserts quite correctly that moral virtue is a necessary condition for the exercise of prudence.[201]

[196] See NE 1143a22-24 (at 129). On equity as superior to justice (owing to the correction of the inappropriate generality of rules and principles), see NE 1137b10-25 (at 112).

[197] See NE 1114b2-4 (at 53).

[198] See NE 1144b30-33 (at 133): 'It is clear, then, on the basis of what has been said, that it is not possible to be good in the authoritative sense in the absence of prudence, nor is it possible to be prudent in the absence of moral virtue.'

[199] See NE 1105b19-27 (at 32).

[200] See NE 1144b13 (at 133).

[201] See NE 1144b30-33 (at 133).

Without benefitting from the blessings of moderation, courage, benevolence or generosity, we would not be able to get the mean even into view.[202]

While moral virtue makes us intuitively aim at the right target, prudence, which is about governing ourselves and others,[203] allows us to select the means conducive to it.[204] Occasionally, Aristotle presents prudence as though it selected the minor premise in a practical syllogism. The second premise provides us with specific information about how the principle spelled out in the major principle is to be realised.[205] This demonstrates that prudence is about particulars. Knowing to select or to recognise the right particulars is a matter that requires age and experience.[206] Since we are dealing with matters that are just as ultimate as the first principles of action (and only located on the other side of the spectrum: not general, but most specific), one must perceive them. Prudence is the 'eye of the soul'.[207] This may mean that people with sufficient experience are able to 'see' what is right even if the grounds of their perception may elude them.[208] What is indispensable, at the end of the day, is paying attention to the undemonstrated assertions and opinions of experienced older people, for 'they have an experienced eye' and 'see correctly'.[209]

You'll Never Walk Alone

At the same time, what is virtuous is also determined socially. You become virtuous by acting like other virtuous persons providing a role model for

[202] See NE 1144a35-37 (at 132): 'For corruption distorts and causes one to be mistaken about the principles bound up with action. As a result, it is manifest that it is impossible for someone who is not good to be prudent.'

[203] See NE 1141b29-34 (at 124).

[204] See NE 1144a8-10, 1145a5-8 (at 131, 134). This not to say that prudence is mere 'instrumental rationality'. Prudence is internally tied to the realisation of good ends. See Wolf, n 166, 156–57. See also G Striker, 'Two Kinds of Deliberation' in her *From Aristotle to Cicero: Essays on Ancient Philosophy* (Oxford, Oxford University Press, 2022) 142–61, 148.

[205] See NE 1141b19 (at 124).

[206] See NE 1143b7-8 (at 130).

[207] See NE 1144a32-35 (at 132).

[208] Aristotle actually speaks of perception (*aisthesis*). See NE 1141b27-30 (at 126). There are different ways to resolve his puzzling reference to the triangle as the ultimate figure that we can only intuit and what it means in the context of practical philosophy, see Wolf, n 166, 151–53.

[209] See NE 1143b11-14 (at 130). See also J MacDowell, 'Virtue and Reason' in his *Mind, Value, and Reality* (Cambridge, MA, Harvard University Press, 1998) 50–73, 73; and, somewhat critically, G Striker, 'Aristotle's *Ethics* as Political Science' in her *From Aristotle to Cicero: Essays on Ancient Philosophy* (Oxford, Oxford University Press, 2022) 128–41, 133–34.

you.[210] This explains why social standing and the question of shame are not by accident of the greatest significance in Aristotle's ethics.[211] What others think of you matters for the determination of virtuous conduct.[212] This does not mean that all conduct is entirely about going with the crowd. People can appeal to seemingly attitude-independent principles in a context of mutual recognition. Whether one succeeds in not inviting rebuke or resistance to one's claims depends on one's social standing and reputation.[213] If, by contrast, you are a lowly member of the pack, you can be safe only by heeding the advice and encouragement provided by others.

A conventional morality can guide us only if some people enjoy the authority to make first-person plural statements. Not by accident, conventional morality and social hierarchy easily mesh. The advice of friends is necessary for good action to come to pass.[214] The substantive dimension of our moral judgement is essentially mediated by the social dimension.[215]

[210] Outward conformity is, however, not enough. See NE 1105b5-9 (at 31–32): 'Matters of action are said to be just and moderate, then, when they are comparable in kind to what the just and moderate person would do. And yet he who performs these actions is not by that fact alone just and moderate, but only if he also acts as those who are just and moderate act.'

[211] See NE 1116a27-29 (at 58).

[212] It is, in particular, so for the young people who are guided by their sense of shame. See NE 1128b10-15, 20 (at 88).

[213] Korsgaard, n 156, 197, suggests that being motivated by honour is not yet the mark of mature virtue. Yet it is safe to assume that drawing on one's reputation in order to state what 'we' believe is all there is.

[214] See NE 1170a1-3 (at 204).

[215] For a further elaboration of these points, see my *The Legal Relation: Legal Theory after Legal Positivism* (Cambridge, Cambridge University Press, 2017) 71–72.

7

Natural Law: Its Problem

What We Are Looking for

If one expects to receive from Aristotle more guidance than the advice to follow the lead of people who are regarded as well-bred or decent and to heed the advice of prudent friends, one must leave his philosophy with at least a modicum of disappointment. One may even feel oneself to be at a complete loss. It may match the regret on the part of law students who do not receive from legal philosophy what they expect, namely, elaborate 'right answers' in hard cases or clear definitions of cloudy concepts such as human dignity, let alone compelling deductions of human rights from some first principle. There is not a trace of an explication of natural law in Aristotle. One departs, therefore, from his study of the governance of soul and city with the impression that, from a normative angle, it simply falls short.

It may seem, however, that the most prominent school of thought emerging in the wake of Aristotle's declining Lykeion, the Stoics, fills this normative void by identifying, proudly, the natural law. This is quite vividly revealed in the works of a Roman devotee of Stoic doctrines, Marcus Tullius Cicero. Here are citations from *De legibus* and *De re publica*:

> … I find that it has been the opinion of the wisest men that Law is not a product of human thought, nor is it any enactment of peoples, but something eternal which rules the whole universe by its wisdom in command and prohibition. Thus they have been accustomed to say that Law is the primal and ultimate mind of God, whose reason directs all things either by compulsion or restraint. Wherefore that Law which the gods have given to the human race has been justly praised; for it is the reason and mind of a wise lawgiver applied to command and prohibition.[1]

> True law is right reason in agreement with nature; it is of universal application, unchanging and everlasting; it summons to duty by its commands, and averts from wrongdoing by its prohibitions. … And there will not be different laws at Rome and at Athens, or different laws now and in the

[1] Cicero, De legibus II.8, cited after Cicero, *De re publica, De legibus* (trans CW Keyes, Cambridge, MA, Harvard University Press, 1928) 379–80.

> future, but one eternal and unchangeable law will be valid for all nations and all times, and there will be one master and ruler, that is, God, over us all, for he is the author of this law, its promulgator, and its enforcing judge. Whoever is disobedient is fleeing from himself and denying his human nature, and by reason of this very fact he will suffer the worst penalties, even if he escapes what is commonly considered punishment …[2]

If anything looks like natural law theory, this does, doesn't it? One encounters portentous words and high promises. The law is unchangeable and, hence, always and everywhere the same. What is more, the final sentence of the second paragraph suggests that those failing to obey natural law will at the end of the day harm themselves. Natural law promises to be self-enforcing by visiting misery on those turning a blind eye to it.

Stoicism

Upon closer inspection, however, at least the early Stoa[3] was far less 'legalistic' than one would expect from a theory that proudly addresses the cosmic law.[4] This is apparent already in the equation of law with Zeus and reason.[5] It indicates that the law is a manifestation of a divine intellect in which human beings participate.[6] It is an active principle.[7] Moreover, the law permeates nature and is, thus, of a physical kind.[8] It does not descend down to us from heaven like a lightning bolt trailed by rumbling thunder. Rather, the cosmic reason in which we humans participate is something that emerges within us by nature and involves our paying attention and being responsive to the

[2] Cicero, De re publica III.33, cited after Cicero, *De re publica, De legibus*, n 1, 211.

[3] On the different periods of Stoic philosophy, see, for example, B Inwood, *Stoicism: A Very Short Introduction* (Oxford, Oxford University Press, 2018). See also KM Vogt, 'The Stoics on Virtue and Happiness' in C Bononich (ed), *The Cambridge Companion to Ancient Ethics* (Cambridge, Cambridge University Press, 2017) 183–99, 183.

[4] The following paragraphs are deeply indebted to the magnificent study by KM Vogt, *Law, Reason, and the Cosmic City* (Oxford, Oxford University Press, 2008). The Stoics may have taken their cue from Plato, *Laws* (trans T Griffith, Cambridge, Cambridge University Press, 2016) 897b-c (at 383–84). See J Annas, *Virtue and Law in Plato and Beyond* (Oxford, Oxford University Press, 2017) 167–68.

[5] See Vogt, n 4, 4.

[6] See Cicero, De legibus 1.22, n 1, 321. See also Vogt, n 4, 16.

[7] KM Vogt, 'The Stoic Conception of Law' (2021) 38 *Polis: The Journal for Ancient Greek and Roman Political Thought* 557–72, 559. The passive principle is matter (ibid 560). As an active principle the law is also a soul in its best form, namely, reason (ibid 561). See ibid 562, 'Stoic law has nothing above it; via its identification with Zeus, it is the highest living being. … Stoic law is the law of the world, rather than being attached to any nationality or territory. Like a prince who is a living law …, Stoic law is a soul.'

[8] See Vogt, n 7, 558, 570. The cosmic law is the law that moves the universe and that is at the same time normative for us. It is a corporal principle pervading the world. On the normativity of the law for both us humans and the cosmos, see Annas, n 4, 174–75, 186.

clues and cues that nature provides for our conduct.[9] Nature is our reliable guide; it even makes us acquire evaluative and normative concepts, which initially grow out of the useful.[10] Nature ensures that we develop preconceptions of what there is and what is good for us, even if these rough ideas require further refinement.[11]

We are naturally disposed to preserve our existence. If we follow what nature expects us to do, we are thereby incorporating the preservation of our physical existence into our reasons for action and hence into something we care about. Explaining the matter in terms of the discussion of reasonableness in chapter 4, it is as though human beings originally did not even have person-relative reasons and had to turn free-floating desires into those by befriending their interests.[12] The Stoics referred to this process as *oikeiôsis*.[13] The making of something into something that we care about as 'our own' is repeated when we are dealing first with our parents and later with offspring. The process can be imagined as emanating outwards in concentric circles until we regard the lives of all human beings as relevant to us.[14] Our moral reasoning is then, using contemporary parlance, replete with neutral reasons. Health, wealth and life are relevant concerns for us, for they relate to our self-preservation and to the preservation of those who are dear to us and about whom we care.[15] All human lives matter to us, even though Stoics do not deny that there is merit to the existence of more closely knit and more local communities[16] whose members are closer to each other than complete strangers.[17]

Nature thus assists us, first by means of emotional endearment, in a process of rational discovery, for we, if we succeed at approximating the

[9] See Vogt, n 4, 200.

[10] ibid 185. See also G Striker, 'Two Kinds of Deliberation' in her *From Aristotle to Cicero: Essays on Ancient Philosophy* (Oxford, Oxford University Press, 2022) 142–61, 152.

[11] See Vogt, n 4, 14, 55, 164, 166, 168.

[12] There is great wisdom in this idea. Of all the incentives storming through my head, I need to figure out which of those do indeed belong to me or are reflections of what others expect me to do. I find myself burdened with this problem all the time.

[13] See Vogt, n 3, 189.

[14] See Vogt, n 4, 201.

[15] Vogt, ibid, who explains this as follows: 'Most generally put: whenever we regard something (our body, our brothers, etc) as "belonging to us", we take whatever it is that sustains it or is an impediment to it as relevant considerations for our deliberation. If this is so, we can see why, for example, "honoring our parents" is dictated by reason, just as much as "taking care of one's health".'

[16] See ibid 202, on the relevance of both universal and special obligations.

[17] See Cicero, *De re publica* 6.13, n 2, 265–67, on how pleased the supreme God is about the existence of local and bounded political communities. On Cicero's position, see M Schofield, *Cicero: Political Philosophy* (Oxford, Oxford University Press, 2021) 111–12.

ideal of the sage,[18] realise that we are part of a larger whole, which is the *cosmos*.[19] This concerns our relationship to other human beings too. We are always and already part of a cosmopolis. The cosmos has laws and is therefore like a city.[20]

Cosmic Law Is Not a Code

According to Vogt's interpretation,[21] the law of the cosmos is not a system of rules but rather the perfection of naturally acquired reasonableness[22] that manifests itself in the decisions we arrive at after engaging in a deliberative process.[23] In a similar vein, Vander Waerdt explains that not until the time of the late Stoa was natural law imagined to be general abstract norms resembling legal rules. Rather, natural law is constituted by the sage's rational disposition.[24] Both are joined by Asmis, who also observes that Stoic law is a mental state of perfect rationality. Written laws, by contrast are neither a mental state nor capable of telling individuals what they ought to do.[25]

For the Stoics, value and disvalue are facts of nature.[26] Life in agreement with nature is perfectly integrated into the cosmos like a planet staying within its orbit.[27] It observes cosmic law. What right reason says is an expression of it.[28] Every single command is its manifestation. The law is not a rulebook that we apply but a systematically developed and refined reasoning process.[29] The wisdom of the ideal sage is manifest in the virtues of prudence, moderation, justice and courage.[30] These virtues are subfields of

[18] None of the Stoics claimed to be an embodiment of the sage. See Vogt, n 3, 184.

[19] See Vogt, n 4, 66–67.

[20] See ibid 80.

[21] Vogt, n 7, 566 fn 39 lists the authors following the 'rules interpretation' of Stoic law.

[22] See Vogt, n 4, 179; Vogt, n 7, 566–67. The right reason of the wise person is not a set of general rules but beyond rules and in the mind of that person. It is still called law because of the normativity of the reasons for action that it determines. See Annas, n 4, 182, 185.

[23] According to Vogt, n 3, 196, the end in itself of human life is to become a good deliberator, the attainment of which gives rise to happiness.

[24] See PA Vander Waerdt, 'Zeno's Republic and the Origins of Natural Law' in P Vander Waerdt (ed), *The Socratic Movement* (Ithaca, NY, Cornell University Press, 1994) 272–308, 287. On the controversy that has arisen over this view, see B Straumann, *Roman Law in the State of Nature: The Classical Foundations of Hugo Grotius' Natural Law* (Cambridge, Cambridge University Press, 2015) 112, fn 35.

[25] See E Asmis, 'Cicero on Natural Law and Laws of the State' (2008) 27 *Classical Antiquity* 1–33, 19.

[26] See Vogt, n 4, 17, 178.

[27] See Vogt, n 7, 566.

[28] See Vogt, n 4, 185. Vogt, n 7, 567, puts it as follows: 'There is no legal code, set of customs, or advice by others that can replace our correct thinking.'

[29] See Vogt, n 4, 162, 215.

[30] See Vogt, n 3, 186, 190.

systematically developed wisdom,[31] which is also informed by the principles of logic and physics.[32] Wisdom and virtue as a whole are thus 'the perfection of naturally acquired reasonableness'.[33] Vogt sums up the matter as follows:

> But to be able to live by the law is to understand nature fully, to acquire a substantive body of knowledge that will constitute the perfect disposition of one's soul. And this is different from obeying a law that is external to oneself, or adhering to formal principles of reasoning.[34]

Impressions and Indifferents

The process of practical reasoning begins with 'impressions' that, if affirmed, are turned into impulses. The similarities to the model that we discussed in chapter 4 are striking. In contrast to animals that lack reason, human impressions possess propositional form.[35] The impressions relevant to action ('hormetic impressions') present humans with 'to-be-doneness', which means that they present certain courses of action as appropriate.[36] As rational animals, humans either assent to impressions or reject them.[37] The assent gives rise to an impulse that is immediately followed by action if no further obstacle impedes it.[38] The assent is articulated in the form of an imperative or a summons. The agents prescribe action to themselves.[39] In this way, the dictate of right reason represents what 'the law' prescribes.

Put differently, the law is the set of systematically adjoined responses that feed into a well-reasoned justification of action.[40] These responses are built and refined by taking so-called 'indifferents' (*adiaphora*) into account.[41] As values or disvalues they are relevant to any action that realises *oikeiôsis* as to the interests of oneself or others. Health, wealth and life are neutral

[31] See ibid 191.

[32] See ibid 188–89. Virtue is the unified perspective on the world. The sage has a complete system of knowledge. See ibid 184, 186. See Vogt, n 7, 571: 'To follow the law is not more and no less than to act based on comprehensive knowledge of the universe.'

[33] Vogt, n 4, 179.

[34] ibid 216.

[35] ibid 167.

[36] ibid 14.

[37] ibid 169.

[38] ibid.

[39] On *autopragia* with which agents move themselves by virtue of their own reason, see Vogt, n 7, 563; Vogt, n 4, 172. Rational agents have the capacity to move themselves.

[40] According to Asmis, this was also the understanding of law that emerges from the first book of Cicero's *On Laws*. See Asmis, n 25, 18.

[41] Indifferents are of two different types, one relevant to action, the other not. See Vogt, n 3, 193.

values that nature makes us disposed to prefer; illness, poverty and death are what we are equally ready to avert. While, at the end of the day, the Stoic wise, when it comes to their happiness, remain unaffected by fortune or misfortune[42] and therefore, owing to their exclusive concern with virtue, are indifferent as between health and sickness or poverty and wealth, reconciling oneself with nature nonetheless requires that actions be informed by the goods signified by *adiaphora*.[43] But the wise would not be unhappy if for some reason they ended up being sick, disabled or destitute.[44] One can be happy without getting what one prefers.[45] The wise can still master adverse situations owing to their prudence, courage, moderation or resilience.[46] Virtue – in fact, the ability to deliberate well[47] – is what accounts for their happiness. One can be happy without wealth, but one could not be if one did not possess virtue.[48]

If things work smoothly, moral goodness is manifest in how we systematically and consistently[49] accord over time preference to one or the other *adiaphoron*, depending on what our opportunities are.[50] We do not weigh them against each other, we just establish conditional relations of preference for certain settings.[51] Hence, what the Stoics have in mind when speaking of 'law' is perhaps best explained by analogy to a coherent set of precedents (and not by thinking of a code of laws). The masters of the relevant reasoning processes are the sages. The reason that they develop is, after all, part of cosmic reason.[52] As Vogt explains:

> [T]he sage's perfect reason, insofar as it is practical, and identical with the law, has developed out of tendencies for action that nature instils in human beings *as part of making them rational beings*.[53]

[42] See Vogt, n 4, 149.

[43] See ibid 59, 108, 176, 178. This is the point of Stoic ethics that receives most critical attention. The idea that the indifferents do not really matter to our happiness, for we can be happy or unhappy with or without them, seems to stem from Socrates. See Plato, Meno 88a-d in *The Dialogues of Plato*, vol 1 (trans R.E Allen, New Haven, CT, Yale University Press, 1984) 173–74. I owe the reference to Plato to A Schriefl, *Stoische Philosophie: Eine Einführung* (Stuttgart, Reclam, 2023) 130–31.

[44] The good of virtue is different from the values designated in indifferents. Virtue is the key unlocking the door to happiness. See Vogt, n 7, 565.

[45] See Vogt, n 3, 193, 195.

[46] ibid 193–94.

[47] This is the end in itself. See ibid 196.

[48] See ibid 194.

[49] See Vogt, n 4, 198, 210.

[50] On the comparison of happiness with the good flow of life, see Vogt, n 3, 194.

[51] See Vogt, n 4, 199–200, 204–05, 210.

[52] See ibid 153.

[53] ibid 179.

Lex aeterna and Other Laws

It may have taken a stronger emphasis on God as the creator of the world to arrive at a more rule-like formulation of the eternal law. While Cicero, as an exponent of 'late' Stoicism, may have already moved in this direction,[54] the matter becomes more forthright in the case of Augustine, who also drew a line vis-à-vis pagan Stoic philosophy.

Generally, monotheism views God in the position of a legislator exercising volition.[55] The conception of nature still remains teleological, in the sense that movement is taken to be governed by the drive to attain some end. Nature is not yet the field of undirected mechanical forces impacting on each other. Creation in general is still considered to be ordered hierarchically.[56] The more a being in question resembles God, the more highly it is ranked on its scale.[57] Each being has its own nature or essence and moves (or even evolves) according to the laws that are part of the eternal laws. Each has its proper place in the hierarchical order of things that begins at the lower end with raw materials and ends, at the top, with human beings and angels who are closest to God.

This teleologically conceived nature is supposedly governed by God's eternal law, which contains *immutabilis regulas*.[58] The relevance of rules indicates a more 'legal' understanding of the Stoic *koinon nomos*, the common law.[59] While Stoic philosophy does not perceive an ontological gap separating Zeus from nature, monotheism began drawing a line between the Creator and the order of the world that is his creation (*natura naturans* and *natura naturata*).[60] In this vein, Augustine conceives of the law as a programme determining order from the realised order itself (*ordo ordinans* and *ordo ordinata*). This law is the *lex aeterna* with its *regulas*. While non-human nature is governed by the *lex naturae*, human beings obtain guidance from the

[54] But see M Schofield, 'Cicero and Plato' in JW Atkins and T Bénatouïl (eds), *The Cambridge Companion to Cicero's Philosophy* (Cambridge, Cambridge University Press, 2022) 88–102, 97–98.

[55] See E-W Böckenförde, *Geschichte der Rechts- und Staatsphilosophie: Antike und Mittelalter*, 2nd edn (Tübingen, Mohr, 2006) 198.

[56] See JB Schneewind, *The Invention of Autonomy: A History of Modern Moral Philosophy* (Cambridge, Cambridge University Press, 2010) 19.

[57] See Böckenförde, n 55, 205.

[58] See Augustinus, *De vera religione*, 2nd edn (ed K Flasch, Stuttgart, Reclam, 2006) XXXI, 58, 163 (at 98). See also Böckenförde, n 55, 204.

[59] This is also manifest in Aquinas' establishing a link between virtue and the observance of rules. See Schneewind, n 56, 20.

[60] See Böckenförde, n 55, 202.

lex naturalis. It is, according to Augustine's famous locution, the imprint left in the human soul by the seal ring of eternal law.[61] Occasionally, he also says that the law has been implanted into the human heart by God[62] and gives rise to our intimate familiarity with, and intuitive application of, the Golden Rule.[63]

Participation in the Eternal Law

Matters become more elaborate in Aquinas' system. In his work we find a combination of Aristotelianism and monotheism that first exposes the tension inherent in natural law thinking. The 'law' is not just the euphemistic designator of perfect practical reason but also some type of rule or code, such as the Decalogue.[64]

Aquinas was a faithful student of Aristotle's philosophy. This explains why we do not see too much discontinuity between the two.[65] It is still the case that human beings supposedly have a social nature. It is still the case that human life is meant to go well, and that it can go well, God's grace permitting, if people exercise their proper function.[66]

Politically, however, things are different. Aquinas favours monarchy, indeed monocratic leadership in all social spheres.[67] What is more, Aquinas fuses Aristotelianism with the belief in the *nomos* governing God's creation and, of course, with the belief in the almighty creator of the world,[68] whose plan for governing the creation is the *lex aeterna*.[69] This plan is, however,

[61] See Augustine, *On the Trinity Books 8–15* (trans S McKenna, Cambridge, Cambridge University Press, 2002) XXIV.15.21, 160; Böckenförde, n 55, 205–06.

[62] See Augustine, *On Free Choice of the Will* (trans T Williams, Indianapolis, IN, Hackett, 1993) I.6., 11. See Böckenförde, n 55, 202. This manner of speaking continues in how Calvin speaks of the presence of God's will in the human heart. See Schneewind, n 56, 33. Apparently, it goes back to Romans 2:14.

[63] See Böckenförde, n 55, 206.

[64] This has been pointed out, more recently, by J Habermas, *Auch eine Geschichte der Philosophie*, vol 1: *Die okzidentale Konstellation von Glauben und Wissen* (Berlin, Suhrkamp, 2019) 749–750.

[65] See C Shields and R Pasnau, *The Philosophy of Aquinas*, 2nd edn (Oxford, Oxford University Press, 2016) 12–13.

[66] ibid 46–47, 246.

[67] See Thomas Aquinas, 'On Kingship, to the King of Cyprus' (excerpts in Aquinas, *On Law, Morality, and Politics*, 2nd edn (trans RJ Regan, Indianapolis, IN, Hackett, 2002) I.1, 203–07. See also Habermas, n 64, 742–43; Böckenförde, n 55, 266.

[68] At the same time, we should not forget that even Plato's and Aristotle's metaphysics recognise a figure akin to the creator of the universe. In the case of Plato, it is the 'demiurge' and in the case of Aristotle the 'unmoved mover'. Neither of them plays, however, the important role that Aquinas attributes to God.

[69] See Aquinas, Summa Theologica I-II Q.91 A.1 in Aquinas, n 67, 16. See also Summa Theologica I-II Q.93 A.1, ibid 31: 'And so, as the plan of divine wisdom has the nature of a craft or type or idea because all things are created through it, so the plan of divine wisdom causing the movement of all things to

not God's command, but it is coextensive with his own eternal existence.[70] The eternal law is what underlies the movement that we observe in historical time taking place within the cosmic order. The cosmos is governed by purposes. The development of a seed is caused by the goal that it develop into a fruit or a tree.[71] *Entelechia* is the force moving substances from their mere potential towards what they are finally supposed to be in actuality. The order of the cosmos is characterised by this type of movement.[72]

We have only limited insight into the plan of the universe as laid out in the eternal law. In a manner reminiscent of Augustine, Aquinas believes that the part to which we have access for the purpose of guiding our conduct, also as members of society, is natural law (*lex naturalis*). Ostensibly borrowing an image that we have already encountered in Augustine, Aquinas characterises natural law as the imprint that the eternal law left on the human soul.[73] This explains why we have access to natural law. Natural reason possesses insight into fundamental practical principles, even if it is unaided by revelation.[74] For Aquinas, these principles are of the same type and reside on the same level as the principle of non-contradiction and other self-evident precepts of theoretical reasoning.[75] Through our natural reason we partake of the eternal law. Remarkably, Aquinas establishes the connection of participation from the perspective of those whose movements are governed by the law. Whoever follows a rule, as it were, 'participates' in the rule.[76] If we follow based on insight, we are part of the eternal law by virtue of our intellect.

That we have such access, and are not left in the dark as to the laws governing our conduct, demonstrates that God provides us with necessary guidance.[77] Aquinas' God is good and benign and not a *genius malignus* deceiving us about the way of the world (a hypothetical possibility

their requisite ends has the nature of law. And so the eternal law is simply the plan of divine wisdom that directs all the actions and movements of created things.'

[70] See Aquinas, Summa Theologica I-II Q.93. A.4 in Aquinas, n 67, 35–36 where Aquinas explains that God's will in relation to himself is not 'normative' because it is simply an expression of who he is. By contrast, in relation to his creatures, it is what governs their conduct and pervades and determines all creation. See also Summa Theologica I-II Q.93 A.3, ibid n 67, 34.

[71] On the priority of the final cause, see Shields and Pasnau, n 65, 51–52.

[72] See, again, Aquinas, Summa Theologica I-II Q.93 A.1 in Aquinas, n 67, 31.

[73] It is implanted in the mind of human beings. See Aquinas, Summa Theologica I-II Q.90. A.4, ibid n 67, 16.

[74] See Aquinas, Summa Theologica I-II Q.79 A.12, ibid n 67, 2; Shields and Pasnau, n 65, 272.

[75] See Aquinas, Summa Theologica I-II Q.94 A.2. in Aquinas, n 67, 42; Shields and Pasnau, n 65, 272.

[76] See Aquinas, Summa Theologica I-II Q.91 A.2 in Aquinas, n 67, 18.

[77] See Shields and Pasnau, n 65 278–79.

contemplated by Descartes in his 'First Meditation'),[78] and also not the demiurge imagined by the Gnostic Marcion qua architect of a hostile universe from which only Christ can redeem us.[79] God makes laws that are good for us and he invests us with the ability to understand natural law, even if he seems to have an interest in seeing us cope successfully with the law of concupiscence or sin.[80] The medium of insight into law is called *synderesis*, and it is basically the equivalent of what we would call conscience, even if *synderesis* is perhaps better understood as the natural disposition to understand first self-evident principles.[81]

There are two more laws to consider in Aquinas' system. Divine laws are part of divine revelation,[82] that is, the 10 commandments and the precept to love God and your neighbours as yourself.[83] Finally, there is positive or human law, *lex humana sive positiva*.[84] Human law is 'determined' by natural law, but not fully determined by it. We will return to the relation between natural and human law below.

A Pithy Slogan and Natural Inclinations

The most basic precept of natural law says that we ought to do good and avoid doing bad.[85] Aquinas regards it as a self-evident principle.[86] Modern readers might be struck by its apparent emptiness. Yet what seems to amount to a truism becomes somewhat less embarrassing when we contemplate that it merely restates a basic feature of human action. We always act in the guise of the good.[87] This means that our actions are purposive, and in pursuing aims we implicitly take it for granted that our objectives are good to pursue. If that were not the case, we should not and would not engage in action. Even if I merely wanted to harm others or to demonstrate to everyone how

[78] See R Descartes, *Meditations on First Philosophy*, 2nd edn (trans J Cottingham, Cambridge, Cambridge University Press, 2007).

[79] See H Blumenberg, *Arbeit am Mythos*, 3rd edn (Frankfurt aM, Suhrkamp 1984) 209–26.

[80] See Aquinas, Summa Theologica I-II Q.91 A.6, in Aquinas, n 67, 25. On the paradoxical nature of this law, see Shields and Pasnau, n 65, 279–80.

[81] Aquinas, Summa Theologica I-II Q.79 A.12 in Aquinas, n 67, 2; Shields and Pasnau, n 65, 272; Böckenförde, n 55, 239.

[82] See Aquinas, Summa Theologica I-II Q.91 A.4 in Aquinas, n 67, 21 (explaining its necessity).

[83] See Mark 12:30–31; Matthew 22:36–40.

[84] In the case of Augustine, it is called *lex temporalis*. See Augustine, n 62, I.6., 8. See Böckenförde, n 55, 206.

[85] See Habermas, n 64, 729–30. It is cited in Shields and Pasnau, n 65, 273 (ST 1a2ae 94.2c).

[86] See Aquinas, Summa Theologica I-II Q.94 A.2 in Aquinas, n 67, 43.

[87] See JD Velleman, *The Possibility of Practical Reason*, 2nd edn (Ann Arbor, MI, Maize Books, 2015) 73–99; J Raz, *From Normativity to Responsibility* (Oxford, Oxford University Press, 2011) 59–84.

much evil I can perpetrate, my demonstration of callousness would still have to be regarded as the 'good' of my action. If asked what my action is 'good for', I would always reply by stating its purpose, which may well be to perform another action.[88] 'Why are you turning this screw'? 'I am disassembling the alarm clock.' The latter action is the good of the former.

Still, we need to know which purposes are morally commendable and which are reprehensible, and we cannot discern these merely by pointing to the teleological structure of action or by saying that whatever happens to be desired is good. For the relation between the good and the desired is the obverse, as Aquinas insisted upon. Things are desired because they are good. Ends are not good because they are desired.[89]

Grounding the good in desires, however, points in the direction of Aquinas' answer, which must remove the equivocation in the relation of the formal purposiveness of action and what we ought to regard as *truly* good (and not merely take to be good when acting). It is also the core of the attempted reconciliation of metaphysics and deontology. In order to find out which actions are right, and which are wrong, we need to attend to our natural inclinations.[90] They have been implanted into us by God and are, therefore, elements of the *lex aeterna*.[91] While they not only propel us towards doing certain things, they nonetheless help us to figure out what to do. They engage our rationality. It falls to reason to allocate to each inclination its proper place and to distinguish between appropriate and inappropriate satisfactions.[92]

Our first natural inclination concerns self-preservation.[93] We want to stay alive. We use our natural reason, then, to figure out what conduct is conducive to attaining the objective of living for as long as we possibly can. We realise that gluttony is bad and that exercise, if not engaged in excessively, is good for us.

Our desire to have sexual intercourse is indicative of the inclination to procreate (at least, this is how Aquinas would have looked at the matter).[94]

[88] See also M Thompson, *Life and Action: Elementary Structures of Practice and Practical Thought* (Cambridge, MA, Harvard University Press, 2008) 85–86.

[89] See Shields and Pasnau, n 65, 252.

[90] See Habermas, n 64, 745, 755–56; Shields and Pasnau, n 65, 275; Schneewind, n 56, 20.

[91] See Aquinas, Summa Theologica I-II Q.93 A.3 in Aquinas, n 67, 34. Franciso de Vitoria, as a representative of the 'late scholasticism' of the school of Salamanca, holds the same view. See Böckenförde, n 55, 347.

[92] See Habermas, n 64, 754, 757.

[93] See Aquinas, Summa Theologica I-II Q.94 A.2 in Aquinas, n 67, 43.

[94] ibid.

This matches how traditional Roman Catholics speak of our sexual appetites. They are supposedly geared towards procreation. I can only speak from the perspective of a white heterosexual man, but I am afraid that Aquinas was mistaken. Sexual desire is about the joint experience of lust. Aquinas would possibly reply that my view is myopic, for the result of unprotected sexual intercourse is pregnancy. If I replied that contraceptives serve to redirect the purpose of intercourse from procreation to the enjoyment of sexual pleasure, then he would most likely retort that doing so is against nature's law.[95]

This simple example demonstrates that natural law arguments share two elementary features. First, they suggest that some conduct comports with the natural order of things even if God has given us the ability to change it. The Catholic natural law theorist says that it is natural for matrimony to be monogamous. But would not universal promiscuity seem more like the natural state? Second, natural law arguments are just that, namely, arguments. The Stoics appear to have understood this. Natural law provides us with a horizon from which we can examine the merits or demerits of certain actions or recommended laws. But *lex naturalis*, particularly if it merely says 'do the right thing', is not, easy cases aside, a code on which we can draw when confronted with more tricky questions.

Incidentally, the third inclination is not surprising.[96] Human beings want to know the truth about God and live in community with others and understand, therefore, that they must not harm others.[97]

The Legislature

Owing to the strange career of Radbruch's theory of 'legislative injustice', we have now come to view natural law through the lens of members of the judiciary who are confronted with the question whether a piece of legislation is to be treated as valid law even though they regard it as gravely unjust.[98] The examples that Radbruch had in mind when he formulated his theory were instances of Nazi policy, for example the prohibition of marriage between 'Arians' and Jews. Radbruch conceded that any piece of

[95] The example is also discussed in Shields and Pasnau, n 65, 277.
[96] See Aquinas, Summa Theologica I-II Q.94 A.2 in Aquinas, n 67, 43–44.
[97] See Böckenförde, n 55, 239.
[98] See G Radbruch, 'Statutory Lawlessness and Supra-statutory Law (1946)' (2006) 26 *Oxford Journal of Legal Studies* 1–11 (trans B Litschewski Paulson and SL Paulson).

positive law is of value, not least because it clarifies what people ought to do. It creates, as Radbruch put it, 'legal certainty'. However, the value of legal certainty may in certain cases be outweighed and fall by the wayside in the face of a substantive injustice contained in the norm (such as the prohibition of interracial marriage in Germany).

Radbruch's philosophical reflections from the post-war period were remarkably successful. They were used both by the German Supreme Court and by the German Constitutional Court to declare certain instances of National Socialist legislation retroactively invalid.[99] To this day we look at natural law from the perspective of judges who are hypothetically confronted with the question whether a piece of legislation is too gravely unjust to be valid law. This has created the impression that natural law is of peripheral importance and relevant to a legal system only in the catastrophic case that the law supports regimes of apartheid or even genocide.

We tend to forget, therefore, that natural law was from medieval times onwards directed at the legislature. It is supposedly relevant to all kinds of political projects and not at all limited to averting catastrophes.

At the same time, the image of natural law as the last normative resort for invalidating positive law has also obscured how natural law and positive law are supposed to interact according to Aquinas' system. We ignore that historical experience, local knowledge and their respective specialisation are also part of God's creation and therefore no less essential to the actualisation of natural law than any contemplation of the proper satisfaction of *inclinationes naturales*. The relation between natural law and positive law is one of *determinatio*.[100] In this relation, natural law provides us with a rough sketch of how things ought to be; nonetheless, the prudence, experience, historical trajectory and local knowledge of the legislature is equally indispensable for fleshing things out at a level of greater detail.

How *determinatio* works is explained by Aquinas in two ways.[101] The first form of determination amounts to a deduction from principles. We realise that we should not injure others because this would harm them, and harming others is wrong. The second form of *determinatio* is, taking up Aquinas' own example of a builder, explained with reference to the relation

[99] For an introduction, see PE Quint, 'The Border Guard Trials and the East German Past – Seven Arguments' (2002) 48 *American Journal of Comparative Law* 541–72.
[100] See Böckenförde, n 55, 240.
[101] See Aquinas, Summa Theologica I-II Q.95 A.2 in Aquinas, n 67, 54.

between a family who wishes to build a home and an architect who is able to arrive at a blueprint. The family members have a rough idea, but they need the expertise and assistance of the architect (or of a builder) to arrive at a clearer and more detailed conception of what they really want.[102] This second form of determination resembles the way in which 'craftsmen in the course of exercising their skill adapt general forms to specific things'.[103] This requires, as Aquinas explains with explicit reference to Aristotle's prudence, experience and deference to the judgement of those who have already distinguished themselves in their craft.[104]

There is hardly ever any ready-to-use natural law without the interposition of the legislature.

A Twofold Tension

Hans Kelsen indicted natural law theory for mistakenly inferring 'ought' from 'is'.[105] Undoubtedly, if one isolates the link that teleological arguments establish between what there is and the further steps that that which is must take to attain perfection, then their reasoning appears to be ostensibly faulty. From the mere fact that we wish to be happy, it does not – not without anything further, at any rate – follow that we ought to be happy.

The intellectual fate of natural law demonstrates, contrary to Kelsen's simplistic objection, how mistaken it is to draw a sharp line between is and ought. Natural law theory would have fared better, had it stayed on the Stoic track. We shall see, indeed, that it is best to have alleged natural laws dissolve into the consistent operation of practical reason. Remarkably, an author most ignorant of the natural law tradition, Ronald Dworkin, appears to have divined this, even if only as though he had done so by the grace of God.

Matters have never been as simple as Kelsen imagined them to be. The relevance of our inclinations was based on metaphysical premises explaining their normative force. God has created us such that we want to preserve ourselves and live happily with and among others.[106] Our inclinations are

[102] For a resumption of this tradition, see A Vermeule, *Common Good Constitutionalism: Recovering the Classical Legal Tradition* (Cambridge, Polity, 2022) 44–47, 151–54.

[103] Aquinas, Summa Theologica I-II Q.95 A.2 in Aquinas, n 67, 54.

[104] See ibid 55.

[105] See, for example, H Kelsen, *Introduction to the Problems of Legal Theory* (trans B Litschewski Paulson and SL Paulson, Oxford, Clarendon Press, 1992).

[106] See Shields and Pasnau, n 65, 275.

expressive of who we essentially are as part of creation. Goodness and badness are predicates that also apply to entities, thus designating their 'ontological qualities'.[107] Inasmuch as a being falls short of the fullness of being it could possibly attain, it is 'bad'. Someone or something can be better or worse, more perfect or less perfect, at being who or what they are supposed to be. Any emerging or remaining difference is explicable as a *privatio boni* (*ens et bonum convertuntur*). Actions are good if in light of the highest good – which is the face-to-face encounter with God *post mortem*[108] – they are oriented towards the appropriate end.[109] This means that actions have to accord with natural and with divine law (the Decalogue, in particular).

Aquinas still believes in the full congruence of the intelligible natural order and God's will. What is more, his teachings suggest that God relies on forms for this creation that are just as eternal as he is himself. The eternal law comprising these forms is immediately manifest in his creation. He has not chosen to create it. The created order is coextensive with who he is.[110]

Monotheism and traditional metaphysics, however, can only arrive at an uneasy synthesis.[111] While the original tension between the law and reason appears to be resolved by regarding the law as written into the human soul, it remains difficult to imagine how the eternal forms of being could prejudice God's will and for what reason God should be constrained to using them, rather than conceivable others, for the purpose of creation.[112] This marks one of the points at which monotheism threatens to be destructive of natural law.

Another tension, however, is of equal significance and points to the same root. Practical reason is a matter of insight into our nature and our place in the world. Lawfulness is the product of yielding to the right instincts based on the light cast on the *conditio humana* by natural reason. But *lex* is also of divine origin and, hence, attributable to a command of God.[113] In the latter case, the participation in the law is mediated by apprehending this law with trepidation.[114] This suggests a rift between the *lex* as a

[107] See Habermas, n 64, 731–32.
[108] ibid 781.
[109] ibid 734 (Summa Theologica I-II, Q.3, A.8).
[110] See F Oakley, 'Medieval Theories of Natural Law: William of Ockham and the Significance of the Voluntarist Tradition' (1961) *Natural Law Forum* 65–83, 81.
[111] On the following, see also F Oakley, *Natural Law, Laws of Nature, Natural Rights: Continuity and Discontinuity in the History of Ideas* (New York, Continuum, 2005) 46–51.
[112] See Oakley, n 110, 82.
[113] See Habermas, n 64, 752–53.
[114] ibid 753–54. There is an unresolved tension between the in-built inclination to observe the natural law and the control of our impulses by rational means (see ibid 753, 757).

standard and its human addressee. The law is *external* to the regulated being that had traditionally been taken to be responsive, even if only moderately, to the guidance obtained naturally from inclinations in the light of natural reason.[115] What we encounter here already is the prefiguration of the deontological normativity of norms: its claim to be binding, regardless of whether what is bound by it is naturally aligned to it or tied to it based on an approbation of appetites.[116]

Both tensions can be explained by the uneasy alliance between the legacy of the necessitarianism of Greek metaphysics that treats essences and their entelechial force as eternal and the contingency pervading a universe that originates *ex nihilo* from God's will.[117] It is this tension between the unchangingly reasonable and the voluntary part of creation[118] that not only Duns Scotus, but also the late scholastic philosophers of the Salamanca school addressed in subtle attempts to contain voluntarism.[119] They struggled with sustaining both, for example, by distinguishing the 'demonstrative' from the 'preceptive' function of natural law[120] or the use of the distinction between *potestas ordinata* and *potestas absoluta*[121] to relegate God's free will to deviations from his earlier established order[122] and to estop him from

[115] Möhle explains this difference by contrasting the Aristotelian model of action, which perceives a cooperative activity between the intellect and a naturally functioning appetitive power, and Scotus' emphasis on having the intellect present the commendable actions and the will acting independently of inclinations as the effective cause. The will can determine itself to action in complete independence of a final cause. See H Möhle, 'Scotus' Theory of Natural Law' in *The Cambridge Companion to Duns Scotus* (Cambridge, Cambridge University Press, 2003) 312–31, 323–24.

[116] For a slightly different way of stating this matter, see Habermas, n 64, 748–49.

[117] See Oakely, n 110, 67. It will be seem that, as Möhle explains, Scotus still tried to steer a middle course between both ways of modelling reasonableness. See Möhle, n 115, 313.

[118] See Oakley, n 111, 46–48.

[119] De Vitoria, for example, still regarded natural law simply as a precept of reason. See F de Vitoria, 'On Law: Lectures on ST I-II. 90–105' in *Political Writings* (ed A Pagden and J Lawrence, Cambridge, Cambridge University Press, 1991) 153–204, § 121, 155.

[120] See F Suárez, Treatise on Law and God the Lawgiver, in *Selections from Three Works* (trans GL Williams et al, ed T Pink, Carmel, IN, Liberty Fund, 2015) 5–755, 58–59 (I.IV.6). Suárez, for example, tried to accommodate God's will by claiming that if knowledge of what is right does not in and of itself give rise to law, there must be a divine precept to make a law binding. The reason is that without that condition, God would be subordinate to such knowledge. See further n 156. At the same time, Suárez' demonstrative function of law permits him to sustain the idea of natural law as a signifier of eternal law, and of human judgement and conscience as modes of participating in this eternal law. See Schneewind, n 56, 63–64; Böckenförde, n 55, 383.

[121] On the distinction, see J Duns Scotus, *Selected Writings on Ethics* (trans T Williams, Oxford, Oxford University Press, 2017) 94 (Ordinatio I d. 44 q. un. 3), according to whom ordered power is, seemingly paradoxically, the power to do what one has been ordered to do. Absolute power is the power not to. See Suárez, n 120, 164 (II.II.4). As Möhle, n 115, 317 explains, someone acts by 'ordinate power' if the person acts within an established order and follows its law, whereas the same person acts by 'absolute power' if they transgress this order or replace commands that constitute that order.

[122] See Böckenförde, n 55, 348–49.

making amendments that would introduce a contradiction into the work of his own making.[123]

An Aside on the Onto-theological Paradox

Everything hinges, at the end of the day, on the function played by God the Creator. Medieval natural law theory is based on the onto-theological[124] difference between the totality of being as such, which accounts for the world, and entities existing within the world as part of creation. This ontological difference is manifest in the relation between God and everything he sustains.[125] The difference is, however, also partly rescinded, for the beings that are part of a hierarchically structured cosmic order are believed to partake of God's being depending on the degree to which they approach the level of humanity (humans are the most perfect creatures). While participation is a comparative matter of 'more of less', it nevertheless bridges the ontological difference between the infinite supreme being and its finite creatures. The infinite being exists just as the finite beings exist, and the finite beings are just part of what the infinite being is. The difference between the infinite and the finite is sustained and at the same time levelled. This is the core paradox of onto-theology.[126]

The scholastic theories that we associate with voluntarism and nominalism no longer view the finite and the infinite as different types of entity designated by the concept of 'being'. Duns Scotus' philosophy takes an epistemological turn. The concept of being as such, with its trans-categorical and indeterminate content, is cast as an epistemological condition for the cognition of concrete objects.[127] We must have already understood what being as such is, devoid of further content, before

[123] The matter is not so easily answered in the case of Scotus, who distinguishes between general laws and particular orders. See Scotus, n 121, 97 (Ordinatio I, d 44 q un 11). In principle, Scotus believed that God is unqualifiedly free to make a proposition or its contradictory proposition true; free, in contrast to Aquinas, not only successively but at any point in time. See ibid 90 (Reportatio IA, dd 39–30, qq 1–3, 39). God cannot, however, will both to be true. See ibid 93–94 (Reportatio IA, dd 39–30, qq 1–3, 57). For a very helpful introduction, see T Williams, 'John Duns Scotus' *Stanford Encyclopedia of Philosophy* (2022) at https://plato.stanford.edu/entries/duns-scotus/, 26 (pdf version).

[124] On the following, see Habermas, n 64, 771–85.

[125] ibid 737.

[126] See Habermas, n 64, 772.

[127] See J Duns Scotus, *Philosophical Writings* (trans A Wolter, Indianapolis, IN, Hackett, 1987) 4–8. See also L Honnefelder, *Johannes Duns Scotus: Denker an der Schwelle vom mittelalterlichen zum neuzeitlichen Denken* (Paderborn, Schöningh, 2011) 15.

comprehending concrete beings.[128] Based on this transcendental notion, Scotus no longer distinguishes between an infinite entity and finite entities but regards infinity or necessity – or, on the other side, finiteness and contingency – as modes of trans-categorical being.[129] They are presupposed in the vocabulary that we use when we talk about God or nature, but they do not refer to different entities. All conceptual content is based on the presupposition of 'objectness' as such. The qualities of the infinite being have to be determined by theology, based on revelation.

One result of this is, in the nominalist context, the de-essentialisation of being. The world of nature is reconceived as being composed of internally unrelated things that are at best connected by causation.[130] The first concept of God that philosophy can arrive at is the notion of a trans-categorical 'something' that is substantively indeterminate in its determinate existence. This move, apparently, prepares the contingency of creation.[131]

Limiting God's Freedom

Hitherto, natural law theory had assumed that natural law qua dictate of right reason maps the part of the cosmic order that is accessible to us. It is, in contrast to divine law, without a source. One can even attribute[132] to Aquinas the view that what is commanded in the Decalogue is good not because it is commanded but because it is good in itself.[133] God is manifest in his reason. He could not rise above it without losing himself.

Duns Scotus can be credited, if what he did is at all meritorious, with elevating freedom into God's first attribute and with viewing his free will as still subject to internal constraints. The precepts of natural law are part of these constraints. The scope of strict natural law is manifest in commandments that are valid on the grounds of conceptual necessity.[134] The *lex aeterna* has already gone out of the window. Natural law prescribes what is unqualifiedly necessary to observe. The core commands of natural law

[128] See Habermas, n 64, 778–79.
[129] See Scotus, n 127, 8–9; Habermas, n 64, 779.
[130] See on what Charles S Peirce would regard as the threat of nominalism in P Foster, *Peirce and the Threat of Nominalism* (Cambridge, Cambridge University Press, 2011) 4–7.
[131] See Scotus, n 121, 89 (Reportatio IA, dd 39–40, qq 1–3, 38).
[132] As is done by Schneewind, n 56, 23.
[133] The question was first raised in Plato's *Euthyphro* 10a. See Plato, *The Last Days of Socrates: Euthyphro, Apology, Crito, Phaedo* (trans C Rowe, London, Penguin Books, 2010) 17.
[134] See Möhle, n 115, 315–16.

have God as their object. God is only one. God is to be loved because he is the best being.[135] From this nature of God follow the first two commandments of the Decalogue.[136] Scotus adjusts the third precept to fit the other two. In the Decalogue, the third commandment demands that the Sabbath be kept holy. Clearly, it is not on the same level of 'necessity' as the first two commandments and appears to be contingent. Scotus recasts it as the precept that God is not to be hated.[137]

This comprises natural law in the strictest sense.[138] The first three commandments are ordained by God because they are genuine natural law, that is, good.[139] They cannot be changed even by him. God cannot will anything going against his own nature. The Almighty cannot will himself to be not almighty; the infinite cannot will itself to be finite. God cannot want us to worship other gods and not be loved by us. Remarkably, he also cannot will two contradictory propositions to be true.[140]

Consistency and avoiding of contradictions are of great relevance to natural law in a wider sense, which has to be ordained by God, such as the other seven commands of the Decalogue.[141] These other precepts of divine law could have been willed differently by him.[142] For example, he could have permitted adultery, polygamy or murder.[143] According to Ockham, not Scotus,[144] God could have even ordered us to hate him.[145] In any event, what God commands is good because it has been laid down by him and not because of the nature of what is commanded or its consequences.[146]

135 See Scotus, n 121, 172 (Ordinatio III d 27 q un 53); Schneewind, n 56, 23.

136 See Duns Scotus, n 121, 252–53 (Ordinatio III, d.37, q un 16–29). For a helpful interpretation, see Williams, n 123, 24–26 (pdf view).

137 See Williams, n 123, 24–25 (pdf view).

138 See Möhle, n 115, 316.

139 See Schneewind, n 56, 23–24.

140 See n 123 and Möhle, n 115, 318, who notes that self-contradiction is outside of God's infinite power.

141 See Schneewind, n 56, 24.

142 See Williams, n 123, 26 (pdf view). This traditional voluntarist rendering of Scotus' doctrine has been challenged more recently by T Borland and TA Hillman, 'Scotus and God's Arbitrary Will: A Reassessment' (2017) 91 *American Catholic Philosophical Quarterly* 399–429 and TM Ward, 'A Most Mitigated Friar: Scotus on Natural Law and Divine Freedom' (2019) 93 *American Catholic Philosophical Quarterly* 385–409.

143 This view is rejected by Suárez, n 120, 329 (II.XV.4).

144 See the references cited in n 136.

145 See Schneewind, n 56, 24–25. On this consequence, see AS McGrade, 'Natural Law and Moral Omnipotence' in PV Spade (ed), *The Cambridge Companion to Ockham* (Cambridge, Cambridge University Press, 2006) 273–301, 280, 284.

146 See McGrade, n 145, 280.

Nevertheless, whatever is ordained by God cannot be entirely arbitrary, for it has to be consonant with strict natural law[147] and meet requirements of consistency and coherence. Apparently, strict natural law requires that God lay down coherent orders; and if he changes his mind on certain issues, he cannot simply introduce a dispensation but must change the general principles of the order by creating a new one.[148] Yet, in this context, both Scotus and Ockham distinguish between an absolute power and ordained power.[149] The latter is the order of God's creation to which we still have access with our natural reason,[150] whereas the first had been coined in order to account for exceptions that God makes for laws, for example by working miracles or granting dispensations. In Scotus' case, *potentia ordinata* is manifest in whole orderings, not in single laws.[151] The distinction between *potentia ordinata* and *absoluta* resolves the difficulty that while there is natural law in the wider sense qua ordained power, it must not be regarded as God's final word. On the contrary, as it is taken for granted that God can abrogate the ordained laws,[152] this implies that the teleological and logical connections between elements of the world become fragile and lose their apparent naturalness. In the face of the threat of chaos, Scotus attempts to retain the emphasis on order by extending the criterion of non-contradiction to various orderings. Indeed, natural law theory should be able to elaborate the principles that can be reconciled differently in different orderings. The place that the emerging matrix of orderings leaves for God's free will is then manifest in the weight that he accords to one principle or purpose rather than another. The institution of matrimony can serve the purposes of either maximising offspring or preventing unchastity. If God decided that the former purpose carries more weight than the other, then God would permit polygamy. In the reverse case, monogamy would give rise to greater chastity.[153] Apparently, wider natural law theory can be developed into a

[147] See Möhle, n 115, 316.

[148] ibid 318–19.

[149] See Duns Scotus, n 121, 85–87 (Ordinatio I d 44 q un 3–11); Schneewind, n 56, 24–25; Oakley, n 110, 70–71.

[150] Ockham, indeed, regards our natural reason as tacitly ordered by the divine will. We are following God's law even if we do not apply divine commandments and merely use our natural reason. For an account of how this can be understood, see McGrade, n 145, 277–79.

[151] As Möhle, n 115, 319 explains, '[I]f God were to create an ordering that contained precepts that could not be reconciled with one another, a contradiction would thereby exist.'

[152] Matters are complicated of course, as regards the matter that God can abrogate. Also, it should be borne in mind that God cannot but act normatively, which explains why the exercise of absolute power is also the exercise of ordained power. See Duns Scotus, n 121, 96–97 (Ordinatio I, d 44, qu un 5, 11).

[153] See Möhle, n 115, 321–22.

theory of possible divine laws by viewing God as free to tip the balance of reasons in favour of either. The advantage that Scotus' approach offers is to prevent voluntarism from running rampant by taking God's will to amount to inscrutable commands. God is neither determined nor inscrutable because we can appreciate the significance of his choices.[154]

Even though the *lex aeterna* is consumed by the *legislator aeternus*,[155] in Scotus' case the link to the intellect is not entirely severed, even if it is no longer tied to eternal essences.[156]

Under the preponderance of God's will, it must be assumed that each single being is the contingent product of God's will.[157] But it opens the door to seeing all the connections that we perceive between events as of our making. Nominalism[158] and empiricism are of a piece with onto-theological voluntarism. Universal concepts no longer refer to essences that are active in nature; they are the product or generalisation of empirical realities.[159]

The Voluntarist Sting

But even with Scotus' precautions and elaborations in place, God's will is independent of reason, not only in the sense of its ability to act contrary to ordained reason, but also ontologically speaking.[160] Of the possible worlds that God could have created, the creation of this particular world becomes groundless.[161] Oakley observes for the moral domain that, in the final consequence, all moral laws are eventually expressive or derivative of 'inscrutable commands'.[162] That the world is no longer embedded in an

[154] ibid 322.
[155] See Böckenförde, n 55, 284.
[156] This severance is in principle also sustained by Francisco Suárez, who argued that even though God's knowledge of eternal essences is eternal, knowledge alone cannot suffice to impose natural law, for God would then be bound by it. But God cannot be subordinated to anything because God has no superior. See Suárez, n 120, 212 (II.VI.6) See also Schneewind, n 56, 60. Yet Suárez does not fully buy into voluntarism. Certain conduct is inherently evil. God only adds his own command. Once he has done so, he cannot go against himself, because once ordained he cannot refrain from willing to forbid the intrinsically evil act. God has created us to do good things and changing this would defeat his own purpose. See Suárez, n 120, 217–19 (II.VI.11). See also Schneewind, n 56, 60–61.
[157] See Böckenförde, n 55, 278, 301–02.
[158] The opposite, realism, appears more elusive to us now. But the core idea is straightforward. Womanhood exists. The universal is manifest in various individuals in which the universal is combined with something particular. The universal that exists outside the mind is repeatable in them. See also Williams, n 122, 18 (pdf view).
[159] See Böckenförde, n 55, 280, 303–05.
[160] See Honnefelder, n 127, 27.
[161] See Habermas, n 64, 784.
[162] Oakely, n 110, 73.

intellect that provides it with ontological stability also has consequences for what we regard as reason.[163] Not only is it we who now need to establish the connections between what we encounter; we also have to take it for granted that everything is subject to God's masterly control (see 'The Heart of the Matter: Mastery' below). If we eliminated Scotus' precautions, we could not be assured of the consequences that really follow even from a given set of premises, for it would be possible for God to ordain at any time an exception. If whatever God wanted is necessarily registered in our intellect as 'good',[164] our relation to the world would match the attitude we have to adopt in common law systems in which a new case that misapprehends the significance of existing precedents still alters the whole body of case law. We needed to rationalise chaos and attempt to arrive at a different sense of coherence. The equivalent to this in civil law systems would be situations in which a case that would ordinarily be regarded as easy and clear is claimed to present an unprecedented set of facts requiring a new and 'creative' solution. In these contexts, everything that we have called reason disintegrates because reasoning is set loose to move in a variety of directions.

Voluntarism, even if it seems to call for mere obedience, is a deep and profound challenge to reason.[165] Ultimately, it perceives God choosing a universe of thought in the act of creation.[166] This universe is susceptible to contingent amendments. Nature is neither inherently nor unequivocally reasonable.[167] Morality loses its ontological moorings in the teleological realisation of essences. Practical reason is directly exposed to God's authority demanding obedience.[168] The link between justice and the natural order of things is broken:

> The principle of natural law, to do good and refrain from doing evil, can no longer be concretized with regard to the metaphysically recognized species nature of man according to natural aspirations and a corresponding diversity of basic goods.[169]

[163] See Honnefelder, n 127, 28.

[164] On the following, see McGrade, n 145, 280–82, 287.

[165] And to the idea of God, for if followed through consistently, the God of voluntarism can be substituted with chance. See H Blumenberg, *Die Legitimität der Neuzeit: Erneuerte Ausgabe* (Frankfurt aM, Suhrkamp, 1988) 165.

[166] See Habermas, n 64, 784. See also Böckenförde, n 55, 289, claiming that according to voluntarist doctrine, the reasonableness inherent in God's creation is contingent and dependent on God's will.

[167] See Habermas, n 64, 785.

[168] ibid 790.

[169] ibid 802: 'Das Prinzip des Naturrechts, Gutes zu tun und Schlechtes zu unterlassen, kann nicht mehr mit Blick auf die metaphysisch erkannte Artnatur des Menschen gemäß natürlichen Strebungen und einer entsprechenden Vielfalt von Grundgütern konkretisiert werden.'

As Möhle explains, the will can determine itself to action in complete independence from a final goal.[170] Human beings possess free will,[171] as Scotus tried to demonstrate by perceiving them as invested with the freedom to choose a course of action, such as the pleasurable or the just.[172] The intellect is passive. It is necessitated by the object to which its attention has been directed to recognise what this object is. The will is free with regard to both its objects and the act of volition. It enjoys the liberty whether and what to will. It is, therefore, invested with an element of self-reflexivity that subjects first-order volition to second-order volition.[173] As Möhle explains, 'The will that wills an object also always wills its willing of that object.'[174] Such a will has always the power to suspend and to abandon its willing. Set free from natural constraints, such as inclinations, the reasonableness of the will is entirely dependent on being amenable to 'reason'.[175] God's freedom and the freedom of humans[176] introduce, as Habermas puts it, a 'double contingency' into the world. Both God and human beings have power to make new beginnings.[177] It can be reined in only by the principle of consistency with which God, in order to will anything, must tie himself to his orders, and by the commitment made by human beings, who are free to observe the natural law. The basis of this obligation is insight into what God has commanded humans to do.[178] Theoretical reason seems to precede its practical counterpart. God's command commits us without being aided and abetted by human inclinations.[179]

Voluntarism will run rampant in Protestant theology.[180] The impenetrability of God's will becomes stressed to an extent that attains absurd proportions. The anti-Pelagian[181] stance conceding God unrestrained power

[170] See Möhle, n 115, 324.
[171] See Honnefelder, n 121, 25.
[172] On the distinction between the *affectio commodi* and the *affectio iustitiae*, see Scotus, n 121, 112–18 (Ordinatio II d 6 q 2, 39–63). See Schneewind, n 56, 31; Williams, n 123, 28 (pdf view). Without such a choice, we would be driven only by appetites and could not sin.
[173] See Möhle, n 115, 325–26.
[174] ibid 326.
[175] ibid 328.
[176] See Scotus, n 121, 89 (Reportatio IA dd 39–40 qq 1–3 n 38).
[177] See Habermas, n 64, 796, 800.
[178] See J Habermas, *Auch eine Geschichte der Philosophie*, vol 2: *Vernünftige Freiheit. Spuren des Diskurses über Glauben und Wissen* (Berlin, Suhrkamp, 2019) 85.
[179] See Habermas, n 64, 790.
[180] On Luther and Calvin, see Schneewind, n 56, 29–32.
[181] For an introduction, see E Nelson, *The Theology of Liberalism: Political Philosophy and the Justice of God* (Cambridge, MA, Harvard University Press, 2019) 2–3. According to the teachings of the Irish monk Pelagius, we could assure ourselves of our salvation by means of good deeds. The guarantee of being saved on the ground of our works, however, implied that God would have to observe something like the rule of law and be bound to reward us for what we believe ourselves to have merited. Already Augustine

to elect those who are saved invites hard questions, such as why we are not exonerated given that God has created us to be sinners, with the claim that God's intellect is inaccessible to human understanding. The natural law that is written into our hearts and elucidated by the Decalogue is groundless. The function of positive law becomes, aside from educating the elect about their duties, to deter the unregenerate and to instil in sinful creatures a sense of shame by reminding them of their lowliness and inability to live up fully to God's heartless precepts.[182]

Rights and the Social Contract

The scholastic edifice crumbles even more if voluntarism becomes diffused into God's free creatures.

The first noteworthy development concerns the emergence of the concept of *ius* in the sense of a right held by individuals, and of the idea that individuals have *dominium sui*, which prefigures, in Suárez' *ius naturale concessivum*,[183] the idea of private autonomy.[184] De Vitoria views it as emerging in the context of the property right, which invests subjects with freedom of choice.[185] Both anticipate therewith the equal external freedom of all as the new fundamental principle of law. Suárez, however, does not view this liberty as an inalienable right. People are free to dispose of it.[186]

The second development concerns the changing status of the social contract. Some form of social contract has always played a peripheral role in explaining how human beings move beyond the family and form larger communities.[187] The ideas have stayed, however, within the framework developed by Aristotle, who had also explained at the beginning of *Politics* how smaller human communities unite and form larger units until they

objected that this implication would run foul of God's free judgement. Only God can determine who is saved and who is not. A consequence of the opposition to Pelagius is the doctrine of prevenient grace. Why God has chosen to save one and not the other is inaccessible to the human intellect. See Augustine, *Four Anti-Pelagian Writings* (ed JA Mourant, Washington, DC, Catholic University of America Press, 1992).

182 See Schneewind, n 56, 34.

183 See Suárez, n 120, 386 (II.XVIII.2). Böckenförde, n 55, 385–86.

184 See Habermas, n 178, 88–90, 95.

185 See F de Vitoria, 'On the American Indians' in *Political Writings*, n 119, § 20, 247. For a far more elaborate account of the whole history, see AS Brett, *Liberty, Right and Nature: Individual Rights in Later Scholastic Thought* (Cambridge, Cambridge University Press, 1997).

186 See Böckenförde, n 55, 386.

187 See on Suárez and de Vitoria, Böckenförde, n 55, 356–58, 388.

reach the level of the polis.[188] The chief motive attributed to the relevant social actors is that they seek the benefits accruing from cooperation on a grander scale.[189] This explains why they form 'social contracts'.

From the scholastic standpoint, the arrangements formed by the commonwealth are merely the material causes of the effective cause that is God's eternal law.[190] Against this background, the individuals are still just exercising what God has ordained them to do, and all political authority remains entirely derivative of God's will.[191] As soon as this metaphysical context falls by the wayside and the decisive ground of authority is the reciprocal self-interest of autonomous individuals, the point of the social contract changes. As a hypothetical arrangement among individuals, it becomes the yardstick of political legitimacy.[192] The compact, however, is no longer a covenant between a people that is underwritten by a covenant with God; it is a contract that is concluded among the members of the political community themselves. The foundation of law then becomes secular.[193]

Political order thus becomes attitude-dependent,[194] though based upon reciprocal recognition among equals. Mutual recognition is then taking the place of attitude-independent authority.

The Heart of the Matter: Mastery

With the demise of medieval natural law we encounter, for the first time, a problem that afflicts all normativity. The most straightforward explanation of the binding force of directives says that they are binding because – and as long as – we take them to be binding. This explanation is, however, self-defeating, for if obligations can be rescinded at any time for any or even no

[188] See Aristotle, *The Politics*, 2nd edn (trans C Lord, Chicago, IL, Chicago University Press, 2013) 1252b10-30 (at 2–3).

[189] See, for example, Aquinas, n 67, 204. See Böckenförde, n 55, 358.

[190] See Suárez, n 120, 437–40 (III.III.5–7).

[191] See F de Vitoria, 'On Civil Power' in *Political Writings*, n 119, §§ 3 and 6, 6, 10, who regards natural necessity as the final cause of civil government and God as its efficient cause. He spells out what this means as follows (ibid 10): '[P]ublic power is founded upon natural law, and if natural law acknowledges God as its only author, then it is evident that public power is from God, and cannot be over-ridden by conditions imposed by men or any positive law.' See also Böckenförde, n 55, 362, 388.

[192] See Habermas, n 178, 93.

[193] ibid 94, 96.

[194] Much to the dismay of L Strauss, *Natural Right and History* (Chicago, IL, University of Chicago Press, 1953).

reason at all, they are not what they purport to be.[195] We owe nothing to anyone.

This explains why we have for the greater part of human history sought to invest obligations with a more reliable mooring, such as nature, eternal forms or the *koinos nomos*. What these have in common is to designate some attitude-independent authority that does not depend on being taken to be authoritative by the subordinates.

The God ('Lord') of voluntarist metaphysics represents what Brandom, following Hegel, calls 'mastery',[196] namely, the authority to attribute statuses and responsibilities to others without having to shoulder any responsibility oneself. God is completely independent, and since he is not accountable to his creatures, he may as well remain entirely inscrutable to them.

The major step, taken in modernity, is the attempt to conceive of authority as attitude-dependent, that is, on acceptance by the subordinates, without thereby sacrificing its bindingness. The key thereto is that people pull themselves up by their bootstraps and make the authority to attribute authority to others dependent on their recognition of such authority.[197]

[195] See J-J Rousseau, *The Social Contract* (trans C Betts, Oxford, Oxford University Press, 1994) 57, I.7.
[196] See R Brandom, *A Spirit of Trust: A Reading of Hegel's* Phenomenology (Cambridge, MA, Harvard University Press, 2019) 314–15.
[197] ibid 321.

8

Natural Law: Trajectories

Why Natural Law Theory Is Bound to Be Somewhat Trivial

There is a false expectation of natural law theory growing out of a professional deformation of lawyers. Against the odds of their own professional experience, they occasionally develop an insatiable appetite for arguments that are supposedly so compelling as to settle a case.[1] This peculiar outlook explains why lawyers notoriously would have natural law amount to an ultimate source of law that, if tapped, removed all gaps and undraped the right answer. Natural law would thus be like an uncommanded command, as clear and determinate as an imperative, without, however, having been issued by someone.

But natural law, if it existed, could never be like this. It is, above all, a modelling of practical reason and to a large extent, therefore, an attempt to explain what we already know. When we watch in documentary movies how members of the SS had Jewish prisoners jump into ditches, where they were killed and subsequently buried on top of layers of other executed bodies, we cannot but react with shock and utter revulsion. The sight of such evil kindles an emotional response revealing our firm belief that cold-blooded atrocities of this kind are fundamentally wrong. Natural law, if it existed, would then speak from the midst of our moral experience.

Killing is wrong, cruelty is bad. This seems trivial. The impression of triviality is, however, itself not trivial. We could not live without sharing an elementary understanding of right and wrong. Natural law is what makes survival and human flourishing possible. Its precepts must be effectively observed, at least largely, to facilitate what matters to us: friends, family, gainful activity, political power, honour and glory. We are aware of the normative conditions of our life, which explains why natural law

[1] According to Stanley Fish, the selfsame expectation feeds into the type of formalism that identifies the normativity of law with the clarity of legal norms. See S Fish, 'The Law Wishes to Have a Formal Existence' in his *There's No Such Thing as Free Speech* (New York, Oxford University Press, 1994) 141–79, 142–43.

should be largely uncontroversial. Triviality is essential to its function. If, by contrast, arguments that purport to state natural law are self-consciously bold and provocative, they are often also outrageous and difficult to accept. Contemporary Christian natural theorists provide us with examples, such as Robert George's claim that sexual acts are morally right only within marriage and that oral or anal sex, for example, are against nature.[2] Such 'natural law' arguments do in fact speak to partisans seeking to reassure themselves of their righteousness.

Etsiamsi daremus

Bidding goodbye to God has never been easy. This is epitomised in Nietzsche's 'crazy man', who makes his appearance in *Gay Science*. His lament is a reminder of how essential God has been as the anchor of order and law. Without God there are no more grounds because there is no ultimate ground to sustain them:

> What did we do when we unchained this earth from its sun? Where is it going now? Where are we going? Away from all the suns? Are we not constantly falling? And backwards, sideways, forwards, to all sides? Is there still a top and a bottom? Are we not wandering through an infinite nothingness? Doesn't empty space breathe on us? Hasn't it got colder? Isn't the night always coming and more night?[3]

It should not come as a surprise that, in the case of natural law theory, this immense and horrific unhinging had to be prefaced with a subjunctive. Secular natural law is first introduced with circumspection: even if we conceded what cannot be conceded, namely, that God does not exist, there would be something to guide us.[4] Grotius, who formulated this subjunctive, hastened to add, of course, that there is ample proof for the existence of the Creator and that his free will is another source of law aside from our interest in the 'maintenance of social order'.[5] The latter is due to 'an impelling desire

[2] See R George, *In Defense of Natural Law* (Oxford, Oxford University Press, 1999) 161, 170.

[3] See F Nietzsche, *Die fröhliche Wissenschaft*, 2nd edn (Leipzig, EW Fritsch, 1887) § 125, 154: 'Was thaten wir, als wir diese Erde von ihrer Sonne losketteten? Wohin bewegt sie sich nun? Wohin bewegen wir uns? Fort von allen Sonnen? Stürzen wir nicht fortwährend? Und rückwärts, seitwärts, vorwärts, nach allen Seiten? Gibt es noch ein Oben und ein Unten? Irren wir nicht durch ein unendliches Nichts? Haucht uns nicht der leere Raum an? Ist es nicht kälter geworden? Kommt nicht immerfort die Nacht und mehr Nacht?'

[4] See H Grotius, *On the Law of War and Peace* (student edn, ed SC Neff, Cambridge, Cambridge University Press, 2012) 4 (prologue).

[5] ibid 3.

for society' (*appetitus societatis*),[6] which is a natural trait of human beings. Grotius goes on to specify this desire further by saying that humans do not desire just any society but a society that is 'peaceful, and organized according to a measure of human intelligence with those who are of his own kind'.[7] Grotius coordinates the two sources, the trait of humans that provides them with 'a strong bent towards social life'[8] and God's will, by recognising God as the creator of such traits.[9] This apparent voluntarism is, however, in light of the initial subjunctive, entirely inconsequential. What anchors natural law are the desire for society and the requisite intelligence possessed by human beings (and not by other animals)[10] to determine and to agree on what it takes to fulfil it.[11] Grotius is not a theological voluntarist.[12]

Voluntarism remains a challenge, but in a manner not giving rise to perturbation, involving the source of obligatoriness. Suárez, who is also not a voluntarist, claimed that precepts of natural law are about what is really right and wrong; in order to be binding upon us, however, they need to be backed up by God's command. If such a command were lacking, they would remain on the level of counsel,[13] that is, on the same plane as principles possessing weight.[14] Peremptoriness requires God's will. What this view amounts to is beautifully summarised by Darwall, stating that God's commands do

[6] ibid 2.

[7] ibid 2. In the 2nd edn this sentence is followed by a reference to the Stoic *oikeiôsis*, which is apparently translated in English editions as 'sociableness'. I owe the reference to the 2nd edn to R Tuck, *The Rights of War and Peace: Political Thought and the International Order from Grotius to Kant* (Oxford, Oxford University Press, 1999) 99. An elaborate exploration and explication of the Ciceronian roots of this reference is provided in the magisterial study by B Straumann, *Roman Law in the State of Nature: The Classical Foundations of Hugo Grotius' Natural Law* (Cambridge, Cambridge University Press, 2015) 90–102.

[8] Grotius, n 4, 3.

[9] ibid 4.

[10] Human beings possess *ratio et oratio*, reason and speech, which are also constitutive of the special community they occupy vis-à-vis other animals. Grotius thus deviates from Ulpian, for whom natural law is also to be found among other animals. See Straumann, n 7, 91, fn 17; 94–95. The view that natural law is, in the case of Grotius, based on the *appetitus societatis* is also held by S Darwall, *Modern Moral Philosophy: From Grotius to Kant* (Cambridge, Cambridge University Press, 2023) 63 (contrasting Pufendorf and Grotius).

[11] Grotius' ambivalent relation to voluntarism is summed up by Schneewind with reference to the fear that God might be irrelevant to morality: 'Grotius' refusal to call openly either on the voluntarist God who creates morality by fiat, or on the intellectualist God who keeps the moral universe in moral order, gives point to this fear'. JB Schneewind, *The Invention of Autonomy: A History of Modern Moral Philosophy* (Cambridge, Cambridge University Press, 2010) 75.

[12] See Darwall, n 10, 19.

[13] See F Suárez, 'Treatise on Law and God the Lawgiver' in *Selections from Three Works* (trans GL Williams et al, ed T Pink, Carmel, IN, Liberty Fund, 2015) 5–755, 24, I.1.8; 217, I.18.10.

[14] It may be recalled by readers that the normative force of the mind of the Stoic sage who is invested with right reason does not rise above this 'softer' level of normativity. See E Asmis, 'Cicero on Natural Law and Laws of the State' (2000) 27 *Classical Antiquity* 1–33, 6–7, 18–19.

not make wrong what is wrong, they add the obligation to avoid what is wrong independently of the command.[15] The challenge of voluntarism is compounded in the case of Grotius, for he appears to be the first 'modern' moral theorist.[16] He no longer grounds the obligation to follow natural law in the pursuit of one's own good, that is, *honeste vivere* in the pursuit of eudaimonia.[17] The common good is also no longer considered, without anything further, to be part of the personal good of the agents, that is, as comprising their good life.[18] Rather, now the contrast arises between rationality and reasonableness, that is, a gulf separating the agent's self-interest from the interest of all. While the problem is not as clearly revealed in Grotius as it is in Hobbes, it is quite obvious that the theory of natural law is confronted with the collective action problem, for which morality provides the solution.[19] Everyone is better off if everyone follows the moral law, while each would be better off individually by departing from it.[20] The contrast between what is good for each and what is good for all, points to the Each–We Dilemma that not least Hobbes attempted to resolve.[21] Why is it in my interest to comply with what is good for all even if in some instances it is not good for me, individually considered? Why is the former interest the source of moral obligation? Indeed, as is underscored by Darwall, the point of the undertaking is to show that morality exists only if eudaimonism is false.[22] The approach is internalist.[23] The reasons for acting morally or reasonably have to move people to act accordingly.

Sociability

Grotius' beginning seems to be an example for how trivially natural law can be 'derived' from trivial premises.[24] There is human nature and from its existence follows natural law:

[15] See Darwall, n 10, 20.

[16] As Darwall, ibid 19, explains, following Sidgwick, that morality is a source of normative reasons in addition to, and at their root independent of, the reasons appealing to the agent's good.

[17] This is, of course, a major difference with regard to Aquinas or Suárez. See Darwall, ibid 20, 26.

[18] ibid 20.

[19] ibid 27.

[20] See, generally, on Each–We dilemmas, D Parfit, *Reasons and Persons* (Oxford, Oxford University Press, 1986) 93.

[21] On Hobbes' 'fool', see T Hobbes, *Leviathan* (ed I Shapiro, New Haven, CT, Yale University Press, 2010) 89–90, [73].

[22] See Darwall, n 10, 30.

[23] ibid 29–30.

[24] Grotius' natural law theory looks quite secular, but there are strong Christian elements retained in it. See Schneewind, n 11, 68–70.

> For the very nature of man, which, even if we had no lack of anything, would lead us into the mutual relations of society, is the mother of the law of nature.[25]

Of course, there was a point to how Grotius conceived of this nature. With the Stoics, he held against the Epicureans that not the experience of pleasure but living peacefully among others is what humans are naturally after. While the point against the idea that our first aim is pleasure can be relatively easily argued based on the first consequence of *oikeiôsis* qua 'recognition and appreciation of something as belonging to one',[26] namely, the striving for self-preservation, it is more difficult to derive our readiness to incur sacrifices from our drive to live in harmony with all other citizens of the cosmopolis.[27] For it seems that the second drive is less manifest than the first. Frequently, we have the impression that respect of others, let alone solidarity with them, is easily outdone by the desire to enjoy even simple pleasures.

Pufendorf appears to make a quite similar entry. Even though he also accords to the Creator pride of place and views him as the ultimate source of law,[28] the sociability of man looms large, even if it is seen in a more instrumental connection to the mutual satisfaction of wants that arise from human self-love.[29] We need to be smart enough to understand that we are all better off if we cooperate peacefully, in fact, we would be too weak to survive without others.[30] We should therefore strive to perfect our *socialitas*,[31] at which we will succeed only if we observe natural laws out of rational insight into their necessity and for their own sake and not only if they happen to be to our advantage.[32] The development of an understanding of the reciprocity

[25] Grotius, n 4, 5.

[26] See G Striker, 'The Role of *oikeiôsis* in Stoic Ethics' in her *Papers in Hellenistic Epistemology and Ethics* (Cambridge, Cambridge University Press, 1996) 281–97, 282.

[27] See, on self-preservation, Straumann, n 7, 114, 118.

[28] See Schneewind, n 11, 122; Darwall, n 10, 61–62. Nevertheless, according to Hochstrasser, Pufendorf appeared to have contempt for innate natural law. See TJ Hochstrasser, *Natural Law Theories in the Early Enlightenment* (Cambridge, Cambridge University Press, 2000) 89, 94.

[29] See S Pufendorf, *On the Duty of Man and Citizen According to Natural Law* (trans M Silverthorne, Cambridge, Cambridge University Press, 1991) 35, I.7: 'Man, then, is an animal with an intense concern for his own preservation, needy by himself, incapable of protection without the help of his fellows, and very well fitted for the mutual provision of benefits. Equally, however, he is at the same time malicious, aggressive, easily provoked and as willing as he is able to inflict harm on others. The conclusion is: in order to be safe, it is necessary for him to be sociable; that is to join forces with men like himself and so conduct himself towards them that they are not given even a plausible excuse for harming him, but rather become willing to preserve and promote his advantages [*commoda*].'

[30] ibid 33, I.3.3.

[31] ibid 35, I.3.9.

[32] For an excellent discussion showing that Pufendorf distinguished clearly between the mere fear of sanctions and self-judging oneself as worthy of censure, while he also seemed to grant that avoidance of social disapprobation may well be the ulterior motive, see Darwall, n 10, 69, 95, 80, 84–85.

of advantages and disadvantages seems to be of paramount concern. In a like manner, Grotius had conceded that 'expediency' assists the realisation of natural law, even though he strongly denied that it has its base in it.[33]

The Basic Tension

The approach seems to be unsophisticated enough. Natural law is manifest in the rules that permit us to reap the benefits that accrue from peaceful cooperation.[34] A predicament remains, nonetheless, that is for both Grotius and Pufendorf inherent in our self-love. According to Pufendorf, it is so strong that 'all other passions give way before it', and Grotius realised that our self-love makes us 'quarrelsome'.[35] Human nature does not provide us with the conditions that translate the recognition of natural justice into sweet harmony of agreement. Matters are more complicated than the appeals to the maintenance of society and sociability suggest.

Interestingly, the matter has been pronounced most eloquently by someone whose theory of natural law is based not on combining traits of humans with the deployment of the intellect but on an a priori principle of law. In his philosophy of history, however, Immanuel Kant speculated about the 'end of nature' that can be reflectively attributed to the evolution of human societies.[36] Since in the case of history, Kant is concerned with facts and not with moral principles, it makes sense for him to focus on human nature as the source of the energy driving the historical process. Interestingly, sociability and quarrelsomeness become fused in Kant's text into one feature of the human condition that, if this were traditional rationalist natural law theory, would amount to its most fundamental principle. Kant calls it 'unsocial sociability'.[37] Unsocial sociability is manifest in – citing the precise words that Schneewind uses to characterise Grotius' position – 'our natural unsuitability for the sociable living that we naturally need'.[38]

[33] See Grotius, n 4, 5.

[34] See Pufendorf, n 29, 35, I.3.8: 'The laws of this sociality [*socialitas*], laws which teach one how to conduct oneself to become a useful [*commodum*] member of human society, are called natural laws.' It is, at the end of the day, a combination of sociable instinct and the calculation of self-interest that motivates us rationally to observe natural law. See Hochstrasser, n 28, 62–63, 90.

[35] See Grotius, n 4, 24, I.1.1. See also Schneewind, n 11, 72.

[36] See I Kant, 'Idea for a Universal History from a Cosmopolitan Perspective' in *Toward Perpetual Peace and Other Writings on Politics, Peace, and History* (trans DL Colclasure, ed P Kleingeld, New Haven, CT, Yale University Press 2006) 3–16, 4.

[37] ibid 6. The attribution of the same basic theme to Pufendorf is made in Hochstrasser, n 28, 90.

[38] Schneewind, n 11, 130.

Again, the matter is ostensibly trivial, but it is not so trivial as to what it entails. Kant presupposes that nature expects humanity at large to develop its potential, which would be manifest in the fact that human beings control and create the conditions of their existence: food, dwellings, enjoyment, the arts and the sciences, all these things are at the end of the day of human design. The production of artifacts flatters human self-love, inasmuch as rational self-esteem is satisfied only if human beings are the artificers of what they inhabit, that is, their cultural space.[39] Kant even seems to anticipate Wilhelm von Humboldt[40] with his assertion that the development of human faculties and capabilities is only possible under the antagonistic conditions we associate with rivalry and ambition. If humans would not compete for wealth or power they would possibly 'live the arcadian life of shepherds, in full harmony, contentment and mutual love', but owing to their lack of ambition their talents would lie dormant and be squandered in idleness.[41] They would perhaps be as good-natured as sheep, but their lives would also not be of greater value than those of their domesticated animals.

Human nature prevents underdevelopment, as we are doomed to compete with one another, not least due to our 'lust for honor, power, or property'.[42] We desire, Kant says, obviously echoing Rousseau's Second Discourse,[43] to outshine others whom we dislike but on whom we also depend. We depend on them, for only under conditions of increasingly elaborate division of labour are we able to discover and to strengthen what we can do best; yet we also remain repulsed by them and tend to keep to ourselves because we always and everywhere encounter resistance. We cannot do without others,[44] but we do not really enjoy being among them:

> Humans desire harmony, but nature knows better what is good for their species: it wills discord. Humans wish to live leisurely and enjoy themselves,

[39] See Kant, n 36, 6.

[40] See W von Humboldt, *The Limits of State Action* (ed J Borrow, Cambridge, Cambridge University Press, 1969) 19.

[41] See Kant, n 36, 6.

[42] Kant, n 36, 6.

[43] For an illuminating interpretation, see F Neuhouser, *Rousseau's Theodicy of Self-Love: Evil, Rationality and the Desire for Recognition* (Oxford, Oxford University Press 2010); F Neuhouser, *Rousseau's Critique of Inequality: Reconstructing the Second Discourse* (Cambridge, Cambridge University Press, 2014).

[44] In a sense, Kant's remarks on our desire to live with others against all odds echoes the Stoic *oikeiôsis* doctrine as developed by Grotius into our desire to live in society. See Straumann, n 7, 93.

> but nature wills that human beings abandon their sloth and passive contentment and thrust themselves into work and hardship, only to find means, in turn, to cleverly escape the latter.[45]

This is the final elaboration of a core idea of secular natural law, but with one important modification. Pufendorf and Grotius believed that natural law allows us to deal with the tension between self-love and the necessity to be sociable. For Kant, by contrast, unsocial sociability is the natural mechanism that will in the final event lead to the realisation of systems of law that regard each and every one as free and equal, provided that they are also self-activating and sufficiently independent.[46] Antagonism is the condition making us jockey for what is required by reason anyway. Kant therefore views the conditions established by human nature and the ascribed natural teleology inherent in unfolding the potential of the human species as the background for historical processes of legal experimentation that will either founder on the ground of offending human self-love and pride or find acceptance as reciprocally based on the balance of power that underpins social arrangements.

Two Lines of Proof

Kant thereby merely articulated more clearly an element that is inherent in natural law systems that acknowledge the basic tension between self-love and sociability or, put differently, between rationality and reasonableness. The perfection of sociability in human history is subject to historical elaboration.[47] This element is already present, however, in the somewhat hapless empiricism of Grotius' and Pufendorf's thinking.

According to Grotius, the law of nature is subject to 'two lines of proof'.[48] The a priori proof rests on the 'necessary agreement or disagreement of anything with a rational or social nature'.[49] A posteriori proof demonstrates that the relevant law or principle is practised or believed among all nations,

[45] Kant, n 36, 7.

[46] On these three conditions, in particular civic independence, see I Kant, 'On the common saying: That may be correct in theory, but it is does not apply in practice' in *Kant's Political Philosophy* (trans HB Nisbeth, Cambridge, Cambridge University Press, 1970) 61–92, 87.

[47] See Kant, n 36, 8: 'All the culture and art that decorates humankind, as well as its most pleasing social order, are fruits of an unsociability that is forced by its own nature to discipline itself and thereby develop fully the seeds that nature planted within it by means of an imposed art.'

[48] See Grotius, n 4, 31, I.1.12. On the following, see Straumann, n 7, 66–68, 84.

[49] Grotius presents what he does in mathematical terms in the sense that his thinking is not tied to particular events. See Grotius, n 4, 19 (prologue).

at any rate, those possessing a more advanced civilisation.[50] Natural law is thus to be inferred from testimony provided by philosophers, historians, poets or orators.[51] Should this law, which is still universally observed, not also be supported by an a priori argument then it belongs to the 'law of nations' only and has on its face its obvious base in 'the free will of man'.[52] This is not a substantive deficiency.[53] Rather, a universal effect must have a universal cause, and this suggests that it reflects the 'common sense' of mankind.[54] Arguably, its existence may be indicative of a stronger premise that we are as of yet not able to identify.

The a priori proof asks whether something is consistent with our sociable nature, in other words, what it takes for us to get along. The modern, deontological answer given by Grotius focuses, according to Darwall, on what it takes for us to get along in the most elementary fashion. It amounts to staying out of each other's way, respecting each other's choices, minding our own business and accepting that others have standing to demand non-interference from us as long as they are ready to accept such a demand themselves.[55] The a posteriori path is empirical, however, it coincides cunningly with what is sought after along the path of a priori reasoning. It teaches also what must and likely will be accepted if we are making claims on others. It merely arrives at it using a comparative, possibly 'shallower', route.[56]

The Strategy

As Straumann explains, both forms of proof reflect the ancient rhetorical strategy pursued by Grotius.[57] He offers *probationes* for natural law, which

[50] ibid 31, I.1.12.

[51] ibid 12 (prologue). For example, Grotius states that 'authorities' assign to wars three justifiable causes: defence, recovery of property and punishment. See ibid 82, II.1.2.

[52] ibid 12 (prologue).

[53] According to Straumann, n 7, 79, Roman rhetoricians had the status of an unquestionable basis of proof.

[54] See Grotius, n 4, 32, I.1.12.

[55] This is, of course, a highly 'Darwallian' way of interpreting Grotius, as it highlights the second-personal dimension of morality. See Darwall, n 10, 22, who interprets sociability as 'standing to make reasoned claims and demands of one another' that underlies the more specific rights. See also ibid 33: 'This suggests that we might best understand Grotius as holding that the law and right of nature are grounded in the capacity of rational sociable persons to recognize their common competence and authority to make reasoned claims and demands against one another and to live with one another on terms that respect this common standing.' See generally S Darwall, 'Authority and Second-Personal Reasons for Acting' in his *Morality, Authority, and Law: Essays in Second-Personal Ethics I* (Oxford, Oxford University Press, 2013) 135–50; and S Darwell, *The Second-Personal Standpoint: Morality, Respect, and Accountability* (Cambridge, MA, Harvard University Press, 2006).

[56] See Darwall, n 10, 36.

[57] See Straumann, n 7, 63.

may even succeed by reasoning from examples, judgments or *juris consulta*.[58] As an exercise in speaking, as it were, the proofs are addressed to someone. It is therefore important to take into account that the Grotian arguments are a reply to the objections made against universal justice by the ancient academic sceptic Carneades.[59] They were to be found in a work that was of the utmost importance for Grotius, namely, in Cicero's *De re publica*.[60] The objections are composed of two elements.[61] The first element consists of empirical evidence that diachronically and synchronically people disagree about justice. The diversity indicates, second, that people adopt laws because it is in their self-interest. Those who do not see this are fools and believe that what others claim to be just is indeed just. They harm themselves in acting against their best interest. Rationality is all there is.

Both forms of proof address this challenge. The a posteriori proof of natural law draws on sources that demonstrate convergence. Not all sources matter, to be sure. Grotius refers only to what he takes to be the best cultures – ancient Greece and Rome – when these were in their prime.[62] It is not really clear whether through reference to philosophers, historians, poets and orators Grotius really suggests that he is providing empirical proof of natural law or merely of the law of nations, for that matter.[63] One could indeed claim that he is tapping literary sources and views of philosophers as mere expressions of belief and, hence, as at best indicative of natural law. Admittedly, natural law and the law of nations are difficult to disentangle in Grotius' work, not least because the authority of Roman law is believed to be rooted in its superior quality. No longer is its authority mediated by the myth of the *translatio imperii*.[64]

If, based on selective 'testimonials', the first part of Carneades' objection is refuted, after evidence has been put on the table strongly indicating consensus rather than diversity of opinion, it can still be reasonably

[58] ibid 71.

[59] What Carneades claims echoes ordinary Sophistic wisdom, as it is, for example, articulated by Glaukon in Plato's *Republic*. See Straumann, n 7, 89; See also Darwall, n 10, 16. See also R Tuck, *Philosophy and Government 1572–1651* (Cambridge, Cambridge University Press, 1993) 55–58, 175.

[60] Cicero's *De re publica* was lost and had to be partly recompiled from quotations from it in other literary sources. Grotius had to rely on what Lactantius had reported from Cicero on Carneades. See Straumann, n 7, 58.

[61] See Cicero, *De re publica, De legibus* (trans CW Keyes, Cambridge, MA, Harvard University Press, 1928) 193–210, III.8–20. For a concise summary, see Straumann, n 7, 59, 83, 89.

[62] See Straumann, n 7, 81.

[63] The latter is what Straumann, ibid 84, seems to believe.

[64] See F Wieacker, *Privatrechtsgeschichte der Neuzeit: Unter besonderer Berücksichtigung der deutschen Entwicklung*, 2nd edn (Göttingen, Vandenhoek & Ruprecht, 1967) 289–90; Straumann, n 7, 78.

conjectured that the relevant views are quite possibly more than merely an accidental convergence of whims. Even if the source of their validity is thus left open,[65] owing to the wealth of materials and the comparative dearth of a deductive argument from self-evident principles, the a posteriori mode of proof may effectively be more 'popular' than its a priori counterpart.[66]

The a priori proof, by contrast, has to demonstrate the 'fitness' of an action or norm with the reasonable or social nature of human beings.[67] Undeniable and fundamental conceptions are involved in such a proof. They are 'almost' as evident as the things that are perceptible to the external senses.[68] The elements of natural law that Grotius mentions after introducing the 'maintenance of social order' as the 'source of natural law', indicate that individual rights[69] may well be the principles from which everything else follows:[70] abstentions from taking what belongs to others, restoration of damages or unjust enrichment, the obligation to fulfil promises and the infliction of punishment in proportion to desert.[71] Grotius hastens to add that only corrective, and not distributive, justice is part of natural law,[72] and that the law is not at all about the education of virtue.

From Virtue to Rights and Roman Law

This points to the major break with older Stoic doctrines, a break that Grotius may have extracted from Cicero.[73] The latter seems to have already replaced the Stoic focus on virtue, which indicates the second stage of *oikeiôsis* that makes us embrace other human beings as belonging to ourselves,[74] with

[65] Hence, a posteriori arguments can establish only the probability of their validity (and truth). See Straumann, n 7 (fn 17).

[66] See Grotius, n 4, 31, I.1.12.

[67] ibid. See Straumann, n 7, 68, 84.

[68] See Grotius, n 4, 12 (prologue).

[69] On the major shift in Stoic doctrine that would originally have accorded to the development of moral virtue a central role towards the adoption of one of the indifferents, namely, private property, as the focus of morally correct conduct, see the lucid analysis by Straumann, n 7, 108–13.

[70] This is my interpretation of a doctrine that does not emerge quite clearly from the best commentaries. But see also Tuck, n 59, 197.

[71] Grotius, n 4, 3 (prologue). Indeed, the persons in the state of nature regard each other as equals. See Darwall, n 10, 34.

[72] See also Straumann, n 7, 4, 119–20, 123. Distributive justice is a matter for the household only. See Darwall, n 10, 29.

[73] See Straumann, n 7, 96, 103–04, 107, 109, 117. Or possibly it was Cicero and the Digest, see ibid 121.

[74] See Straumann, n 7, 104–06, 118, on the first stage that involves self-preservation and the second, higher stage that involves reasonable insight into the *honestum* vis-à-vis others.

respect for the rights of others.[75] What is sustained, however, is that rights as instances of the *honestum* – even if simple transplants of Roman *actiones* into a state without a *praetor* or judiciary – are considered to be of greater weight than mere appeals to self-preservation.[76] Any form of self-preservation needs to avail itself of a *justa causa*,[77] which is, aside from self-defence, recovery of property or punishment.[78] Indeed, Grotius followed Alberico Gentili and some ancient Roman jurists in regarding Justinian's Roman law as 'declaratory' of natural law, a matter that earned him criticism from John Selden and Robert Filmer.[79]

In any event, the moral virtue and judgement of the sages – as opposed to the opinions of the deplorable fools – is no longer decisive for judgements and actions to pass as emanations of natural law. The *honestum* is equated with the observance and administration of justice, that is, respecting rights and obligations and accepting accountability to the harmed party.[80] The obligatoriness of justice is severed from an internal connection with human happiness and motivationally suspended from the thin air of the *appetitius societatis*.[81] Simply put, a decisive step down is taken from striving for *eudaimonia* to elementary non-interference. Respect for property rights becomes the linchpin of justice.[82] The 'protoliberal' thrust of his theory is further reinforced by its deontological makeup.[83] Since there is no more eudemonistic justification of natural law,[84] the right is prior to the good, a priority that is pushed so far that not only are individuals free to choose their good, but peoples are also entirely free to choose their government.[85] It does not even matter whether it is to the benefit of the governed.[86] What,

[75] The matter is historically complicated and contested, not least because Cicero himself failed to clarify the precise relation between universal natural law and Roman law. According to Annas, Cicero regarded in *De legibus* his idealised version of Roman law as the best interpretation of ideal right reason. See J Annas, *Virtue and Law in Plato and Beyond* (Oxford, Oxford University Press, 2017) 183–84. Annas, however, also grants that the universal laws of nature, even according to Cicero, were not supposed to have a law-like form. Rather, natural law is right reason in the wise person (ibid 182). See also Asmis, n 14, 19, 28.

[76] See Straumann, n 7, 164.

[77] ibid 117.

[78] ibid 161.

[79] ibid 132, 148.

[80] See Darwall, n 10, 22, 33, 38. On the importance of rights, see also R Tuck, *Natural Rights Theories: Their Origin and Development* (Cambridge, Cambridge University Press, 1979) 66–67, 73.

[81] See Straumann, n 7, 86, 88, 139.

[82] ibid 109.

[83] See the very precise observations by Straumann, ibid 85, 87.

[84] There is also no teleological account of human nature. See ibid 87.

[85] See Grotius, n 4, 51–52, 1.3.8.

[86] ibid 54.

indeed, supposedly motivates humans to observe natural law is not their desire for happiness but their 'antecedently given natural instinct, [their] *appetitus societatis*'.[87] This is not much.

Rights exist in a state of nature, that is, no polis is needed for their validity or for effectiveness.[88] They are enforced with war-like means. The right-holders are free to take the law into their own hands. Regardless of whether Richard Tuck[89] is right in claiming that Grotius and others modelled the state of nature on the international relations among states, or whether the legal situation of states was, somewhat conversely, modelled on Roman private law,[90] Grotius has law prior to the state. This priority is sustained in Pufendorf, even though the approach is markedly different.

At the same time, strangely enough, owing to the existence of the right to punish, which can be exercised by anyone without its having to be the injured parties themselves,[91] the members of the state of nature belong to a moral community for which the mutual respect for rights is some form of common concern.[92] The individuals not only have authority to have their own rights respected, they also have the authority to protect the integrity of the legal regime in which they count as 'mutually accountable equals'.[93]

Terrible Animals with Voracious Appetites

The tension between self-love and *socialitas*, which Kant later synthesised into unsociable sociability, appears in a most pronounced form in Pufendorf's work.[94] Self-love is the most obvious fact about us,[95] and in light of the other fact, that it is for our own benefit to cooperate with others, it also poses an almost intractable problem. Animals also possess self-love

[87] Straumann, n 7, 86.
[88] Both Grotius and Pufendorf distinguish between perfect and imperfect rights and, correspondingly, perfect and imperfect duties. The perfect rights are enforceable, and the corresponding duties are omissions. Imperfect rights are mere moral obligations of commendable acts, for example acts of assistance. See Darwall, n 10, 21, 62–63; Schneewind, n 11, 78–80. Sociability cannot be manifest in a duty of benevolence, for duties of benevolence are imperfect. See Darwall, n 10, 37. In Pufendorf's work, the distinction reflects the difference between obligations that have to be enforced for society to exist at all and others the fulfilment of which merely leads to its improvement. See Schneewind, n 11, 133.
[89] See Tuck, n 7, 8–9, 84, 96.
[90] See Straumann, n 7, 147.
[91] See Grotius, n 4, 271, II.20.3.
[92] See Darwall, n 10, 34.
[93] ibid.
[94] See Hochstrasser, n 28, 90.
[95] See Pufendorf, n 29, 33, I.3.2: '[M]an holds nothing more dear than himself …'.

and desire to have their various hungers stilled, but we humans are spoiled and indulging. 'Tickled by the itch for lust', we are constantly pursuing sexual adventures, tend to overeat, and are always eager to come out ahead of others and tormented by an unquenchable thirst for recognition.[96] By comparison, animals are so much more sociable than we are. Human beings are the major obstacle to human happiness, the attainment of which requires each 'to be a fit member of society'.[97] For indeed, we have a superb ability to benefit each other and to reap the benefits of mutual cooperation.[98] Our excessive self-love, however, threatens to subvert these gains, for it disposes us to inflict harm on others.[99] Humans can be safe only if they understand that it is their first duty to become sociable[100] and to cooperate peacefully and on fair terms with others:

> The laws of this sociality, laws which teach one how to conduct oneself to become a useful member of society, are called natural laws.[101]

More precisely, adopting a sociable attitude towards others means to master certain normative understandings ('moral entities'[102]) that are requisite to getting along with others. Living peacefully involves the mutual recognition of equal dignity, the rights of others and our duties to assist them where possible.[103] As the most fundamental principle of natural law, *socialitas* is so important that it is the source not only of duties towards others (not to harm others, to respect their equality and to be useful to others, when possible),[104] but also of duties that we have towards ourselves. The duty to invest effort into our own perfection is also based on the duty to be a fit member of human society.[105]

There is, of course, a difference between having reason to do something and being obligated to do it. Pufendorf leaves no doubt that there is no duty

[96] ibid 34, I.3.4.
[97] ibid 46, I.5.1.
[98] ibid 35, I.3.7.
[99] ibid 34, I.3.4. In the preface (ibid 10), Pufendorf says that human beings are animals 'seething with evil desires'. Without being really privy to Protestant anthropology, this strikes me as a rather Protestant statement, nonetheless.
[100] ibid 35, I.3.9: '[T]he most fundamental natural law is: every man ought to do as much as he can to cultivate and preserve sociality.'
[101] ibid 35, I.3.7.
[102] Pufendorf regards all normative conceptions (rights, obligations, roles, etc) as imposed on the natural world. They are divine and human constructs. See Darwall, n 10, 67; Schneewind, n 11, 120–21.
[103] See Darwall, n 10, 71–74.
[104] See Pufendorf, n 29, 56, I.6.2; 61, I.7.1; 64, I.8.1.
[105] ibid 46, I.5.1–I.5.2. See Schneewind, n 11, 140.

without an imperative and no imperative without an imperator: 'An obligation is introduced into a man's mind by a superior …'[106] In a manner that must have inspired John Austin,[107] Pufendorf adds that the superior must have the capacity to inflict some injury on 'the recalcitrant'.

But this is only one condition for the existence of the obligation; the other is that an order or imperative must be based on a good reason for interference with the liberty of the addressee. The dual condition is explained by Pufendorf as follows: if the norm were merely backed up by a threat of sanctions, it would not be *rational* to obey it in the absence of such a threat; were it not supported by a good reason, it would not be *reasonable* to hold me to account for not doing what I had been ordered to do. Obviously, rationality matters from the first-personal perspective of the addressee, whereas reasonableness is of relevance from the viewpoint of the second or the third person. The normative demand exists by virtue of the good reason, the authority to enforce it, however, makes it stick. This is also the case for the obligations that we have towards God. They are based on a combination of reverence and fear.[108]

This understanding of obligation, even if not at all unsound, gives rise to the following perplexity. If the reason for action protected by a sanction is a necessary, but not a sufficient, condition for an obligation, this means that, if it were not for the sanction, the proposed course of action should nonetheless elicit the free acceptance of the obligated. Otherwise, we would be left with a mere threat and with the bare fact of one person's causally influencing the conduct of another. That which makes the obligation into what it is, is the reason and not the threat. Pufendorf's conception of obligation as something that presupposes one person's, the superior's, controlling another, the inferior, is thereby strangely reversed.

Still, people are, according to Pufendorf, free to choose even between good and evil. There is nothing to necessitate the choice of the good. This implies that in order to make people do what we believe they ought to do, we need a threat of sanctions. This is the way of motivating good behaviour on the part of those who happen to be unmoved by proper insight, because they either do not have it or are prey to different motives.

[106] Pufendorf, n 29, 28, I.2.5.
[107] See J Austin, *The Province of Jurisprudence Determined* (ed WE Rumble, Cambridge, Cambridge University Press, 1995) 22–23.
[108] See Schneewind, n 11, 136.

But this implies, again, that obligations can also be independent of free acceptance by the obligated. We have come full circle. An obligation exists for persons of unsound mind if persons of sound mind would be ashamed of not doing what they believe they would have reason to do were they in the situation of the former. But does this imply that the sound-minded can self-righteously create obligations for those whom they take to be unsound-minded by the mere use of force? Are they free to exercise mastery? How could we tell the difference between sound-mindedness and mere *de facto* superiority? Hobbesians, at any rate, would stick to the latter.[109]

The perplexity does not even end here. For if human beings can choose not only what is good, but also what is bad for them, it remains inexplicable why and how the threat of sanctions can ever oblige. Fear would ultimately have no power over the human will.[110]

The Questionable Authority of Natural Law

This muddled understanding of normativity must cast a long shadow of doubt on the authority[111] of natural law. Its most fundamental principle says that any disturbance or violation of sociality is forbidden. Everything else supposedly follows from it.[112] The medium to apprehend these self-evident truths is 'the natural light that is native to man'.[113] Indeed, Pufendorf uses formulations reminiscent of medieval natural law theory by quoting the scripture according to which natural law is 'written into the hearts of man' and so deeply engrained in our mind that its precepts are so plain and clear as to be met with immediate assent.[114] But how can this be law? Where is the superior?

[109] See, on the 'sovereign by acquisition', Hobbes, n 21, 105, 123 [88], [104].

[110] See Schneewind, n 11, 137. Pufendorf's non-reductionist concept of obligation confronts us with the challenge to view obligation as voluntary and involuntary at the same time. We agree to be bound by something freely and vouchsafe fear in order to take away our liberty to disobey. Perhaps this is the whole idea of normativity. We are freely convinced of the correctness of an idea so that we surrender to it our liberty to reject it.

[111] The reasons for authority that Pufendorf, n 29, 28, I.2.5 mentions are: (i) conferral of an exceptional benefit; (ii) benevolence and superior ability to serve the addressees' interests; (iii) reciprocal admission of authority to the addressees; and (iv) voluntary submission.

[112] ibid 36, I.3.9.

[113] According to Hochstrasser, n 28, 86–87, Pufendorf did not believe that natural law was an innate system of propositions, and insight into it required a mature mind.

[114] See Pufendorf, n 29, 37, I.3.12.

Pufendorf resorts to a remarkably voluntarist theology to resolve this problem.[115] Even though we can elaborate by means of inference all natural laws on the ground of their obvious utility, they attain the force of law only because He 'has enjoined the human race to observe as laws those dictates of reason which He has Himself promulgated by the force of the innate light'.[116] This is, in a sense, the forced marriage between Stoicism,[117] according to which whatever emanated from the reasoning process of the sage is the law or Zeus,[118] and theological voluntarism. The imprint of reason is a promulgation of law. This does not make much sense, for Pufendorf also says that if humans elaborated natural law guided by the principle of utility alone, they would merely produce good advice.[119] Conceded that there is a difference between an advice and an order, this difference does not matter to the use of reason alone. The production of advice and the emanation of natural law from our reasoning process do amount to the same. There is no perceptible difference. Pufendorf's way out, however, is to regard reasoning as the manifestation of a reasonableness ordained by God. God wills that humans ought to use the light of reason to conduct themselves according to natural law. Fear of the Deity is, according to Pufendorf, a clear indication that social life has been imposed upon man by God's authority.[120] Humans would not be sociable if they were not imbued with religion and, hence, fear of God.[121]

This raises the question what natural law is, after all. Pufendorf explains that natural law is neither positive nor human law.[122] Positive law is the law that is not derivative of the common condition of human nature and merely based on the will of the legislature. All human law, strictly speaking, is positive. Divine law, by contrast, can be either natural or positive. What is laid down in the scripture and not natural is positive law. But where is the 'naturalness' in all of this? This remains just as unclear and elusive as the two other major issues burdening Pufendorf's project.

[115] See Darwall, n 10, 61–62.
[116] Pufendorf, n 29, 36, I.3.10.
[117] On Pufendorf's self-ascribed Stoicism, see Hochstrasser, n 28, 70.
[118] Asmis, n 14, 19, sums up the Stoic position, which was also shared by Cicero, nicely as follows: 'Stoic law is a mental state of perfect rationality, which tells the wise individual precisely what to do or not to do on each occasion, whereas written laws are not a mental state nor can they tell individuals how to act correctly on each occasion.' See also Annas, n 75, 186.
[119] See Pufendorf, n 29, 36, I.3.10.
[120] ibid 36–37, I.3.11.
[121] ibid 37, I.3.13.
[122] ibid 32, I.2.16.

The first is what sociality, with its inbuilt mutual respect for others,[123] amounts to if the requirement of respect is ultimately imposed by God.[124] We ought to grant others standing to make claims on us merely because God has ordered us to do so.[125] This is not tantamount to regarding them as *worthy* of esteem. This is equal to being kind to someone because your mother expects you to be. The kindness is not genuine. Divinely ordained sociality is secondhand.[126] Matters are even worse for Pufendorf, considering that God's will to create us as beings who are constantly torn between social and anti-social impulses – while also invested with the capacity to develop our sociality – remains inscrutable. Schneewind has pointed out what the consequence of such voluntarism is. The contingency of morality leaves it without foundation. Neither is natural law inherently rational nor does it rest on self-evident principles.[127]

Second, Pufendorf's theological voluntarism raises intractable questions concerning God's authority.[128] God can have the authority to make natural law binding upon us only if there is between Him and us a prior relation explaining our subjection. Where does this prior relation come from? One may want to reply that it must in turn be from God. As soon as God ordains natural law, He also creates the relation of subjection. This act, however, could not itself be based on prior authority but only on God's pure power to do so, that is, God's power to create 'moral entities' (norms, roles, normative relations). In contrast to sheer power, however, authority is relational and therefore subject to mutually recognised limits. Whoever exercises authority must be amenable to being held to account for its proper exercise. If God's authority is derivative only of His power, God retains power to undo it any time. Mere power cannot out of nothing give birth to authority. It can merely stubbornly assert power.[129]

Pufendorf's way out of this predicament is to base God's authority on the gratitude owed by creatures to the Creator.[130] God makes a good

[123] See Darwall, n 10, 40.
[124] ibid 75–79.
[125] ibid 68.
[126] See Kant, n 36, 12: 'All that is good yet is not based on morally good convictions is nothing but pure outward show and shimmering misery.'
[127] See Schneewind, n 11, 140.
[128] On the following, see also the critical discussions in Darwall, n 10, 70, 80–81; Schneewind, n 11, 135.
[129] This explains why Darwall, n 10, 70, stresses that God's authority to obligate by imposing His will must be normatively independent of its exercise.
[130] See n 111 on the grounds of authority mentioned by Pufendorf.

life possible for us humans, provided we try hard enough to be sociable among other sociables. The only way to express our gratitude to someone who has everything is to obey their orders.[131] But, again, this raises the question whether the obligation of gratitude is something imposed by God out of nothing and hence an exercise of groundless might. In addition, gratitude is an imperfect duty within Pufendorf's system. It is not sufficient to provide the basis of an obligation to observe natural law.

Voluntarism, Utility and Rights

Three themes seem to predominate natural law theory after Grotius and Pufendorf, even if theories place varying emphases on each: voluntarism, utility and rights.

Lest someone object that Grotius' contemporary Hobbes[132] is omitted from the following – admittedly, already highly cursory – precis of natural law, I should like to mention that I am deliberately postponing the engagement with *Leviathan* to chapter 9 on authority, not least because Hobbes, more than anyone else, anticipated the attitude-dependent framework of constitutionalism. The following spotlights of an abundant tradition will be complemented with an analysis of Hobbes' thinking later.

Both rights and voluntarism play an important role in John Locke's political and moral philosophy. His Second Treatise[133] is in fact very much indebted to the 'Grotian problematique'.[134] The law of nature is prior to the establishment of civil government. War is not, in contrast to Hobbes, a natural consequence of the exercise of natural rights.[135]

Again, in contrast to Hobbes,[136] human beings are deemed to be naturally sociable, not least because God instilled in them the inclination to

[131] See Schneewind, n 11, 136.

[132] There is a long debate over whether Hobbes built on Grotius' framework or developed his own original theory. For a critical review of this debate, see M Harvey, 'Grotius and Hobbes' (2006) 14 *British Journal of the History of Philosophy* 27–50.

[133] See J Locke, *Two Treatises of Government* (ed P Laslett, Cambridge, Cambridge University Press, 1960).

[134] See Schneewind, n 11, 142–43. After all, Locke also establishes a link between law and our quarrelsome nature that jeopardises the pursuit of our own good and undercuts our inclination to live with others. Schneewind, ibid 156, also observes correctly that the evolution of society in the state of nature and the institution of government have probably been taken from Pufendorf.

[135] See Hobbes, n 21, 77–78 [61]–[62]. Locke is quite adamant about the state of nature's not being without anything further a state of war. See Locke, n 133, 280, II. § 19. Locke concedes, however, that within a state of nature, lawless violence can give rise to a state of war.

[136] See Hobbes, n 21, 77 [61], 'men have no pleasure, (but on the contrary a great deale of griefe) in keeping company, where there is no power to over-awe them all'.

live among others and to talk to them.[137] Of the rights that people enjoy by nature,[138] property is of paramount importance, because the freedom and physical integrity of humans are lumped into the same overarching category.[139] People own themselves,[140] aside from – and on top of – the stuff they have legitimately appropriated. Such has been ordained by God. Somewhat paradoxically, those who are self-owning vis-à-vis others are in turn the property of God.[141] The Almighty owns us all. From this somewhat perplexing proposition follow duties and rights to defend ourselves against attacks and to punish criminal offenders even if the crime has been committed against someone else. Indeed, the rights we enjoy as self-owning property owners are consistent with our status as God's creatures. God provides us with the freedom to do as we please,[142] but our freedom comes to an end when we interfere with what others do, for they are also God's property and invested by him with the same freedom. There seems to be a tacit connection between God's owning of free creatures and their self-ownership vis-à-vis others. Property rights are what it takes to protect their freedom and integrity – and therewith God's property – vis-à-vis others. While the property of humans is not directly deduced from God's ownership of us, there is an intelligible connection between our rights and the inviolability of God's property.

Rights are all there is. As in the case of Grotius, there is no overarching highest good that all people are supposed to aspire to.[143]

This bold opening aside, Locke's moral universe is amazingly bleak.[144] When it comes to the origin of the law of nature, he professes extreme voluntarism. The law is what it is simply because God wills it such. God's law may well be entirely arbitrary and raise the spectre of tyranny.[145] Property and justice are merely part of God's plan and not an expression of

[137] See Locke, n 133, 318–19, II. § 77.

[138] See ibid, 271, II. § 27: 'The *State of Nature* has a Law of Nature to govern it, which obliges every one: And Reason, which is that Law, teaches all Mankind, who will but consult it, that being all equal and independent, no one ought to harm another in his Life, Health, Liberty, or Possessions.'

[139] ibid 350, II. § 123.

[140] ibid 287, II. § 27.

[141] ibid 271, II. § 6: 'For Men being all the Workmanship of one Omnipotent, and infinitely wise Maker; All the Servants of one Sovereign Master, sent into the World by his order and about his business, they are his Property, whose Workmanship they are, made to last during his, not one anothers Pleasure.'

[142] See ibid 269, II. § 4.

[143] See Schneewind, n 11, 144.

[144] Apparently, it is also muddled, see ibid 144–56.

[145] ibid 150, 158.

natural reason.[146] Furthermore, divine impositions require punishment for their execution. Men act entirely out of their self-interest and need to fear sanctions in order to observe moral constraints.[147] Locke is an inveterate defender of moral externalism. Moral thoughts, even though they exist, are 'motivationally inert'.[148] He goes even so far as to claim that the human soul must be immortal to make God's commands stick in the face of impending eternal damnation.[149] As Darwall concludes, 'It is because God's sanctions connect natural law to agent's *goods* that they become practical.'[150]

Christian Wolff, to whom we shall return momentarily, would have in principle agreed. An obligation is created by giving a human being a motive for willing something.[151] But this is not to say that coercive threats alone trigger such motives. According to Wolff, as explained by Schneewind,[152] the 'availability of increased perfection' moves people to do the right thing. Amazingly, one encounters here again the basic Stoic idea, even if outside the Stoic context, that the law of nature is tantamount to what we take to be reasonable, from which follows that a reasonable man needs no external laws, for he is a law unto himself.[153] The virtuous will know what to do and pursue virtue out of a desire to perfect their nature. As in the case of Stoicism, happiness is the reward for virtue, the pursuit of – and the encounter with – perfection is what gives them pleasure.[154]

The distance to the basic Pufendorfian contention that obligation involves the threat of an evil is even greater in the case of Thomasius, who teaches that God rules unlike a despot and more like a father.[155] His laws are therefore not enforced by means of punishment and in fact more like

[146] See, on the contrast to Suarez, Darwall, n 10, 92.

[147] Hence, human beings would be incapable of overcoming their collective action problems if it were not for the commands of a benevolent commander in heaven. See ibid 94–95.

[148] ibid 100.

[149] ibid 94.

[150] ibid 97.

[151] See C Wolff, *Vernünftige Gedancken von der Menschen Tun und Lassen*, 7th edn (Halle, Rengerische Buchhandlung, 1743) 8, § 8. Interestingly, we cannot but act for a reason, according to Wolff. Free volition that is not triggered by some, even if unconscious, preference is inconceivable for him. See C Wolff, *Vernünftige Gedancken von Gott, der Welt und der Seele des Menschen*, 8th edn (Halle, Rengerische Buchhandlung, 1741) 312–23, § 511.

[152] See Schneewind, n 11, 438.

[153] Wolff, *Tun und Lassen*, n 151, 18–19, § 24; Schneewind, n 11, 439.

[154] See Wolff, *Seele des Menschen*, n 151, 247, 255–57, 260–62, §§ 404, 417–18, 422 respectively. Schneewind, n 11, 436.

[155] See C Thomasius, *Foundations of the Law of Nature and Nations (Selections)* in C Thomasius, *Institutes of Divine Jurisprudence* (trans T Ahnert, Indianapolis, IN, Liberty Fund, 2011) 612–14, chapter V, §§ 33–42); Schneewind, n 11, 161–63.

guidelines issued by counsellors. Like Wolff,[156] Thomasius believes that wise human beings consider their inner duties as superior to directives backed up by force,[157] even though, to be effective, the law requires this type of backing.

Thomasius differentiates between different spheres of normativity of which the law is merely one.[158] The law occupies the domain of justice without which society would be impossible. The most fundamental principle of natural law – echoing Hobbes, to whom we shall return below – says 'Whatever you do not want to have done to you, do not do it to others.'[159] By contrast, the rules of propriety or decorum are similar to Grotius' law of love,[160] that is, recommendations for how we might assist others in improving their condition, aided and abetted by the self-interested motive to prevent that they might grow ill-willed towards us. The principle of universalisation shifts from omissions to commissions: 'Whatever you will that others should do to you, do to them.' This principle is again different from the principle governing the honourable, which simply states 'Whatever you will others should do, do yourself.'

The honourable and the proper give rise to merely imperfect duties.[161] This does not mean that the relevant obligations are of minor importance: on the contrary, according to Thomasius, the imperfect duties are 'more perfect' and more important to the wise person. The inner obligation felt by human beings forestalls the importance of autonomy qua self-legislation.[162] But, again, a self-interested motive, also familiar from Hobbes, is of relevance here too, for the fulfilment of imperfect duties entitles people to gratitude and promotes solidarity within a group.[163] The overarching perspective of natural law is, after all, to render 'the life of man maximally long and happy'.[164]

Christian Wolff, even though of paramount significance to the German philosophy of his time, presents us with a rather peculiar case. It makes good

[156] See Wolff, *Tun und Lassen*, n 150, 28–29, § 38; Schneewind, n 11, 439.
[157] Wolff and Thomasius clearly relax the voluntarism by claiming that laws of nature are justified in terms intelligible to us. They are not simply inscrutable commands. See Schneewind, n 11, 160.
[158] See Thomasius, n 155, 574. On the following, see Schneewind, n 11, 163–64.
[159] See also Thomasius, *Institutes*, n 155, 131, chapter I, § 18).
[160] See Grotius, n 4, 35, I.2.1.
[161] On the distinction, see n 88.
[162] See Schneewind, n 11, 165.
[163] See Thomasius, *Institutes*, n 155, 203, chapter II, §§ 50–55; see also Schneewind, n 11, 165.
[164] See Schneewind, n 11, 160.

sense to view his practical metaphysics as aligned with the camp that puts a premium on the overall happiness that a cooperative society is likely to beget. In his case, however, happiness is mediated by the pursuit of, and the encounter with, perfection, which is epitomised by complex entities, the parts of which work harmoniously together.[165] We encounter perfection in the harmony of the manifold.[166] Both the attainment and the comprehension of greater perfection make us happy. That happiness is all the greater if we not only have clearly pleasurable experiences, but also understand what it is about them that gives us pleasure, and if we therefore are in a better position to bring about actively what pleases us.[167] Wolff believes that we are under an obligation, ordained by God, to pursue our own perfection, which is implicated in our becoming more self-determined and enhancing our experience.[168] Since living among others and contributing to their perfection is an integral component of our own perfection, all the duties that we have towards others are derivative of the duties that we have towards ourselves.[169]

Finally, the most successful models of natural right theory remain theories of rights.[170] They are deontological and their orientation is not informed by a conception of the good life. In a way, it makes sense to call them 'liberal' if by that we mean that they are about the 'side-constraints'[171] that actors must observe in pursuing what they take to be their own good. Contributing, driven by sympathy and concern, to the good of others is neither a duty of citizens nor a task of the state. Nowhere are both themes more clearly articulated than in Kant's legal and political philosophy.[172] Not by accident, his theory of law goes to some length to distinguish between perfect and imperfect duties, a theme that already surfaced in Grotius' work[173] and was

[165] There is ostensibly resonance of this idea in the work of von Humboldt, n 40, 17–18.

[166] See Wolff, *Seele des Menschen*, n 151, 78–79, § 152 (explaining by example of a watch working perfectly owing to the perfect fit of its component parts). See Schneewind, n 11, 436.

[167] See Wolff, *Seele des Menschen*, n 151, 298–99, 464, 466, 469, §§ 491, 744, 748, 755–56, respectively; Schneewind, n 11, 437.

[168] See Schneewind, n 11, 437.

[169] See Wolf, *Tun und Lassen*, n 150, 539, § 767.

[170] See Tuck, n 80, 82.

[171] See R Nozick, *Anarchy, State, and Utopia* (New York, Basic Books, 1973) 28–29.

[172] See Kant, n 46, 74.

[173] See Grotius, n 4, 35, I.2.1: 'According to the diversity of the matter, that which we call moral goodness at times consists of a point, so to speak, so that if you depart from it even the least possible distance, you turn aside in the direction of wrong-doing. [A]t times it has a wider range, so that an act may be praiseworthy if performed; yet, if it be omitted altogether or performed in some other way, no blame would attach, the distinction being generally without an intermediate stage, like the transition from being to not-being. Between things opposed in a different way, however, as white and black, a mean may

to be picked up by Pufendorf too.[174] While Kant's account is undoubtedly muddled and shifting its focus from one work to the other,[175] it is fair to say that legal obligations are, first, subject to 'external' legislation,[176] which means that they concern the observable content of actions – what people perceptibly do or do not do – and not the choice of their aims. More precisely, external actions impact like 'facts' on one another's conduct, while the aims pursued by those creating these facts remain immaterial. The reason why legal obligations in contrast to obligations of virtue occupy this province is that the law is all about removing obstacles to external freedom according to general laws.[177] The means thereto (preventive and restorative) is coercion.[178] Rights and the permission to resort to coercion 'amount to the same'.[179] The law – and a fortiori the state – has no business in lecturing people about the projects they ought to pursue. Adopting an aim is not subject to coercion.[180] The coercive nature of law is of elementary significance for its domain. It may also explain why, second, already in the *Groundwork*,[181] Kant uses a different distinction, namely that between perfect obligations, which are unequivocal and apply without exception, and their imperfect counterpart.[182] The ground of this distinction is, apparently, the lack of strictness of imperfect obligations. They leave obligated individuals with sufficient leeway to dispose of their responsibilities subject to available opportunities, means or in light of the comparative urgency to fulfil other duties. Imperfect obligations are prima facie duties only and, using

be found either by effecting a combination of the two or by finding an intermediate between them. / It is with this latter class of actions that both divine and human laws are wont to concern themselves, in order that those acts which were in themselves merely praiseworthy might become also obligatory.'

[174] See n 88.

[175] See C Horn, *Nicht-Ideale Normativität: Ein neuer Blick auf Kants politische Philosophie* (Berlin, Suhrkamp, 2014) 145–69. Horn identifies four different, yet heterogeneous, criteria with which Kant distinguished legal from ethical obligations: latitude and discretion in the case of ethics versus strictness of legal obligations (148, 166), the relevance or irrelevance of motivation (151), whether or not a duty is correlated with another's right (155), and an element of supererogation in the case of ethical duties (158–59).

[176] See I Kant, *Die Metaphysik der Sitten* in *Werke in zwölf Bänden*, vol 8 (ed W Weischedel, Frankfurt aM, Suhrkamp, 1968) 347 (AB 47).

[177] In addition, obligations of virtue concern the choice of ends and are subject to the application of the categorical imperative with a focus on a potential 'contradiction in will'. For an illuminating analysis, see O O'Neill, *Acting on Principle: An Essay on Kantian Ethics*, 2nd edn (Cambridge, Cambridge University Press, 2013) 178–84.

[178] See Kant, n 176, 329–30 (AB 35).

[179] ibid 340 (AB 36), 'bedeuten also einerlei'.

[180] ibid 510–11 (A 5–6).

[181] See I Kant, *Grundlegung zur Metaphysik der Sitten* (ed B Kraft and D Schönecker, Hamburg, Meiner, 1999) 45–46.

[182] See Kant, n 176, 520 (A 20); Horn, n 175, 148.

more contemporary parlance, do not apply in an all-or-nothing fashion.[183] Strictness ('all or nothing'), by contrast, easily attaches to duties that are correlated with rights. Since rights are permissions to coerce others, and coercion may be used only to remove obstacles to freedom, rights must give rise to determinate obligations to refrain from illicitly interfering with the freedom of others. The law is the domain of negative freedom and as such devoid of positive obligations of solidarity.[184] You omit doing the wrong thing that the legal obligation prohibits, regardless of whether this wrong thing is in the end an omission or commission.

Kant's Hobbesian Liberalism

The coevolution of natural law and liberalism appears to come to its conclusion in Kant's work.[185] In his political writings, notably in his essay 'On the Common Saying', Kant identifies three principles of a civil constitution, the establishment of which is a duty.[186] The constitution is supposed to secure the external freedom by means of coercive laws in such a way that the freedom of each is compatible with the equal freedom of all. The three principles, unsurprisingly, comprise freedom, equality and independence.

Freedom is manifest not only in a principle of mutual independence, according to which nobody is subject to direction by others unless they have agreed to it, but also in the absence of a caring state pursuing the well-being and happiness of all. Kant is clearly opposed to a 'paternal government' that treats its subjects as 'immature children who cannot distinguish what is truly useful or harmful to themselves'.[187] Under such a government, people would be forced to reside in a state of passivity, for they had to rely on the judgement of the head of state with regard to what makes them happy. The entire freedom of the subjects, in the sense of independently identifying and pursuing their self-interest, would thereby be 'suspended'. They would have no rights whatsoever.[188]

[183] See Kant, n 176, 520–21 (A 21).
[184] See Horn, n 175, 154–55. But see n 190.
[185] See, generally, A Ripstein, *Force and Freedom: Kant's Legal and Political Philosophy* (Cambridge, MA, Harvard University Press, 2009).
[186] See Kant, n 46, 73.
[187] ibid 74.
[188] By contrast, Kant regards a 'patriotic government' as supported by the attitude pursuant to which the commonwealth is taken to be 'a maternal womb' and the land a 'paternal ground' from which the citizen sprang, which everyone 'must leave to his descendants as a treasured pledge'. See ibid 74.

Equality means that all are – with the only exception being the head of state – subject to the same coercive laws, and that distinctions between and among citizens are permissible only if they are 'earned' on the grounds of talent, industry or good fortune.[189] State services to the poor play a residual role in Kant's system, but they are nevertheless grounded in the hypothetical original contract's containing a pledge to sustain those members of society who cannot preserve themselves.[190] Hereditary prerogatives are inconsistent with equality.[191]

Independence finally comes into play in Kant's discussion of public law, which is his name for the positive law laying down what ought to be done legally by all.[192] Since such a will must not commit injustice, and injustice is ruled out when one voluntarily acts towards oneself (*volenti non fit injuria*), one individual will cannot legislate for all. Rather, public law needs to have its roots in the *unity* of the will of all the members. Since it is a synthetically unified general will that is supposed to authorise all laws, the hypothetical[193] original contract (*pactum sociale*) provides the critical standard of all legislation. The unity requisite thereto, however, requires, aside from freedom and equality, the independence of all voters. If voters were not independent, they would in their judgement not aim at the point at which their wills indeed become unified. Citizens have to be property owners and be their own masters.[194]

Two consequences follow from this. The first is that Kant restricts political participation to those whom he deems to be independent. The criterion used by him to distinguish the dependent from the independent is ludicrously formalistic. The question is whether one creates works that one then sells to others or is employed under the supervision of a boss. In an age in which even the most menial labour is done by people who are self-employed (eg, the people in the business of delivering food and all kinds of commodities), this distinction no longer carries any intuitive appeal. Kant himself already admitted 'that it is somewhat difficult to define the qualifications which entitle anyone to claim the status of being his own master'.[195]

[189] ibid 75.
[190] ibid 446 (B 216–17). See Ripstein, n 186, 272–86.
[191] See Kant, n 46, 75.
[192] ibid 77–78.
[193] ibid 79.
[194] ibid 78.
[195] ibid, final sentence of the asterisked footnote.

The second consequence of Kant's ideal of legislation is that laws that a people with mature reason could not adopt for themselves need to be rejected. This is the criterion for the critical appraisal of all legislation. Kant's examples demonstrate that what he had in mind were discriminatory unequal treatments[196] and severe inferences with liberty, such as the introduction of an established religion.[197] It may be safely concluded, then, that the expectation that legislation live up to fundamental rights is a consequence of the application of hypothetical contract.

While all of this sounds like liberalism with an edge, and even though Kant exposes his ideas under the heading 'against Hobbes',[198] the matter must appear like impotent handwringing from the perspective of Hobbes' political philosophy. Like Hobbes, Kant believes the sovereign to be exempt from all laws[199] and, like Hobbes, that any forceful alterations of constitutional arrangements would lead only to unnecessary turmoil and disorder.[200] Like Hobbes, Kant denies citizens any rights of resistance (other than the 'freedom of the pen'),[201] with arguments that would have found much support by Hobbes, for the control of the sovereign by another would imply splitting it in half, which is an impossibility.[202]

Indeed, considering that prudent Hobbesian sovereigns would observe to the best of their abilities the 19 laws of nature, the society envisaged by Kant would be almost identical to Hobbes' with the exception, though, that the Kantian polity would recognise freedom of speech.

Anti-positivism

In retrospect, it may seem that theories of natural law that flourished in the seventeenth century had completed their work, not least because their results, putting it cautiously, coincided with declarations of the 'rights of man'.[203] As these rights entered the first modern constitutional charters, usually in their first part, they fed into the slow development of fundamental

[196] The existence of a hereditary aristocracy countervenes the original contract. See ibid 79.
[197] ibid 85.
[198] ibid 73.
[199] See Hobbes, n 21, 106 [89].
[200] See Kant, n 46, 81–83. See Hobbes, n 21, 106 [88].
[201] See Kant, n 46, 85.
[202] ibid 84. See Hobbes, n 21, 90 [73], 113 [95].
[203] On the 'rights of man' as predecessors of modern human rights, see S Moyn, *The Last Utopia: Human Rights in History* (Cambridge, MA, Harvard University Press, 2010) 11–12, 20–32, 35–36, 40–50, 81, 85, 92–93.

rights law. It would take a separate, albeit rewarding, chapter to explore how natural rights thinking is nowadays again nesting in the opinion of courts that have made it their agenda to push the development of human rights law forward.[204] The focus on rights that governments must protect and not illicitly interfere with is also consistent with the focus on what makes government authority legitimate. Habermas points out, correctly, that later natural law theory is no longer concerned with the composition and government of the civitas.[205] The attention shifts to the justification of authority. The one instrument that is supposed to guarantee such justification is the written constitution. We shall see in chapter 9 why the justification of authority and of its constitution is where the action is.

This does not mean that the natural law tradition comes to a close with its 'translation' into modern constitutionalism. On the contrary, it continues to this day and is manifest in a whole variety of all approaches that refuse to draw a sharp line between law and morality.[206] But with the emerging predominance of legal positivism, this refusal begins to have a different point. It is the opposition to legal positivism that matters the most. Therefore, with the noteworthy exception of some Christian theorists, natural law theory is no longer part and parcel of practical philosophy or, put differently, of a theory of practical reason. Rather, it retreats to demonstrating that the legal positivists' view of the law qua system of authoritative directives needs at least to be amended, if not even scrapped altogether.

Three different approaches stand out, of which the first is the most original. It identifies morality with what constitutes the form of law as a practice of governing that differs from others. We find this idea articulated in the work of Lon Fuller.[207] The second approach continues natural law in the vein in which it had been conceived by scholastic philosophers,

[204] On international law as a tradition of idealism and progress, see already H Lauterpacht, 'The Grotian Tradition in International Law' (1946) 23 *British Yearbook of International Law* 1–53, 48.

[205] See J Habermas, *Auch eine Geschichte der Philosophie*, vol 2: *Vernünftige Freiheit. Spuren des Diskurses über Glauben und Wissen* (Berlin, Suhrkamp, 2019) 105.

[206] To this day, there is natural law theory with the ambition to be relevant to the legislature. It often, however, appears in the disguise of an 'ethical approach' to law. See, most prominently, Dietmar von der Pfordten, *Rechtsethik*, 2nd edn (Munich, CH Beck, 2011) and n 208 below on Messner. The relevant contributions to the genre of *Rechtsethik*, however, often endorse a particular focus of moral reasoning – mostly of either a Kantian or a utilitarian persuasion – and are linked to certain spheres of human activity, such as modern medicine, scientific research or immigration. In a more degenerate form, which largely abstains from self-reflection, one encounters *Rechtsethik* in the context of agenda scholarship. Human rights enthusiasm and gender studies occasionally offer examples of this mindset, which speaks exclusively to fellow-travellers and comrades rather than the scientific community.

[207] See, notably, LL Fuller, *The Morality of Law*, 2nd edn (New Haven, CT, Yale University Press, 1969).

namely as an account of how we ought to live. This is the path taken by Roman-Catholic thinking on the subject, of which John Finnis' work today is the specimen most widely referred to.[208] The third approach is most vividly manifest in the work of Ronald Dworkin,[209] in which the Stoic idea of natural law qua deposit of our practical reason has come to live again. Hercules, his mystical judge, is nothing short of a revenant of the Stoic sage.

The Form of Law

Lon Fuller's contribution to natural law theory is quite unique. He offers an account of the 'internal' or 'inner' morality of law.[210] He does so in reply to legal positivism, however, not by focusing on adjudication but by asking what kind of features a system of governing needs to possess in order to pass as a law. Fuller believed that eight features provide us with the elementary qualities that any system that claims to be a legal system needs to possess. His account of natural law is not about fundamental rights and not about distributive justice; rather, it is concerned with the form of law.[211]

These are the eight principles:

(1) The law is composed of rules and not of a motley array of ad hoc decisions.
(2) The rules are publicly known.
(3) The rules are known in advance of action and there is no retroactive legislation.
(4) Rules are comprehensible.
(5) Rules do not contradict one another and are not internally contradictory.
(6) Rules do not demand the impossible.
(7) Rules are not so frequently changed that obtaining guidance from them becomes impossible.

[208] See J Finnis, *Natural Law and Natural Rights* (Oxford, Clarendon Press, 1980). It is, however, also the case that of late, the work of Johannes Messner has been receiving attention from contemporary Christian theorists. Messner is the author of one of the most comprehensive systems of natural law of all times that promises to be of relevance to every field of social policy making. See J Messner, *Social Ethics: Natural Law in the Western World*, 2nd edn (trans JJ Doherty, St Louis, MO, B Herder Book Co 1965). For the contemporary reception of his work, see A Vermeule, *Common Good Constitutionalism: Recovering the Classical Legal Tradition* (Cambridge, Polity Press, 2022) 188, 226.

[209] The most elementary exposition of his work is still to be found in his *Taking Rights Seriously*, 2nd edn (Cambridge, MA, Harvard University Press, 1978).

[210] See Fuller, n 207, 9, 41–44, 131–32.

[211] He also calls it 'procedural natural law'. See ibid 96–97.

(8) There is congruence between the announced rules and their administration.[212]

Evidently, what Fuller has in mind is largely coextensive with our ideal of the rule of law,[213] even if he does not include judicial review of government action. But we can imagine that Fuller, in order to secure the impartial application of the said principles, would amend the list with another maxim requiring the impartial review of the observance of the elementary eight principles. What is more, while the principles seem largely to call for effective government action, Fuller indicates that their application, in particular the principle rejecting retroactivity, implicates the autonomous planning of conduct. Our autonomy would be thwarted if we ended up with different legal consequences of our action than the ones we had a fair opportunity to anticipate at the time of action. Hence, Fuller can rightly claim that what underpins the morality of law is indeed the important moral principle of autonomy.[214]

It is a slightly different matter whether an authoritarian regime might be better off governing by means of rules. The subjects would be aware of their obligations and comply out of fear of sanctions. Tasks could be delegated to ordinary officials. Bound by rules and subject to review, they would not have to be government loyalists and still reliably carry out their mission. Provocative arguments along these lines were proffered by Matthew Kramer.[215] They point in a direction that is similar to the transformation of the rule of law into a rule *by* law in China.[216] The law is a convenient means for steering members of society into a direction desired by government. Kramer's claims were met with incessant criticism by Nigel Simmonds, who argued that no smart authoritarian regime would tie its actions to rules and thereby divest itself of opportunities to deal with enemies as the situation

[212] ibid 38–39.

[213] See K Rundle, *Forms Liberate: Reclaiming the Jurisprudence of Lon L Fuller* (Oxford, Hart Publishing, 2012) 151.

[214] See Fuller, n 207, 162. Drawing on an observation made by the German sociologist Georg Simmel, Fuller also claims that the government's commitment to act according to rules laid down in advance indicates the existence of reciprocity in the relation between the government and its citizens: 'Government says to the citizen in effect, "These are the rules we expect you to follow. If you follow them, you have our assurance that they are the rules that will be applied to your conduct". When this bond of reciprocity is finally and completely ruptured by the government, nothing is left on which to ground the citizen's duty to observe the rules'. ibid 39–40.

[215] See M Kramer, 'On the Moral Status of the Rule of Law' (2004) 63 *Cambridge Law Journal* 65–97.

[216] See JA Cohen, '"Rule of law" with Chinese characterisics: Evolution and manipulation' (2021) 19 *International Journal of Constitution Law* 1882–87.

seems to call for.[217] There is, hence, a moral element in the form of law, which makes it unattractive for authoritarian government to be constrained by its rigour.

Fuller, to be sure, rested even more faith in the morality of law. He believed that racial discrimination would be inconsistent with the principles of legality.[218] In his view, it is based on ideas so crude and incoherent that they could never give rise to any predictable practice. This is a high hope, but possibly it was in vain. The law has been able to absorb racism quite capably and even predictably, alas.

Fuller was aware that there is possibly no single legal system that meets all the criteria of the morality of law to a full extent. This made him speak of a 'morality of aspiration'.[219] Some systems will live up to the idea more fully than others. Viewed from that angle, we end up with better and worse legal systems. There is, however, an indeterminate line distinguishing the law from other modes of governing humans, such as managerial discretion or the creation of followership by means of 'good communication' or neuro-linguistic programming. To make us aware of the relevant differences is the great merit and achievement of Fuller's legal philosophy.

Natural Law Theory as Ethics

One of the few remaining theorists whose natural law theory work sweeps so broadly as to warrant the description of 'ethics' is John M Finnis.[220] The roots of his work go back to Aquinas,[221] but very much to his credit he has given traditional natural law theory an innovative and, indeed, strongly liberal twist.[222] His work is 'ethics' in the full sense of the term, for it not only concerns what we ought to do in relation to other persons, but also offers an intellectual matrix for thinking about how we ought to live in order to live fulfilling and rich lives.[223]

[217] See NE Simmonds, *Law as a Moral Idea* (Oxford, Oxford University Press, 2007) 85–88.

[218] See Fuller, n 207, 159–62, 183–84.

[219] ibid 5–6, 41–42, 45.

[220] Never mind, however, that part of the thrust of his work is also to present a more plausible alternative to legal positivism. See Finnis, n 208, 3–9, 25–29.

[221] ibid 29–30.

[222] The latter is owing to the fact that Finnis believes in the incommensurability of basic goods, which creates ample room for the free choice of individual pursuits. See N Simmonds and J Neoh, *Central Issues in Jurisprudence*, 6th edn (London, Sweet & Maxwell, 2022) 129–30.

[223] See Finnis, n 208, 23.

Finnis begins with an account of 'basic goods' or values. Systematically, these occupy the place that used to be taken by 'natural inclinations' in Aquinas' theory.[224] They are the goods that we all seek to have in our lives because participation in them is integral to human flourishing.[225] They are desired not because they serve as means to have access to some other good, but rather because they are considered to be good in themselves.[226] Epistemologically, they are supposedly self-evident,[227] and logically they are axiomatic. They are self-evident because any attempt to point out what makes them appealing invariably needs to draw on them. For example, any attempt to show why friendship is of value in our lives must appeal to what it means to be a friend. This meaning cannot be reduced monistically to an elementary quality like 'pleasure'. The values are axiomatic in that they are not derived from any other premise. It is good to be alive. Period. It is good to have friends. Full stop. The goods that Finnis identifies are the following: life and health, knowledge, play, aesthetic experience, sociability, practical reasonableness, and religion.[228]

These goods are, Finnis claims, equally fundamental.[229] None is more basic than any other, in the sense that we can always imagine occasions on which we are ready to sacrifice one in order to enjoy another. Life, admittedly, appears to be most basic, but we can nevertheless imagine situations where we would say that it is understandable to put one's life at risk for the sake of another good, such as, for example, the independence of one's country. Conversely, the loyalty to one's country will likely come to an end when the fake facts of its national history are fabricated by officials in the employ of the ministry of truth.[230]

Indeed, once our focus comes to rest on one of these goods, it immediately, but often falsely, claims priority over others.[231] This indicates that the goods are incommensurable with one another. Borrowing Raz's characterisation of incommensurability, this means that no good is better or worse than any other and that they are also not of equal value.[232] There is no scale

[224] ibid 60–62.
[225] ibid 67, 87.
[226] ibid 80–83.
[227] ibid 64–69.
[228] ibid 85–90.
[229] ibid 92.
[230] See G Orwell, *Nineteen Eighty-Four* (London, Penguin Books, 1983).
[231] See Finnis, n 208, 93.
[232] See J Raz, *The Morality of Freedom* (Oxford, Clarendon Press, 1986) 322, 325.

on which to compare them. In particular, it is not possible to express the degree of realisation or possession of one good in the degree of realisation or possession of another. It is also impossible to compensate the felt lack of one good through quantities of others. The great health that you are in cannot console you over having no friends.

By attending to these goods or values, we can make human action intelligible. We can see why people believe that what they do is worth their while.[233] It may still be the case that the lives people lead strike us as completely unbalanced, for example on the ground of their largely ignoring the arts and devoting all their time to their family. But it remains intelligible what the good is such people pursue.[234] Whether it is also right to live in such a way is a question that concerns the application of one of these goods, namely, our practical reasonableness.[235] That the latter is a good itself is shown by the fact that we don't want to have our actions determined by someone else. We want to take charge of our own life, and our self-control will likely not go awry if we possess the 'good' – the dianoetic virtue – of practical reasonableness.

Finnis arrives at a number of precepts of practical reasonableness, the most important of which are the maxims to form a plan of life[236] (subject to revision) and to avoid sacrificing completely the pursuit of any one good to the pursuit of others. Our lives would be less complete and well-rounded if we lacked any one of these goods. A plan of life involves commitments.[237] Of course, Finnis' belief in the incommensurability of values makes it difficult for him to imagine how we could rationally accept any such commitments (for example, the commitment to ancient political theory rather than playing the cello), not least because no good or value endorsed in such a commitment can be rationally preferable to any other. Obviously, rationality can be guaranteed only by taking one's own capacities and circumstances to enjoy particular goods into account. While the capacity to enjoy goods is important, it is not, at the end of the day, the value ultimately guiding our choices.[238]

Finnis avoids the question of how rational it is to be reasonable by including sociability, and therewith matters such as matrimony, friendship

233 See Finnis, n 208, 83.
234 Life plans have to be selective. See ibid 105.
235 ibid 100–03.
236 ibid 103–05.
237 ibid 109.
238 See the perceptive observation by Simmonds and Neoh, n 222, 134.

and community, in the list of self-evident and axiomatic values. Hence, getting along with others is part and parcel of living well. Nevertheless, his conception of the common good reveals that his theory of natural law, despite having roots in medieval theology, is firmly placed within the modern liberal camp. Owing to the incommensurability of goods, the commitments made by people depend essentially on their choices. In a liberal vein, then, the common good is understood to amount to the set of conditions that have to be in place for individuals to live their possibly idiosyncratic lives successfully (to 'flourish').[239] Finnis also adds 'subsidiarity' to the principles relevant to the common good, which implies that in the first round, individuals are themselves responsible for obtaining their own good.[240] Larger communities are supposed to step in only where individuals lack the relevant capacities. Natural law and positive law are indispensable for the coordination of our conduct in society and for reaping the benefits of cooperation.[241] While Finnis accords them pride of place in his theory, they somehow dwindle in significance in the face of the more profound questions that ethics seeks to answer.

Perfect Legal Positivism Disavows Itself

Of all rejuvenations of the strong connection between law and morality, the position advocated by Ronald Dworkin is possibly the most aggressive. It is also the most persuasive. This is not least due to the fact that Dworkin has formulated a powerful internal critique of legal positivism.

Legal positivism aims to provide us with the most sober account of the legal system. Sobriety can be achieved by removing from the description of positive law all unnecessary idealisations.[242] Legal positivists believe themselves, falsely, to succeed at this task by drawing a sharp line between law and morality. But in doing so they fall prey to another fatal idealisation, which makes them disposed to misdescribe the realities of the legal systems they want to capture. Legal positivists posit that the legal system is a system of rules.[243] But it is, indeed, not exclusively composed of this type

[239] See Finnis, n 208, 154–55.
[240] ibid 144–45.
[241] ibid 281–91 and throughout chapters VII–XII.
[242] For a further elaboration of this point, see my *Knowing What the Law Is: Legal Theory in a New Key* (Oxford, Hart Publishing, 2021) 71–74.
[243] See, for example, HLA Hart, *The Concept of Law* (Oxford, Clarendon Press, 1961).

of normative standard. Judges also rely on policy arguments and principles. This is the core of Dworkin's objection.[244]

Appeals to rules are about 'all or nothing'. A rule is either applicable or it is not. Arguments from policies or principles invoke a different normative force. Both policies and objective principles have a 'weight' and must be balanced against other standards of this type.[245] Dworkin goes to great lengths to explain why positivists mistakenly ignore these arguments by relabelling them as exercises of judicial discretion.[246] He argues, convincingly, that they thereby arrive at a distorted account of the legal system. Positivism, therefore, ignores an important dimension of legal practice and originates from grafting on social realities the idealised image of law qua system of rules.

Once Dworkin has made this elementary point, he goes on to explain that arguments from principle (they are about asserting an individual right, in contrast to policy arguments that simply point to desirable states of affairs in the aggregate)[247] not only draw on 'institutional support' in the legal materials.[248] The fundamental rights contained in a Bill of Rights, for example, represent principles laid down in a Charter. It can also happen, however, as Dworkin explains, that principles assert their relevance by emerging from the broader moral background of the law. This happened in the case of Elmer, who killed his grandfather in order to inherit the estate.[249] Even though the killing of the testator was not mentioned in the relevant New York statute as a ground for forfeiting a claim to inheritance, the Court appealed to the principle that nobody must benefit from their own wrong to reject Elmer's claim to the estate. Dworkin takes this case as a strong proof that we had better account for the legal system in a manner that includes moral background principles, even if they are not buttressed by a source of law. Surprisingly, therefore, cancelling the separation of law and morality gives us the more accurate picture of legal practice.

Dworkin is right about this. Most legal scholars, if asked, would likely claim that they are 'legal positivists' but still argue in a manner that Dworkin

[244] The article, entitled 'The Model of Rules', in which Dworkin developed his objections is reprinted in Dworkin, n 209, at 14–45.

[245] See Dworkin, n 209, 24–26.

[246] ibid 31–39.

[247] ibid 90.

[248] ibid 100–01.

[249] ibid 23.

would find congenial.[250] They are doing so because they simply follow the established practice of legal argument that is often oblivious to the dividing line between law and morality.

Natural Law as Reason

At the same time, it must be granted that Dworkin is an unusual natural law theorist. There is no appeal to eternal law, no God, no conception of human nature, not even a more elaborate moral theory undergirding his enterprise, merely rather tiresome adjurations and erratic explications of moral objectivity.[251] He seems to believe that the reason of law resides in its practice.[252] Such practice is what German idealistic philosophy, following Hegel, would call 'objective spirit'.[253] It is a practice that develops conceptions of itself that are in turn folding back into it.[254] A practice that is guided by interpretations of its point is 'interpretive'. It is informed by accounts of what best explains its existence, which points, in the field of human agency, to its purpose. The purpose of the practice of observing holidays is to let commercial life come to a rest and give people the opportunity to repose in more serene pursuits.

Interpretations of practices that we designate with concepts result, if all goes well, in more elaborate conceptions.[255] In the case of law, this concerns primarily certain partitions of law, such as freedom of speech or freedom of contract. The point of elaborating a conception (or a 'soundest theory' of the partition in question[256]) is to have adjudication continue in light of its best justification. This explains why interpretations necessarily avail

[250] 'Inclusive legal positivism' was later developed to bridge this gap. For the first sketch, see J Coleman, "Negative and Positive Positivism" (1982) 11 *Journal of Legal Studies* 139–64. The whole approach was later subjected to a strident critique by Ronald Dworkin. See his *Justice in Robes* (Cambridge, MA, Harvard University Press, 2006) 187–222.

[251] For a particularly cumbersome example, see R Dworkin, 'Objectivity and Truth: You'd Better Believe It' (1996) 25 *Philosophy and Public Affairs* 87–139. For a powerful critique, see S Street, 'Objectivity and Truth: You'd Better Rethink It' (2016) 11 *Oxford Studies in Metaethics* (ed R Shafer-Landau, Oxford, Oxford University Press) 293–334.

[252] This is what one must take away from Dworkin's *Law's Empire* (Cambridge, MA, Harvard University Press, 1986).

[253] See T Pinkard, *Hegel's Phenomenology: The Sociality of Reason* (Cambridge, Cambridge University Press, 1994) 123–24; RB Pippin, *Hegel's Practical Philosophy: Rational Agency as Ethical Life* (Cambridge, Cambridge University Press, 2008) 242.

[254] See Dworkin, n 252, 48, 66–67.

[255] ibid 70–72.

[256] ibid 105.

themselves of the two dimensions of 'fit' and 'justification'.[257] They need to be plausibly tied to what has been done before and still aim to continue by casting the existing practice in its best possible light. Owing to this normative dimension, 'fit' can never be total but only partial.

On a larger scale, one encounters attempts to arrive at the best possible interpretation of law in justifications of legal practice as a whole. The point of law is to justify acts of coercion.[258] Of these conceptions Dworkin finds 'law as integrity' most convincing, which demands that the law speak with one voice and treat everyone with equal respect and concern.[259] In order to bring about such univocity, the legal materials must be reconstructed from the perspective of morally significant principles, and it must be shown how these principles hang together.

The model agent for bringing about coherent interpretations of fields of law and of legal practice as a whole is Hercules,[260] a mystical judge invested with supranatural powers. His task is to synthesise the legal materials along horizontal and vertical lines in a manner also bestowing upon it the best possible moral appeal. With that, however, natural law theory seems to have recovered its original form. It touches base again with the ideal of the Stoic sage. The law is not manifest in various rules and precedents, even though these are of necessity for some of its component parts. What holds the law together and keeps it alive, however, is the reasoning process of the sage, who manages to distinguish cases and to arrange adequate replies to practical challenges into a coherent whole.[261] Reason is thus embedded in the law and not operating on it as if it were a foreign guide.

[257] ibid 223–28.

[258] ibid 94.

[259] ibid 188–89.

[260] First introduced in Dworkin, n 209, 104. On his task, see ibid 116–17.

[261] See KM Vogt, *Law, Reason, and the Cosmic City: Political Philosophy in the Early Stoa* (Oxford, Oxford University Press, 2008) 198–200.

9

The Enigma of Authority

Validity and Authority

Legal positivists usually speak, when addressing the authority of law, of 'legal validity'. What they mean thereby is either of two things.

First, a norm is 'valid' if it is to be regarded as a standard governing the adjudication of the relevant issues in a certain jurisdiction. If asked by an external observer, judges would reply that, indeed, valid law is what they are supposed to cite in deciding cases. It is a duty incumbent on them. It's their job.[1] What legal positivists would deny, however, is that ordinary people are obligated to comply with what judges use as valid law. Invariably, they must merely face the consequences of their failure or refusal to do so. Legal validity is not, therefore, an expression of a general obligation to obey the law.

Second, by 'validity' of norms can be understood their belonging to the set of normative standards comprising the legal order.[2] While in the former understanding a normative element is still retained, inasmuch as legal validity is relevant to the obligations of judges, validity is in this case entirely drained of its normative dimension. It merely designates the membership of norms to a set and is stripped of any connection to human conduct.

The first understanding of legal validity concerns obligations of judges, possibly based on existing conventions; the second understanding evades the question of authority completely. In the latter case, the concept of validity is an expedient used by legal positivists to deflect attention from the core normative issue, which is the question of whether the law imposes obligations on us. If the state uses my taxes to subsidise the installation of photovoltaic systems in private homes, this raises the question whether the transfer of wealth from non-owners to owners is fair and just. Can it be law? Or is the inequity so egregious that the government's laws and actions must be considered null and void?

[1] See HLA Hart, *The Concept of Law*, 2nd edn (Oxford, Clarendon Press, 1994) 116.

[2] See, even though Kelsen does not highlight the difference from obligatoriness, H Kelsen, *Pure Theory of Law* (trans M Knight, Berkeley, CA, University of California Press, 1967) 10.

The question of authority is whether someone has the power to create obligations for us even though we regard the resulting duties as wrong. This is the genuinely interesting question to ask in lieu of engaging in the perfunctory talk concerning legal validity.

Practical Authority

Joseph Raz – one of the most eminent legal positivists of all times – deserves credit for having reintroduced the concept of authority, viz practical authority, to the study of law.[3] His quite elaborate conceptual analysis, to which we shall return below, builds on the simple idea, which was first clearly articulated by Hobbes,[4] that someone has practical authority if others have to do something simply because that someone has ordered them to do so.

> 'Why do I have to clean up my room?'
>
> 'Because Dad said so.'

Hobbes' and Raz's analyses aside, any claim to authority arguably involves three elementary features. The first is the peremptoriness or pre-emptive quality of authoritative enactments. An appeal to authority supposedly overrides and precludes other considerations or potential objections.[5] Second, whoever exercises authority expects others to follow without regard to the underlying substantive reasons. If the speed limit is 30 mph, drivers need to comply. There is no hope of wrenching concessions from adjudicators by pointing to lower traffic or greater driving experience. An authority can be substantively wrong or lay down inflexible rules and still validly exercise its power. Third, authority is a status that a person or an institution might possess. This status is often relative to certain issues or to certain tasks. That the government has authority to lay down traffic regulations does not mean that its authority also extends to regulating the purchase of vehicles.

Relevant in our context is, of course, practical authority, which is the authority to create and to enforce obligations for others. This type of authority needs to be distinguished from epistemic authority that concerns what we had better believe.[6] Many people who surround us possess epistemic

[3] See J Raz, *The Authority of Law*, 2nd edn (Oxford, Clarendon Press, 2009).

[4] See T Hobbes, *On the Citizen* (trans R Tuck and M Silverstone, Cambridge, Cambridge University Press, 1997) XIV.1, 153–54.

[5] ibid 154.

[6] See, again, on the distinction between 'advice' and 'command', ibid 153–54.

authority that does not in and of itself extend into the practical sphere. Medical doctors, financial advisers or mentors provide us with advice to heed, but the determination of what we have reason to do is ultimately left to us. The line, concededly, dividing epistemic from practical authority is not always easy to make out, and it can happen that in certain circumstances epistemic authority bleeds into its practical counterpart. If people are injured in an accident, we are morally obligated to do the best we can to help. Should medical doctors be present in a such a situation, however, we have reason to follow their orders, for their epistemic authority is decisive for determining the most effective course of action.

Consent and Contract

Since we have lost faith in authority that exists by virtue of God's grace and believe no longer, without anything further, in having to pay deference to 'the better sort', the most promising account of authority appears to be the consent of the governed.[7]

It is important, at this point, to distinguish between *de facto* and *de jure* authority.[8] De facto authority is exercised by anyone who is *believed* to possess real authority by their followers. If people comport themselves in accordance with the orders of someone pretending to be a military commander, then that person possesses *de facto* authority. Persons enjoying the voluntary support of their followers possess *de facto* authority. They rule based on the consent of the governed. In the context of a discussion of party coalitions, David Hume claimed that the sole sources of the authority of government are precedent and the opinion of right that is reflected in the readiness to succumb to present practice.[9] Authority rests on opinion,[10] but opinion[11]

[7] For a very useful introduction to the topic, see AJ Simmons, 'Authority' in D Estlund (ed), *The Oxford Handbook of Political Philosophy* (Oxford, Oxford University Press, 2012) 23–39. On the emergence of the idea in Tudor and Stuart England, see D Herzog, *Happy Slaves: A Critique of Consent Theory* (Chicago, IL, University of Chicago Press, 1989) 182–96.

[8] See Simmons, n 7, 25.

[9] See D Hume, 'Of the Coalition of Parties' reprinted in *Political Writings* (ed SD Warner and DW Livingstone, Indianapolis, IN, Hackett Publishing, 1994) 142–49, 144: 'The only rule of government … known and acknowledged among men, is use and practice: Reason is so uncertain a guide that it will be always exposed to doubt and controversy …'.

[10] See, famously, D Hume, 'Of the First Principles of Government' in his *Political Essays* (ed K Haakonssen, Cambridge, Cambridge University Press, 2012) 16–19, 16. As is well known, the quip that opinion of the governed is the foundation of government was appropriated by Madison. See J Madison, *The Federalist* (ed C Sunstein, Cambridge, MA, Harvard University Press, 2009) no 49, 332.

[11] Clearly, Hume speaks of 'mere' opinion in contrast to some philosophical truth. See E Vollrath, 'That All Governments Rest on Opinion' (1976) 43 *Social Research* 46–61, 54–57.

is determined by the salience of a moderately well-working tradition. According to Hume, however, such *de facto* authority also always exists *de jure,* for in his view any dissension over rightful authority would lead to turmoil and civic strife. Consequently, deference towards already existing authority is underpinned by the general utility to which such deference gives rise.[12] In a sense, it is a self-fulfilling prophecy. Hume thus, seemingly paradoxically, argued that debating the rightfulness of authority is a perilous misapprehension of the fact that *de jure* authority is inherent in its existence *de facto.* This way of thinking is, of course, not consistent with the contractualist tradition.[13] From its point of view, authority would be rightful and merit the dignified appellation of *de jure* only if the consent of the governed were based on good reasons that emerge under ideal counterfactual conditions ('if people were all equal and free …'). De facto people may follow the orders of their rulers because they wrongly attribute to them supranatural powers. The rulers enjoy the consent of the governed, even if it is rooted in mere gullibility. De jure authority – far from designating authority that is conferred by positive law – concerns the grounds of *legitimate* authority. Such authority must be based on convincing arguments for supporting its powers. If that is the case, the authority is legitimate. Legitimacy means that a ruler or a regime *deserves* recognition.[14]

Hence, the idea that legitimate governmental authority rests on the consent of the governed may seem superficial, and for that reason also misleading. Consent cannot be a sufficient condition of legitimacy. Stupid or fainthearted acquiescence can confer *de jure* authority only if one shares Hume's view that as long as submission underpins order, we are better off than under conditions of widespread discord. What is more, actual consent may not even be a necessary condition. Is a liberal government illegitimate because it does not enjoy the support of that part of a population that harbours racist and sexist attitudes? Any consent that might be forthcoming must be based on the right reasons. We speak of consent and *a fortiori*

[12] See D Hume, 'Of the Origin of Government' in *Writings*, n 9, 194–97.

[13] See D Hume, 'Of the Original Contract' in *Writings*, n 9, 164–82, 171.

[14] I am taking my cue from Jürgen Habermas, who famously stated 'Legitimität bedeutet, dass der mit einer politischen Ordnung verbundene Anspruch, als richtig und gerecht anerkannt zu werden, gute Argumente für sich hat; eine legitime Ordnung verdient Anerkennung. *Legitimität bedeutet die Anerkennungswürdigkeit einer politischen Ordnung.*' In English, 'Legitimacy means that the claim associated with a political order to be recognised as right and just is supported by good arguments; a legitimate order deserves recognition. *Legitimacy means that a political order is worthy of recognition.*' See J Habermas, 'Legitimationsprobleme im modernen Staat' in his *Zur Rekonstruktion des Historischen Materialismus* (Frankfurt aM, Suhrkamp, 1976) 271–303, 271.

of a social contract only because of reasons that can be shared, subject to reciprocity, by people who are free and equal. Legitimate authority is a matter of general or universal rationality or reasonableness. This, and nothing else, is the core idea underlying the 'social contract', understood as a hypothetical agreement among the governed. This agreement is, however, if it is anything at all, nothing but the *implicit* mutual pledge to observe the normative constraints of human reasoning before consenting. Consent must never be based on considerations that are entirely frivolous or even foolish.

From *de jure* to *de facto* Authority and Back

The question of authority arises in consequence of a predicament that natural law theory cannot resolve. In it inheres a basic incapacity, not least because it must recoil from admitting the obstinacy of the problem. Granting that natural reason provides us with insight into what is right or wrong, it still needs to be determined who ought to have the power to ascertain – and to give effect to – what reason requires with relevance for all. The matter is as paradoxical as it is exigent. It is paradoxical, for natural law theory is supposed to render the second step redundant. Natural law is *natural* and therefore amenable to rational insight by all. Anyone should be able to say what it is. Its recognition must be person-neutral. What the stories told about the hypothetical state of nature reveal, however, is that owing to the influence of passion, self-interest, rivalry and the very generality of its principles, people are likely to disagree over what such natural law requires. The enduring conflicts over what comports with right reason explain why authority is necessary to put controversy to an end.

But might the authority also get it wrong – legitimately, that is? Can what is wrongly cast as natural law be binding?

Interestingly, authority does not sever the connection with reason. The validity of its directives is based on the double bind of their having to be correct and being authoritative even if they are not.[15] They depend on reflecting sound reasons while pre-empting the relevance of inquiries into their existence. The double bind explains why, with the turn to the justification of authority, the underlying understanding of reasonableness becomes profoundly altered. Now the decisive question is under what conditions

[15] See, on the dependence thesis and the pre-emption theses, respectively, Raz, n 3, 47, 57–58.

the status of authority is immune from nullification, even if we come to believe the authority to be wrong in some instances. Since the question would recur indefinitely if we allocated the adjudication of authoritativeness to another, higher authority,[16] the recognition of authority becomes, lest authority be authoritarian,[17] attitude-dependent. Authority exists where we believe ourselves to have reason for its existence.[18] Invariably, therefore, a *de facto* element enters into our determination of *de jure* authority.[19]

Attitude-dependence, however, is also relevant for what the authority regards to be right reason. We take to be law what the authority believes to be such because we consider authority to be authority. The double bind, sketched above, marks the break with the natural law tradition. The authority of law is historical. Reasonableness concerns the conditions for accepting practical authority. Since, owing to the attitude-dependence of the recognition of authority, we have to make the relevant determinations ourselves, the conditions of reasonableness are set out in the course of collective self-determination.

The Hobbesian Gambit: Rationality

There are many reasons to regard Thomas Hobbes as one of the most outstanding legal and political philosophers of all times.[20] There are the wit and humour inherent in his style of exposition,[21] and the unmatched radical consequence to which he pushed the alternative between peace

[16] See Hobbes, n 4, VI.17, 88.

[17] See my analysis in 'Delegation and Authority: Authoritarian Liberalism Today' (2015) 21 *European Law Journal* 340–60.

[18] In a remarkable analytical hairsplitting exercise, Placani distinguishes between the belief in the legitimacy of authority and the acceptance of authority as if it were legitimate. The only progress made in this context is the admission of attitude-dependence of attributions of authority. See A Placani, 'Joseph Raz's Service Conception and the Limits of Knowablity' (2021) 34 *Ratio Iuris* 207–23, 219–16.

[19] This may explain why Norberto Bobbio believed that, in the case of Hobbes, all law is positive law and natural law only the basic norm of the positive legal order. See his *Thomas Hobbes and the Natural Law Tradition* (trans D Gobetti, Chicago, IL, University of Chicago Press, 1993) 141, 148.

[20] The British, somewhat understatedly, usually claim that Hobbes was the greatest political philosopher of the Anglophone tradition. See M Oakeshott, *Rationalism in politics and other essays* (Indianapolis, IN, Liberty Fund, 1991) 223. See also, from a Canadian perspective, D Gauthier, *Moral Dealing: Contract, Ethics, and Reason* (Ithaca, NY, Cornell University Press, 1990) 11.

[21] See, for example, his explanation of the state of war: 'For WARRE, consisteth not in Battell onely, or the act of fighting; but in a tract of time, wherein the Will to contend by Battell is sufficiently known: and therefore the notion of *Time*, is to be considered in the nature of Warre; as it is in the nature of Weather. For as the nature of Foule weather, lyeth not in a showre or two of rain; but in an inclination thereto for many dayes together: So the nature of War, consisteth not in actuall fighting; but in the known disposition thereto, during all the time there is no assurance to the contrary. All other time is PEACE.' T Hobbes, *Leviathan* (ed I Shapiro, New Haven, CT, Yale University Press, 2010) 77–78 [62].

and returning to the 'natural' situation of war. While all of this confers on his work unique marks of distinction, his greatness inheres in fusing the arguments from rationality and reasonableness into one. Putting it more cautiously, Hobbes' arguments in support of the existence of authority can be presented as appeals to our self-interest in a context in which rational conduct yields reasonableness as its supervening result. Conversely, they implicitly engage our reasonableness – that is, our sense of reciprocity – by suggesting that its absence would harm our self-interest.

The first is obvious in his presentation of the state of nature.[22] Hobbes begins with our inclination to pursue our self-interest, the desire for self-preservation being paramount, based on our natural freedom to do what we want.[23] He casts this freedom, the 'right of nature',[24] as a 'right to everything',[25] which is, in Hohfeldian terms, a mere privilege, for it is not correlated with a duty.[26] Everyone can do anything they deem necessary to serve their rational self-interest; however, they can, at the same time, be prevented by everyone else, with all possible means, from attaining their objectives.[27] As is well known, the unsafety inherent in such a situation makes it rational to engage in pre-emptive strikes against others.[28] Since all are simultaneously going to do the same, the resulting situation amounts to a war of everyone against everyone else.[29] Life is, as the possibly most often-quoted line from *Leviathan* illustrates, 'solitary, poore, nasty, brutish and short'.[30]

We need not dwell on what is well known about Hobbes' theory, namely that the state of nature is overcome by the surrender ('laying down')[31] of the right to everything and the submission to unconstrained sovereign power,

[22] ibid 78–79 [63].
[23] See Hobbes, n 4, XIV.3, 156, where he characterises 'right' as a natural liberty created not by law but by the absence of restriction.
[24] See Hobbes, n 21, 79–80 [64].
[25] ibid 80 [64].
[26] See JJ Thomson, *The Realm of Rights* (Cambridge, MA, Harvard University Press, 1990) 49–50.
[27] See Hobbes, n 4, I.12, 29.
[28] See Hobbes, n 21, 77 [61].
[29] ibid 79 [63].
[30] ibid 78 [62].
[31] See ibid 81 [65]. It should be noted, however, that only as much liberty is to be surrendered as is necessary for the sake of peace, and the surrender is subject to reciprocity. Human beings ought to content themselves with as much liberty against others as they would be willing to concede to others towards themselves. This is Hobbes' second law of nature. See ibid 80 [64]–[65]. See also Hobbes, n 4, II.3, 34. See also S Darwall, *Modern Moral Philosophy: From Grotius to Kant* (Cambridge, Cambridge University Press, 2023) 42.

that is, to the one whose right to everything remains unscathed.[32] What is remarkable, from our perspective, is the minimalism of Hobbes' argument In contrast to Grotius and his followers, there is no – decidedly no – reference to an innate social appetite.[33] Likewise, there obtains no prior connection, as in the Aristotelian polis, among the people.[34] Human beings are essentially unrelated.[35] A society is the product of self-love, not of the love of friends.[36] Of *oikeiôsis* remains, hence, only its most rudimentary, yet also most tenacious, instantiation, namely self-preservation.[37] The hypothetical war situation first and foremost appeals to our self-interest.

A law of nature, Hobbes explains, is merely a general rule, discovered by reason, telling humans what they ought to do or omit to preserve their lives.[38] Laws seem to appeal to *rationality* only, and amount to saying that in the long or even shorter term we would all be worse off if each and every one of us availed ourselves of the right to everything. Hence, we had better trade this for the peaceful coordination of conduct subject to the conditions laid down by sovereign power.[39] Interestingly, behind the use of calculating

[32] See Hobbes, n 21, 108 [90], 160 [137]–[138]; Hobbes, n 4, I.14, 31.

[33] See Hobbes, n 21, 77 [61]: '[M]en have no pleasure, (but on the contrary a great deal of griefe) in keeping company, where there is no power able to over-awe them all.' For an illustration of this point that sounds bitter because Hobbes reports how much people enjoy putting one another down, see Hobbes, n 4, I.2, 22–23.

[34] See Hobbes, n 21, 103–04 [86], where Hobbes explains why human beings, unlike ants or bees, are not political animals. First, humans continually compete for honour and dignity. The envy and hatred that results from this leads to war. Second, there is no organic connection between the private and the common good.

[35] See Darwall, n 31, 40.

[36] See Hobbes, n 4, I.2, 24.

[37] See Hobbes, n 21, 79–80 [64]; Hobbes, n 4, I.7, 27, where Hobbes compares the drive for self-preservation to the law of gravity. It is, he claims, a 'real necessity of nature as powerful as that by which a stone falls downwards'.

[38] See Hobbes, n 4, II.1, 33; Hobbes, n 21, 80 [64]. Laws are only conclusions or theorems concerning what is conducive to self-preservation. See Hobbes, n 21, 98 [80]. See also ibid 126–27 [107]. where Hobbes claims that the skill of making and maintaining a commonwealth consists of certain rules, as do arithmetic and geometry. Laws properly so called are only the sovereign's command. See ibid 98 [80].

[39] In a similar vein, Schneewind concludes that normative laws reflect psychological necessities. We are necessitated by fear to preserve peace. See JB Schneewind, *The Invention of Autonomy: A History of Modern Moral Philosophy* (Cambridge, Cambridge University Press, 2010) 90. In spite of what Hobbes himself says about self-preservation as a 'real necessity of nature' (see n 37), it is possible to conceive of it also in normative terms, hence as a mandatory aim – and it may be regarded as a strength of Hobbes' theory that it can *also* be construed as an obligation that is backed up by the fear of death and that the issue does not have to be settled whether self-preservation is a mechanical or teleological law (and as the latter subject to reflective endorsement). After all, there is no other way of accounting for real obligations in a Hobbesian context than the fact of required conduct's being backed up by strong passions, of which fear of death is arguably the strongest. Thus understood, the right of nature vis-à-vis others is a right that all have to have in order to fulfil the obligation to preserve themselves, an obligation that humans have either towards themselves or towards the Creator. It bears mentioning that a correlation of a duty towards the Creator and the liberty towards others would later be established for freedom of religion

rationality lurks the tension between, and complementarity of, reason and passion.[40] While people are amenable to being governed by rational insight, reason could not motivate lest it be supported by passions. Passions are generally more potent than reason.[41] The laws of nature are contrary to the natural passions that carry us to partiality, pride and revenge.[42] Passions must therefore be counterbalanced by other passions to make rational behaviour possible. Fear is one of the most powerful of these. Hence, it is necessary to steer us towards conduct that is rational vis-à-vis the laws of nature. This explains why Hobbes believes all true obligation (*foro externo*)[43] to be based on fear.[44] Only the public sword has the force to oblige.[45]

Hobbesian Gambit: Reasonableness

At the same time, however, the state-of-nature argument also demonstrates that exercising one's right to everything is also *unreasonable*, for it cannot be universalised.[46] This can be clearly seen by recasting Hobbes' hypothetical experiment[47] in the terms of Kant's first test for the universalisation of maxims under the categorial imperative.[48] It amounts to examining whether a maxim suffers from what O'Neill calls a 'contradiction in conception'.[49] One needs to imagine what the overall social situation would be like if the maxim or

by James Madison in his 'Memorial and Remonstrance Against Religious Assessments' in *Writings* (ed J Rakove, New York, Library of America, 1999) 29–36, 30.

[40] See Hobbes, n 21, 79, 114 [63], [96].

[41] ibid 114 [96].

[42] ibid 102 [85].

[43] According to Hobbes, ibid 97 [79], the laws of nature oblige only *foro interno*, and 'bind to a desire they should take place'. If they are backed up by sanctions, they are also applicable *foro externo*.

[44] See ibid. Of course, Hobbes mentions other passions that incline humans to peace, such as the desire of things necessary for leading a comfortable life and the hope to obtain them by one's own industry. See ibid 79 [63]. Evidently, people possessed by religious zeal, racial hatred or a desire to restore the glory of their nation are not amenable to Hobbes' argument in favour of a social contract.

[45] See ibid 107 [89]. In *On the Citizen*, n 4, XIV.2, 155, Hobbes explains, with an eye to the original compact, that man is obligated by an agreement but kept to his obligation by law, ie the fear of penalty.

[46] This explains why there is another strand of Hobbes' interpretation that emphasises the important role of reciprocity in Hobbes' theory. See S Lloyd, *Morality in the Philosophy of Thomas Hobbes* (Cambridge, Cambridge University Press, 2009); Darwall, n 31, 54–55.

[47] See, however, on the state of nature in 'the Americans', Hobbes, n 4, I.13, 30. See also Hobbes, n 21, 78 [63].

[48] See I Kant, *Grundlegung zur Metaphysik der Sitten* (ed B Kraft and D Schönecker, Hamburg, Meiner 1999) 47. For a useful introduction, see R Johnson and A Cureton, 'Kant's Moral Philosophy' in *Stanford Encyclopedia of Philosophy* at https://plato.stanford.edu/entries/kant-moral/ 17–19 (pdf view).

[49] See O O'Neill, *Acting on Principle: An Essay on Kantian Ethics*, 2nd edn (Cambridge, Cambridge University Press, 2013) 152–58. For a highly useful explanation of the 'test' of maxims pursuant to Kant's explication of the categorical imperative, and the contradiction in conception component in particular, see Johnson and Cureton, n 48.

rule underlying one's own conduct were to be realised by all as though they were puppets on the strings of a relentless universal law of nature.[50] While the right to everything can be regarded as our maxim, the consequence of its realisation as a universal law would be that nobody could enjoy it. What purports to be a natural right is unreasonable. Such a right cannot be part of the *law* of nature.[51]

Avoiding the state of nature is, therefore, not only a maxim of rationality but also a matter of reasonableness.[52] In the first round, concededly, we are motivated to follow the laws of nature on rational grounds. The state of nature (or its anticipation) forces us to act according to the first law of nature, which requires us to seek peace if we can be reasonably confident of attaining it.[53]

The second law of nature demands accepting as much natural liberty of others as one would like to enjoy oneself. This is not a matter of mere rationality. The latter would only call for the maximisation of one's own freedom, requiring concessions to others only to the extent necessary to keep them down and calm. At the same time, the second law of nature needs to be complemented with the third,[54] which makes the performance of the reciprocal deal also rational by backing it up with irresistible sovereign power. The realisation of reasonableness, were it not assisted by rationality, would be constantly upset by passions and the lure of short-term advantages.[55] Fear is the cunning emotional instrument of reason, which motivates rationality to pull, like a reliable mule, its cart.[56] In the civil state, the fear of others is replaced with the fear of sovereign power.

The reasonableness of the commands of the sovereign, by contrast, is vouchsafed by the reasonableness of the sovereign's authority.[57] We thus rationally create or yield to what is reasonable.

[50] What is so fascinating about Hobbes' argument is that there is a natural inclination on the part of humans to act, where state authority does not exist, as though they had a right of nature. Uninhibited by rational insight, the situation of war is the universal law of nature. All human beings are born unfit for society and have to be made fit for it by training. See Hobbes, n 4, I.2, 25.

[51] The science of the laws of nature is the 'only Moral Philosophy'. Hobbes, n 21, 97 [79].

[52] Schneewind, n 39, 84, fn 5, points out that Hobbes' political philosophy serves a conservative function. It is about avoiding falling into the state of nature; it can scarcely show fanatics who have already fallen into it a way out.

[53] See Hobbes, n 4, II.2, 34.

[54] See Hobbes, n 21, 88–89 [71]–[72]; Hobbes, n 4, XIV.12, 158.

[55] See Hume, n 9, 49.

[56] Fear of death is, however, complemented occasionally by the craving for glory. See Hobbes, n 4, IV.21, 64. See also Schneewind, n 39, 87.

[57] See Hobbes, n 4, XIV.10, 158–59, where Hobbes explains that the obligation to obey the law is 'older' than the positive law itself, for it is part of the original covenant. Therefore, no civil law can be contrary to natural law (even though Hobbes makes a remarkable exception for blasphemy).

And yet neither Hobbes nor we can be too sure that Hobbes was right about that. We are going to return to this matter below.

Gauthier's View of Supervenience

Undoubtedly, David Gauthier's crisp and sharp analysis of Hobbes' moral theory offers an erudite account of what is involved in reasonableness supervening on rationality, even if Gauthier does not use the distinction between these types of reasoning and speaks instead of 'natural' and 'conventional' reason.[58]

In his view, moral conventions have the laws of nature as their grounds, of which the second law is the 'cornerstone'.[59] Gauthier understands conventions in Lewisian terms.[60] A convention is some rule followed because, owing to its coordinative function, its observance by all is in the interest of each. An example of conventions are traffic regulations. Generally, conventions would be, Gauthier explains, pointless if following them did not benefit the actors; they would be redundant if the actors did what conventions stipulate anyway without heeding their existence, and also if others did not do the same.[61] The concern with seeing conventions observed reflects the actors' interest in not falling prey to the treachery of others. Following a convention can be in the agent's self-interest only so long as others reliably observe it too.[62] Otherwise, it would be redundant.

Obviously, there is the always present lure of defection, which means that it may be in the agent's self-interest to ignore a convention, without being found out, while others adhere to it. We shall return to this problem posed by Hobbes' 'fool' (see 'Another Taxing Situation' below). This explains why conventions are often unstable.[63] In the state of nature, the laws of nature bind only *foro interno*,[64] and this may give everyone reason to suspect non-compliance with conventional standards by others. Indeed, everyone must expect that people will not do what is required by

[58] See Gauthier, n 20, 21.

[59] ibid 15. Strangely, Gauthier, ibid, claims that the laws of nature are not themselves moral principles. This contention is very difficult to square with their ostensible moral content, not least with the reciprocity condition already inherent in the second law, let alone in matters such as 'complaisance' or respecting the equality of others.

[60] See D Lewis, *Convention: A Philosophical Study* (Oxford, Basil Blackwell, 1968). See also A Marmor, *Social Conventions: From Language to Law* (Princeton, NJ, Princeton University Press, 2009).

[61] See Gauthier, n 20, 16, 48.

[62] See A Marmor, *Philosophy of Law* (Princeton, NJ, Princeton University Press, 2011) 74–75.

[63] See Gauthier, n 20, 49.

[64] See Hobbes, n 21, 97 [79].

a convention if doing so promises them some personal gain.[65] Anticipating shirking by others, it becomes ever more rational to default on conventional behaviour oneself.[66]

Stated in Gauthier's terminology, this is a consequence of the prevalence of 'natural reason'. It is manifest in the type of instrumental reasoning underpinning the right of nature qua licence to do whatever one may find conducive to one's own preservation and good. Gauthier therefore suggests that covenanting and the original compact must involve the transmutation of reason into a 'conventional' format.[67] In our terms, this means shifting from rationality to reasonableness.

Conventions are relevant in two different ways.[68] First, the conventions of morality reflect, according to Gauthier, the laws of nature; second, the conventional form of reasoning is necessary to overcome the situation of war to which we would remain forever locked owing to our natural reason (ie, rationality). Gauthier designates this transition by pointing to the change of objective. One transcends simple self-preservation as the standard of reason in favour of the broader objective of peace. In covenanting and, hence, laying down one's right to everything, 'one has renounced natural reason as the court of appeal, in favor of a reason that dictates to every man what all agree is good'.[69] Gauthier explains that this involves a change in the trump card winning the reasoning process. The subjectivity of our ends makes natural reason unfit to give rise to peace, for – as the instability of moral conventions indicates, which persists as long as they are not supported by conventional reason – it makes us revert invariably to the situation of war. Only if each takes peace to be trumps can this situation be overcome. One adheres to a convention, even if one might in an extant situation benefit from its breach, with the understanding that its stability is good for all, including oneself as an element of all. This signifies the shift from hostility to sociability.[70] Moral conventions must be buttressed by overcoming the gravitational pull of natural reason. They demand that we pursue our interest only by also taking the interest

[65] As Gauthier, n 20, 19, points out, morality would not constrain if doing what is morally required would always be to one's own advantage.

[66] Gauthier, ibid 18, describes the situation as follows: 'Each may pretend peace, but only the better to anticipate his fellows. The laws of nature offer no escape from the ills of our natural condition.'

[67] In another context, Gauthier speaks of a shift from straightforward to constrained maximisation as the shift from economic to political rationality. See ibid 232, 346–47, 349.

[68] Gauthier, ibid 12, speaks of a 'dual conventionalism, in which a conventional reason, superseding natural reason, justifies a conventional morality, constraining natural behavior'.

[69] ibid 21.

[70] ibid 348.

of all others into account. While it is, in light of attaining one's long-term objective of safety (which is broadly understood by Hobbes),[71] rational to *become* reasonable, there may be many instances in which we sense that it is not rational to comport ourselves reasonably, given that some small advantage can be reaped from an infidelity.[72]

'Peace' is an end that we share, and it is in light of this objective that desires and interests of others become *equally real for each*. This, indeed, can be seen as marking the point at which self-concerned rationality is 'superseded'[73] by reasonableness, for if people are interested in peace, they must take interests of others into account. The interest in peace is 'rational', but not rational in terms of the right of nature. In addition, people accept the means, the laws of nature, that are necessary to attain survival as an end or, more precisely, as categorical imperatives formulating *deontological constraints*.

What does not become fully clear in Gauthier's reconstruction, however, is how reciprocity enters the picture. Why do human beings, using their natural reason, arrive at the second law of nature? Why do reciprocity and the recognition of natural equality[74] occur to them as pointing the way forward? It may well be the case that the contending persons simply rediscover something they have experienced already in more intimate settings[75] and project it to a situation in which they encounter each other as strangers. Since reciprocity appears to be decisive, one must be sceptical of the idea that moral constraints are 'conventions', for it is the mark of conventions to involve substantive arbitrariness. Yet it is quite inconceivable that the transition to reasonableness could be made based on haphazard standards.

Another Taxing Situation

Hobbes claims straightforwardly that the 'terror of some power' is needed for covenants to be fully binding: 'And Covenants, without the Sword, are

[71] See Hobbes, n 4, XIII.4, 143–44.

[72] The matter is very succinctly captured by Gauthier, n 20, 232–33. What is needed, according to Gauthier, is a 'conventional rationality' that calls for adherence to agreements against the dictates of individual utility-maximisation. The rationality is, however, grounded in such maximisation. See ibid 346–47.

[73] ibid 22.

[74] See the eighth and ninth law of nature in Hobbes, n 21, 94 [76]–[77].

[75] See Gauthier, n 20, 352–54, where he claims that contractarian thinking exposes love as an opium of the people that makes them unduly sacrifice their interest to those of others, but which is nonetheless functionally necessary to sustain systems of constrained rationality or reasonableness. Contractarian ideologies are, therefore, practically incoherent.

but Words, and of no strength to secure a man at all.'[76] This statement is, however, underinclusive from the perspective of the argument that supports it. It does not pay heed to another situation in which rationality is supposed to bring about the reasonable result. This is the situation of the 'fool'. It is discussed after Hobbes introduces the third law of nature, saying that men ought to perform the agreements that they conclude among themselves. This law is, according to Hobbes, the 'Fountain & Originall of JUSTICE'.[77] While there can be no injustice where there is no original covenant,[78] the non-performance of contractual obligations is the very definition of injustice.[79]

Against this background, the 'fool' stands for persons realising that it may be to their own advantage – and hence rational – to default on contractual obligations.[80] All people pledge to pay a certain amount of money into a fund, depending on their circumstances.[81] Every smart person has a reason to cheat as long as they are not likely to be found out. Hobbes claims that such behaviour is irrational, for such fools cannot reckon with others' being so easily deceived and should expect their machinations to become publicly exposed at some point. If that happened, nobody would want to cooperate with them any longer.[82] Interestingly, Hobbes says that this is also of relevance for the state of nature where everyone depends on the support of confederates to prevail over enemies. This would seem to imply, contrary to what Hobbes claims on other occasions about the powerlessness of mere promises, that even in the state of nature, agreements can be binding and give rise to an obligation to perform, at least as long as there is no reason to suspect that by doing so one is likely to fall prey to others who will subsequently renege.[83]

This situation matches almost exactly the one referred to by Kant to demonstrate that breaking promises cannot be universalised. Kant's argument may appear stronger than Hobbes' on the ground of using a publicity

[76] Hobbes, n 21, 102 [85]. See also ibid 89 [73].
[77] ibid 88 [71].
[78] ibid 89 [72].
[79] ibid 88 [71]. See, however, Hobbes, n 4, IV.21, 64, where Hobbes claims that mere external obedience is not morally meritorious and 'unjust'.
[80] See Hobbes, n 21, 89 [73]. See also the summary in Darwall, n 31, 52–53.
[81] Think of the small donations made during religious services.
[82] See Hobbes, n 21, 90 [73].
[83] Hobbes' statements are not easy to reconcile with one another. See Hobbes, n 21, 84–86 [68]–[69]. The adequacy of the concern that others will not perform is to be determined by the parties themselves. See Hobbes, n 4, II.11, 37.

condition.[84] Suppose that everyone knew that fools are not honouring their contractual obligations; it would be clear to everyone that one should avoid concluding contracts with them or not rely on a fool's word. The internal contradiction of the conduct is more clearly revealed if the conduct of the fools is hypothetically imagined to be a universal law of nature. If all contractual obligations were consistently and persistently breached, the institution of contract would disappear altogether. One cannot give and breach one's word and thereby create a social setting in which, if universalised, the institution of promise would vanish due to the promisees' widespread distrust in the faithfulness of promisors. Again, we encounter in Hobbes a tacit appeal to reasonableness, which is cast in the idiom of rationality. Owing to the risk of being exposed and ostracised as a defector, one is rationally required to behave reasonably. At the same time, Hobbes' way of presenting the argument is not entirely persuasive. Depending on the circumstances, it may well be rational to bet on the gullibility of promisees.

Representing the Reasonable and Rational

In *De Cive*, Hobbes seems to believe, at least as long as one's own survival in the state of nature is at stake, in an obligation to perform and to make the first move unless one has indications that others will likely not reciprocate.[85] One cannot be expected to make oneself into the prey of others and to procure one's certain ruin.[86] This condition appears to be plausible. Yet it nonetheless follows that covenants must be binding in a state of nature, for otherwise there would be no way out of this adverse condition.[87] The covenant is irrevocable[88] and, in the civil state, its unilateral renunciation would amount to treason.[89]

Again, rationality is supposed to make us converge on the reasonable result. Kant's universal-law-of-nature test and Hobbes' state of nature are devices for eliminating maxims in a manner resembling Rawls' original

[84] See Kant, n 48, 47.

[85] See Hobbes, n 4, II.11, 37.

[86] See Hobbes, n 21, 97 [79].

[87] ibid 90 [73]. See Darwall, n 31, 53.

[88] Hobbes' statements are somewhat ambivalent. On the one hand, he says that the transfer of full power to the rulers (which in fact merely leaves them with their right to everything) is not unilaterally revocable, but he also insinuates that a unanimous revocation of consents might be possible, even if he considers its occurrence to be unlikely. See Hobbes, n 4, VI.9, 69 and VI.9, 89: 'By no stretch of the imagination could it ever happen that all citizens together would unite in conspiracy against sovereign power, without one single exception.'

[89] ibid XIV.20, 165. This act is punishable by natural right. See ibid XIV.21, 166.

position. The latter is a hypothetical situation of deliberation constructed to deduce principles of social justice from a point of view supposedly yielding impartial results.[90] The deliberating parties are prevented from knowing the social positions and views of the good life of the people whom they represent, and hence are ignorant of the persons' race, sex, ethnic group or various endowments such as strength or intelligence. The parties are, figuratively speaking, behind a 'veil of ignorance'. Interestingly, this idea can be given a Hobbesian twist by stipulating that the represented are allowed to lie about their circumstances and who in fact they are. The wealthy could claim to be needy and the inept boast about their genius. In such a situation of universal uncertainty and distrust, the parties would have to proceed as if they were behind such a veil of ignorance. Universal impartiality would again be a product of universal strategic partiality. What makes the matter noteworthy is that reasonableness would even here supervene on rationality.[91]

Given both the universal exercise of the right to everything and the problem of the fool, it becomes all the more plausible that Hobbes takes for granted the convergence of rationality and reasonableness when he asserts, first, that the laws of nature are instruments for the pursuit of one's own interest,[92] and, second, that the easiest way to remember their content is to remember not to do to others what you would not do to yourself.[93] He continues by claiming that, in studying the law of nature, we have nothing else to do than to reverse the perspective between ourselves and others such as to wash out all elements of self-love and partiality.[94] Unsurprisingly, the Hobbesian laws of nature confront us with elementary demands of reciprocity or even of unrequited kindness, such as a return of some benefit upon the receipt of a gift,[95] the obligation of 'complaisance', which is the equivalent of Pufendorf's sociability, namely, one's aptness to society,[96] to abstain

[90] See J Rawls, *Justice as Fairness: A Restatement* (ed E Kelly, Cambridge, MA, Harvard University Press, 2001) 15.

[91] Darwall, n 31, 58 suggests, however, that 'individuals who recognize and know one another to recognize only reasons of self-interest cannot covenant'. By using the verb 'supervene' I mean to refer to an occurrence of 'supervenience', ie some new type of being emerging from the ground of other already existing beings. See D Davidson, *Essays on Actions and Events* (Oxford, Oxford University Press, 1980) 214.

[92] See Hobbes, n 21, 98 [90].

[93] ibid 96 [79]. The laws of nature, Hobbes repeats later (ibid 163 [140]), need neither publishing nor proclamation, for they are 'contained in this one Sentence, approved by all world, Do not that to another, which thou thinkest unreasonable to be done by another to thy selfe'. And he summarises the second law of nature by appeal to this law of the Gospel (ibid 81 [65]). See also Hobbes, n 4, IV.23, 65.

[94] See Hobbes, n 21, 96 [79].

[95] ibid 92–93 [75]–[76].

[96] ibid 93 [76].

from amassing so much superfluous wealth that others become envious,[97] or the obligation to forgive offences repented by the offending parties (pardon is the granting of peace).[98] For Hobbes, the laws of nature are immutable and eternal.[99] He ends with the following final gloss with which he summarises their import in the language of individual virtue:

> For Injustice, Ingratitude, Arrogance, Pride, Iniquity, Acception of persons and the rest, can never be made lawful. For it can never be that Warre shall preserve life and Peace destroy it.[100]

The Problem of Sovereign Authority

The laws of nature give us the substance of reasonable arrangements among human beings. The question remains, however, of who is going to flesh out their meaning and implications in particular circumstances. This is the question of authority. Since the major *substantive* issue is the preservation of peace, the calibration of authority's scope must be severed from its dependence on the judgement of those subject to it. This is what makes Hobbes' approach both fascinating and enigmatic. Whoever possesses authority is supposed to make right choices pursuant to natural laws; but in order to sustain peace, whosoever is responsible for its exercise must be immune from any external review on the ground of these laws.[101] The tension can easily be increased to a point at which it becomes paradoxical. Then it means that you have authority only if you make the right decisions, but taking you to be right depends on disabling everyone else from reviewing, judging or evaluating your choices. This is a game that the sovereign is positioned to win with ease.

Hobbesian sovereigns must not be partners to an agreement but merely beneficiaries of an authorisation[102] or of a multilateral submission to the power of another.[103] Hobbes understands, however, that by virtue of

[97] ibid.

[98] ibid.

[99] See Hobbes, n 4, XIV.4, 156, where Hobbes explains that natural law is of divine origin since it is the manifestation of God's eternal word that is innate in the natural reason of human beings. It is from God and therefore divine law. The divine law that has been revealed by Jesus, the prophets and the apostles in the Bible is positive divine law, which is, as Hobbes goes to some length to demonstrate, fully congruent with natural law. See ibid, IV.1, 58; XIV.4, 156; and IV.2-24, 59–65.

[100] Hobbes, n 21, 97 [79].

[101] See Hobbes, n 4, VI.17, 88.

[102] See Hobbes, n 21, 104–05 [87].

[103] See Hobbes, n 4, V.7, 72. The matter is slightly different, however, in the case of sovereignty by acquisition, where the vanquished unilaterally surrender to the victor. See Hobbes, n 21, 131–32 [111]–[112]. The surrender is followed by a covenant in which the sovereign is given full control over the

authorisation or submission, the sovereign then comes to formulate a will that is common to all subjects. Sovereignty is indispensable for creating a single will in human beings on matters such as safety and defence.[104] It is by means of sovereign authority that the members of the multitude are able to make themselves into one author and one agent.[105] It would be a grave mistake, therefore, to assume that outside of such constituted authority the authentic representatives of the 'true people' might be encountered in some rebellious or otherwise unruly crowd.[106]

Were the sovereigns partners to agreements, they could be held to account for what they do.[107] But sovereigns could never be partners to such an agreement, for they could not even conclude it with the multitude as a whole. Before being represented by the sovereign, the multitude does not exist as a united body.[108] Moreover, if the sovereign concluded an agreement with members of the multitude severally, not only would they contract with themselves (and could per sovereign power release themselves from their duty against themselves),[109] but they would also not be in a position to complain about an act of the sovereign they have authorised.[110] In whatever the sovereign does or ordains, it is their will that they encounter. The people 'own' the actions of the sovereign: *volenti non fit injuria.*[111]

The link between authority and the sovereigns' power to adopt as civil law their own views of natural law is the preservation of peace. For if the sovereign were bound to observe certain conditions, not only would this undermine sovereign authority as such, but the ensuing disputes would also

subjects who are then regarded as his servants – servants, but not as slaves kept under physical control. See ibid 123 [103]–[104]. The consequence of sovereignty is the same for sovereignty by institution and sovereignty by acquisition: absolute power. See ibid 124 [104]. For a discussion of these issues, see E Fox-Decent, 'Hobbes' Relational Theory: Beneath Power and Consent' in D Dyzenhaus and T Poole (eds), *Hobbes and the Law* (Cambridge, Cambridge University Press, 2012) 118–44, 122–23.

[104] See Hobbes, n 4, V.6, 72.

[105] See Hobbes, n 21, 105 [88].

[106] ibid 113 [95]. See also ibid 111 [93]. See also Hobbes, n 4, XII.8, 137.

[107] See Hobbes, n 21, 106 [89].

[108] See Hobbes, n 4, V.9, 73; Hobbes, n 21, 107 [89]. This is difficult to reconcile with Hobbes' contention that once the original contract has been concluded, the bearer of sovereign authority is selected by majority vote. Even those who were defeated in this vote are bound by this selection. See Hobbes, n 21, 107 [90]. Does the institution of the office of the sovereign unify the people without there being a sovereign in person? See ibid 105–07 [88]–[90]. This is also different from the view that he articulated in *De Cive* where he insists – on the occasion of debunking sedition – that it is not a 'natural rule' to take consent of the majority for the consent of all. A rule of this kind must be laid down by sovereign authority. See Hobbes, n 4, IV.20, 89.

[109] Nobody can bind himself. See Hobbes, n 21, 160 [137]–[138].

[110] ibid 106 [88].

[111] ibid 108 [90].

likely lead to outright rebellion and war. This would be substantively wrong. Nothing could be more foolish, according to Hobbes, than to attempt to alter one's form of government, possibly taking one's cue from neighbouring nations, for any such attempt invariably leads to the dissolution of state authority.[112] All opposition is irrational.[113] Hence, the people, in establishing sovereign authority, must divest themselves of their constituent power.[114] The social contract is the abdication of the multitude qua mere heap of people.[115]

The Fate of Natural Law

Peace, the overarching goal of the civil pact, can only be attained based on unconditional surrender. If that principle is sound, it implies that the laws of nature are entirely at the mercy of the sovereigns.[116] Even though it is incumbent on them to respect these laws,[117] in substance they can only amount to what the sovereigns take them to be, since sovereigns are not bound to abide by anyone else's interpretation. Permitting that the principle of unconditional surrender is sound, would this be an acceptable implication? More precisely, should this implication not give us reason to reject the principle?

Undoubtedly, John Locke believed that absolute sovereign power is entirely unacceptable. Here is how he famously stated the objection:

> As if when Men quitting the State of Nature entered into Society, they agreed that all of them but one, should be under the restraint of Laws, but that he should still retain all the Liberty of the State of Nature, increased with Power, and made licentious by Impunity. This is to think that Men are so foolish that they take care to avoid what Mischiefs may be done them

[112] ibid 203 [177]; Hobbes, n 4, XII.13, 140–41.

[113] Hobbes uses the metaphor of different magnifying glasses used by the people. See Hobbes, n 21, 112 [94]: 'For all men are by nature provided of notable multiplying glasses, (that is their Passions and Selfe-love,) through which, every little payment appeareth a great grievance; but are destitute of those prospective glasses, (namely Morall and Civill Science,) to see a farre off the miseries that hang over them, and cannot without such payments be avoyded.'

[114] ibid 106 [88].

[115] In a way, this anticipates Rousseau's idea that the social contract involves a transformation of human beings into citizens. See J-J Rousseau, *The Social Contract* (trans C Betts, Oxford, Oxford University Press, 1994) II.7, 76.

[116] While the safety of the people is the supreme law, the other natural laws are also binding on the sovereigns. The duties are, however, imperfect and cannot be enforced by anyone. See Hobbes, n 4, XIII.2, 143.

[117] ibid XIII.2, 143.

> by *Pole-Cats*, or *Foxes*, but are content, nay think it Safety, to be devoured by *Lions*.[118]

The matter is thus put bluntly: Why trust one beastly creature that is invested with unlimited authority?

Hobbes appeared to believe that checks inherent in rational conduct would take care of the issue,[119] which is in part reflected in his preference for a monarchical sovereign. He believes that monarchical sovereigns will make sure that their people will prosper and enjoy 'innocent liberty',[120] for this will make these sovereigns look good in the eyes of their peers.[121] One could extrapolate from this the idea that prudent sovereigns would do everything in their power to make sure that people can 'hope' to obtain by their industry such things as are necessary to 'commodious living'.[122] Hobbes' understanding of 'safety' sweeps quite broadly, such as to include, beyond survival, 'a happy life so far as that is possible'.[123]

The incredulity with which we must view Hobbes' pre-emption of judging and constraining sovereign authority[124] has recently led to an interesting attempt to reinterpret the Hobbesian project in Lockean terms. Evan Fox-Decent's interpretation of sovereign power puts a premium on

[118] J Locke, *Two Treatises of Government* (ed P Laslett, Cambridge, Cambridge University Press, 1960) 328, II. § 93.

[119] The sovereigns are, of course, interested in preventing revolt (Hobbes, n 4, XIII.2, 143) fuelled by sentiments of frustration and dissatisfaction.

[120] See ibid XIII.6; XIII.15; XIII.17, 144, 151–52. The 'innocent liberty' is linked to the reliable enjoyment of legal rights. Hence, the rule of law appears to be part and parcel of such liberty. See also ibid XIII.16,151. Compromising the independence of the judiciary would lead to war. See Hobbes, n 21, 95 [77]. See also Fox-Decent, n 103, 143. On Hobbes' endorsement of the rule of law, see D Dyzenhaus, 'Hobbes' Constitutional Theory' in Hobbes, n 21, 453–80, 474. A more nuanced picture is drawn by Poole, n 147, 85–87, 94, who suggests that while Hobbes supported legal form in order to bring about stability and tranquility, and believed it to be beneficial for the purpose of government effectiveness, there remained enough space for 'absolute prerogative', in particular the dispensing power, to function as the 'dark matter' of Hobbes' political universe (ibid 90).

[121] See Hobbes, n 21, 114 [96]. It is quite obvious that Hobbes is not terribly fond of multitudes or assemblies of people. They give rise to the desire to outshine others, rhetorical contests, favoritism, factionalism and strife. They are incapable of arriving at sound conclusions. See ibid 101 [83], 103 [86], 114 [96]. Hence, collective sovereigns ought to be avoided. A popular commonwealth lacks cohesion, in his view, and has to be held together by such factors as a common enemy, eminent leaders or the mutual fear of factions. See ibid 159 [136].

[122] ibid 79 [63]. See Hobbes' list of the goods that the citizens expect to enjoy in Hobbes, n 4, XIII.6, 144.

[123] Hobbes, n 4, XIII.4, 143.

[124] Most interestingly, the pre-emption by sovereign power extends to our own judgement. Originally, in the state of nature, we are ourselves the ultimate arbiters of what we regard as either rational or reasonable. See Hobbes, n 4, I.9, 27–28. This changes in the civil condition. Obedience to the civil law is part of the law of nature: Hobbes, n 21, 161 [138] (a clear instance of how pre-emption overrides any concern with substance). Once sovereign power has been established, what accords with reason is publicly determined by the sovereign. See Schneewind, n 39, 93.

trust and fiduciary obligations.[125] As is clear from Hobbes' treatment of the vanquished and the conquering sovereign, the sovereigns grant their subjects liberty. They leave them control over their body. The subjects, in turn, trust the sovereign to respect and to protect their physical integrity.[126] Hobbes actually posits that the vanquished conclude an agreement, at any rate tacitly, to obey the sovereign.[127] But since the attribution of tacit agreements is an all too facile contrivance to avoid more meticulous explorations of actual consent, Fox-Decent reconstructs the relation between sovereigns and their subjects as one of 'trust'.[128] Trust can arise even without the beneficiaries' doing anything to bring it about.[129] The trustees must merely be established by someone demanding that their capacity be exercised in the interest of the beneficiaries.[130] The state and its institutions can thus be taken to stand in a fiduciary relation towards the people.[131] Fox-Decent believes, somewhat remarkably, the concept of automatic trust not to be 'as strained' as the concept of tacit consent.[132] While the reasons undergirding his belief are not easy to parse, the perspective appears to be consistent with two themes undoubtedly to be encountered in Hobbes.

The first is that Hobbes' laws of nature, in particular those concerning the mutual recognition of the covenanters as equals and the adjudicator's commitment to impartiality,[133] are not so easily reconciled with their alleged rational connection to self-preservation.[134] Conceivably, parties would surrender their right to everything, from an entirely self-interested perspective, even in conditions under which they would, for the sake of peace, be worse off or better off than more audacious or more timid parties,

[125] There are traces of this idea to be found in Hobbes' writings, to be sure. See Hobbes, n 4, XIII.4, 144.

[126] See Fox-Decent, n 103, 125.

[127] See Hobbes, n 21, 123 [103]–[104]. The text remains unclear as to whether the vanquished covenant with the sovereign or among themselves, which would be more consistent with the aim of authorisation without strings attached. The vanquished would thus either accede to the covenant providing the basis of the sovereign's authority or use it as a boilerplate. In these agreements the subjects are taken to consent to the original covenant.

[128] A chief anchor of this interpretation is the opening paragraph of chapter 30 of the *Leviathan*, where Hobbes explains that the sovereign was entrusted with sovereign power to protect the safety of the people. See ibid 201 [175].

[129] See Fox-Decent, n 103, 127.

[130] ibid 124. On agents of necessity (*negotiorum gestio* in Roman legal terms), see ibid 127.

[131] ibid 128.

[132] ibid 127.

[133] The commitment to equality is manifest in the 9th and 10th law of nature; the 17th to 19th laws address matters of judicial impartiality. See Hobbes, n 21, 94 [76]–[77], 96 [78].

[134] See Fox-Decent, n 103, 132–33.

or such parties that are momentarily more or less powerful. This, at any rate, has been the point driven home by James Buchanan in his public-choice-informed account of hypothetical original agreements.[135]

Second, Hobbes indicates, on several occasions, that the sovereigns themselves are subject to the law of nature.[136] While it may seem that this obligation exists only towards God,[137] it may make sense, Fox-Decent suggests, to view it in light of the condition under which the laws of nature are suspended owing to the preponderance of the right of nature. These are the conditions of war. Once the sovereigns rule with an iron fist and sustain peace, it is by virtue of their success that they become bound to observe natural law towards their subjects.[138] If they failed to observe it, their authority would disappear and the subjects would return to the state of nature.[139]

Fox-Decent thus retracts the pre-emptive effect of sovereign authority considerably to restore its substantive dependence on faithfulness to the laws of nature. This comes at a cost, however, and the price is the assimilation of Hobbes to Locke.[140] Sovereign authority 'dissolves' at the moment the sovereigns violate their fiduciary obligations.[141] Whether one has been returned to the state of war by whoever wields state authority is left to the

[135] See J Buchanan, *The Limits of Liberty: Between Anarchy and Leviathan* (reissued, Indianapolis, IN, Liberty Fund, 2000).

[136] See Hobbes, n 21, 136 [116]; 195 [169]: 'It is true, that Soveraigns are all subject to the Lawes of Nature; because such Lawes be Divine, and cannot by any man, or Common-wealth be abrogated.' See also Hobbes, n 4, XIV.3, 155, where he claims that civil law cannot permit what is prohibited by divine law. See M Loughlin, *Foundations of Public Law* (Oxford, Oxford University Press, 2010) 87–98.

[137] See Hobbes, n 21, 121 [109].

[138] See Fox-Decent, n 103, 136–37. Fox-Decent, however, bases his argument on the condition under which contractual obligations are also binding *foro externo* in the state of nature, namely, when there is no reason for concern that the other party may renege on their promise. Once sovereign power has been established, sovereigns do not need to worry about their subjects' unilaterally defecting. They simply can't defect owing to the power of the sovereigns. One may well wonder why this same principle can be so easily transferred to non-contractual fiduciary contexts.

[139] ibid 143. It is at this point that the transformation of Hobbes into Locke becomes particularly obvious. This matches precisely how Locke describes the situation in which the dissolution of state authority remits the subjects to the situation of war. See Locke, n 118, 412, 416, 419, II. §§ 221, 226, 232.

[140] Locke was also a proponent of a social contract theory, but his conclusions are radically different from those of Hobbes. According to Locke, people in the state of nature have a right to life, physical integrity, liberty and private property. This right is rooted in the divine law of nature (this sounds familiar to students of medieval natural law theory). Property is acquired originally by mixing one's labour with nature and later transferred by means of trade and barter. Initially, in the state of nature, people need to take the law into their own hands. The partiality with which they assert their rights results in violent conflicts. Therefore, the people decide to entrust to the state their right to protect and to enforce their rights. If that state breaches that trust, the society that has concluded the civil compact has a right of resistance. See Locke, n 118, 270–72, 280, 288, 330–31, 350, 400, 426, II. §§ 6, 19, 27, 95, 124–125, 202, 241.

[141] ibid 407, II. § 212.

subjects themselves to determine.[142] It is exactly this independent judgement that Hobbes abhorred, in particular when it would be, as favoured by Locke,[143] accompanied by an appeal to religious authority.[144] The assimilation of Hobbes to Locke eases the tension between the substantive justification and the pre-emptive effect of sovereignty to the point at which it sacrifices, conversely, the latter for the sake of the former.

Civil Law: Hobbes' Wavering

Hobbes contends, oddly, that there are two ways of making natural law known: the Golden Rule and civil law.[145] Even more puzzlingly, he claims that '[t]he law of Nature, and Civill Law, contain each other, and are of equal extent'.[146] Hobbes hastens to concede, immediately, that the laws of nature are not 'properly laws' but attitudes disposing human beings towards peace, such as equity, justice or gratitude. At this point, Hobbes even reduces natural law to virtues, the prescriptive import of which is binding on people only after having been commanded by sovereign power. A threat of punishment is required.[147]

As to its pedigree, civil law is part of the law of nature, for the law of nature demands that the civil covenant be adhered to.[148] The covenant is given effect because we are afraid of one another.[149] In the civil condition, the fear of one another is replaced with fear of the sovereign.[150] With that Hobbes returns to the core issue.[151] Does the pre-emption inherent in the

[142] ibid 427, II. § 241.

[143] ibid 427, II. §§ 241–242.

[144] See, on erroneous conscience, Hobbes, n 21, 194 [168]–[169]. See also his rejection of William Ames' idea that people should be free to follow their own account of divine law, ibid 173 [149]. This rejection is, however, accompanied by the concession that in all matters of interpretation of divine law, the subjects are bound to follow the opinions of the sovereign, as long as these are not contrary to natural law. See also Schneewind, n 39, 93.

[145] See Hobbes, n 21,163 [140].

[146] ibid 161 [138]. This equation is dismissed as untrue by Harrison, for it remains inconsistent with Hobbesian principles. Natural law is only of advice to the sovereign as to what our obligations ought to be. Law laid down by the sovereign is what is ultimately binding on the subjects. See R Harrison, 'The Equal Extent of Natural and Civil Law' in Dyzenhaus and Poole (eds), n 103, 22–38, 38.

[147] See Hobbes, n 21, 161 [138]; Harrison, n 146, 25. See also T Poole, 'Hobbes on law and prerogative' in Dyzenhaus and Poole (eds), n 103, 68–96, 70.

[148] Hobbes, n 4, XIV.10, 158–59 puts the matter as follows: the obligation to obey the law implies that no civil law can be contrary to natural law, for the obligation to obey positive law is the supreme principle of all law.

[149] See Hobbes, n 21, 86 [69].

[150] ibid 102 [85].

[151] ibid 161 [138].

constitution of sovereign power consume its dependence on the substance of the natural law to which its exercise ought to be committed?

Hobbes' account of what it takes to have true normativity obscures the underlying issue. Hobbes seems to think that only if the required behaviour can be reliably induced by a coercive threat can we speak of a genuine obligation. He therewith renders the 'ought' in indicative form. This is why pre-emption by sovereign authority, which is also not bound by its own laws,[152] eclipses the relevance of the law of nature. Systematically, however, this is not entirely sound. The genealogical significance of this law for the constitution of sovereign authority cuts even deeper than to the third law of nature that requires that covenants be duly observed and is alleged to be 'the fountain of all justice'.[153] The second law of nature demands that everyone be willing to lay down the right of nature, which is the right to everything,[154] to the extent necessary for peace, and to be contented with as much liberty against others as one would concede to others towards oneself.[155] What appears here, for the first time, is the Golden Rule, which Hobbes takes to be shorthand for all natural law.[156] This confirms that the law of nature comprises the terms of the covenant concluded among the subjects.[157] Pursuant to the third law of nature, the covenant ought to be kept. It is therefore difficult to understand why sovereign authority that exists for the sake of securing the mutual bargain should be free to ignore it. It would be like commissioning people to carry out a certain task while at the same time releasing them from the obligation to perform it. It would be flat-out absurd.

The dependence of the constitution of sovereign authority on natural laws may explain why Hobbes constantly wavers between their relevance and the pre-emptive overriding force of sovereign commands.[158] This is most clearly revealed in his account of civil law.[159] While civil law is positive law and exists only at the pleasure of the sovereign,[160] he believes the

[152] ibid 160 [137]–[138].
[153] ibid 88 [71].
[154] ibid 79–80 [64].
[155] ibid 80 [64]–[65].
[156] See Hobbes, n 4, IV.23, 64.
[157] See Hobbes, n 21, 79 [63].
[158] This wavering is a consequence of the double bind identified in 'From De Jure to De Facto Authority and Back' above.
[159] The matter is put more cautiously by Poole, n 147, 95, suggesting that, in the case of Hobbes, law and equity obtain a 'complex relationship'.
[160] See also, for natural law, Hobbes, n 21, 166 [143]. See, on natural law's validity as dependent on the consent of the sovereign, Harrison, n 146, 29.

unwritten law of nature to be relevant for purposes of adjudication.[161] While Hobbes is vehemently opposed to Coke's concept of 'artificial reason'[162] and to a system of precedent,[163] he believes that anyone of sound mind is capable of resolving cases based on natural reason.[164] The first quality of a good judge, Hobbes suggests, is the right understanding of equity, which is dependent not on the long study of scholarly legal commentary but on the capable exercise of natural reason.[165]

Ineluctably, the relevance of authorisation must return as the core issue. The wavering continues. The adjudicators must be authorised by the sovereign to say what the law is.[166] Private commentaries on the law are subject to capricious subtlety ('cavil') and hence likely to cloud the issues in obscurity.[167] At the same time, Hobbes even suggests that natural law might be used to correct statutory language and that it would amount to an insult ('contumely') to suggest that the sovereign did not intend to have a statute construed in a manner that is consistent with natural reason.[168] These are astounding concessions to the idea that the exercise of sovereign authority must involve the use of right reason.[169]

The Problem of Rationality

The problem inherent in Hobbes' wavering can be explored at a more general level, not least because it points to the problem why we, after having chosen sovereigns to deliver safety, should obey them if they fail to make us safe. Obviously, the pre-emptive nature of authority poses the problem of

[161] See Hobbes, n 21, 164 [141]. This is clearly so where civil law is silent on the issue. See Hobbes, n 4, XIV.10, 159. This unwritten law, which is amenable to rational insight, in particular by those lacking legal training, is also assimilated to 'equity', which had its formal base in the Court of Chancery. But Hobbes casually blends the common law ('civil law') with equity to an extent that the common law ('civil law') becomes 'swamped' by equity. See Poole, n 147, 90–93.

[162] See Hobbes, n 21, 162–63 [139]–[140]. See also his *A Dialogue between a Philosopher and a Student of the Common Laws of England* (ed J Cropskey, Chicago, IL, University of Chicago Press, 1997).

[163] See Hobbes, n 21, 167 [144]. See also Poole, n 147, 92.

[164] See Hobbes, n 21, 170 [146].

[165] ibid 170 [146].

[166] ibid 165–67 [142]–[143]. Judges exercise delegated authority. See Dyzenhaus, n 120, 464–65. Generally, Hobbes was not fond of individual opinion, in particular of regarding individuals as entitled to their own views of religious doctrines. See Poole, n 147, 71–74.

[167] See Hobbes, n 21, 168 [144]. See also ibid 166 [143], where Hobbes complains of the fact that the unwritten law of nature has become prey to passionate and interested interpreters. It must be rescued from being rendered obscure by 'able interpreters'. Hobbes does not explain, alas, who these interpreters might be.

[168] ibid 169 [145]–[146].

[169] See Poole, n 147, 91, who correctly cautions the reader that it is merely a presumption that the sovereign wishes to legislate in accordance with the principles of equity.

irrationality.[170] We surrender our judgement to someone who orders us to do things and are not supposed to put the orders in question. But what if the authority is mistaken?

In order to address this objection to the sway held by authorities, one can consult a theory of authority that asks why authority can be legitimate only so long as it assists us in doing the right thing. Joseph Raz, the proponent of the so-called 'service conception' of authority,[171] has explored the legitimacy of authority along these lines. The core question to be asked about authority is whether it assists us in doing what we ought to do anyway, from a moral point of view. Raz characterises this basic idea as the 'normal justification thesis', which says that

> the normal way to establish that a person has authority over another person involves showing that the alleged subject is likely better to comply with reasons which apply to him (other than the alleged authoritative directives) if he accepts the directives of the alleged authority as authoritatively binding and tries to follow them, rather than by trying to follow the reasons which apply to him directly.[172]

Underlying the normal justification thesis is what Raz calls the 'dependence thesis'. It claims that 'all authoritative directives should be based on reasons which already independently apply to the subjects of the directives'.[173] The core idea is that, from a moral point of view and with the same set of substantive reasons, it might be better for us to have someone else determine our behaviour than to pass judgement on the merits ourselves. The existence of authority, therefore, pre-empts our independent judgement. In other words, the judgment of authority excludes the set of reasons that apply to us independently of its directives. Raz calls this the 'pre-emption thesis'.[174]

The determination that someone possesses authority cannot be made in an ad hoc manner, for if it could, authority would not differ from occasionally following the advice of others. Authority must amount to a status.[175] The

[170] See Simmons, n 7, 32.

[171] For a brief statement, see J Raz, 'The Problem of Authority: Revisiting the Service Conception' in his *Between Authority and Interpretation: On the Theory of Law and Practical Reason* (Oxford, Oxford University Press, 2009) 126–65, 139–40.

[172] J Raz, *The Morality of Freedom* (Oxford, Clarendon Press, 1986) 53 (emphasis omitted).

[173] ibid 47 (emphasis omitted).

[174] ibid 42, 46, 59.

[175] See J Raz, 'Authority, Law, and Morality' in his *Ethics in the Public Domain: Essays in the Morality of Law and Politics* (rev edn, Oxford, Oxford University Press, 1995) 210–37, 215. Amazingly, the question is discussed by Placani, n 18.

status needs to be earned based on the service that the authority provides. If an institution or person qualifies as an authority, then yielding to authority facilitates doing what we have good reason to do. We can, however, attain this goal only by having our own reasoning pre-empted. As Raz explains:

> The whole point and purpose of authorities … is to pre-empt individual judgment on the merits of a case, and this will not be achieved if, in order to establish whether the authoritative determination is binding, individuals have to rely on their own judgments of the merits.[176]

The recognition of authority is therefore based on an exclusionary reason[177] not to follow one's own judgment (or instinct, for that matter), but rather to do as we are told to do by authority.[178] Supposedly, authority is in a position to assist us in doing the right thing owing to greater expertise, greater capacity to coordinate conduct or its ability to overcome collective action problems. Authority loses this standing, however, as soon as one of these reasons for accepting the exclusionary reason is no longer applicable. If the collective action problem of keeping our environment nice and tidy is no longer resolved by following authoritative directives because the requisite rules are neither followed nor enforced, then I am no longer obligated to obey these rules. The authority has, in such a case, disappeared.[179]

The question is, of course, how long we may be warranted in ascribing practical authority to a body that is neither issuing sensible directives nor capable of resolving coordination or collective action problems. This points to the justification of authority, a matter, as Raz acknowledges, that is based on dependent reasons. We correctly ascribe authority if we can be sufficiently confident that the person or body is more likely than we are, within its domain, to get things right: 'At the level of general justification, the pre-empted reasons have an important role to play.'[180]

[176] Raz, n 172, 47–48.

[177] See J Raz, *Practical Reason and Norms*, 2nd edn (Princeton, NJ, Princeton University Press, 1990) 39, where Raz explains that '[a]n exclusionary reason is a second-order reason to refrain from acting for some reason'.

[178] In more recent work, Raz has counterbalanced the 'normal justification thesis' with an 'independence' thesis that suggests that we can have reason (indeed?) to have reasonable acceptance of authority overridden out of concern with the independence of our judgement. See Raz, n 171, 137, 149. An attempt to strike a balance between reasonable acceptance and independence may involve a problem of incommensurability. See Placani, n 18, 218, 221.

[179] See J Raz, 'The Obligation to Obey: Revision and Tradition' in his *Ethics in the Public Domain*, n 175, 341–55, 347.

[180] See Raz, n 175, 215.

But it is at this level that we encounter at least three problems, as a result of which the service concept quickly loses its, admittedly, technocratic charm.

The first is of a Hobbesian variety, namely whether I am making myself a prey to others if I am the only one who acts on an attribution of authority and begins to obey. It suggests that some coordination or consensus is needed for a submission to authority to be sufficiently *reasonable*, at any rate in matters affecting any coordination of conduct or joint action.

The second problem is whether, in the face of different opinions as to the capacities of candidates for authority, we do not need some decision-making rule to arrive at an *authoritative* answer. Again, this engages Hobbesian sensibilities, since we have to know, in advance, whether it would be more beneficial to have some authority rather than none. The matter is thoroughly Hobbesian, for the answer to this question again presupposes a second-order authority that determines the scope within which other authorities should or may be established. In other words, we have to have a political domain determining the scope of authorities. This domain must possess *Kompetenzkompetenz*.

The third problem is an offspring of the second. It concerns a potentially infinite regress. How are we to determine, based on dependent reasons, whether a body possesses authority if there is no authority to assist us in answering this question? The quest for authority indicates, after all, that we are unsure about how to resolve the substantive issue. If we lack expertise as to the substance question, how are we to determine who is more capable than others as regards its exercise?

We can move forward only by recognising that we are independent. Put less euphemistically, it requires accepting that we are on our own. There is no other way to stop the regress. Our own judgement – our own attitude – matters. This casts the dependence thesis into doubt, for the attribution of authority turns out to be more a matter of choosing than of judging wisely. Dependence evaporates in the betting on those to whom we entrust offices. What remains is our joint attitude, for which we cannot but accept our joint responsibility. We determine authority ourselves. Authority is possessed by whomever we take to possess it. The only alternative thereto would be authoritarianism, namely, a blind faith in rulers telling their subjects that obedience is good for them, even if they remain incapable of understanding why.

From Natural Law to the Legal Relation

We can now pull both strings together – the wavering between dependence and pre-emption, on the one hand, and the uncertainty about the dependent grounds of pre-emptive authority, on the other.

Hobbes reluctantly embraced the transition from the person-neutral determination of natural law by anyone to its autonomous determination by the sovereign. He was somewhat uneasy about severing the justification of authority from what he believed to be its root, namely, the rational 'theorems' amounting to the laws of nature.[181] Nonetheless, it turns out, as regards sovereigns, their having a *view* of natural law is all that we can hope for. The relevance of anyone's person-neutral natural reason *itself* is spurious. What *leges naturales* require can be rendered differently, depending on time and place. Natural law is mediated by what it is not. Particularity claims its relevance.

The transition to pre-emption is eased by the predicament inherent in the justification of authority. Hobbes aside, there can be no other way of protecting us against ending up with an irrational bargain than the confidence in our *capacity* to establish *and* to disestablish authority. The social covenant needs to cede its place to some 'constituent power', no matter how ill-defined the latter may be.

Attitude-dependence offers the remedy for Hobbesian wavering. What we must consider to be law depends on what the lawmakers take to be good law. The authority of the lawmakers, in turn, depends on whom we regard as such.[182] Public power rests on the 'opinion and belief' of the people.[183] This is how we get beyond Hobbes.

Since the justification of conduct remains essential, the relevant opinions and beliefs must not be hostile to reasonableness and therefore be amenable to universalisation.[184] With the focus on universalisation, natural

[181] See M Loughlin, 'The Political Jurisprudence of Thomas Hobbes' in his *Political Jurisprudence* (Oxford, Oxford University Press, 2017) 22–34, 32.

[182] See, with an eye to Hobbes, ibid 33–34.

[183] See T Hobbes, *Behemoth or The Long Parliament* (ed F Tönnies, reprint Chicago, IL, Chicago University Press, 1990) 16.

[184] The core idea is, not by accident, intrinsic to Kant's idea of the original compact qua regulative ideal guiding all legislation. See I Kant, 'On the Common Saying: That may be correct in theory, but it does not apply in practice' in *Kant's Political Philosophy* (trans HB Nisbeth, Cambridge, Cambridge University Press, 1970) 61–92, 79. It obliges every authority to 'frame … laws in such a way that they could have been produced by the united will of a whole nation' (ibid 79). Kant, however, retains the idealisation and thereby reopens the wavering between the ideal and real will of the legislature. This is something he

law becomes condensed to the *form of law*. As will be further elaborated in chapter 10, from the joint self-reflection on an antinomy of moral judgement emerges a structure of interaction in which the social dimension of moral judgement provides the major underpinning of authority and pre-emption.[185] The thrust of natural law theory is thereby reversed. Instead of some substantive truth determining what we ought to believe, some shared beliefs underpin the authority to say what is right or wrong. While this may still sound trivial at this point, it will be shown how self-reflective universalisation lays bare the form of the legal relation, which is manifest in interactions between and among people who no longer confront each other directly with moral demands but instead take it for granted that they might have any. The uncertainty about the dependent grounds of authoritative pre-emption can thereby enter the very justification of authority itself.

From Natural Law to Constitutional Cancel Culture

The relational approach puts the social dimension – consent and opinion – ahead of substance. It is therefore, though perhaps surprisingly, wedded to constitutionalism as a model of reasonableness. While what is laid down in a constitution is at least in part intended to amount to a declaration of 'natural law', its authority is derivative of having been adopted by a people. The people have the power to establish and to undo, and what they create or dismantle does not turn on being consistent with some ideal social contract. Facts make law.[186]

It may thus seem as if, with the end of the wavering, we descend into the bleak immanence of 'might makes right'. But this would fail to capture an essential feature of constitutional orderings. They internalise the relations of transcendence. To see how they do, one merely has to recognise appeals to an alleged natural law 'by their fruits'[187] and to focus on their

inherited from Rousseau, who also believed that the legislature could judge wrongly what the general will is. See Rousseau, n 115, II.6, 75.

[185] Hobbes' vacillation between dependence and pre-emption will remain relevant to the discussion that follows in chapter 10. Transposed to the level at which the substantive and social dimensions of moral judgement can be distinguished, it can be seen that these dimensions are essential to a proper understanding of the constitution of the legal relation.

[186] See my slender essay 'Ex facto ius oritur' in N Bersier-Ladavac, C Bezemek and F Schauer (eds), *The Normative Force of the Factual* (New York, Springer, 2019) 121–34.

[187] See Charles S Peirce's biblical explication of pragmatic maxim in 'What Pragmatism Is' in *Selected Writings* (ed PP Wiener, New York, Dover Publications, 1966) 180–202, 181.

practical effect. The person-neutral invocation of natural law by anyone can in the end only serve the goal of rendering null and void any offending positive law. Constitutionalism transplants this idea to the sphere of souverain authority and attempts to specify – to the greatest possible extent – the cancelling agents and relevant norms.[188] While such internalisation is not – decidedly not – embraced in Hobbes' work,[189] it recognises that limits on sovereign authority can only be integral and never be external to it.[190] Only by means of the internal structuring of authority within a constitutional 'cancel culture'[191] is it possible to mitigate the impertinence inherent in pre-emption. Not by accident is it a major point of constitutional systems to bring about reasonableness through some clever arrangement of offices.[192] Essential to such an arrangement is, of course, that incumbents are made to observe the limits set to their powers. The constitutionalist way of addressing this problem is epitomised by an obsessive focus on the voidness and annulment of acts.

This much is already clear from Hobbes' treatment of sovereign power. For example, he claims that the rights of sovereigns cannot, unless they consented to, be transferred to others, nor can they be forfeited vis-à-vis the subjects.[193] Sovereignty is inalienable. The rights of the sovereign – which consist of several immunities, liberties and plenipotentiary powers[194] – are

[188] See A Hamilton, J Madison and J Jay, *The Federalist* (ed C Sunstein, Cambridge, MA, Harvard University Press, 2009) no 51, 341–42. Admittedly, wavering cannot be really ended. In fact, one major engine of constitutional law is jurisdictional self-authorisation on substantive grounds. Institutions or officeholders occasionally arrogate to themselves authority to enforce constitutional norms vis-à-vis their peers, even without express authorisation. The latest example is the European Court of Justice vis-à-vis Member States for the purpose of protecting the rule of law. While such arrogations are means of enhancing one's power, they need to be argued on constitutional grounds, for they must be claimed to be consistent with an existing order. In this respect, there is a difference from outright appeals to natural law and justice.

[189] This has to do with his rejection of ancient political thought. See Hobbes, n 21, 196 [170]–[171].

[190] Hobbes is dead set against the latter (but also the former) option. See ibid 196 [170]. See also Rousseau, n 115, II.6, 55.

[191] Constitutionalism essentially is a cancel culture. Foreigners have no voice. Elections serve to eliminate parties from the political process. Various legislative procedures, in particular in the European Union, bar from participation some who are believed to be holding a stake in certain issues. Resolutions of one body can be cancelled by means of the veto of another. Decisions of institutions can be overridden. Officeholders can be removed by a vote of no confidence or by manipulating the limit of their term. Deliberations and negotiation are conducted in the shadow of the ever-looming threat of exclusion (eg, shift to a different partner) or cancellation (eg, re-election). See my 'Parchment Barriers: The Constitution as Law' (2024) 20 *European Constitutional Law Review* 120–45.

[192] See, generally, A Vermeule, *The Constitution of Risk* (Cambridge, Cambridge University Press, 2014); A Vermeule, *The System of the Constitution* (Oxford, Oxford University Press, 2011).

[193] See Hobbes, n 21, 170 [102]. See also Hobbes, n 183, 118.

[194] See Hobbes, n 21, 108–10 [89–92].

all indispensable and hang together. Any transfer of one of these rights to a different institution or person, unless it amounts to a wholesale transfer of sovereignty, must be void.[195] For obvious reasons, the other grand proto-constitutionalist, Locke, for whom political authority is about the protection of property and based on the fiduciary exercise of the originally private powers of legislation and punishment, goes to great pains to underscore that any excess of authority leads to the absence of governmental authority. Excessive uses of powers transform what is intended to be public acts into void private actions.[196] In addition, Hobbes distinguishes between acts that are attributable to the office of the sovereign, and hence the body politic, and actions that the sovereign engages in as a private person.[197] This shows that he implicitly relies on the concept of public power. Hobbes also recognises the existence of 'fundamental laws'[198] that, if taken away, would lead to the dissolution of the commonwealth. They are the sinews of the body politic.[199]

Law is what sovereign authority believes it to be. What Hobbes, owing to his belief in the necessity of strong central authority, did not explore, not least owing to his rejection of the mixed constitution,[200] is how a cancel culture can be used to have partial perspectives interact within a political process with the aim of facilitating well-balanced, rational and equitable results. The function of separation of powers as a synthesising factor is often eclipsed by the mind-numbing importance attributed to the reasonableness inherent in general laws.[201] But legislation is merely the end-product of a process in which social and governmental actors need to ruffle agreement. Their perspectives, considered in isolation, would remain one-sided if they were not tempered through mutual interaction and comity.[202] Reasonableness is supposed to result from a process of collective self-determination.

[195] ibid 111 [93].

[196] See Locke, n 118, 398, 400, 412–13, II. §§ 199, 202, 222.

[197] See Hobbes, n 21 at 136 [116]. See also Poole, n 147 at 84.

[198] On the notion in the context of 17th-century common law, see G Burgess, *Absolute Monarchy and The Stuart Constitution* (New Haven, CT, Yale University Press, 1996) 142.

[199] See Hobbes, n 21, 174 [150]. Hobbes lists, as belonging to the fundamental laws, the power of war and peace, the power of adjudication and election of officers, and the right and power of doing whatever the sovereign deems to be necessary to be done for the public good.

[200] ibid 111 [93].

[201] Here is the major culprit: Rousseau, n 115, II.4, 69; II.6, 73.

[202] This is something that the major culprit nonetheless understood. See ibid II.3, 66–67.

At the same time, authority is dependent on its recognition and acceptance by those whom it governs. Submission to authority is rational for agents to accept only if others submit to such authority too. The latter has also been Hobbes' view. What merits emphasis, nonetheless, is that at the heart of his conception of public authority already lies collective self-determination. Not only is everyone the author of everything the sovereign does,[203] but the constitution of authority is also brought about by us, united in the face of the sovereign.[204]

Again, Hobbes aside, collective self-determination is a permanent feature of constitutional systems and not just an evanescent flicker emanating from a founding bang. The constituent power loses its mystical air once we focus on the obvious. The ideas inherent in a modern constitutional system have from its very outset been subject to partisan articulations. Political parties, according to Edmund Burke's famous characterisation, are poised to promote the national interest subject to some particular principle on which its members agree.[205] Constitutions have often been brought about, and are undoubtedly sustained, by parties joining their forces. They must agree on what they want and share ideas concerning its significance. The constituent power resides, thus, not in parties severally but in their systematic correlation. The readiness among partisans to cooperate is what constitutes and sustains the constitutional order and its law.[206] The potential ratification by the people adds additional varnish to this indispensable primer. This view of the constituent power is consistent with core ideas of political liberalism. The whole cannot but be conceived of from within its parts. The whole is constituted and sustained by the interaction among parts that claim to represent most appealingly the whole. Anyone participating in sustaining this order is collectively self-determining so long as they accord precedence to the life of a whole. The latter is moved by the majority to which in the case of defeat all partisans yield. Being a people is an achievement that stems from the mutual readiness to accept the defeat of one's own party.

[203] See Hobbes, n 21, 108 [90].

[204] Mind that officeholders are determined by majority vote, according to Hobbes. This cannot be reconciled with his contention that the multitude cannot act as one body unless represented by the sovereign.

[205] See E Burke, *Select Works of Edmund Burke: Thoughts on the Cause of the Present Discontents and the Two Speeches on America* (Indianapolis, IN, Liberty Fund, 2014) 150.

[206] See my 'Real Constitutional Law: A Revised Madisonian Perspective' in C Bezemek, M Potacs and A Somek (eds), *Vienna Lectures in Legal Philosophy*, vol 2 (Oxford, Hart Publishing, 2020) 161–83.

Concluding Thought

The first conception of reasonableness that we examined in this work perceived reason as the part of the soul charged with governing the not so rational parts, from which living beings, nonetheless, derive their energy and most of their aims. Reason, albeit commissioned with taking the lead within both the individual soul and the city, is confronted with the reflective task of guiding, without asphyxiating, its complementary impulses as conditions of human action. What remained largely open, however, was what the rules might be that reason is supposed to follow. It appeared that reasonableness was manifest in sound situational judgement – *phronesis*, to use the Aristotelian term.

The natural law tradition, building on the somewhat contrary intuition of the early Stoa, attempted to articulate the rules to which the exercise of natural reason gives rise. What this tradition did not bring into focus clearly enough was the question of authority. Undeniably, there were theories of legitimate resistance against usurpers and tyrants.[207] The authors of the relevant texts were clear in their opposition to the full acceptance of the pre-emptive force of authoritative enactments. While Hobbes took this step and endorsed the latter, he did so reluctantly. It is possible to accommodate this reluctance by giving the move to authority a constitutionalist twist. The new form of reasonableness that arises therefrom can be cast in the formula of 'I yield to what you take to be right, subject to reciprocal conditions.'

The big question that remains to be answered is how we arrive at these conditions without taking our cue from natural law.

[207] See, notably, Stephanius Junius Brutus, *Vindicae Contra Tyrannos* (2nd trans and ed G Garnett, Cambridge, Cambridge University Press, 2008).

10

Relational Approaches

Introduction

The one author with whom we associate, at any rate in the Anglophone tradition,[1] the relational approach to law,[2] is Wesley Newcomb Hohfeld.[3] He taught us to analyse 'jural relations' by paying attention to how second-personal demands imply correlations and oppositions between distinct normative statuses. A claim right on the part of the plaintiff is correlated with an obligation on the part of the defendant, while the opposite of having a right is to have none. If someone lacks the legal power to alter the normative status of others, then that person suffers from an inability, while those whose rights cannot be altered by the disenabled person enjoy a correlated immunity.[4]

The great merit of this approach – and this is possibly also the explanation of why it enjoyed traction among legal realists[5] – is that it provides us with a pragmatic perspective on the legal system. It perceives the legal system as a repository of reasons we use to make or to reject interpersonal claims. If drawing on this repository amounts to a justification of interferences or omissions, then what is implicitly presupposed in Hohfeld's view is a certain understanding of the law. It is a particular form of relating to one another within a practice where we make or reject demands backed up with references to rights, obligation or immunities. The practice of raising and refuting claims forms the core and centre, if anything, of the concept of law, and the various ontologies developed by legal positivists and natural law theorists alike about rules, values or hierarchies of norms

[1] On Georg Jellinek as the author who may deserve credit for introducing it to the field of public law, see n 10.

[2] See now the most recent and comprehensive introduction by E Jeuland, *Theories of Legal Relations* (Cheltenham, Edward Elgar, 2023).

[3] See WN Hohfeld, *Fundamental Legal Conceptions as Applied in Judicial Reasoning* (ed WW Cook, New Haven, CT, Yale University Press, 1964).

[4] ibid 36.

[5] Possibly, the influence was limited to his former Yale colleague Arthur L Corbin. See L Kalman, *Legal Realism at Yale: 1927–1960* (Chapel Hill, NC, North Carolina University Press, 1986) 98–101, 120.

are, at best, secondary, if not even misleading. Misleading they are, indeed, if they become frontloaded into the characterisation of the law. Pragmatically considered, our legal systems are not in and of themselves systems of rules, nor hierarchies of laws, but first and foremost systems of rights; and since rights are asserted under conditions of correlativity, rights need to be viewed against the larger background of the legal relation.[6]

Nineteenth-century German jurisprudence deserves special mention for the emphasis it laid on the relational quality of law.[7] Fichte's theory of 'natural right' aside,[8] the most prominent member of the historical school of jurisprudence, Carl Friedrich von Savigny, gave pride of place to the legal relation – *das Rechtsverhältnis* – in his *System of Contempoary Roman Law*.[9] While, as Savigny explains, a 'right' is a sphere in which human volition rules, any right needs to be perceived against the legal relation of which it is a component. It is the relation as a whole that needs to be considered in order to determine its content.

A true milestone in the development of relational thinking, however, was Georg Jellinek's *System of Public Rights* of 1892.[10] First, Jellinek articulated what has become the core creed of all relational approaches. All law, he asserts, is 'a relation of legal persons', and if the relational aspect were absent, the law would disappear.[11] Second, he developed, long before Hohfeld embarked on his pathbreaking essays,[12] a first analysis of the jural relations. He termed the basic statuses, somewhat confusingly, strong and weaker permission, capacity and 'granting',[13] and insisted that all rights against the state involve that grant of the capacity to initiate their enforcement.[14] While

[6] I fully agree with Pavlakos that the existence and relevance of the legal relation does not presuppose a statal legal system. See G Pavlakos, 'Redrawing the Legal Relation' in JL Fabra-Zamora (ed), *Jurisprudence in a Globalized World* (Cheltenham, Edward Elgar, 2020) 174–94.

[7] For a broadly sweeping account of the history, which also explores the Romanic legal cultures and the Anglo-American tradition, see Jeuland, n 2, 25–45.

[8] See JG Fichte, *Foundations of Natural Right According to the Principles of the Wissenschaftslehre* (trans M Baur, Cambridge, Cambridge University Press, 2000) 49.

[9] See CF von Savigny, *System des heutigen Römischen Rechts*, vol 1 (Berlin, Veit & Comp, 1840) 7–8.

[10] See G Jellinek, *System der subjektiven öffentlichen Rechte*, 2nd edn (Tübingen, Mohr, 1905).

[11] ibid 50.

[12] As far as I can see, Hohfeld did not study German sources. Apparently, he designed his analytical grid taking his cue from John William Salmond's theory. See JW Salmond, *Jurisprudence, or the Theory of the Law*, 2nd edn (London, Steven and Haynes, 1907). See JW Singer, 'The Legal Rights Debate in Analytical Jurisprudence from Bentham to Hohfield' (1982) *Wisconsin Law Review* 975–1059, 1048–50.

[13] See Jellinek, n 10, 49.

[14] For a succinct analysis, see W Pauly, 'Georg Jellineks "System der subjektiven öffentlichen Rechte"' in SL Paulson and M Schulte (eds), *Georg Jellinek – Beiträge zu Leben und Werk* (Tübingen, Mohr, 2000) 227–44, 235–36.

the details of his views are of no concern here, Jellinek's legacy is manifest in how he developed the jural relations into a theory of the statuses that human beings occupy vis-à-vis the state. We enjoy *status negativus*, for example, when we remain free from state interference, and *status activus* when we have rights of political participation.[15] In German public law, the relational approach has seen its ups and downs. Nevertheless, to this day it has been kept very much alive by scholars such as Norbert Achternberg[16] and, most recently, Andreas Wimmer.[17]

Across the Atlantic, the relational approach reappeared in a feminist guise in Jennifer Nedelsky's powerful study.[18] Based on relationalist feminist theory,[19] Nedelsky seeks to develop an alternative to the traditional liberal view of human subjectivity, which she characterises as 'bounded' selfhood, consecrated on rights protecting against interference.[20] She contrasts this with an understanding of the self as constituted within relations, to which she adds the contention that relationships are necessary for human beings to flourish.[21] Her work is thus a testament to the quest to develop a new image of that self 'for which boundary is not an apt metaphor'.[22] Conducive to the development of human autonomy is not the protection against intrusion but the cultivation of constructive relationships.[23] For the interface with which we interact with others, the human skin, rather than a wall, appears to be the adequate simile, for it suggests both flexibility and a sensitive connection to the world.[24] The idealism inherent in this approach should not go unnoticed. Nedelsky seems to believe that a cure for the social ills associated with liberal legal selfhood lies in altering the idealisation we use to interpret social facts. Everything will be good once we begin viewing ourselves as

[15] See Jellinek, n 10, 87, 103, 136–37. For a very helpful critical discussion of Jellinek's status doctrine, see R Alexy, 'Grundrecht und Status' in Paulson and Schulte (eds), n 14, 209–25.

[16] See N Achterberg, *Die Rechtsordnung als Rechtsverhältnisordnung: Grundlegung der Rechtsverhältnistheorie* (Berlin, Duncker & Humblot, 1982).

[17] See A Wimmer, *Rechtsverhältnisse im öffentlichen Recht: Ein Perspektivenwechsel* (Vienna, Verlag Österreich, 2019).

[18] See J Nedelsky, *Law's Relations: A Relational Theory of Self, Autonomy, and Law* (Oxford, Oxford University Press, 2013). For a brief introduction, see Jeuland, n 2, 61–67.

[19] For a classical statement, see C Gilligan, *In a Different Voice: Psychological Theory and Women's Development* (Cambridge, MA, Harvard University Press, 1982) 79, 94.

[20] See Nedelsky, n 18, 4, 91.

[21] ibid 5.

[22] ibid 91.

[23] ibid 98.

[24] ibid 107.

'inseparable from other beings in the universe'.[25] The belief that we change the world by changing our attitudes appears to have deep Christian roots.

In what follows, I would like to focus, first, on two more recent and particularly salient contributions to the relational account.[26] They do not dwell on the technical details of correlatives and opposites, even though there is undoubtedly merit in this,[27] but translate basic German philosophical ideas into an Anglo-American idiom. The link to philosophy explains why the relational approach is thus elaborated from the perspective of justice, on the one hand, and from the perspective of the independence that people retain in horizontal relations, on the other. An examination of Ernest Weinrib's core ideas will be followed by a quick tour of Michael Oakeshott's perspective on the rule of law. While both accounts are intellectually powerful and appealing, they are too narrowly concerned with private law and, at least in the case of Oakeshott, unconvincingly opposed to government intervention. Weinrib, moreover, does not rely on the conception of legality in the Kantian sense[28] in order to explain the attitude with which we respect the authority of law. Elements of both accounts, however, deserve preservation.

Weinrib

Weinrib's work allows us to make a quick transition from Hohfeld, for Weinrib also highlights the correlative nature of rights and obligations.[29] In his view, this correlativity is decisive for the structure of the legal relation, at any rate in the context of private law.[30] He elaborates the normative

[25] ibid 116.

[26] I recognise, of course, the importance and great merit of the work of Jennifer Nedelsky. In a typically North-American vein, however, she does not draw a line between law and morality, and places legal relations very quickly in a large sociological and psychological context. It obviously embraces a social conception of freedom. It is merely the case that she is heading in a different direction. See also, on the 'social conception' of freedom, A Honneth, *Freedom's Right: The Social Foundations of Democratic Life* (Cambridge, Polity Press, 2014).

[27] See, for example, A Halpin, *Rights and Law: Analysis and Theory* (Oxford, Hart Publishing, 1997).

[28] For different understandings of the term of 'legality', see my 'Legality and the Legal Relation' (2020) 33 *Ratio Iuris* 307–16. According to Weinrib, 'legality' is a whole ensemble of components that integrate the transactional relation into a normative unit. See EJ Weinrib, *The Idea of Private Law*, 2nd edn (Oxford, Oxford University Press, 2012) 86, 92.

[29] See EJ Weinrib, 'Correlativity and Personality' in his *Corrective Justice* (Oxford, Oxford University Press, 2016) 9–37, 10; ibid 20: 'Unlike need and virtue, a right is an intrinsically relational idea that immediately signifies the existence of a duty correlative to it.'

[30] See Weinrib, n 28, 2. The legal relation of private law is, according to Weinrib, a direct relation between persons, whereas public law is omnilateral by connecting each person to all and all to each. See

significance of this 'bipolar',[31] correlative relation in terms of 'corrective justice'.[32] For Weinrib, it stands for a structural principle – not a particular content – that is manifest in the type of justification that pervades the laws of voluntary obligations and of torts.[33] Its baseline is an understanding of equality according to which people are equal if they each have what is rightfully their own:

> An injustice occurs when, relative to this baseline, one party realizes a gain and the other a corresponding loss. The law corrects this injustice when it re-establishes the initial equality by depriving one party of the gain and restoring it to the other party.[34]

It is essential, however, that a connection is established between the parties, and what establishes this connection is the wrong committed by one party that is equivalent to the injury suffered by another.[35] If this connection that gives rise to correlativity is ignored, the private legal relation becomes inconceivable.[36] Weinrib claims, therefore, that '[c]orrective justice is the form of the private legal relationship'.[37]

The major idea is straightforward.[38] When an indigent defendant causes damage to the wealthy plaintiff, we may be inclined to ask, from a utilitarian perspective, whether it would not be more equitable to let the damage lie where it has fallen. After all, waiving the compensation would rectify an already existing maldistribution of wealth, whereas the reverse transfer would merely restore it. The higher marginal gain on the part of the defendant would outweigh the relatively minor marginal loss on the part of the plaintiff.[39]

EJ Weinrib, *Reciprocal Freedom: Private Law and Public Right* (Oxford, Oxford University Press, 2022) 70. Since public law, aside from securing rights that would remain provisional in the state of nature (ibid 68) is also in charge of realising distributive justice, it links people only indirectly inasmuch as they merit an allocation of goods or services that are drawn or dispensed from a (limited) fund (Weinrib, n 28, 8, 19, 57, 62, 71).

[31] See Weinrib, n 29, 19; Weinrib, n 28, 63.

[32] Actually, Weinrib, n 29, 10, puts it the other way round. The core of corrective justice is correlativity.

[33] See ibid 21.

[34] ibid 16. Weinrib, n 28, 64, also says that prior to compensation, doing and suffering are unequally divided.

[35] See Weinrib, n 29, 17: 'In bringing an action against the defendant the plaintiff is asserting that they are connected as doer and sufferer of the same injustice.'

[36] See Weinrib, n 28, 9, 11.

[37] ibid 75.

[38] ibid 8, 19, 57, 71.

[39] This is what, at any rate, the principle of diminishing marginal utility suggests.

Weinrib submits – correctly, in my view – that we would not regard a system of compensation as a system of tort law if it employed the perspective of distributive justice.[40] This is, however, what the above recommendation does. It treats accidents and other damages as occasions to re-examine the distribution of wealth. But if the application of the distributive perspective gives rise to a redistribution that is called for in any event, it no longer functions as a system of tort law, not least because it severs the *direct* connection between wrongdoer and sufferer. What matters, instead, is their relative position within a system that distributes and redistributes wealth. A tort would then be an occasion to re-evaluate such a position rather than a relation that is established between plaintiff and defendant through the wrong committed by the defendant.

There are more subtle ways in which Weinrib seeks to drive home his point. One is product liability.[41] The existence of product liability provides producers with an incentive to seek insurance against damage claims brought by those having endured harm from defective products. This is even more advisable if product liability is strict. In this case, however, the cost of insurance ends up being borne by the consumers at large, for producers are going to mark up the price of the product by including the insurance rate. The correlativity between doing and suffering and the correction of relational injustice is thereby cast asunder. Weinrib even goes so far as to claim that distributive and corrective justice, even though both internally coherent and comprehensive modes of external ordering, are mutually incompatible. Any attempt to combine them destroys at least the internal rationality of corrective justice and leads to irrationality.[42]

Such examples support our intuition that a damage is an event through which a doer and a sufferer are tied together based on the principle of corrective justice.[43] Weinrib goes to extraordinarily great, and somewhat tiring, length to argue that it constitutes an identical relation that can be viewed from two different sides:

> Liability consists in a legal relationship between two parties each of whose position is intelligible only in light of the other's. … Justifications for holding someone liable that exhibit the parties as the doer and sufferer of

[40] See Weinrib, n 28, 72.
[41] ibid 49.
[42] ibid 72–75. Weinrib also denies steadfastly and obstinately any priority of distributive justice. See Weinrib, n 29, 28.
[43] See Weinrib, n 28, 73.

> the same injustice render the law both coherent and fair. Legal reasoning composed of such justifications treat the parties' relationship as a normative unity that embraces them both rather than as a hodgepodge of factors separately relevant only to one or the other of them.[44]

It is always the case that the injustice suffered matches the unjust exercise of freedom on the part of the tortfeasor. In a sense, by damaging a resource, for example, tortfeasors are taking away an action from the tort victims that would have been exclusively theirs to perform.[45] The equality that matters for the purpose of corrective justice is the equality of doing and suffering that is restored by making the doers suffer to the same extent to which they have made the sufferer suffer.

This system is, as Weinrib explains, implicit in private law as a practice and not dependent on endorsing a particular philosophical theory of law.[46] Indeed, in this respect it resembles Rawls' political conception of justice as a module that fits various comprehensive doctrines.[47] It gives rise to a coherent justification of what we demand from one another in private law.

So much for the structure of the relation, which is basically composed of rights and obligations. But Weinrib also suggests something about the substance of these rights and duties, which must be consistent with the correlative structure of private law.[48] While this substance is not derivative of the structure, the substance needs to be compatible with the reciprocity inherent in the correlative relation. Weinrib argues that even though private law is about gains and losses, it is not about wealth. It is not, simply because *damnum* can be done by competitive means as long as one does not commit any *injuria*.[49] Furthermore, if wealth were the ultimate substantive focus of private law, it could give rise to positive obligations to foster it in others. None of this is, however, the case.[50]

Weinrib regards 'personality' as the most general substance of private law.[51] The unifying idea comprising rights and duties is the capacity of persons to engage in purposive action. On the duty side this is manifest in the presupposition that the defendant must have committed a certain

[44] See Weinrib, n 29, 1.
[45] See Weinrib, n 28, 62.
[46] ibid 23–24; Weinrib, n 29, 27.
[47] See J Rawls, *Political Liberalism* (New York, Columbia University Press, 1991) 12.
[48] See Weinrib, n 29, 15, 21.
[49] ibid 26.
[50] ibid.
[51] ibid 25. He thereby unwittingly echoes Jellinek, n 10, 52.

act, while on the rights side of the equation it is obviously 'the capacity for purposiveness without regard to particular purposes[;] no obligation exists to exercise this capacity towards a particular end'.[52] Personality is purposiveness in the sense of freedom of choice, in the case either of the doer or of the sufferer. It is about the capacity to pursue objectives, that is, any permissible objective and regardless of an ultimate aim. Personality finds its expression in rights, which are in turn an essential element of the correlative structure of corrective justice.[53]

The Gulf

Weinrib's theory offers an elaborate rejuvenation of paleo-liberal private law theory, of which Arthur Ripstein has given another – mitigated – account in his reconstruction of Kant's doctrine of law ('right').[54] It is based on the premise that corrective justice is not secondary to distributive justice in the sense that, for its operation to begin, some prior allocation of resources has to define the correct initial endowments pursuant to a distributive criterion.[55] Rather, Weinrib suggests the complete independence of these ways of ordering, for otherwise corrective justice would likely be considered as merely ancillary to sustaining distributive objectives.[56] Both types of justice represent different ways of conceiving of what unifies people. In his view, the criterion of distributive justice expresses 'the group's collective unity'.[57] It says, for example, that we belong together because we all need healthcare and should have access to it; or it says, choosing a different example, that

[52] Weinrib, n 29, 25, where he goes on to explain: 'Among these rights are the right to the integrity of one's body as the organ of purposive activity, the right to property in things appropriately connected to an external manifestation of the proprietor's volition, and the right to contractual performance in accordance with the mutually consensual exercises of the parties' purposiveness. The existence of these rights gives rise to correlative duties of non-interference whose content and application depend on the nature of the right.'

[53] Weinrib, ibid 29, overstates his point by claiming that correlativity and personality mutually imply each other. There is no way to get from personality to correlativity, even if Weinrib claims that 'personality represents the parties in their interrelation'. He has not at all shown why the parties necessarily relate to one another in a way so that personality follows from it.

[54] See A Ripstein, *Force and Freedom: Kant's Legal and Political Philosophy* (Cambridge, MA, Harvard University Press, 2009). In *Private Wrongs* (Cambridge, MA, Harvard University Press, 2016) 6–14, Ripstein explains how his views differ from Weinrib's. The mitigation of paleo-liberal theory concerns the fact that taking care of the poor and less fortunate is not left to private charity but regarded as a matter of right.

[55] Weinrib, n 28, 79.

[56] ibid 78–79.

[57] ibid 72–73.

for us competitive racers, our rank may depend on how little time we need to finish a set of laps. By contrast, the unity of corrective justice lies in the correlativity of doing and suffering harm. The criteria that constitute merit for the purpose of various contributions – such as virtue, need, social status or wealth – are eclipsed in the context of corrective justice. They are irrelevant to how we are regarded within the legal relation. We are cast as agents capable of engaging in purposive action. Various aspects about us that may be relevant in a variety of distributive contexts do not and must not matter. Tort liability, that is, cannot be evaded by being an accomplished runner, a celebrity or a member of a historically disadvantaged group. If that were possible, what is hidden behind the mask of personality would come to be revealed for the purpose of overwriting correlativity with distributive objectives. As a result, distributive justice would 'split … corrective justice asunder'.[58] This would be the case not only because a concrete feature of the persons concerned was accorded major importance, but also because the criterion of distributive justice could possibly even select a feature that is relevant to merely one party to the transaction. The unity of the correlative relation would thus be demolished.

Weinrib is correct that the equality of the parties to the transaction is in part constituted by abstracting from the particularities of their rank or moral character. What he cannot explain – at any rate, not in his early work – is how a potential conflict between distributive and corrective justice can be settled without preferring one of the two perspectives by fiat. If there is nothing to bridge the gulf between the two incommensurable types of justice, then external distributive corrections of correlativity must always and necessarily offend corrective justice. Likewise, the operation of corrective justice can always result in unjust distributions of wealth. One can complain equally from either perspective about the other, but there is no overarching perspective to settle the issue. Against this background, the paleo-liberal bias of Weinrib's theory is thrown into sharper relief. People can escape the lack of power that they endure in private relations among formally equal transactional partners by political means, for example, by supporting protective legislation. In early works, Weinrib seems to abhor the idea, for it results in an unprincipled overwriting of correlativity with distributive considerations. Yet, viewed from this angle,

[58] ibid 75.

he lacks any grounds for rejecting the corrective by means of social justice other than the sanctity of the coherence of justifications in the realm of private law. Indeed, the recalcitrance to accept any form of political meddling with private law is not only reminiscent of German ordo-liberal views of *Privatrechtsgesellschaft*;[59] it also suggests that we are essentially private people and not citizens capable of rising above horizontal relationships and ordering them from above. In Weinrib's case, private law is utterly bourgeois. At best, it seems that the early Weinrib leaves us with an existential choice similar to the one that Sidgwick presents us with in his *Method of Ethics*, namely, the choice between being a self-interested or an altruistic maximiser.[60]

Is There a Bridge?

In a more recent work, Weinrib has attempted to identify an overarching perspective that spans both corrective and distributive justice.[61] Not by accident, it is linked to what is probably the most general principle of Kant's legal philosophy, namely, the principle of reciprocal independence.[62] According to Weinrib, this principle, which in the context of Kant's work simply requires independence of the '*nötigenden Willkür*' of others,[63] has both a negative and a positive dimension.[64] Negatively, it designates the freedom from 'being non-reciprocally bound by another'; positively, by contrast, it requires that people be able to have their fate in their own hands.[65] One is, accordingly, 'entitled to be one's own master (*sui iuris*) and therefore to assert oneself in one's relation to others', which 'encompasses the power to make one's way in life in at least a minimally decent and satisfactory manner'.[66] While Weinrib still insists that corrective and distributive justice are 'mutually irreducible' and 'categorically different',[67] he claims that there

[59] See, for example, K Riesenhuber (ed), *Privatrechtsgesellschaft* (Tübingen, Mohr, 2009).

[60] Sidgwick distinguishes between egotistic and universalistic hedonism. See H Sidgwick, *The Method of Ethic*, 7th edn (Indianapolis, IN, Hackett Publishing, 1981) 411, 487.

[61] See Weinrib, *Reciprocal Freedom*, n 30.

[62] ibid 101, 108.

[63] See I Kant, *Metaphysische Anfangsgründe der Rechtslehre* (ed B Ludwig, Hamburg, Meiner, 1986) 47.

[64] See Weinrib, *Reciprocal Freedom*, n 30, 100.

[65] Whether this positive condition of reciprocal independence is genuinely Kantian may be duly doubted. At the same time, whether one is or is not a follower of a Kantian approach is relevant to a philosophical argument.

[66] Weinrib, *Reciprocal Freedom*, n 30, 105.

[67] ibid 96.

is a 'conception of juridical unity'[68] that elucidates their connection. This intelligibility is mediated by a 'conceptual sequence'[69] in which distributive justice becomes introduced at a later stage in order to address a deficiency that may arise as a result of a system of private transactions.[70] This deficiency concerns the positive dimension of reciprocal independence. Private legal relations might give rise to such inequalities in the distribution of resources that leaves some with no alternative other than to surrender their activities to masters paying them wages. They may no longer be able to make their own way in life. Weinrib acknowledges that 'private law … creates the possibility of systemic subordination that distributive justice alone can address'.[71] If it were not for protective labour legislation, subordinates would be reduced to the level of mere instruments of their bosses.[72] While having to enter a condition of subordination is 'unimpeachable' pursuant to the principles of private transactions,[73] it runs foul of the overarching principle of reciprocal independence.[74] It involves, more precisely, the loss of its *positive* dimension. This deficiency that arises within the context of private ordering may be legitimately addressed by public law that has to possess powers to mitigate dependencies.[75] Since mitigating actions are taken within the civil condition (and not in the state of nature in which property relations are entirely provisional), the emerging reconstructed independence is different in kind from its original form. It concerns the legal relation between each individual and all others qua participants in the civil condition ('omnilateral' relations) and lends a new quality to independence that is captured in the term 'human dignity',

> a term that refers in the most abstract way to the normative idea that governs the relationship between an individual and the commonwealth of right-holders that constitutes the civic condition.[76]

In a typically Kantian vein, Weinrib characterises this guarantee of dignity as encompassing the power 'to make one's way in life in at least a minimally

[68] ibid 97.
[69] ibid 99.
[70] ibid 100.
[71] ibid 109.
[72] See, in this respect, on 'masterly' as opposed to 'political' or 'kingly' rule, Aristotle, *Politics*, 2nd edn (trans C Lord, Chicago, IL, University of Chicago Press, 2013) 1254b5, 1255b17, 1278b30–40, 1259a38–40, 1324b25 (at 8, 11, 72, 21, 191).
[73] See Weinrib, *Reciprocal Freedom*, n 30, 104.
[74] ibid 152.
[75] ibid 106.
[76] ibid 105.

decent and satisfactory manner';[77] from which it can be inferred that protecting dignity would not amount to guaranteeing equality of condition.[78]

The situation to be mitigated based on a distributive justice principle such as 'need'[79] or other principles[80] is not one in which the *legal* independence of a person has been interfered with illicitly; rather, what is to be remedied is a situation of *economic* dependence. If, however, dignity is supposed to address the problem of economic dependence, then the overarching principle of reciprocal independence gives the state unrestricted power to overwrite the operation of corrective justice by drawing on its distributive counterpart. The reason is straightforward. As Hegel memorably observed in his philosophy of law, civil society is a sphere of mutual interdependence.[81] This interdependence affects our lives so deeply that it even determines what we take to be our needs. We develop needs (or 'preferences') in light of the resources we might have to fulfil them. What is more, the internal logic of economic activity requires that we maximise our assets and resources. As Christoph Menke pointed out in his theory of liberation, this is the case not because the maximisation of wealth is the central objective of all participants of the economic system; rather, it is the other way round: maximisation is imperative because it is the only way to guard ourselves against always unpredictable devaluations of our assets and resources. Whatever it may be that is our asset or resource, it can have value for us only if such value is attributed to it by others. Economically considered, we are not the masters of what we own.[82] The market economy, in which all of us are cast as *legally independent*, is a system of universal mutual *economic dependence*. Owing to this universality, it is unclear at what point the power of the state to mitigate economic dependence would have to come to an end. Not by accident, Weinrib attributes 'broad latitude' to the legislature when it comes to mitigating dependence.[83] There is no reason to stop at the level of guaranteeing minimal subsistence. Why not protect whole industries against 'unfair' competition from abroad? Hence,

[77] ibid 105; see Ripstein, n 54, 286.

[78] In fact, Weinrib just lists the usual repertoire of social welfare states as options to mitigate dependence. See Weinrib, *Reciprocal Freedom*, n 30, 113–14.

[79] ibid 106.

[80] On the multiplicity of principles and possible distributions, see ibid 111.

[81] See GWF Hegel, *Elements of the Philosophy of Right* (trans HB Nisbet, Cambridge, Cambridge University Press, 1991) 224, § 187.

[82] See C Menke, *Theorie der Befreiung* (Berlin, Suhrkamp, 2022) 314, 317–18, 323, 496.

[83] See Weinrib, *Reciprocal Freedom*, n 30, 112.

corrective justice and distributive justice remain irreconcilable,[84] with the latter always threatening to wipe out the operation of the former. Any line-drawing is historically contingent and must appear more or less arbitrary from the point of view of the latter. One cannot but regret that Weinrib's liberalism is at the end of the day too fainthearted to embrace the harsh normative conclusions that follow from the ideology of corrective justice.

Oakeshott

Of the few writers emphasising the relational character of law, the British philosopher Michael Oakeshott did so by distinguishing types of relationships and identifying the type of persona that we create within them.[85] Within a transactional relationship, he claims, we appear to one another in the persona of someone who is merely interested in some substantive benefit that is not necessarily personal. The same persona also matters in the context of various joint ventures.[86]

The ethos of transactions and personally disengaged cooperation is explained by Oakeshott with reference to the normative set-up of games.[87] Games actually cast us in the guise of two different personae, one appearing in the foreground of the interaction and the other staying in the background. As participants in games, we are frequently cast as competitors. But we do not merely interact as competitors; we also mutually pledge to behave fairly and to abide by the rules. We are in a relationship that is mediated by the recognition of the game's norms. In this respect, games and their rules resemble the rule of law.

While in the case of games the rules are freely adopted, for the law they are not accidental. The substance of law seriously affects what kind of relationship is to be established by those recognising one another as free and equal. Law therefore necessarily possesses a moral dimension. The *lex* of positive law is based upon the principles of good law, *ius*. The proscriptions

[84] This is revealed, again, in the aversive manner, in which Weinrib approaches the horizontal (third-party) effect of fundamental rights. See ibid 152–53.

[85] On the following, see M Oakeshott, 'The Rule of Law' in his *On History and Other Essays* (Indianapolis, IN, Liberty Fund, 1999) 129–79.

[86] In their case, however, the engagement between and among persons may already become tighter, closer to reaching the level of team players or comrades. See ibid 133. A person may thus easily become entangled in a common task, a joint venture, a common project and so forth. What happens in such a case, of course, is that the social relationship begins to engulf a person more comprehensively.

[87] See M Oakeshott, *Rationalism in Politics and Other Essays* (Indianapolis, IN, Liberty Fund, 1991) 427–32, 141.

and prescriptions of *ius* do not, however, extend beyond what Fuller would have called the 'inner morality' of law (matters concerning predictability, publicity, etc).[88] Nevertheless, legal rules are moral rules in the sense of not being merely of instrumental significance. Instrumental rules govern the effective pursuit of an external objective. Non-instrumental rules, by contrast, concern the conditions of the fair pursuit of any objective.

Remarkably, Oakeshott believes that the only reason why morality and law are really different is that the validity of moral rules is dependent not on 'authenticity' but on their substantive correctness.[89] Law, just like the rulebook of games, can be traced back to some historical origin. Morality, by contrast, has no such source. Some of its demands are necessary, but not sufficient, conditions for the existence of law.

Just like rules of the game, the law does not prescribe what kind of moves one ought to perform in order to attain a goal, for example the rather obvious goal of winning. The law merely prescribes what Oakeshott somewhat strangely calls 'the adverbial conditions' under which persons are permitted to pursue their own ends.[90] Here is one of Oakeshott's formulations:

> Here, then, is a mode of human relationship, distinct from others and, like others, abstract: a relationship not of persons but of personae. Association, not in terms of doing and the enjoyment of the fruits of doing, but of procedural conditions imposed upon doing: laws. Relationships, not in terms of efficacious arrangements for promoting or procuring wished-for substantive satisfactions (individual or communal), but obligations to subscribe to non-instrumental rules: a moral relationship. Rules, not in terms of the alleged worth, 'rationality' or 'justice' of the conditions these rules prescribe, but in respect of the recognition of their authenticity.[91]

From the non-instrumental character of the 'adverbial conditions' (when, how, where?) of conduct, Oakeshott comes to far-reaching conclusions against any substantive external morality of law (such as the protection of human rights) or the 'technological state' that adopts all kinds of regulations in the pursuit of allegedly common objectives. A state of this type interferes with human conduct for the sake of our health, safety or moral decency. In

[88] See LL Fuller, *The Morality of Law* (New Haven, CT, Yale University Press, 1969) 33–44, 152–77.
[89] See Oakeshott, n 85, 147, 151.
[90] ibid 148.
[91] ibid 161.

Oakeshott's view, this is not warranted by the civil condition[92] staked out by the rule of law.

Incoherent Conservatism

But this conclusion cannot be right.

First, Oakeshott himself has to concede that 'common substantive satisfactions may be supplied as a by-product of the operation of the legal conditions imposed upon the self-chosen conduct of the associates'.[93] What Oakeshott has in mind here is the maintenance of a stable currency or the prevention of monopolies. This is a very thin and liberal idea of the common good, and it is not at all clear why monopolies as merely one instance of unequal bargaining power should be more intrinsically inimical to the rule of law than the disparity of power in the relationship between capital and labour.[94]

Second, Oakeshott's diatribe against the 'technological state' involves a much more fundamental and fatal misunderstanding. He assumes that the legal relation is just as socially straightforward as any other relationship and should be kept in a relatively unaffected state. This ignores that the legal relation is a reserve and default position that we invoke when we believe that things have gone awry in our informal dealings. The air of warm kindness surrounding interactions suddenly disappears. The relation then comes to be inhabited by tokens of the types that the law uses in order to characterise the rights and responsibilities of partners engaged in some transaction (eg, 'buyer', 'seller', 'lessor', 'lessee'). That this is the case is actually indirectly captured in how Oakeshott describes the front-back relation between the two relations in a game:

> The players of a game are, then, related in two categorically distinct modes of association. One is an actual, terminable relationship of assignable contestants identified in their several powers to pursue, in a succession of self-chosen actions, a substantive outcome. It is a relationship located in respect of a place and a time and it is exhausted on the occasion. The other is an ideal relationship, invoked on the occasion of a substantive contest, but subsisting in advance and independently of any such occasion. And it is

[92] See, more generally, M Oakeshott, *On Human Conduct* (Oxford, Oxford University Press, 1975) 128–29.

[93] See Oakeshott, n 85, 176.

[94] But see Oakeshott, n 87, 431–33.

> this second relationship that affords us a glimpse of a mode of association expressly and exclusively in terms of the recognition of rules.[95]

The legal relation is a specimen of the 'ideal relationship'. The 'real relationship' between contestants may be one of long-standing animosity or camaraderie, which may, in the latter case, go along with some care for the well-being of the other. The difficulty involved in insisting on the observance of rules in the real relation indicates what is at stake. It is necessary and entirely unobjectionable that, in order to get along with others, we remain oblivious to the legal relation, provided that we retain the power to invoke and thereby to elicit the 'ideal' within 'real relationships'. It is great to be loyal and dependable as long as one can prevent exploitation by invoking the cold legal relation in which we appear as faceless bearers of rights.

Oakeshott seems to have believed that this latter relation is entirely overridden when the state makes us 'work' towards certain beneficial objectives. But becoming enlisted to a project is entirely unobjectionable if we retain rights that allow us to raise the question whether anyone who has the obligation of doing x must also do y. It did not occur to Oakeshott that participation in common pursuits is not inconsistent with asserting one's rights.

Where They Are Falling Short

Weinrib's difficulty to integrate distributive justice and Oakeshott's misconceived aversion to the 'technological state' aside, both approaches to the legal relation suffer from two major shortcomings.

First, the relation between law and morality is not entirely clear but somewhat muddled. Weinrib claims, on the one hand, that legal relations are 'external' and distinguished from ethics, by which he means that morally praiseworthy objectives cannot justify malfeasance or damage done to others. He presents, on the other hand, correlativity as a special morality.[96] It is, at any rate, not clear enough why private law is supposedly ethically neutral *and* simultaneously an instantiation of morality. Oakeshott, again, does not explain what we are supposed to do if *lex*, that is positive law, conflicts with the moral rules governing *ius*, that is good law. This raises the

[95] ibid 138.
[96] See Weinrib, n 28, xii, xvii.

core question whether the law possesses authority vis-à-vis what we take to be right or wrong.

Second, neither Weinrib nor Oakeshott explains how and why we enter a legal relation in the first place. It does not occur to either of them that external freedom or freedom of choice might be social achievements. Worse still, Weinrib even regards the external freedom of the parties as 'inborn'.[97]

The analysis that follows is based in the conjecture that the constitution of the legal relation and the relation between law and morality are intertwined. We can understand one adequately only by understanding the other.

[97] ibid 85.

11

The Enigma of Morality

Reconstructing Know-how

'Rational reconstruction' is the name that Jürgen Habermas has given to various attempts at making sense of our know-how for saying or doing certain things. Key to such a reconstruction is the identification of the normative structures that facilitate individual capacities.[1] They are about what we must be able to master in order to attain the status of a competent speaker of a language or of a responsibly moral agent. According to Habermas, theories of moral development such as Piaget's and Kohlberg's are chief examples of this type of undertaking, as are Chomsky's linguistics and Searle's speech act theory.[2] What must have intrigued Habermas, in particular, is that the resulting accounts of potentially universal structures of communication and interaction originate from empirical studies that reach out to philosophical reflection.[3] All the same, the relevant reconstructions abstain from claiming boldly to amount to unearthing conditions of possibility for which there are no alternatives. By seeking to achieve something more modest and contextual than a transcendental deduction, they do not posit the universal necessity of the forms to which normative structures give rise.[4] They are not, however, overtly modest in relation to hermeneutics and history, for rational reconstructions do not merely try to understand what agents believe themselves to be knowing or doing; they are concerned with what is going on behind their backs and what makes their knowing and doing possible. Nor do they offer a history qua chain of events with the aim of explaining how something has come about. The rational reconstruction of structures that constitute capacities – such as for knowing how to

[1] See J Habermas, *Moralbewusstsein und kommunikatives Handeln* (Frankfurt aM, Suhrkamp, 1983) 40–48; J Habermas, *Der philosophische Diskurs der Moderne* (Frankfurt aM, Suhrkamp, 1985) 350. See already his *Erkenntnis und Interesse*, 2nd edn (Frankfurt aM, Suhrkamp, 1973) 411–12.

[2] See Habermas, *Erkenntnis und Interesse*, n 1, 412.

[3] Indeed, the processes of psychological and linguistic reconstruction originate from amidst the world we inhabit in our daily routines.

[4] See J Habermas, *Wahrheit und Rechtfertigung: Philosophische Aufsätze* (Frankfurt aM, Suhrkamp, 1999) 27–28.

say or to do certain things – explores their evolution with an interest in understanding how one stage gives rise to the other, thereby suggesting that each new stage enables subjects to engage in problem-solving that would have remained impeded at the stage that preceded it. It thus develops an account of what we are thinking and doing by examining how we could have reasonably come to hold the beliefs we happen to have or to adopt the attitudes we take.

It is with the task of rational construction in mind that I am turning to how we constitute a relation that we eventually call 'legal'. It emerges, ideally, from a type of moral problem-solving that is essentially 'political'.

Authority, Again

I begin with what Waldron memorably has referred to as the 'circumstances of politics'.[5] They are composed of two features that simultaneously pull in the direction of action and inaction. There is, first, the practical urgency to get to joint action or to settle on a scheme for the coordination of conduct and, second, the empirical unlikeliness of attaining, even among reasonable people, agreement over what ought to be done.[6] Reasonableness obtains if people do not lightly put their own well-being ahead of others but attempt to approach others based on what they believe to be fair terms of cooperation. That is, they treat others as equally real.[7]

Examples of this type of situation abound in our societies. Imagine a people attacked by a terrorist group. What is taken to be an adequate response depends on the relative hawkishness of one's disposition. Sidewalks are nowadays battlefields raided by cyclists, e-scooters or e-rollers menacing the few remaining pedestrians. Everyone wants to use sidewalks. But whom would it be fair to exclude for the sake of traffic safety? Competition can be mutually ruinous for market participants. But which rules are supposed to govern contenders for profit? Should economic efficiency be of paramount concern?

We all know the way out of the impasse designated by the circumstances of politics. It is a decision. But there is the rub. How could a decision ever be legitimate in the face of a persistent disagreement even among reasonable people?

[5] See J Waldron, *Law and Disagreement* (Oxford, Oxford University Press, 1999).

[6] There are philosophical accounts of this unlikeliness, such as Rawls' ideas concerning 'burdens of judgment'. See J Rawls, *Political Liberalism* (New York, Columbia University Press, 1991) 56–57.

[7] See the references to Nagel in chapter 3.

What we clearly encounter, therefore, is the problem of authority in its most pronounced form. We have already had the opportunity to explore it in chapter 9, where we encountered Hobbes' wavering between dependence and pre-emption. The question is why you should do something because someone else has said so, even if you believe the directives you are given to be wrong? How could legitimate authority originate from an apparent contradiction ('It is right to follow orders even though they are wrong')? It was mentioned, in the same chapter, that being at a loss as to what the substantive reasons are for ascribing authority to someone may well be the condition for its possibility. This hypothesis is further elaborated below in the sections 'From Others to Self' and 'The Emergence from Morality'.

Two Dimensions of Moral Judgement

This is precisely the point at which the rational reconstruction sets in.

Our moral judgement possesses two salient dimensions. *Substantively*, moral judgements are about what is – all things considered – right or wrong. *Socially*, they are uttered with the (initially deontically unspecified) expectation of eliciting agreement and voluntary compliance.[8] From the perspective of morality, we consider the social dimension to be dependent on its substantive counterpart. Good reasons force everyone to consent without anyone's being coerced into doing so. The expectation of agreement is decidedly more cognitive in its orientation if the judgement wittingly or unwittingly serves as a reminder of what we are supposed to share in belief ('Torture is wrong'). By contrast, it is wearing a more normative face if the claim serves as an injunction issued to assuage doubts ('This *is* an act of torture').

The distinction between the substantive and social[9] explains why any authority must necessarily prioritise the social dimension of judgement, possibly even at the cost of overriding its substantive counterpart. The task of authority is to elicit acquiescence and compliance. Subject to authority, one must do something simply because someone else has said so.

Therein lies a reversal in the relation of moral grounding. Morality is supposedly the sphere in which we share reasons for action (and reasons

[8] We shall return to this point. What I am taking for granted here is how moral judgements appear on their surface. With the disintegration of *Sittlichkeit*, however, their social function changes from eliciting agreement to reassuring groups of their own righteousness.

[9] For a slightly different take on this distinction under the heading of 'facticity and validity', see J Habermas, *Faktizität und Geltung: Beiträge zur Diskurstheorie des Rechts und des demokratischen Rechtsstaats* (Frankfurt aM, Suhrkamp, 1992) 18–19, 31.

for judging actions). Substantive reasons ought to facilitate such sharing. We believe that bullying is wrong. Putting people down in front of others makes them look weak. It detracts from their social standing and is, therefore, harmful. Harming others is bad. It impinges upon their happiness. Ordinarily, at any rate, we take it for granted that the substantive reasons we share account for our agreement, and possibly even for our basic readiness to do what morality requires. Consent is grounded in substantive reasons.

Good Reasons

It is often said that the reasons to which we ought to respond with assent must be 'good'. What earns reasons this ennobling distinction is expected to reveal itself in ideal situations of calm deliberation, possibly with others. Good reasons presumably present themselves to those engaged in serious efforts to discover what they are, for example in the course of examining and debating pros and cons. It does not matter whether one is a realist about reasons, and hence convinced that we end up being awestruck by them,[10] or a constructivist contending that one always and already needs to possess some beliefs in order actively to endorse others.[11]

No matter how much the quality of reasons depends on the subject under consideration, there is a formal threshold that all moral reasons need to pass in order to earn themselves the predicate 'good'. It is the condition of universalisation. Universalisation is supposed to elicit universal assent. It bridges the gap between the substantive and the social dimension. Three of its elements can be distinguished.

The first element is the injunction against self-exemption for the simple reason that one is 'special', without offering a sufficient reason for why one may indeed be in a particular situation or amount to a special case.[12] The injunction extends, in reverse gear, to discriminating against other people, for example on the grounds of their gender or complexion ('But she is a woman!'; 'What the deuce, he is black!').

The second element is related to the first and demands that reasons for action say what is right for all, that is, not just in a particular instance but for

[10] See TM Scanlon, *Being Realistic about Reasons* (Oxford, Oxford University Press, 2014) 30.

[11] See S Street, 'How to be a Relativist about Normativity' at www.academia.edu/19887937/How_to_Be_a_Relativist_About_Normativity, 10.

[12] See JL Mackie, *Ethics: Inventing Right and Wrong* (London, Penguin Books, 1990; 1st edn 1977) 83–85.

any instance that is a token of the relevant type.[13] They then say that those finding themselves in situations of type x are supposed to do or to endure y. If moral judgements did not involve that claim, they would be consumed by their own particularity and, effectively, establish an exemption for the extant case. If it were not for such generality, one would be absorbed by one's spontaneous reactions to situations. This would, eventually, entail sacrificing agency. As Korsgaard explains with regard to such 'particular willing', that

> willing would be a matter of willing a maxim for exactly this occasion without taking it to have any implications of any kind for any other occasion. You will a maxim thinking that you can use it just this once and so to speak discard it; you don't even need a reason to change your mind.[14]

In other words, the agents would make themselves into beings whose character is just as evanescent as the extant situation.

The third element of universalisation requires that the situation of the people affected by rule-oriented action be taken into account by asking whether they, albeit taking all affected interests impartially into account, would have reason to reject such action and the rule on which it would be based.[15] A good example of what is vulnerable to reasonable rejection is the haughty attitude that seems to have prevailed among the upper class

[13] See the discussion in CM Korsgaard, *Self-Constitution: Agency, Identity, and Integrity* (Oxford, Oxford University Press, 2009) 73–76. On the convergence of objectivity and universality, see AW Wood, 'Deduction of the Summons and the Existence of Other Rational Beings' in G Gottlieb (ed), *Fichte's Foundation of Natural Right* (Cambridge, Cambridge University Press, 2016) 72–91, 73.

[14] CM Korsgaard, *The Constitution of Agency: Essay on Practical Reason and Moral Psychology* (Oxford, Oxford University Press, 2008) 123.

[15] I am condensing ideas of Hare and Scanlon. See RM Hare, *Moral Thinking: Its Levels, Method, and Point* (Oxford, Oxford University Press, 1982) 92; TM Scanlon, *What We Owe to Each Other* (Cambridge, MA, Harvard University Press, 1998) 213–23. The formulation alludes to Scanlon's 'contractualism', which he basically characterises like this (ibid 189): '[W]hen we address our minds to a question of right and wrong, what we are trying to decide is, first and foremost, whether certain principles are ones that no one, if suitably motivated, could reasonably reject.' For a useful discussion of this idea, see H Pauer-Studer, *Einführung in die Ethik*, 3rd edn (Vienna, Facultas, 2020) 135–37. Mind that the 'contradiction in conception' test for the categorical imperative integrates the rejection by others into the first-personal perspective of the agent. See I Kant, *Grundlegung zur Metaphysik der Sitten* (ed B Kraft and D Schönecker, Hamburg, Meiner, 1999) 47. For a useful analytical explication, see O O'Neill, *Acting on Principle: An Essay on Kantian Ethics*, 2nd edn (Cambridge, Cambridge University Press, 2013) 152–58. The test requires adopting a maxim and imagining what the world would be like if everyone else acted or had already acted on it (one should imagine it as operating like a law of nature). I could not carry out my plan to rob a bank, for as a result of frequent robberies there would be no more banks to rob, or banks would have taken such enormous precautions that robberies would be impossible. The precautions by the bank are the equivalent of reasonable rejection, for there is no reason for banks to let themselves be robbed by me. Likewise, as Hobbes already observed in his discussion of the 'fool', not keeping promises is subject to reasonable rejection, because once people learn that one fails to keep one's word they will not accept promises from notoriously unfaithful promisors. Hence, the fool cannot carry out his plan. The reasonable rejection is again manifest in conduct of others that, from the first-personal perspective,

of Victorian England, reassuring one another that deprivation and squalor were not experienced as abjectly by the lower classes as they would have been by themselves.[16] They smothered their feelings of guilt with a rationalising prejudice about the riff-raff's lesser sensibility. On roughly the same level of moral insensitivity resided Nietzsche's contention that the sacrifices of slaves, servants and members of the working class were a harsh necessity of life that made the work of great artists and thinkers possible.[17]

Particular Universalisation

It is the case, however, that not all failures to come to terms with the third element are attributable to a lack of empathy and an attendant failure to show equal respect. There are cases in which people deeply disagree over what it takes to demonstrate such respect. A simple example may illustrate this point. Hard-nosed libertarians, for example, believe that nobody should have a right to social assistance. They believe that leaving people to their own devices forces them to discover their hidden strength. Feeling the urge of necessity is a condition of freedom and growth. Far from denying that we ought to respect individual dignity, libertarians believe that the mode of recognising this very dignity requires leaving people with no other choice than to empower themselves – protecting them against being mired in dependence. As is well known, social democrats find this attitude repugnant and possibly even hypocritical. They contend that those finding themselves in dire straits have a right to state support.

The example is trivial, to be sure. But it explains why the disagreeing parties inhabit different normative worlds[18] or, alternatively put, different systems of morality in the sense of *Sittlichkeit*.[19] What underpins the

changes the world in a manner that makes the pursuit of a plan impossible. See T Hobbes, *Leviathan* (ed I Shapiro, New Haven, CT, Yale University Press, 2010) 89–90 [73].

[16] See G Orwell, *The Road to Wigan Pier* (London, Penguin Books, 1989) 16.

[17] See F Nietzsche, *Unzeitgemäße Betrachtungen*, vol 2, 8th edn (Leipzig, CG Naumann, 1899) 56, 58–59.

[18] However, the normative presuppositions indicate different, as regards the persons concerned, unalienable conceptions of accomplishing selfhood. They collide in the context of universalisation. See C Menke, 'Liberalismus im Konflikt: Zwischen Gerechtigkeit und Freiheit' in M Brumlik and H Brunkhorst (eds), *Gemeinschaft und Gerechtigkeit* (Frankfurt aM, Fischer, 1993) 218–43.

[19] The tacit reference, which is in fact a mere allusion, is, of course, to GWF Hegel, *System der Sittlichkeit [Critik des Fichteschen Naturrechts]* (ed HD Brandt, Hamburg, Meiner, 2002). The main text above renders the predicament in Hegelian terms. It can also be spelled out, however, in the idiom of Schelling's late philosophy. Then the discrepancy can be attributed to the influence of 'burdens of judgment', which we have already encountered in chapter 1. See J Rawls, *Political Liberalism* (New York, Columbia University Press, 1991) 56–57. They concern manifest but inscrutable circumstances making

opposing universalisations are a number of presuppositions that remain largely implicit in its course.[20] Libertarians believe that it would be wrong to deny people opportunities to discover their potential. Individual responsibility and strength are derivative of the 'tough love' of not helping those who falsely believe themselves to be dependent and powerless. The attitudes of libertarians and social democrats are also associated with different understandings of society.[21] For libertarians, society is the space where individuals meet to engage in exchanges. It does not amount to more than a marketplace and is, owing to its being a mere mechanism for the coordination of individual conduct, not capable of exercising agency itself. Ontologically speaking, society is a mere aggregation of individuals. Social democrats, by contrast, believe that society is a system of cooperation, the revenue of which is to be distributed according to some patterned principle of justice. Society acts through the state and must provide individuals with conditions under which they can flourish.

For each position, these presuppositions amount to a moderately coherent whole and involve certain ideas concerning virtues people

us judge in one way or another. They mediate moral conviction, even though they can be pointed to only by using somewhat elusive notions such as 'one's assessment of evidence' or the 'life experience' that happens to channel one's perception of situations. These 'burdens' are, in a sense, the dark matter of practical reason, or – in language more congenial to Schelling – something that is not thought (*Denken*) but being (*Sein*) that mediates thinking. See F Wilhelm Joseph Schelling, *Ages of the World* (trans J Norman, Ann Arbor, MI, University of Michigan Press, 2001). I can only refer to rewarding introductory readings. See J Habermas, 'Dialectical Idealism in Transition of Materialism: Schelling's Idea of a Contraction of God and its Consequences for the Philosophy of History' (trans N Midgley and J Norman) in J Norman and A Welchman (eds), *The New Schelling* (London, Continuum, 2004) 43–89; S Zizek, *The Indivisible Remainder: On Schelling and Related Matters* (London, Verso, 2007); SJ McGrath, *The Dark Ground of Spirit: Schelling and the Unconscious* (London, Routledge, 2012).

[20] From a Kantian point of view, one might object that the libertarian position amounts to what Kant would call a 'contradiction in will'. See Kant, n 15, 48 (AA 423–24). If the persons acting take into account that they are rational persons pursuing goals, and that they can pursue goals in a situation in which they are helpless only if they are helped by others, they must want the rule that provides for help in an emergency for everyone. See O'Neill, n 15, 183–84. Alternatively, but still put in Kantian terms, if seeking your own happiness is a necessary end to have then universalisation requires that we ascribe having the same end to others. Therefore, it is reasonable to help in situations where the pursuit of one's own happiness would depend on feasible assistance too. For a helpful analysis, see R Johnson and A Cureton, 'Kant's Moral Philosophy' in *Stanford Encyclopedia of Philosophy* at https://plato.stanford.edu/entries/kant-moral/, 15, 20–21 (pdf view). Even if one considers this reasoning to be sound, the libertarian's conviction is based on the conjecture that the omission of help is a prerequisite for people to discover their inner strength and to overcome dependence. They thus acquire self-respect and become independent. It is the libertarian path to happiness. The conflict can therefore also be understood as concerning the way in which help must to be provided, even if, paradoxically, in the libertarian case, it is by not helping. No less a figure than Wilhelm von Humboldt argued along these lines See W von Humboldt, *The Limits of State Action* (ed J Borrow (Cambridge, Cambridge University Press, 1969) 24–26.

[21] For a succinct analysis, see P Koller, 'Gesellschaftsauffassung und soziale Gerechtigkeit' in G Frankenberg (ed), *Auf der Suche nach der gerechten Gesellschaft* (Frankfurt/Main, Fischer, 1994) 129–50.

ought to possess, such as, in the case of libertarians, being tough and unrelenting. While Kant undoubtedly believed that there are virtues we ought to develop because their realisation facilitates the pursuit of other ends (such as cultivating our talents or assisting the needy in order to be assisted in turn),[22] it is fair to say that the choice of attitudes and traits is largely inherent in particular ways of life. They are part of small-scale 'systems' of morality. What is more, the libertarian and the social democrat each satisfy all three elements of universalisation, of which the third merely turns out to be *socially* dependent on a particular point of view.[23] Neither of them exempts themselves from the application of the general rule they propose. This is clear in the case of social democrats, who would be happy to receive assistance if it was needed. But libertarians would also, were they sincere, clench their teeth and attempt to help themselves. The first two elements of universalisation are fully met. Both also satisfy the third element, but only *within* their own system of morality. The universal is thereby not denied but rather *mediated* by particularity. Universalisation turns out to be relative to a particular point of view and thus dependent on the attitude of those who share it. But this does not detract from its nature. Both believe that everyone else *ought* to share their point of view.

The problem that arises is that moral judgement does not work in the direction in which we suppose it to work, namely, *from* the substantive *to* the social dimension. Were this route open, the social democrats and the libertarians would be able to confront each other with their arguments and, depending on ideal conditions of conversation, reach agreement. One of them would end up revising their view. But it is not clear why this would be the case. They do not share a conception of what the recognition of human dignity requires. Indeed, it is a type of disagreement we are inclined to call 'reasonable', for people can disagree over whether we ought to treat people by default as strong or as weak creatures. Neither position is obnoxious, let alone bizarre.

The example shows that the substantive dimension is dependent on its social counterpart. Some agreement at a more 'fundamental' level facilitates agreement in particular cases.

Whatever relation may obtain at the end between the libertarian and the social democrat cannot be internal but merely 'external'. It would be

[22] See the discussion in O'Neill, n 15, 176–78.

[23] On the 'nesting' of the social dimension in the substantive, see 'Five Consequences' below.

internal if they continued to persuade each other (and thereby adopted what Habermas calls the 'performative attitude'). The shift to the external relation is marked by either mere mutual causal impact or by the attribution of status to determine the matter for the other. Brainwashing the social democrat into a libertarian would be an example of the former, while granting one of them power to decide the matter would be an example of the latter. The difference between these two forms of external relations is that ascription of status and the corresponding subordination is the mode of resolving an antinomy of morality. The antinomy is manifest in the fact that simultaneously, both and none of the conflicting positions are right, for they each involve universalisations that nonetheless remain particular.

Coherence and Reciprocity

The problem cuts even deeper, and at this deeper level the perplexity of universalisation is reminiscent of Hegel's vehement opposition to Kant's principle of morality – the categorical imperative, that is.[24]

It is indeed very difficult to imagine how the universalisation of a rule could ever be completed if it were placed on a clean slate. Traditionally, there is, if it still exists, compulsory military service for young men only, but not for young women, who by now enjoy the right to enter the military forces if they desire to do so and after passing a physical fitness test. On its face, a norm making service compulsory only for men, but not for women, would ostensibly collide with the first element of universalisation. Yet we may be comfortable with it, for reasons having to do with the inherited allocation of tasks between the sexes, the tenacity of habits inherent in the operation of the military forces, and possibly even with the idea that it is not unfair to impose a greater burden on men owing to the fact that they, as a group, do not have to bear the brunt of pregnancy and childbirth or suffer the attendant adverse effects on their careers. The exemption of women from compulsory service could then be regarded as 'making up' for disadvantages suffered by women owing to the fateful determinants of biology.

[24] See, for example, GWF Hegel, 'Über die wissenschaftlichen Behandlungsarten des Naturrechts, seine Stelle in der praktischen Philosophie und sein Verhältnis zu den positiven Rechtswissenschaften' in GWF Hegel, *Werke in zwanzig Bänden*, vol 2 (ed M Moldenhauer and KM Michel, Frankfurt aM, 1969–71) 434–30, 460–64.

If factors such as these rescue the rule from being dismissed on moral grounds, its universalisation depends on a number of empirical and normative premises. One of these would be the normative principle according to which a disadvantage imposed by a rule may well be evened out by an existing social practice that is not subject to universalisation but – at any rate, for the time being – taken for granted.[25] In the context in which the question of universalisation arises, we treat it as a given and, most importantly, do not call it into question when the imposition of a disadvantage is at issue. For their operation, universalisations presuppose something 'consented' (the *de iure* or *de facto* quality of which remains unaccounted for).[26] This is reflected in Hegel's belief that one can identify reasons for action only as a participant in social practices. A thicker and richer context invests subjects with standards, allowing them to figure out what ought to be done while drawing on implicit knowledge of what is already practised.[27]

Universalisation and Social Freedom

Of course, this example demonstrates only imperfectly why taking certain matters for granted is a necessary condition of universalisation.[28] Universalisation is the form of moral problem-solving that we engage in only when matters become controversial. Unsurprisingly, it is most relevant when sacrifices are being called for. Nobody wants to put up with receiving the raw end of the deal. Yet the reciprocity that everyone expects to be met may not materialise in a direct consideration but in the accrual of other and more remote benefits by virtue of one's participation in social institutions. Men, to a lesser extent than women the slaves of biology, are compensated for their military service in a variety of ways.

Universalisation can also be mediated by the mutual support of individual freedom. The freedom of children to explore the world or to qualify for a profession could scarcely be realised were they left to their own devices. Their actions are facilitated by the choices of others, such as their parents, who support them. Parents are more than happy to sacrifice time

[25] See Scanlon, n 15, 214.

[26] Hegel, n 24, 463, objected that universalisations generally confer universal validity on elements of a contingent institutional setting. He may have thereby alerted us that we must not mistake the taken-for-granted attitude towards those elements as a claim to their validity.

[27] See C Menke, *Autonomie und Befreiung: Studien zu Hegel* (Berlin, Suhrkamp, 2019) 27–30.

[28] On the following, see A Honneth, *Die Idee des Sozialismus: Versuch einer Aktualisierung* (Berlin, Suhrkamp, 2015) 42, 47–48, 51–52, 122.

and resources, not least because they take an interest in the success of their offspring. Their efforts may be rewarded many years later in ways they may have been unable to anticipate. The relation between parents and children is an example of how the demand of universalisation can be satisfied in structures of 'social freedom'. Parents facilitate the educational choices of their children; yet they can succeed at being good parents, which is their very own ambition, only if children are prudent and therefore also amenable to guidance and advice. The realisation of the freedom of one depends on the apt realisation of the freedom of the other.

Viewing the realisation of freedom as extending beyond individual actions, and hence as essentially 'social', can be expanded to include larger structures of social cooperation. For example, my freedom to write about topics of my interests is made possible by many people (administrators, technicians, librarians, research assistants) providing me with the conditions requisite thereto. Presuming that what they intend to do, among other things, is also to support my actions, they can be regarded as the hidden co-authors of my actions. My work is possible because it is, as to what effectively grounds it, *our* work. Their incomes, in turn, help them to sustain their families or allow them to do things they deem valuable in their leisure. The fact that they are employed by an organisation that also employs me, makes me, however at a greater remove, into someone whose freedom contributes to their own. My benefits accruing from their toil are justified because the income that they earn enables them to enlist my actions indirectly to enjoy their freedom in the private domain.

While it is tempting to overstretch the organicism inherent in the conception of 'social freedom', it demonstrates, nonetheless, that the contemplation and justification of sacrifices must be seen in a broader context in which the realisation of individual freedom depends on extended and more complex relations of mutuality.[29] One arrives thereby, applied on a larger social scale, at the type of reasoning encountered in theories of distributive justice. Whether or not it is fair to impose a higher tax rate on higher-earning members of society depends on whether this facilitates the freedom of those who are worse off. But such support also facilitates the freedom of the former. Increasing the tax rate in higher tax brackets can be viewed as justified, again, by taking certain things for granted in a society, such as existing

[29] ibid 52, 54.

socio-economic hierarchies or a specific division of labour and a sense of solidarity underpinning transfers.[30]

The Substantive Is Social

The organicism inherent in the social conception of freedom explains why it cannot so easily be transposed to societies in which people reason from a variety of heterogeneous social perspectives. For libertarians, for example, the tax paid in support of the worse off simply counts as an unrequited sacrifice. In their case, universalisation can only be successful vis-à-vis those who *de facto* happen to share their point of view. It is *particular*. Their moral judgement is universal *for itself*, but it is not so *in itself*. With regard to everyone and anyone, it is at least held in abeyance. If, by contrast, it just happened to be *de facto* commonly accepted, the lack of universality would be hidden underneath its generality.[31]

If all converted to libertarianism, the judgement would be general. From the vantage point of the substantive dimension, one could still raise the question whether what is general is indeed universal, namely, an expression of what all would *have* to agree to. And yet the consequence of all having to do so could also only be stated in social terms. Pragmatically speaking, persuasion is about making people believe what you believe. If you succeed, they become a little bit like you.

This – using Brandom's concept[32] – 'attitude-dependence' of universalisation could be overcome only by eliminating the perspectival 'for itself'. It would involve a quest for some unknown objectivity, the encounter with which is so compelling as to knock all dissenters down. Good reasons, to repeat, would force everyone to consent without coercing anyone into doing so. This seems to be what moral realists are after.[33] But its significance can be restated in social terms.[34] In the final event, everyone would end up being persuaded. This suggests, indeed, that the 'in itself' is eventually a

[30] The only alternative way to account of trade-offs would be the utilitarian calculus. But the problem is why maximisation should matter.

[31] In other words, the judgements would be universal only for all *of them*, but there is no guarantee that *anyone else* must agree.

[32] See R Brandom, *A Spirit of Trust: A Reading of Hegel's* Phenomenology (Cambridge, MA, Harvard University Press, 2019) 263, 265–66.

[33] See Scanlon, n 10, 25, 31, 69, 105.

[34] The late Dworkin appears to have been this type of realist (despite remaining in denial). See his *Justice for Hedgehogs* (Cambridge, MA, Harvard University Press, 2011).

manifestation of what things are 'for others'.[35] Possibly, the gap separating universality from generality is not as wide as it seems.

Five Consequences

The social nests in the substantive. The first consequence that can be drawn from this hypothesis is that if the heterogeneity of substantive moral perspectives has to be taken for granted as an independent variable of action, we are only, but nonetheless, entitled to endorse particular universalisations. We stand vindicated before ourselves, at any rate, no matter what others say. Morality thus becomes an essentially personal affair, even though this does not entail that people must abstain from efforts to garner followership and support. People are free to walk around assured of their righteousness and to proselytise. There is no objection to having particularism outgrow itself into generality, even if by virtue of such growth it would never become truly universal.

We shall see whether this conclusion warrants moral relativism. There are reasons to doubt it.

The second consequence is that, if heterogeneity as a circumstance is to be taken into account in the context of moral judgement, then attaining agreement is not morally necessary. Aiming at agreement might even be false, not least because one must suspect any agreement to be based on some form of intimidation or other asymmetries of power. It seems that the conclusion that needs to be drawn is reminiscent of Pyrrhonic scepticism. The wise person suspends judgement and does not care whether it is possible to find a right answer in the future.[36]

The third consequence is detachment from action. Particularistic moral judgements are unfit to serve as the cement of society. While those raising claims are formally assured of their righteousness and meet the expectation of insiders, what they thereby provide for outsiders are neither summons nor directives but merely reports of what they take to be right or wrong. They demonstrate attitudes and stop short of engaging anyone's 'performative attitude'.[37] Habermas observed keenly that the morality of modernity

[35] See Brandom, n 32, 280.

[36] See KM Vogt, *Belief and Truth: A Skeptic Reading of Plato* (Oxford, Oxford University Press, 2012) 115–16.

[37] The expression in inverted commas pays tribute to Jürgen Habermas. I hasten to add that demonstrations of attitudes can be so unnerving that they evoke performative attitudes in any event.

is a 'system of knowledge', owing to its aloof detachment from the motives driving the conduct of people who are exposed to the harsh realities of competition and experience the need to make accommodations and to settle on compromise.[38] People are able to confront each other with what they take to be universal *for themselves*. Morality is thereby transformed into what Hegel analysed with exasperation in the *Phenomenology*[39] and the *Philosophy of Law*.[40] Detached from the world of action, morality is, in certain social situations, turned into a rhetorical device with which bystanders needle and wheedle those who shoulder responsibility and take action. A moral judgement that never gets off the ground is by its very nature hypocritical, for it fails to put itself on an equal footing with real agency. It claims superiority while faintheartedly judging from a place located outside of practice. Basing moral evaluation on such a safe bet is craven and mean.

The fourth consequence is that, nonetheless, a world inhabited by moral particularists assuring themselves by means of universalisation of their righteousness contains, indeed, the seed for the transformation of morality into the legal relation. The step that needs to be taken thereto, however, consists of moving forward to the universalisation of particular universalisations. We shall return to this below in 'From Others to Self'.

The fifth and most important consequence, however, is that the third element of universalisation that appeals to 'acceptability' from the perspective of variously affected people explicitly mentions a social component that resides in the substantive dimension. What morality requires 'in itself' turns out to be a disguised form of the 'for itself'. More precisely, the third element introduces a distressing undecidedness into the substantive dimension that we have already encountered in its social counterpart (see 'Two Dimensions of Moral Judgement' above). In fact, this amounts to an invasion, as it were, of the wavering between the cognitive and normative orientation[41] inherent in the latter. Do reasonable people *have to* agree or is reasonableness *constituted* in the absence of objections? The question must be, of course,

[38] See J Habermas, *Faktizität und Geltung: Beiträge zur Diskurstheorie des Rechts und des demokratischen Rechtsstaats* (Frankfurt aM, Suhrkamp, 1991) 145.

[39] See GWF Hegel, *Phänomenologie des Geistes* (ed H-F Wessels and H Clairmont, Hamburg, Meiner, 1988) 395–426.

[40] See GWF Hegel, *Elements of the Philosophy of Right* (trans HB Nisbet, Cambridge, Cambridge University Press, 1991) 170–84, § 140.

[41] It should be noted that the cognitive orientation is the consequence of accepting pre-emption. The normative orientation prioritised the dependence on good reasons. Evidently, the problems of authority that we discussed in chapter 8 are derivative of problems of morality.

whether, if an occasion for reasonable rejection arises, any objection must pass as a valid veto (the latter alternative: pre-emption) or whether the judging person retains the right to set the conditions governing the appropriateness of objections (the former: dependence on substance). Putting the matter more precisely, the question is whether objectors may give effect to a rejection of their own accord or whether the judgers retain authority to determine its validity.[42] This alternative reflects the wavering between the cognitive and the normative orientation (between pre-emption and substantive dependence). Obviously, recognition is decisive here, for the question is, indeed, whether the objectors need to put up with the authority of the judgers or the other way round. Authority is, however, a matter concerning the social dimension.

From this it follows that the priority of the substantive dimension must, if its significance is – in the spirit of pragmatism – clearly stated, embrace its negation and reversal. Boldly and simply put, for morality to possess substance it needs to be buttressed by some acknowledgement of authority. Universal endorsement is what the substantive dimension promises to deliver without being able to ground it.[43] Any spontaneous consent is ungrounded. It appears to be a sibling of Schopenhauer's will;[44] or, cast in Hegelian terms, a substance, that is, that which is of itself what it is.

Why Relativism Does Not Offer a Solution

The first consequence of particular universalisation is that the moral judgements in which it is manifest are correct only substantively but not socially. If any universalisation is as good as any other then, in the end, socially, there is none. There is moral objectivity for particular subjects only. We arrive at an antinomy. Its significance is often misunderstood. The result of this misunderstanding is moral relativism.

[42] The assertion of dependence on substantive reasons pre-empts pre-emption. From this it follows that pre-emption involves a self-authorisation of dependent reasons to pre-empt other reasons. Mind that this pre-emptive effect is built into the very idea of a reason. A good reason precludes the relevance of other reasons. What matters here, however, is that the divide between pre-emption and dependent reasons is thrown into relief in situations in which the pre-emptive effect of good reasons can no longer be taken for granted because one is confronted with a variety of plausible reasons.

[43] Autonomous acceptance is integral to reason. One may wonder whether reasonable people do not have to accept something if something is reasonable. But why do they have to *accept* it (and not just do as they are told)? It is because we only encounter reason in the reasoning of individuals. See I Kant, *Kritik der reinen Vernunft* (ed J Timmermann, Hamburg, Meiner, 1998) 784–85 [A 738–39].

[44] See A Schopenhauer, *Die Welt als Wille und Vorstellung*, vol 1.1 (ed A Hübscher, Zürich, Diogenes, 1977) 150–51.

According to the relativist outlook, as reconstructed by Boghossian,[45] the truth conditions of moral statements depend on the framework from within which they are made. This implies that any moral claim that *straightforwardly* asserts something to be right or wrong misrepresents its own truth conditions. While the claim appears to say something about the world (eg, 'this' is wrong), it must be translated into what it can legitimately state, namely, that something is right or wrong *within* a particular framework or *from* a certain point of view. This explains why Boghossian characterises moral relativism as a form of relationalism. Making a moral claim is tantamount to a logical statement claiming that an act is right or wrong within a certain framework.

Relativism, however, misrepresents the antinomy of moral judgement, for it cannot account for the existence of disagreements.[46] If relativism indeed translates the *de re* 'folk'[47] moral judgement that slavery is wrong into the *de dicto* statement that most folks believe that slavery is wrong according to their particular moral code, then this finding is merely a statement of what follows from their code. If someone objected that the relevant moral code did not indict slavery then this disagreement would not be about slavery but about the import of the code.[48] Controversy over the substantive issue, namely, whether slavery is *really* wrong, would be resolved by attributing the divergent views to the application of different codes or, at any rate, to different interpretations of what they imply. Everyone could understand why others see it differently. Consequently, however, differences of opinion on moral issues would be ruled out. If we all had reciprocal access to our respective codes, we could all understand why, from a certain point of view, one must have a certain view. Relativism fails to explain the problem it purports to answer. It does not explain why we ought to respect a relative point of view at all and within which limits. It does not even give us reason to endorse any point of view, for each is equally unreasonable.

Elaborating the Inverting Invasion

We can now return to elucidating the substantive dimension of moral judgement through the lens of its social counterpart. The latter is implicitly

[45] See PA Boghossian, *Fear of Knowledge: Against Relativism and Constructivism* (Oxford, Oxford University Press, 2006) 48–52.

[46] See PA Boghossian, 'Three Types of Relativism' in S Hales (ed), *A Companion to Relativism* (Oxford, Wiley-Blackwell, 2011) 53–69.

[47] See CB Miller, 'Moral Relativism and Moral Psychology' in Hales (ed), n 46, 346–67, 348.

[48] See Boghossian, n 46, 58.

present in the former, for the third element of universalisation demands that a rule or practice has to be acceptable from the perspective of persons affected. This condition suggests that persons judging morally need to concede to others who happen to be in different situations some form of veto power. But since egocentric or frivolous vetoes would be unacceptable, the objectors must be held to a standard agreeable to everyone else, the judgers included. After all, the objectors should also ask themselves whether their rejection could elicit agreement from those who are in, again, other situations.[49] They must, in other words, not carve out a privilege for themselves.

The substantive condition can be further spelled out in social terms by taking one's cue from the 'mechanics' of constitutional arrangements.[50] Impertinent objections can be discouraged if the objectors' veto power is matched with a power of override on the part of the judgers. Nevertheless, the issue remains of who should have the ultimate authority to determine whether an objection is unacceptable.

From the perspective of the social dimension, the exercise of both powers is attitude-dependent.[51] While both may recognise the commitments following from their entitlement to either veto or override, the exercise of these powers depends on what each *takes* to its appropriate use. There is no guarantee of their sharing a substantive criterion independently of what judgers and objectors take it to be. Such a criterion, if it existed, would, conversely, be attitude-independent.[52]

As we will explore below, the only way out of this impasse is to externalise (see 'Particular Universalisation' above) the internal relation. What the objectors take to be serious demur must be accepted by the judgers by virtue of taking the objectors as having the power to determine the matter. The objectors, in turn, not only need to recognise the status of the judgers to invest them with such power, but they also have to accept that their stating of *valid* objections depends on the judgers' recognition of their status as objectors.

[49] See Scanlon, n 15, 191.

[50] Again, it is obvious that what we encounter here is a wavering between dependent reasons and pre-emption. The enigma of authority that we studied in chapter 8 has its root in the enigma of morality.

[51] On the concept, see Brandom, n 32.

[52] Under conditions where one must reckon with social heterogeneity, criteria that *seem* to be attitude-independent are *de facto* reflective of a convergence of attitudes. Universality is in fact generality and generality is seeming attitude-independence.

Pure Independence (and Why It Fails)

The veto power conceded to objectors must be limited. Were the judgers to concede to the objectors unlimited discretion then the objectors would enjoy absolute independence or 'mastery'. Remarkably, such status is a *social* equivalent to the attitude-independence implicit in how we ordinarily conceive of the substantive dimension of moral judgement. The objectors would always be right and thus turn out to be what Brandom calls 'constitutive takers'.[53] Whatever they take[54] to be right would indeed be right by virtue of their taking it to be so. Matters would count for everyone else as what they are in themselves because of what they are for those[55] who are purely independent and the masters of intelligibility.[56] All others would be stripped of all authority to say what is right and wrong and be required to follow their lead.

Interestingly, such a relation would be *inconsistent* with the third element of universalisation, in particular if one reads it as a version of Kant's means-ends formula of the categorical imperative.[57] People who are consigned to staying mute when their interests are at stake are not treated as ends in themselves.

Before examining this situation further, it should be noted that the practice of moral argument and judgement is permanently affected by asymmetries of power of which such 'mastery' is merely the most extreme expression.[58] Morality is, owing to its dependence on the social dimension, not a sea of tranquility; rather, it is, more often than not, subservient to the exercise of power.[59]

[53] See Brandom, n 32, 330. They are sovereign takers. See ibid 331.

[54] According to Brandom, ibid 245, a 'taker' is an 'institutor of orectic significances'. This means that beings of this kind attribute a certain significance to things from the perspective of what they are striving for. Hungry beings 'take' a loaf of bread to be food.

[55] This is what Brandom, ibid 314–15, calls, following Hegel, 'mastery' *(Herrschaft)*. Whoever takes oneself to be a master is ontologically mistaken.

[56] ibid 275–76, 314.

[57] See Kant, n 15, 53.

[58] See also Brandom, n 32, 340–41.

[59] The idea has been contemplated by Brandom too. See RB Brandom, 'Towards Reconciling Two Heroes: Habermas and Hegel' (2015) 1 *Argumenta: The Journal of the Italian Society for Analytic Philosophy* 29–42, 31–32: 'Perhaps what we are pleased to call "reason" is *just* the distinctly modern form of power relations; politer, no less coercive, and both less honest (in denying that power is being exercised at all) and more encompassing (because penetrating the permeating the discursive core of what the self-conscious modern selves who are subjected to that power are) than premodern forms.'

The full authority enjoyed by a constitutive taker is, of course, both an illusion and an abomination.[60] There is no reason for judgers to have vetoes by objectors pre-empt what they believe to be substantively correct. The power of objectors has to have limits lest they implicitly deny the judgers the authority to attribute independently their status to them. The objectors also cannot on their own initiative turn themselves into constitutive takers.

It is possible, indeed, to be *essentially* a taker.[61] It is essential to self-conscious beings to count as something for themselves, which is – not least because our self-understanding is part of what we are – inherent in what they are in themselves.[62] But one cannot, despite being an essential taker, constitute oneself into a constitutive taker.[63] For if one could, one would never make the experience error[64] and go through processes of self-correction.[65] Indeed, in a relation of mastery it is part of the work of the dependent servants to correct silently the mistakes committed by the masters while sustaining for them the illusion that they are always right.[66] That the servants undergo learning processes in dealing with the world explains why in the long haul they outdo their masters by their wits.[67]

What masters are for themselves – namely, constitutive takers – is part of what they are in themselves (ie the false conception of their authority makes them into who they are). Nevertheless, they are also mistaken about what they are in themselves, for they cannot just turn themselves into such

[60] See Brandom, n 32, 275–76, 336–37, observing that the master is mistaken about what he is in himself, even if being mistaken is part of what he is in himself. He is someone mistakenly taking himself to be a constitutive taker.

[61] Selves are essentially takers, because for them things are what they are for themselves. See ibid 244.

[62] ibid 235.

[63] ibid 332.

[64] ibid 349. What is true is attitude-dependent if it is true by virtue of our taking it to be true. This is, when it comes to a ruling political party, the world of 'Insoc' as horrifically conceived by George Orwell in his disturbing novel *Nineteen Eighty-Four*. What is true is what the party takes to be true, and it makes it true by rewriting historical records. Anscombe's 'direction of fit', according to which descriptive statements have to match the facts and, conversely, facts to comport with prescription, is turned upside down. The facts do not determine the statement; those making the statements eviscerate everything that could be used as evidence against its truth. See G Orwell, *Nineteen Eighty-Four* (London, Harcourt Brace and Co, 1949).

[65] See Brandom, n 32, 235.

[66] ibid 346.

[67] While the master degenerates into a silly consumer: see C Taylor, *Hegel* (Cambridge, Cambridge University Press, 1975) 156.

creatures. In fact, masterly authority depends on unilateral recognition[68] extended by servants,[69] and the satisfaction of the masters' desires would be impossible if it were not for the servants' intelligent labour. This *de facto* reversal of dependence is the key to unlocking the relation of *mutual* recognition.[70] For the masters, the servants are nil. They – the masters – do not view servants as having the capacity, as a status, to ascribe masterly authority to them, for this would be inconsistent with their viewing themselves as constitutive takers. Yet since they cannot create this status by themselves, they depend on the status they deny their servants, namely the status to be equally status-attributing normative beings.[71] Initially, the masters can get on in their deluded universe so long as the servants feign respect for their allegedly correct judgement and tacitly revise their mistaken views of the world. Once the recognition becomes mutual, however, the judgements of neither are considered by default to be either superior or inferior.[72] Dealing with the world becomes mediated by reasoning together, which involves taking the ratiocination of the other as seriously as if it were one's own.[73] Both enjoy independence based on mutual dependence. The relevance of their independently arrived at claims, demurs, conjectures or desires depends on the attribution by the other of the status of responsible peerage in the reasoning process. The attribution of status-attributing status – the attribution of power to confer peerage – remains in their hands.[74] Since both hold this power simultaneously, the relation is symmetrical. Any revocation of status could be requited with the selfsame act. However, the recognition of the status of a reasoner can never amount to granting full power to say what is right, for it would enslave the status-conferring person and thereby divest it of the power to confer status in the first place.

[68] The most elementary attitude of recognition views others not as mere objects but as beings who also possess desires that adopt attitudes such as wanting and apprehension. See RB Brandom, *Pragmatism and Idealism: Rorty and Hegel on Reason and Representation* (Oxford, Oxford University Press, 2022) 69. See also Brandom, n 32, 248: 'Recognizing others is attributing to them the practical significance of exhibiting the triadic structure of orectic awareness: taking them to be takers, subjects for whom things can have a practical significance, relative to a desire, and mediated by an activity.'

[69] See Brandom, n 32, 340. The servant is wrong about what he truly is in viewing himself as a thing. See ibid 344–45.

[70] ibid 343.

[71] See Brandom, *Pragmatism and Idealism*, n 68, 76: 'Not only are commitments or responsibilities attitude-dependent statuses, but so is the authority to institute statuses by one's attitudes.'

[72] ibid 77, 81.

[73] See Brandom, n 32, 254–55.

[74] ibid 345; Brandom, n 68, 77.

Mutual Recognition

Recognition, admittedly, is a darling token of contemporary philosophy and requires, considering the variety of its uses, some clarification. In contrast to the broad use made by Axel Honneth, for whom recognition comprises relations of mutual love, the recognition of persons as legal subjects and the reciprocal appreciation of works or services,[75] what is of relevance in our context are the authority and responsibility to claim, to argue or to decide matters.[76] The relation between judgers and objectors provides an acutely apposite example. If either of them had *natural* authority to determine the conditions under which an objection is reasonable, their authority would be independent of being attributed by another. It would exist and would have to be acknowledged by virtue of its existence.[77] Judgers and objectors would possess this authority not only *for* themselves, but also *in* themselves, independent of relations of recognition.

Among equals, however, authority and status are dependent on attributions. This is what is 'modern' about them.[78] The deference that we owe to those exercising their power of judgement is not just added to what they conceivably already possess; rather, the attribution of that power is indispensable for its existence.[79] It explains why what they say matters to us. Their authority is, however, also independent. Whether or how people exercise their judgement is up to them. Whether or not how we independently evaluate what they say is of relevance to them, is determined by themselves. My independent attribution of status depends on their freedom to let my responses matter to them, while the relevance of their independent statements depends on my making myself freely amenable to it.[80] Such a reciprocal relation represents a structure of 'perfect freedom and

[75] See A Honneth, *Kampf um Anerkennung: Zur moralischen Grammatik sozialer Konflikte* (Frankfurt aM, Suhrkamp, 1992) 153, 173–74, 179.

[76] See Brandom, n 68, 76: 'Recognizing others is taking them to be normative subjects. That is taking them to be subjects of normative statuses and attitudes: able to be responsible and to exercise authority, and both to attribute those statuses to others and to acknowledge, undertake, or claim them themselves'.

[77] This is why, in the case of Kant, the appropriate response to human dignity, which is taken to be a metaphysical fact, is to respect it. The authority to make oneself responsible by taking oneself to be responsible is a given. See Brandom, n 32, 265, 269, 271, 278. See also Brandom, n 68, 72.

[78] Brandom, n 68, 84–85.

[79] See Brandom, n 32, 280.

[80] As Brandom, ibid 284, explains, '[r]ecognizing … is the attitude of attributing the status of authority to institute statuses by one's attitudes, when those attitudes are suitably complemented'.

independence', in which the 'I' is 'We' and the 'We' is 'I'.[81] The status of those possessing authority depends on others and on their regarding these others as authority-conferring. The authority to institute statuses based on one's attitudes is attributed to others who are taken to possess the self-same authority.[82] As an autonomous being, I can make myself responsible by taking myself to be responsible because others, to whom I attribute the requisite authority, authorise me to do so.

Conceiving of objectivity through the lens of mutual recognition results, in the first round, in admitting the perspectives and experiences of others to the reasoning process. Objectivity becomes explicable as the convergence of attitudes based on reasoning together.[83] Richard Rorty had a dry way of putting the matter: true is whatever your community will let you get away with.[84] But there can be no guarantee of convergence. The encounter between judgers and objectors may result in a dead heat. They may experience a persistent and tenacious divergence of attitudes. In such a case, the recognitional model must be taken to the next level.

A Revised Understanding of Objectivity

We began with a conception of moral objectivity that accorded priority to the substantive dimension of moral judgement. The idea was that the uncoercive force of the better argument would elicit agreement along the social dimension. We can now rephrase what we meant by the substantive dimension through the lens of its social counterpart.

[81] See GWF Hegel, *Phänomenologie des Geistes* (ed H-F Wessels and H Clairmont, Hamburg, Meiner, 1988) 127. As Brandom, n 32, 282–83, explains: 'They do not individually lift themselves up into the normative status of having recognitive authority by the bootstraps of their own recognitive attitudes (attributions of authority). But the recognitive unit they form when their recognition is mutual *does* lift the attitudes of *both*; it does promote their statuses (recognitive authority) that are merely virtual as the objects of their attitudes up to the level of actual normative statuses.'

[82] See Brandom, n 32, 282–83.

[83] Mutual recognition is what warrants objectivity under conditions of attitude-dependence. See ibid 246. If you recognise a recogniser, their judgements are of relevance to you. Recognising recognisers also means that trusting your own judgement depends on frequent confirmation by others. Relations of mutual recognition, to be sure, exceed this elementary function. They constitute the possibility of error in the application of rules. See RB Brandom, *Tales of the Mighty Dead: Historical Essays in the Metaphysics of Intentionality* (Cambridge, MA, Harvard University Press, 2002) 220–21. Their existence also explains the important hermeneutic task of learning more about the world by considering how it is seen by others. Actually, there is nothing outside the difference of perspective of others that would provide us with access to the 'in itself'. But see Brandom, n 68, 58–59, contemplating the possibility that we may confer authority on something outside of our practice, such as oracles, omens or things.

[84] Quoted in Brandom, n 68, 85.

Initially, we tacitly presupposed attitude-independence. We took it for granted that what is morally right is independent of what anyone takes it to be. At the same time, we realised that the third element of universalisation tacitly cedes the ground to the social dimension. By lending credence to rejection from a particular point of view, it highlights the tension between judgers and objectors. The foregoing discussion has not explored the possibility whether either of them might possess by their very nature better judgement and would therefore be invested with *natural* authority to say what is right.[85] The road that has been taken here is decidedly modern and 'anti-authoritarian'.[86] Normative statuses are attitude-dependent, and these attitudes are manifest in social practices. Brandom calls the latter thesis 'social pragmatism about norms'.[87]

The relation between judgers and objectors is one of *both* dependence and independence.[88] The relevance of the objection depends on the indulgence of the judgers. By attributing authority to the objectors, they make themselves responsive to it. The objectors are independent, for they are not obligated to agree with the judgers' opinion. The judgers depend on the objectors, because if their proposal did not require acquiescence on the part of the latter the problem would not arise. But they do not have to accept their objection. They also remain independent.

At this point both parties may part company. But if, as the circumstances of politics indicate,[89] that is not in their joint interest, they can continue in

[85] See ibid 72.

[86] ibid 28–29. See R Rorty, *Pragmatism as Anti-Authoritarianism* (Cambridge, MA, Harvard University Press, 2021).

[87] See Brandom, n 68, 60–61, 65, 73, 75, 81, 83.

[88] This matches the structure of reason that accounts for our authority of reasonable beings. We have this authority attributed to us when we have demonstrated our ability to master the rules of language and inference. Our authority is dependent on the judgement of others. Such a recognition authorises us to confront others with our independently arrived at conceptions of such rules and inferences. Such conceptions are 'attitude-dependent', for they reflect what we *take* to be meanings we share. They may involve normative idealisations of our practices that transcend established routines. George Herbert Mead pointed out that owing to our ability to develop our own best conceptions of our communities, we can transcend our existing social worlds and inhabit an ideal community. This is our independence. In order to enjoy it, however, we need to grant this same independence to others, for nobody would be willing to put up with our occupying the position of the master. It is owing to our subjectivity – our self-consciousness – that transcendence is built into the facticity of our dealings. See GH Mead, *Mind, Self, and Society from the Standpoint of the Social Behaviorist* (ed CW Morris, Chicago, IL, University of Chicago Press, 1934) 272, 382. The norms governing the attribution of authority do not confer status unless they are applied by individuals. The 'We' has to condense into an 'I'; the 'I' has to prove its authority vis-à-vis the 'We'.

[89] See Waldron, n 5.

the face of disagreement by mutually altering their status.[90] This alteration is easily possible, as it merely highlights an aspect of what lending credence to rejection from a particular point of view reveals about what they are in themselves. At this juncture, this aspect (or 'moment') is essential for continuing universalisation in a reflective mode, that is, by submitting it to its own discipline vis-à-vis its particularistic manifestations. The move is dialectical in that it shifts beyond a limit encountered in a way of reasoning – substantive moral discourse in this case – and draws on something that has remained latent in the situation creating the impasse. The impasse is the antinomy of moral judgement. Judgers and objectors acknowledge each other's equal ability to pass judgement on moral matters (they mutually attribute status) while disagreeing substantially. This equality has been already presupposed for any exchange of arguments, for it is based on the idea that owing to the equal capacity for being amenable to the same arguments, everyone will end up being convinced of the same. The status alteration necessary in the face of equally plausible conflicting judgements involves shifting from regarding one another as equally reasonable interlocutors to viewing one another as choosers. As already adumbrated, the internal relation among reasoners is transformed into an external relation. The external relation articulates the mutual attribution of equal judgement ability under the auspices of dissent.

With this move, it must seem as though the three dimensions of universalisation become swallowed up by a black hole lurking in the third. For each agent is cast for the other as invested with freedom of choice. The substantive reasons underlying their choices drop out of the picture. This is the progress that practical reason makes at this point. The transcendental illusion[91] of attitude-independence disappears. Substantive reasons remain relevant only at a remove because respecting choices is the way of accommodating particular universalisation. If people are convinced that abstaining from the consumption of red meat contributes both to animal welfare and to the preservation of the planet, then respecting their choices is a way of respecting what appears universally right to them. At the same time, since the substantive claim to universalisation is thereby also socially retracted, it is

[90] Cast in terms of the legal philosophy that Fichte developed in his *Grundlage des Naturrechts* (see n 97), this means that the moral point of view that is always about the right answer and always about right or wrong, needs to be abandoned in favour of the legal point of view that grants people leeway to be responsive to reasons by their own lights. See JA Clarke, 'Fichte's Independence Thesis' in Gottlieb (ed), n 13, 52–71, 65–66.

[91] On the 'transcendental illusion' concerning the existence of transcendental ideas and its tenacity and persistence, see Kant, n 43, 408 [A297, B353–354].

confined to morality as a mere 'system of knowledge' ('I know that …'). We respect people's *having* of moral beliefs, but we need not kowtow to these beliefs themselves. Like Pyrrhonian sceptics, we are free to hold their claims in abeyance (suspend judgement, practise *epoché*).[92]

Acting on what one takes to be one's own insight is of greatest significance for autonomous beings. But the reasons constituting their insight are not *directly* relevant socially, for they are not – without anything further – binding on anyone else. What is normatively relevant is the fact of their having beliefs – and exactly this is the matter that moral relativism can neither explain nor elucidate. It is a consequence of our regarding one another as autonomous beings.

What remains relevant of others is that they 'choose' to have certain views or certain projects.[93] The others are, therefore, presented as people with the capacity for freedom of choice. Reasons for choices, to be sure, lose their relevance, not least because the basic premise of the now emerging legal relation is that the reasons swaying others may remain strangely inscrutable.[94] The other agents are rendered as 'persons'. Weinrib is right that we ascribe to these constructs the capacity for purposive activity without regard for the end to which it is put.[95] He does not, however, account for its ground. Reciprocal independence[96] is not an 'innate right' but, on the contrary, an intersubjective achievement. Cast in the format of freedom of choice, it is indeed the core of the legal relation. Johann Gottlieb Fichte made this point quite succinctly in his *Foundation of Natural Law*:

> The … relation between rational beings requiring that each limits its freedom by the concept of the possibility of the freedom of the other, under the

[92] See Sextus Empiricus, *Outlines of Skepticism* (ed J Annas and J Barnes, Cambridge, Cambridge University Press, 2000) and the lucid commentary by G Striker, 'Skepticism as a Kind of Philosophy' in her *From Aristotle to Cicero: Essays on Ancient Philosophy* (Oxford, Oxford University Press, 2022) 177–91.

[93] In order to avoid a misunderstanding, I would like to clarify that the positions created by the resolution of the antinomy are not mere *leges permissivae* but most often powers and rights to which are correlated liabilities and duties. The 'permissive' element inherent in rights is, however, that right-holders possess discretion to decide on their exercise. It needs to be added, too, that the adoption of legal solutions does not presuppose the existence of disagreements. It suffices if it protects decisions against disagreements in advance.

[94] The irony inherent in the self's relation to itself should not elude us. The fact that people mutually yield to one another's judgements can be also regarded as a 'summons' to be reason-responsive by one's own lights *and* to respect the independent reason-responsiveness of others. The second condition, however, divests moral reasoning of its rigidity once it becomes applied to oneself. For an interpretation of Fichte's 'summons' as the call for reason-responsiveness that is capable of holding reasons at arm's length, see Wood, n 13, 83.

[95] See, for example, EJ Weinrib, *The Idea of Private Law*, 2nd edn (Oxford, Oxford University Press, 2012) 100, 104.

[96] See I Kant, *Metaphysische Anfangsgründe der Rechtslehre* (ed B Ludwig, Hamburg, Meiner, 1986) 47.

> condition that the former also limits its own by that of the other, is called the *legal relation*; and the formula now established is the *legal proposition*.[97]

The substantive dimension of judgement breaks away 'from below'. We no longer must hanker after an attitude-independent mooring. Freedom of choice – often sneered at as morally deficient or shallow – becomes the new anchor of the moral universe. In a sense, it springs out of mutually recognised equal judgement authority. Free choice advances to a mute token of reasons that may well be either entirely obstruse or carefully considered. The indifference of this difference for freedom of choice explains why this type of freedom is the final place to encounter the 'blinking' between the substantive and the social dimension of judgement – between *de jure* and *de facto*, as it were. The 'blinking' (or wavering), however, is all that remains, and recognising choices is the new objectivity.

From Others to Self, from Reasons to Sources

The position that we occupy in the legal relation explains why, for example, freedom of religion is wearing its well-known double hat.[98] What is not at all lightly 'chosen' from the perspective of the believer is cast towards others as a bare preference simply because nobody is supposed to scrutinise the grounds of religious belief or to ask for an explanation. A most serious matter is thus reduced to a triviality. What is more, the fact that I am related to others legally profoundly affects how I can, if I choose to do so, relate to myself. If I count, in relation to others, as a person with freedom of choice, I can relate to myself wearing the mask of my social persona and attain a more relaxed attitude towards my own pursuits. Owing to the protective shield of the legal relation I become free to lead an unexamined life.[99] This may come as a relief for overly conscientious souls.

Morality thus begins to distinguish itself from itself. It is no longer about right or wrong, all things considered. Rather, the focus shifts to what

[97] See JG Fichte, *Grundlage des Naturrechts nach Prinzipien der Wissenschaftslehre* (ed M Zahn, Hamburg, Meiner, 1979) 52: 'Das … Verhältnis zwischen vernünftigen Wesen, dass jedes seine Freiheit durch den Begriff der Möglichkeit der Freiheit des anderen beschränke, unter der Bedingung, dass das erstere die seinige gleichfalls durch die des anderen beschränke, heißt das *Rechtsverhältnis*; und die jetzt aufgestellte Formel ist der *Rechtssatz*.' For an alternative translation, see JG Fichte, *Foundations of Natural Right* (trans M Baur, Cambridge, Cambridge University Press, 2000) 49.

[98] See J Madison, 'Memorial and Remonstrance against Religious Assessments' in *Writings* (ed JN Rakove, New York, Library of America, 1999) 29–36.

[99] See n 94.

must be regarded as *valid*, regardless of whether it is right or wrong.[100] Validity – *legal* validity, as we will come to call it – signifies what we take to be authoritative by pre-empting inquiries into its merit. Practical reasoning shifts from determining duties to underpinning powers for the determination of such duties.

The constitution of the legal relation takes place long before we encounter a full-blown legal system in the routines of our daily lives. Developed legal systems merely draw on the form that emerges from our interactions.

The judgers and the objectors (who are, of course, also judgers) constitute the legal relation by attributing to each other independence, albeit within limits.[101] This attribution does not come out of nowhere. It is already implicit in raising substantive claims, for doing so posits that the addressees have the capacity to recognise their correctness *on their own*. Independent kowtowing to substance ('reasons' as imagined by moral realists) is thus turned into freedom within limits. With that step, the antinomy of moral judgement is thrown into full relief. While each attributes to the other the equal capacity for judgement and consequently equal authority to decide an issue, they can nevertheless continue to disagree. The antinomy lays the foundation for authority's form.[102]

The question that must arise next is how one arrives at concrete allocations of such authority.

The Emergence from Morality and the Gestalt Shift

The reversal of direction from the substantive to the social dimension takes place in two steps. The first step involves the alteration of status sketched above (see 'A Revised Understanding of Objectivity'). Persons change from being interlocutors to being choosers. Whereas as interlocutors they were burdened with the responsibility to offer reasons for their assertions, as

[100] Not surprisingly, in the *Phenomenology*, Hegel had consciousness enter the status of law (*Rechtszustand*) with the demise of traditional morality. See Hegel, n 81, 316, where Hegel puts the matter thus: 'Das Allgemeine in die Atome der absolut vielen Individuen zersplittert, dieser gestorbene Geist ist eine Gleichheit, worin Alle als Jede, als Personen gelten.' In English, 'The general fragmented into the atoms of the absolute many individuals, this dead spirit is an equality in which all are considered as each, as persons.' See also C Menke, *Tragödie im Sittlichen: Gerechtigkeit und Freiheit nach Hegel* (Frankfurt aM, Suhrkamp, 1996) 137–38.

[101] The motive for doing so may well be that they would like to get to joint action.

[102] Being subjected to authority, to be sure, means to be obligated even if one finds authoritative directives substantively wrong. For an experienced driver like me, speed limits are silly. I know how to adjust my speed to traffic situations. Yet the reasons of authority are content-independent.

choosers they can invoke their right of choice. The second step anchors the mutually recognised new status in factual agreements.

Any spontaneous allocation of authority may initially appear to be based on indeterminate grounds ('You'll decide'). But any such indeterminacy is likely saturated with implicit moral intuitions. It makes sense, therefore, to view the legal relation as steeped in morality in the process of its institution.

We have already observed that any substantive resolution of the question whether a burden or sacrifice is reasonably acceptable must rely, variously and invariably, on presuppositions taken for granted *as shared* by judgers and objectors. The resolution of the core issue may thus depend on unexamined contextual premises (see 'Universalisation and Social Freedom' above). The same can be observed for the determination of authority. People spontaneously grant each other authority ('You'll decide on the route we take', 'You'll decide what we are going to have for dinner'). Such grants rely on implicit knowledge that perhaps nobody wishes to elaborate simply because it is often more conducive to cooperation to leave their substance and status unexplored.

Allocations of authority may in many cases, therefore, reflect shared moral beliefs. Nevertheless, owing to the reversal from the substantive to the social dimension, moral belief is also rendered as the social *fact* of agreement, a matter on which people *happen* to converge. This indicates a gestalt shift. What the parties in a legal relation may be taking for granted as morally appropriate and fair becomes externalised, not least owing to the external character of the relation, into the fact that they agree on something. The law emerges from sources, and sources point to social facts. Most importantly, the source of authority is rendered as *both*, namely as a moral precept and as a normatively haphazard convergence of views. It flickers back and forth between morality and law, which explains why the legal relation, unless buttressed by formal legal institutions, is a fragile and rather ephemeral achievement. Even in the case of more full-blown legal systems the reassimilation of law to morality remains a live possibility.

Phenomenologically speaking, spontaneous coordination draws on implicit moral background knowledge that is a component of the lifeworld of the parties.[103] Such knowledge feeds into what they can do or accomplish by virtue of taking certain things for granted. The moral and

[103] On the following, see J Habermas, *Theorie des kommunikativen Handelns*, vol 2: *Zur Kritik der funktionalistischen Vernunft* (Frankfurt aM, Suhrkamp, 1981) 189–99; J Habermas, *Nachmetaphysisches Denken: Aufsätze und Reden*, vol 2 (Berlin, Suhrkamp, 2012) 22–23.

intellectual resources provided by the lifeworld are, however, subject to disintegration and decay once they become explicit and subject to reflection. Their relevance can be rescued only by recasting them as expressions of what the parties entering a legal relation want. The volition that is thus attributed to parties inherits from the implicit moral knowledge on which it draws an embarrassingly ungrounded quality. This explains why its backing by will is all the more essential for its validity. People can then mutually tell each other that they have *settled* on a certain arrangement ('But didn't we agree that I get to choose the route?') They can regard the principle governing their arrangement as voluntarily endorsed, and therefore as an expression of their common will. This is consistent with two of the fundamental principles of the legal relation, namely, freedom and equality. The third of these principles, reciprocity, can be relied upon to support conditional allocations of authority.

While the flickering of the terms of the legal relation between morality and consent is convenient, it also creates a consistency between form and the substance. The legal relation focuses on choices. Viewing its substance as outgrowth of some natural private law is an insult to the type of freedom inherent in this relation. The terms of the legal relation have to be recast, one after the other, as voluntarily endorsed. This explains why there is this deep connection between the rather anarchical germination of legal relations in our social dealings and having them anchored in a common will. The constitution of the legal relation requires backing by constitutional authority.

The reconsideration of moral substance as sources unleashes the critical potential that is inherent in the legal relation. It explains why it makes sense to regard law as the historical self-critique of practical reason.[104]

Rational Reconstruction and Critique

So far, an attempt has been made to offer a rational reconstruction of how the perplexity inherent in moral universalisation gives rise to the form of

[104] The change of direction from the social to the substantive dimension implies, however, not only that there is a transitive relation from reasons to the requirement to assent, but that accepting and allowing are mediums for developing reasons. This acceptance is mediated by our nature as social beings. We accept reasons because we have to get along with one another. But if reason itself is something that cannot be thought without the social dimension, then the ironically fractured acceptance of the thinking of others is built into the constitution of reason a priori. In this light, Brandom's seemingly strange claim that following rules involves a moment of forgiving the rule-application of others begins to make sense. See Brandom, n 32, 601–06.

law. According to Habermas, such a reconstruction indicates an effort of self-reflection.[105] People possessing know-how arrive at accounts of what makes their knowing possible. In this vein, we have tried to understand how we constitute the legal relation, and have examined carefully how the move from substantive reasons to allocations of authority resolves an antinomy of moral judgement. This move involves an intersubjective correction of first-personal moral beliefs. It reveals the recognitional power-dynamics inherent in moral judgement. It is the task of theory to render these matters visible.

Rational reconstruction is not the only form of self-reflection, though. The other is what Habermas calls 'critique'. It is driven by a desire for emancipation. The point of such critique is to expose what we take to be authority as sham. Rather than reconstructing the conditions of one's capacities, it is about the identification of internal obstacles, questionable beliefs and seeming taboos.[106] Interestingly, this form of critique is inherent in the evolution of the legal relation and manifest in the recalibration of moral intuitions as autonomous acts. Only this step completes the law as a system of freedom that promises to liberate people from false impressions of natural authority, fetishism[107] or other 'hypostatized powers'.[108] We constitute what binds us. This is what it means, eventually, to lend priority to the social dimension.[109]

The legal relation is an alternative to both homogeneous morality and moral relativism.[110] The substance of relations is initially indeterminate. What the persons involved become increasingly aware of, however, is that they regard each other as free to determine this substance, equally so and under conditions of reciprocity.

[105] See his *Erkenntnis und Interesse*, n 1, 411. See also J Habermas, *Der philosophische Diskurs der Moderne: Zwölf Vorlesungen* (Frankfurt aM, Suhrkamp, 1985) 350.

[106] See Habermas, *Erkenntnis und Interesse*, n 1, 413.

[107] See Brandom, n 68, 27, 53, 64, 72, according to whom fetishism means mistaking the products of our own practices and practical attitudes for features of the objective world.

[108] See J Habermas, *Technik und Wissenschaft als 'Ideologie'* (Frankfurt aM, Suhrkamp, 1968) 159.

[109] See Rorty, n 86, 138–43.

[110] Concededly, this may come as a surprise to those who access legal philosophy at a point at which the constitution of the legal relation has already been completed and focus then, for example, on a commander, a legal system or courts.

12

The Indeterminacy of Law

Revisiting the 1980s

Some 40 or almost 50 years ago, the 'indeterminacy thesis' was quite notorious, not least because it served as one of the battle cries of the critical legal studies movement. This current of American legal thought has by now petered out. Indeed, it may have long run its course. Roberto Mangabeira Unger's highly idiosyncratic summary of the movement's shapes and objectives, first published in 1983,[1] marked – at any rate, in retrospect – a moment at which the movement had already inched beyond its climax. What followed afterwards, including Mark Kelman's meritorious book-length exposition,[2] revelled in recounting the movement's brief historical trajectory or, in Kelman's case, continued to engage in the already ongoing struggle with one of its sworn opponents, namely, Chicago-style law and economics.

The self-conscious contributors to critical legal studies believed in exposing a somewhat complacent liberal and conservative American legal culture to 'radical' ideas.[3] While such purport may have passed as obvious where it contrasted with ascendant neoliberalism in matters affecting labour law,[4] rent control[5] or race relations,[6] the 'indeterminacy thesis' was, to say the least, a less obvious candidate for enlistment to a left-wing agenda. One

[1] R Mangabeira Unger, 'The Critical Legal Studies Movement' (1983) 96 *Harvard Law Review* 561–675.

[2] M Kelman, *A Guide to Critical Legal Studies* (Cambridge, Mass., Harvard University Press, 1988).

[3] See M Tushnet, 'Critical Legal Studies: A Political History' (1991) 100 *Yale Law Journal* 1515–40. It gave rise to irritation among progressive liberals. See, for example, A Altman, *Critical Legal Studies: A Liberal Critique* (Princeton, NJ, Princeton University Press, 1993). There has been also a critique from the left. For an example, see DF Brosnan, 'Serious But Not Critical' (1986) 60 *Southern California Law Review* 259–396.

[4] See KE Klare, 'Judicial Deradicalization of the Wagner Act and the Origins of Modern Legal Consciousness, 1937–1941' (1978) 62 *Minnesota Law Review* 265–339.

[5] See D Kennedy, 'The Effect – of the Warranty of Habitability on Low Income Housing: "Milking" and Class Violence' (1987) 15 *Florida State University Law Review* 485–519.

[6] AD Freeman, 'Legitimizing Racial Discrimination through Antidiscrimination Law' (1978) 62 *Minnesota Law Review* 1049–1119.

might wonder, therefore, why it was met with so much resistance, if not revulsion, not only by conservatives[7] but even by centrist liberal scholars?[8]

The indeterminacy thesis defended by critical legal scholars has always been a double-edged sword. It suggests, in the first place, that determinate resolutions of legal questions require an intervention by a force that is generically not legal. In order to be able to say something, the law must surrender to political ventriloquism. Not by accident, the indeterminacy thesis was trailed by the slogan 'it's all politics', and maybe it was the conjunction of the thesis and the slogan that accounted for the outrage. The law is clay in the hands of political machinations. Departing from this relatively simple and straightforward formulation, it was possible to elaborate the thesis further along lines suggesting that exhibiting something as legally required is a ruse for hiding one's true intentions. Or it could be pushed to the hilt by claiming that the law is nothing but an ideological veil adorned with adjurations of neutrality, objectivity and impartiality, diverting attention from the power-driven fabric of social life.[9] These core contentions of critical legal studies were indeed provocative and would, if correct, not at all lack bite today, in particular in contexts where the legal and liberally democratic mainstream is busy defending the rule of law against infidels, who by now have come to adhere to the political right.[10]

This first edge of indeterminacy can be given a less alienating and negativistic twist, however. Roberto Mangabeira Unger's subsequent work, building on his eponymous exposition, suggests that existing legal arrangements are pregnant with institutional variations. They are likely to be found at the 'margins'.[11] Legal institutions are less settled than they appear to be at what we take to be their core. Mangabeira Unger encourages us to engage our institutional imagination by generalising marginal variations and transforming them into potential templates for new

[7] See PD Carrington, 'Of Law and the River' (1984) 34 *Journal of Legal Education* 222–28.

[8] See LB Solumn, 'On the Indeterminacy Crisis: Critiquing Critical Legal Dogma' (1987) 54 *University of Chicago Law Review* 462–503; J Stick, 'Can Nihilism be Pragmatic?' (1986) 100 *Harvard Law Review* 332–401.

[9] JW Singer, 'The Player and the Cards: Nihilism and Legal Theory' (1984) 94 *Yale Law Journal* 1–70. Borrowing an idea from Brandom's reading of Hegel's phenomenology, the 'modernism' implicit in critical unveilings of this type is an instantiation of the verminous attitude of the moral valet who regards all moral justifications of actions as deceitful pretension. See R Brandom, *A Spirit of Trust: A Reading of Hegel's* Phenomenology (Cambridge, MA, Harvard University Press, 2019) 550–51.

[10] See most recently, the anthology edited by G Shaffer and W Sandholz (eds), *The Rule of Law under Pressure* (Cambridge, Cambridge University Press, 2025).

[11] See R Mangabeira Unger, *What Should Legal Analysis Become?* (London, Verso, 1996).

formative frameworks of social life.[12] Efforts to tap inadvertent experimentation for the purpose of social reconstruction are integral, he claims, to the quest to imagine better mitigations of the conflict inherent in the enabling conditions of human self-assertion,[13] namely our dependence on others and the need to emancipate ourselves from the shackles with which such dependence binds us.

The idea that conflict underlies social arrangements, and the conjecture that what appears to be solid and unified is in fact brittle and internally divided, points to the second edge of indeterminacy as understood by critical legal scholars. It is first and foremost manifest in interpretive choices. Duncan Kennedy and his followers argued that it is – at any rate in hard cases – always possible to arrive at constructions of the legal materials that favour either more individualistic or more altruistic solutions.[14] There are no meta-principles warranting either. A 'fundamental contradiction' within our moral consciousness explains why decisions in those cases are ultimately existential leaps in the dark.[15]

This is, arguably, that version of the indeterminacy thesis which is congruent with the widely shared sense that when values conflict, the resolution of the issue depends on a judge's faithful attempt to arrive at a morally defensible solution. While Ronald Dworkin, always a major target of the critical legal scholars,[16] attempted to refute such 'external skepticism',[17] even he often had to concede, albeit merely parenthetically, that at the end of the day, reasonable people may disagree over what the right answer to a legal question is.[18]

While in this rendering the indeterminacy thesis is likely palatable even for mainstream jurists, it is far from formulating a radical claim. It does not speak to workplace democracy, the expropriation of landlords, more

[12] On formative frameworks, see R Mangabeira Unger, *Social Theory: Its Situation and its Task* (Cambridge, Cambridge University Press, 1988).

[13] See R Mangabeira Unger, *Passion: An Essay on Personality* (New York, Free Press, 1986).

[14] D Kennedy, 'Form and Substance in Private Law Adjudication' (1976) 89 *Harvard Law Review* 1685–1778; JM Balkin, 'The Crystalline Structure of Legal Thought' (1986) 39 *Rutgers Law Review* 1–110.

[15] See P Gabel and D Kennedy, 'Roll over Beethoven' (1984) 36 *Stanford Law Review* 1–55.

[16] See JM Balkin, 'Taking Ideology Seriously: Ronald Dworkin and the CLS Critique' (1987) 55 *UMKC Law Review* 329–433; AC Hutchinson, 'Of Kings and Dirty Rascals: The Struggle for Democracy' (1984) 9 *Queen's Law Journal* 273–92.

[17] See R Dworkin, 'Objectivity and Truth: You'd Better Believe It' (1996) 25 *Philosophy and Public Affairs* 87–139; R Dworkin, *Law's Empire* (Cambridge, MA, Harvard University Press, 1986); R Dworkin, *Justice for Hedgehogs* (Cambridge, MA, Harvard University Press, 2011).

[18] See, for example, R Dworkin, *A Matter of Principle* (Cambridge, MA, Harvard University Press, 1986).

participation of students in educational institutions or overcoming the adverse psychological effects of growing up in the nuclear family. It carries no political message whatsoever.

From AD to BC

It cannot be ruled out, however, that the radicalism of the indeterminacy thesis resides in something altogether different from its potential enmeshment with progressive political causes. It may stand for a different kind of radicalism, if by radicalism we mean going to the root of things. This tacit connection could have been grasped by exploring the quite obvious proximity of indeterminacy to Pyrrhonic scepticism.[19] As a 'school' of ancient scepticism, Pyrrhonism became famous for juxtaposing opposing assertions and linking them with arguments and objections. In the face of equipollence, the sceptic recommends the suspension of judgement for the sake of spiritual tranquility. While such a quietist stance ostensibly endorses the opposite of what 'activists' crave – not a way forward but abstention from guiding human praxis (the charge of 'apraxia')[20] – there is something more radical in the position of sceptics than meets the eye of practical-minded people. It is radical, however, not morally or politically but in a metaphysical sense. As Vogt has argued with regard to Pyrrho, this type of scepticism attempts to tease out not an epistemological but an ontological fact. It departs sharply from the metaphysical tradition that takes it for granted that whatever there is, is also determinate even if we fail to grasp how it is.[21] Rather, the world itself is taken to be in an indeterminate state. As Vogt explains:

> Assuming that phenomena of difference are pervasive, every given state of mind is like a freeze-frame: the world looks some specific way to a specific cognizer at a given time, under given circumstances, and so on. If we were to assent to such representations as true, we would be wrong about the world. The world is neither as it looks (sounds, etc) in this freeze frame, nor as it looks (sounds, etc) in some other freeze frame. We cannot perceive the world as it is, namely, indeterminate. But we can infer from phenomena of difference that the world is indeterminate.[22]

[19] For a superb introduction, see KM Vogt, 'Ancient Skepticism' in *Stanford Encyclopedia of Philosophy*, at https://leibniz.stanford.edu/friends/members/preview/skepticism-ancient/; G Striker, 'Skepticism as a Kind of Philosophy' in her *From Aristotle to Cicero: Essays on Ancient Philosophy* (Oxford, Oxford University Press, 2022) 177–91.

[20] See Vogt, n 19, 51.

[21] On this tradition, see G Gamm, *Flucht aus der Kategorie: Die Positivierung des Unbestimmten als Ausgang der Moderne* (Frankfurt aM, Suhrkamp, 1994).

[22] Vogt, n 19, 14.

Without claiming to follow the indeterminacy thesis as it had been expounded by the sceptics in Elis or Alexandria, I would like to use the core idea as a heuristic device. It will bear fruit in the context of law once it is taken into account that the law emerges from indeterminacy and that in the process of growing more determinate, this primordial moral indeterminacy never disappears. Rather, it becomes reproduced and cast in a different format. Whatever comes across as determinate in a legal system remains surrounded by a lack of clarity and a dearth or surplus of meaning. Legal forms work, borrowing Vogt's language, like freeze-frames, and they come and go. My submission is that the relational approach to law is the adequate medium for confronting this reality.

While what this entails may, at this point, still be largely obscure and essentially unrelated to the political agendas that critical legal scholars sought to advance (concerning class, race and gender), the matter is of greatest political significance. At this point the irony should not elude us that, with their indictment of 'liberalism', critical legal scholars missed a deep-seated indeterminacy of the declared foe's project. Rawls put his finger on it when he developed its political outlook.[23] He realised that even if one provided the best account of the principles underlying a truly liberal society, one would have to admit that in a free society even the most reasonable people must enjoy the liberty to remain unconvinced of it. Put in Hegelian terms, this means that what a liberal society is *in itself* is what it is *for its members*. It is essential to a liberal society to generate a variety of perspectives on what explains its appeal. This realisation can be adorned with a nice dialectical stitch. A liberal society can have its solid normative foundation only in an external overlap of the attitudes among its members. The foundation consists in continuous factual convergence. Its status qua authoritative framework is derivative of interlocking incongruent beliefs. Attitudes are, however, contingent and capricious. Consequently, it is quite unsurprising that a liberal society is a place where, when it comes to law, 'you can argue either way'. It is an essentially risky normative project.

Rights and Powers

Our discussion of the resolution of the antinomy of moral judgement has shown that the key to resolving moral collisions without compromising

[23] See J Rawls, *Political Liberalism* (New York, Columbia University Press, 1991).

their substance consists of reconciling the seemingly irreconcilable by means of competence allocation. A and B settle on entertaining separate spheres of *jurisdiction*. By bracketing our substantive reasons for favouring one position over the other – that is, by according priority to the equal capacity and authority of judgement – they can realise that they, while disagreeing on the substantive issue, may well share intuitions[24] over how best to allocate powers to determine individual or joint conduct.

Doing so works most easily in cases in which the moral issue concerns actions that affect predominantly the judging persons themselves. A and B recognise each other's freedom to choose their profession. This does not rule out that A or B may have strong views about what other persons ought to do with their lives. They may even find that their relevant others are judging their own affairs very badly. They are, however, very likely to agree, in the spirit of the harm principle, that each should have full discretion to lead their own lives as they see fit. They will do so, under conditions of reciprocity, not least to secure for themselves a convenient shelter against unsolicited advice.

Once they endorse this solution, the self-reflective universalisation can succeed. Based on conceding each other the equal capacity and authority for judgement, they arrive at solutions that, from the point of view of the other person, are authoritative only because they both need to get along. The conviction of one does not have to be taken seriously by the other. They merely have to put up with what the other happens to decide. 'Putting up with something' is the modality of validity thus constituted, that is, qua abstention from following one's own judgement.

But how are we to address the conflict between the libertarian and the social democrat (see chapter 10)? Their claims concern how the social world as a whole should operate. Their difference cannot be settled by allocating to them different personal spheres so that they can stay out of each other's way. On the contrary, it is part of the substance of their judgement to determine how others ought to live. They are proposing rules for how people are meant to live together in general.

We know how to solve this problem. We grant each an equal chance to succeed in the political process. Again, the equality of persons is decisive here, which explains why the majority principle can serve as the tie-breaker.

[24] As I tried to explain in chapter 10, these intuitions flicker between moral grounds and consent that obtains *de facto*.

It is reasonable of us to submit to it, for it is based on the same principle that is inherent in recognising the judgement of others. No one has greater authority than others. There is no *pars sanior*. Where there is none, the majority must have its way, unless we abstained from acting as one political body altogether.[25]

Reflective universalisation is the intellectual operation constituting the legal relation or the 'form of law'. It stands for how we deal legally with one another in quotidian interactions without paying heed to official legal systems, and how we change as what we appear for each other in its context. Reflective universalisation recognises the different substantive determinations of moral matters and relies for their resolution on the social dimension. This means, however, that what is mutually relevant about persons is not their substantive views but rather the fact that they happen to hold some. In fact, that they might have any.

Reflective universalisation draws on the principles of the therewith emerging legal relation. In addition to equality, at any rate, when it comes to moral judgement, the agents involved presuppose reciprocity as a commitment that is shared by them.[26] That they have also committed themselves to freedom is obvious from their being in the business of determining the limited authority of the autonomous moral insight of each. It is fair to say, thus, that equality, freedom and reciprocity are the 'transcendental' principles of the legal relation.[27] We cannot commit ourselves to anything else without first committing ourselves to these.

Legality and Coercion

The legal relation is defined, as we have seen, by rights and legal powers that are correlated, ordinarily, with duties and liabilities. We have come full circle and returned to Hohfeld.[28] But what Hohfeld did not take into account in

[25] See J Locke, *Two Treatises of Government* (ed P Laslett, Cambridge, Cambridge University Press, 1960) 332–33, II. § 98.

[26] A very clear statement of reciprocity can be encountered in the work of a political scientist. See A Schedler, 'Democratic Reciprocity' (2021) 29 *Journal of Political Philosophy* 252–78. Reciprocity is the obligation to return favours and the permission to retaliate harms (ibid 252).

[27] See G Schönrich, *Kategorien und transzendentale Argumentation: Kant und die Idee einer transzendentalen Semiotik* (Frankfurt aM, Suhrkamp, 1981) 212; AW Wood, 'Deduction of the Summons and the Existence of Other Rational Beings' in G Gottlieb (ed), *Fichte's Foundation of Natural Right* (Cambridge, Cambridge University Press, 2016) 72–91, 75, 77, 86.

[28] See the beginning of chapter 9. WN Hohfeld, *Fundamental Legal Conceptions as Applied in Judicial Reasoning* (ed WW Cook, New Haven, CT, Yale University Press, 1964).

his project, for the simple reason that he did not have to, is that the legal relation is characterised by a specific way of relating to the decisions made by those others exercising rights or powers.

This way of relating is characterised by what Immanuel Kant called 'legality'.[29] It consists of compliance that is by default uncommitted and 'external', in the sense that reasons and motives are immaterial for doing as one is obligated to do. It should not escape our attention what this entails. By treating decisions as legally binding, we do not accept as valid the beliefs harboured by decision-makers who may well take these to be true. We construe a type of validity that brackets, entirely, substantive reasons for action. Not by accident, our engagement with legal norms can therefore be permissibly suffused with irony.[30]

This bracketing of substantive commitments, therefore, affects *how* we want what we are legally obligated to do. We want it, even though we do not share the underlying substantive reasons for action. We are paying our taxes even though we find the rate of taxation brutally excessive. When filing our tax returns, we are doing what we do unwillingly. Apparently, our commitment to legality makes us want it.

Whence does this commitment originate? The paradigmatic instance of involuntary volition is willing under conditions of coercion.[31] A person coercing us makes us want something even though we would never want it if it were not for the credible threat of an even more unpleasant sanction. We would never pay a complete stranger a large amount of money if it were not for disbursing a ransom payment to an abductor. In a like manner, legal validity requires us to do what we would otherwise not do if it were not for surrendering to the demands of the law.

Two consequences follow from the link between legality and coercion. First, 'external' obedience is fully compatible with yielding to mere threats. This does not mean that legal validity is *directly* derivative of coercion.[32] It is

[29] See I Kant, *Metaphysische Anfangsgründe der Rechtslehre* (ed B Ludwig, Hamburg, Meiner, 1986) 29.

[30] For further elaboration of this point, see my *The Legal Relation: Legal Theory After Legal Positivism* (Cambridge, Cambridge University Press, 2017) 57–78.

[31] For a more extended discussion, see my *Knowing What the Law Is: Legal Theory in a New Key* (Oxford, Hart Publishing, 2021) 163–68.

[32] The commitment to legality as the attitude that emerges from entering a legal relation may not be elicited through coercion by another *person*. Being threatened into obedience by a sovereign is not the normative ground of the legal relation. We can secure the commitment to legality by coercive means, and as faithful Hobbesians, we will favour a coercive system in order not to become prey to the defection and machination of others. See T Hobbes, *Leviathan* (ed I Shapiro, New Haven, CT, Yale University Press, 2010) 102 [85].

plain, however, that the normative demands of law are neither affected nor diminished by being backed up with force. Since the substance of norms does not matter, we may as well do what we are forced to do because we are yielding to a coercive threat.

Second, there is nothing wrong in conceding that, as reasonable persons, we are forced *by circumstance* to accept legality. In many instances, social conditions may be such that it makes sense to say that people cannot but choose something, even though they would be happier if they did not have to make this choice. For example, we are not talking nonsense when we say that people are coerced by economic circumstance to take on assignments that they would refuse to carry out if they were financially independent. People accept uncongenial jobs in order to make a living. They would rather not have to, but their *de facto* dependence on wage labour forces them to do so. In a like manner, being in society requires us to accept lawmaking in the face of persistent moral disagreements. We would possibly rather be free to do what we believe to be right or to live among like-minded or even saintly people. But this is not the human condition. Being among others means being forced by circumstance to agree to the existence of legal powers and the rights of others.[33] In our commitment to legality resounds the uneasiness that inheres in having to live among others with whom we potentially disagree. Legality therefore is not only compatible with yielding to threats of coercion, it also reflects being forced by circumstance into accepting the legal relation.

Morality Distinguishing Itself from Itself

Legal relations originate from situations in which people need to settle on modes of cooperation or coordination in the face or in anticipation of disagreement. While they cannot resolve the substantive issue, it may occur to them how they can go on without being of the same opinion. Assume A strongly suggests that B eat only vegan food, while B harbours doubts about whether a diet of this type would provide them with sufficient nutrients. They can resolve this issue based on shared moral intuitions, such as that no

[33] For a similar approach to the legal relation that views it based on a hypothetical imperative that presupposes the goal of living in community with others, see JG Fichte, *Grundlage des Naturrechts nach Prinzipien der Wissenschaftslehre* (ed M Zahn, Hamburg, Meiner, 1979) 10–11, 89–91. See D James, *Fichte's Social and Political Philosophy: Property and Virtue* (Cambridge, Cambridge University Press, 2011) 116–22; F Neuhouser, 'Fichte's Separation of Right from Morality' in Gottlieb (ed), n 27, 32–52.

one should force others to ingest what they – for whatever reason – happen to dislike, or that all ought to be free to handle issues that at least predominantly concern only themselves. They thereby distinguish between the substantive and the social dimension of judgement, partitioning out areas where the will may rule without having to give reasons. They advance from morality to law. They cut out freedom of choice from the moral domain by drawing on moral intuitions that they incidentally share.

Again, using Hegelian language, one can say that with this move, morality begins to differentiate itself from itself by distinguishing law and morality. Inside the discretionary space of freedom is law; outside of it is, at this original stage, still morality. The evolution of law – not in the sense of a historical process, but as a sequence in which participants in a relation bring before themselves what this relation is in itself – is the process of replacing moral presuppositions with sources that regard social facts as grounds of deontic statuses,[34] such as rights and obligations.[35] B eats meat. A must not meddle with that (even though at this point it is not quite clear what this prohibition entails).

Assume that A and B agree to have one of them determine, alternately, what they are going to have for lunch. A decides on Monday, B on Tuesday and so forth. A's and B's conduct is mutually correlated via powers and liabilities. There are three ways in which they can account for the substance of an arrangement that does not directly address the question of what they ought to eat but their mutual acceptance of being at each other's whim. First, A and B could simply welcome the fortunate coincidence of their preferences and mutually congratulate each other on its existence ('glad we found each other'). If that were their attitude, they would leave the sphere of the normative. They would, that is, not get to law and leave matters in an entirely factual state. Second, they could perceive what they agreed upon as a contractual arrangement. For their deal to have normative import, they would have to postulate that contracts are a legitimate way of creating rights and obligations. The force of their special agreement would be derivative of a more general principle governing contractual relations. Third, they may

[34] See chapter 10.

[35] The relational approach does not deny that the law also exists in the form of an object. Contrary to legal positivism, in particular, it does not treat such objectivity as a given. The relational approach considers the 'legal facts' as constituted within a relation that is always already normative. It does not suffer from the defect of having to introduce normativity after it has taken cognisance of legal facts by 'assuming' a *Grundnorm* or contemplating a rule of recognition. This is a major flaw of legal positivism.

well believe that this is the *right* path to take in a situation of this type; that is, they may believe themselves to have a good reason for doing what they do.

What matters the most, at this point, is that the first option is a non-starter, for it cannot give rise to obligations. Both the other options, however, introduce the universality that is characteristic of reasons for action.[36] They remain within the remit of the normative.

In the last two instances – contractual arrangements or the presumptively correct reason – the substance of the emerging legal relation still retains one foot in morality. The self-differentiation of morality is left in its incipient state and gives rise to the 'flickering' analysed in chapter 11. Such a moral pedigree affects the legal relation with an inconsistency. As we have also already seen in chapter 10, the moral rootedness of the arrangement collides with the freedom of choice that it facilitates. The agents are not free to reject it. Within the legal relation, however, what people end up doing depends on their attitude or on the attitude of those whose choices they accept. Moral norms, by contrast, make claims on us regardless of whether we believe in them or have *de facto* chosen to adopt them. They are purportedly attitude-independent and rooted in a status that we possess by virtue of who we are (eg, part of nature or beings that possess dignity).[37] Within the legal relation, reasons operate by making facts about behaviour or utterances relevant to the conduct of others. A is obligated to have lunch at the place that B has selected for them (and the other way round). If it were not for B's decision (based on his favourable attitude towards a certain place), A would possibly have no reason to go there. Borrowing Raz's parlance, the reason is 'content-independent'.[38]

The arrangement between A and B is, however, in the last two cases not content-independent. Initially, they assume that it is good to have contracts or that it is good to have a rule demanding alternation. One would not be bothered by this inconsistency if it were not for a principle implicit in the legal relation, namely, that people are free to accept obligations within the parameters set by the two other principles, that is equality and reciprocity. It is mutually recognised freedom of choice, to be sure, but freedom it is. As a result, the differentiation of morality from itself cannot stop here. It needs to advance further.

[36] See the discussion in CM Korsgaard, *Self-Constitution: Agency, Identity, and Integrity* (Oxford, Oxford University Press, 2009) 73–76.

[37] See Brandom, n 9, 318–19.

[38] See J Raz, *The Morality of Freedom* (Oxford, Oxford University Press, 1986).

Modulations of Indeterminacy

Before we can make some progress at this point, we must perceive clearly how what is about to become 'law' emerges from an indeterminate background.

The most elementary indeterminacy consists of the disagreement between A and B about dietary propriety. To veganism, A says 'yes' and B 'no'. From a combined and unified perspective, the reasons conflict on their merits. No determinate course of action can be found. But even the overlapping intuitions about getting along by means of alternation are affected by a considerable degree of indeterminacy. How far does the agreement extend? Is it an outgrowth of the broader intuition that rotation is a fair way of allocating benefits and burdens among equals? Or is it just some randomly hammered-out compromise? Where do we need to make exceptions? Shouldn't food allergies be taken into account? Hence, regarding its scope, it is not quite clear what the arrangement really requires.

It is important to note that removing the inconsistency within the legal relation, which concerns moral demands versus the free choice of conditions, and the modulation of indeterminacy go hand in hand. The legal relation can differentiate itself from morality if the rule allocating powers and liabilities and rights and obligations can pass as voluntarily endorsed. Everything else would be contrary to autonomy qua attitude-dependence of one's status as bearer of responsibilities.[39] Put in Brandom's terms, autonomous persons make themselves responsible by taking themselves to be responsible. While the will of the contracting parties suffices for a concrete arrangement, both the laws of contract and the purportedly good rule need to be based on a 'common will' with which the parties identify. In other words, it must be a will that they, in one way or another, regard as their own inasmuch as they belong to a collective.[40] The romantic jurists of the nineteenth century spoke in this connection of the spirit of the people (the *Volksgeist*).[41]

Assuming that A and B, for the time being, perceive the matter from a purely intuitive point of view, they seem to regard what they do as

[39] See Brandom, n 9, 316–17.

[40] See J-J Rousseau, *The Social Contract* (trans C Betts, Oxford, Oxford University Press, 1994) I.6, 55–56.

[41] See, for example, KF von Savigny, *Vom Beruf unserer Zeit für Gesetzgebung und Rechtswissenschaft* (Heidelberg, Mohr und Zimmer, 1814) 8–9, 13–14, 33.

something 'we' do or, rather, as consistent with how matters are handled 'around here' or 'among us'. They would thereby implicitly rely on what legal scholars call 'customary law'.[42] This type of law is essentially backward-looking. Its constitutive elements of practice and *opinio juris* are appealed to in statements asserting that 'we' have always believed something to be right or wrong and that 'our' longstanding practice is proof of our having done so.

It should not escape our attention how the indeterminacy of the legal arrangement is matched by the source. Whether A and B do what they do because they regard it as their discrete arrangement or as the application of a broader principle of equal rotation is not yet clear. It may seem, however, as though they took it to be an outgrowth of custom. But customary law is the most elusive source of law. At the level of its form, it is left open how many instances of practice one must have seen for there to be law, and whose views count for the existence of *opinio juris*.

The source is shot through with indeterminacy. This must give rise to the concern that assertions of customary law are modes of dressing up power and privilege in the garb of widely shared and undisputed sentiments. Again, this explains why the source qua form is at loggerheads with a principle of the legal relation, in this case, equality. This is the predicament. Not only does the moral substance of legal relations have to be funnelled into the form of sources, but the sources themselves can also give rise to conflicts with its constitutive principles. The law initially comes to this world in a manner that is at odds with the principles of the legal relation. The history of law is a process of self-critique. At its end, the equal freedom of human beings and the outlines of reciprocal terms of cooperation are recognised in systems of constitutional authority. Modern constitutions, after all, involve the transition from morality to voluntarily adopted sources of law, not least because their authority – appeals to seemingly attitude-independent values notwithstanding – is vested in choices made by a people at particular points of time. Constitutions, however, also explicitly and implicitly establish the limits that are drawn to reasonable disagreements. These limits are, however, to be felt out based on a distinction between reasonableness and unreasonableness that must be made from within the zone of disagreement to which liberal societies cannot offer relief.

[42] On the following, see my *Wissen des Rechts* (Tübingen, Mohr, 2018).

Three Types of Source

The evolution of legal relations is driven by two objectives. First, lines must be drawn between law and morality. The relevance of moral precepts must be substituted with derivations from legally relevant social facts articulating some common will. Second, sources inherit from morality the inconsistency with the principles of the legal relation, even if at the level of sources sheer heteronomy is replaced with asymmetries of power. Asymmetries are nonetheless necessary in the face of moral disagreements.

All sources of law are modes of expressing a common will. At their most general level, sources come in three types.[43] *Customary law* is based on the belief that shared intuitions of law are manifest in general and constituent usage over time. An appeal to customary law is noticeable in the indignation with which people assert that 'they' have never allowed 'something like this' to happen 'here' before. With its invocation they discover that they must have willed something else all along, even if they have long tracked it only unwittingly in practice. *Decisions* state what a group of people want based on allocations of authority to some person or institution to speak on their behalf. An appeal to decisions reminds everyone of clarifications made earlier.

Conceivably, staying faithful to what has been laid down in a source could be left to these two types of sources and to their cross-fertilisation. In both instances, however, the later source immediately swallows up the former. Where customary law is known in the medium of customary law, the purportedly customary recognition abrogates its object, for it creates new and equally authentic custom. If decisions are all we have to remain faithful to, the new decision takes the place of the former. The same is true in the relation of custom to decisions and decisions to custom. If international courts spell out what they believe to be customary law of nations, the precedent that they thereby create matters; yet it is of relevance only so long as it is not eclipsed by subsequent practice. The same is true if the meaning of decisions is articulated in customary law (think of subsequent treaty practice in conventional international law; it overrides the original source).

From this follows that a distinction between what has been laid down in a source and its application in individual cases requires another medium

[43] On the following, see my 'Über die Subjektivität des Rechts' (2021) 76 *Juristenzeitung* 1–7.

to intervene. This is *legal scholarship*, for it opens the space between a norm and its application and takes great pains to elaborate the appropriateness of applications of norms to specific sets of facts. Today, it is unheard of to characterise scholarship as a source of law. A professor's view, the objection goes, could never attain the authority of a court decision. But his objection assimilates scholarship to decisions. Scholarship, however, differs from decisions in how social facts are relevant to it and how it articulates a common will. Decisions are events the occurrence of which is made legally relevant in allocations of authority. The facticity inherent in scholarship is closer to the facticity of custom, for it is manifest in long-standing intellectual routines and habits of analysis that are imparted to initiates through years of training. One might still wonder what the element of common volition is that is supposedly manifest in scholarship. Arguably, it is the attempt to link the differentiation between factual situations with applicable legal norms in a manner that is itself susceptible to universalisation. The systematicity of legal scholarship is the epitome of this aspiration. Therefore, it makes much sense to attribute to legal scholarship the quality of a source. It must not be forgotten, nonetheless, that each type of legal source – customary law, decisions and scholarship – delivers the law in different shapes and links it with different social perspectives. Customary law is congenial to the viewpoint of members of simple communities. Never mind that upon closer inspection it turns out to be amenable to the power of the 'boys' calling the shots. Decisions invoke the perspectives of superior and subordinate. Scholarship, finally, is tied to the perspective of a community that expects to be repaid with equal treatment for being law-abiding.[44]

Full Circle

By arranging sources in a rational sequence, it can be seen how the law simultaneously absorbs and preserves indeterminacy. We move from no rule to a *de facto* arrangement. Its content is fuzzy and its basis obscure. The indeterminacy of the original situation is removed and simultaneously preserved inasmuch as the settlement perceives its ground in customary law, which is fraught with a great number of loose ends. While decisions – more precisely, the procedures governing their adoption – remove the

[44] See my *Rechtssystem und Republik: Über die politische Funktion des systematischen Rechtsdenkens* (Vienna and New York, Springer, 1992).

indeterminacy inherent in the creation of customary law, they give rise to an indeterminacy of their own. General rules, adopted by legislation, do not apply themselves to situations. An intellectual medium needs to intervene, linking rules with the facts to which they apply. Overcoming the indeterminacy inherent in a mere aggregate of general rules gives rise to legal scholarship as a set of historically developed routines to classify legal materials and to connect elements of norms with aspects of factual situations. The core task is to secure equality of application. Once the law has been recast in the medium of scholarly analysis, however, it becomes more 'fluid', for it begins to exist in the form of arguments underpinning or challenging specific claims. This penultimate indeterminacy can be removed only through another decision, the relevance of which for future cases remains subject to debate. The question of what a prior case holds for future cases is indeterminacy's ultimate gestalt.

Recast in the medium of legal scholarship, the law attains its most intriguing form, for the most advanced version of indeterminacy appears to be the revenant of the initial encounter. The moral disagreement returns. It must seem, therefore, as if the original indeterminacy is preserved in unfolding a rather determinate and complex system. Yet its ultimate gestalt demonstrates that is has attained a different shape. The question of what is right or wrong is condensed into the question of the significance of precedents for future cases. This is how liberal societies lend expression to the principle that a liberal society is in itself what it is for its members.

Bibliography

Achterberg, N, *Die Rechtsordnung als Rechtsverhältnisordnung. Grundlegung der Rechtsverhältnistheorie* (Berlin, Duncker & Humblot, 1982).

Ackerman, B, *Social Justice in the Liberal State* (New Haven, CT, Yale University Press, 1980).

Alexy, R, 'Grundrecht und Status' in SL Paulson and M Schulte (eds), *Georg Jellinek – Beiträge zu Leben und Werk* (Tübingen, Mohr, 2000) 209–25.

Altman, A, *Critical Legal Studies: A Liberal Critique* (Princeton, NJ, Princeton University Press, 1993).

Anderson, D, 'Peirce and Pragmatism: American Connections' in C Misak (ed), *The Oxford Handbook of Pragmatism* (Oxford, Oxford University Press, 2008) 38–59.

Annas, J, *Virtue and Law in Plato and Beyond* (Oxford, Oxford University Press, 2017).

Apel, K-O, *Der Denkweg des Charles S Peirce: Eine Einführung in den amerikanischen Pragmatismus* (Frankfurt aM, Suhrkamp, 1975).

Aquinas, T, *On Law, Morality, and Politics*, 2nd edn (trans RJ Regan, Indianapolis, IN, Hackett, 2002).

Aristotle, *Eudemian Ethics* (trans A Kenny, Oxford, Oxford University Press, 2011).

——, *Nicomachean Ethics* (trans RC Bartlett and SD Collins, Chicago, IL, University of Chicago Press, 2011).

——, *Politics*, 2nd edn (trans C Lord, Chicago, IL, University of Chicago Press, 2013).

——, *The Art of Rhetoric* (trans RC Bartlett, Chicago, IL, Chicago University Press, 2019).

Asmis, E, 'Cicero on Natural Law and Laws of the State' (2008) 27 *Classical Antiquity* 1–33.

Augustine, *Four Anti-Pelagian Writings* (ed JA Mourant, Washington, DC, Catholic University of America Press, 1992).

——, *On Free Choice of the Will* (trans T Williams, Indianapolis, IN, Hackett, 1993).

——, *On the Trinity Books 8–15* (trans S McKenna, Cambridge, Cambridge University Press, 2002).

Augustinus, *De vera religione*, 2nd edn (trans K Flasch, Stuttgart, Reclam, 2006).

Austin, J, *The Province of Jurisprudence Determined* (ed W Rumble, Cambridge, Cambridge University Press, 1995).

Bacon, M, *Pragmatism: An Introduction* (Cambridge, Polity Press, 2012).

Balkin, JM, 'The Crystalline Structure of Legal Thought' (1986) 39 *Rutgers Law Review* 1–110.

Balkin, JM, 'Taking Ideology Seriously: Ronald Dworkin and the CLS Critique' (1987) 55 *UMKC Law Review* 329–433.

Barry, B, *Theories of Justice* (Berkeley, CA, University of California Press, 1989).

——, *Justice as Impartiality* (Oxford, Oxford University Press, 1995).

Blumenberg, H, *Arbeit am Mythos*, 3rd edn (Frankfurt aM, Suhrkamp, 1984).

——, *Die Legitimität der Neuzeit: Erneuerte Ausgabe* (Frankfurt aM, Suhrkamp, 1988).

Bobbio, N, *Thomas Hobbes and the Natural Law Tradition* (trans D Gobetti, Chicago, IL, University of Chicago Press, 1993).

Böckenförde, E-W, *Geschichte der Rechts- und Staatsphilosophie: Antike und Mittelalter*, 2nd edn (Tübingen, Mohr, 2006).

Boghossian, PA, *Fear of Knowledge: Against Relativism and Constructivism* (Oxford, Oxford University Press, 2006).

——, Three Types of Relativism' in S Hales (ed), *A Companion to Relativism* (Oxford, Wiley-Blackwell, 2011) 53–69.

Borland, T and Hillman, TA, 'Scotus and God's Arbitrary Will: A Reassessment' (2017) 91 *American Catholic Philosophical Quarterly* 399–429.

Brandom, RB, *Tales of the Mighty Dead: Historical Essays in the Metaphysics of Intentionality* (Cambridge, MA, Harvard University Press, 2002).

——, *Perspectives on Pragmatism: Classical, Recent & Contemporary* (Cambridge, MA, Harvard University Press, 2011).

——, 'Towards Reconciling Two Heroes: Habermas and Hegel' (2015) 1 *Argumenta: The Journal of the Italian Society for Analytic Philosophy* 29–42.

——, *A Spirit of Trust: A Reading of Hegel's Phenomenology* (Cambridge, MA, Harvard University Press, 2019).

——, *Pragmatism and Idealism: Rorty and Hegel on Reason and Representation* (Oxford, Oxford University Press, 2022).

Brett, AS, *Liberty, Right and Nature: Individual Rights in Later Scholastic Thought* (Cambridge, Cambridge University Press, 1997).

Brosnan, DF, 'Serious But Not Critical' (1986) 60 *Southern California Law Review* 259–396.

Brutus, Stephanius Junius, *Vindicae Contra Tyrannos* (2nd trans. and ed G. Garnett, Cambridge, Cambridge University Press, 2008).

Burgess, G, *Absolute Monarchy and The Stuart Constitution* (New Haven, CT, Yale University Press, 1996).

Burke, E, *Select Works of Edmund Burke: Thoughts on the Cause of the Present Discontents and The Two Speeches on America* (Indianapolis, IN, Liberty Fund, 2014).

Carrington, PD, 'Of Law and the River' (1984) 34 *Journal of Legal Education* 222–28.

Castorp, H, 'Wittgensteinsche Einleitung in das Grundlagenfach Rechtsphilosophie' (2021) 76 *Zeitschrift für öffentliches Recht* 467–76.

Christiano, T, 'Disagreement and the justification of democracy' in S Wall (ed), *The Cambridge Companion to Liberalism* (Cambridge, Cambridge University Press, 2015) 237–60.

Cicero, *De re publica, De legibus* (trans CW Keyes, Cambridge, MA, Harvard University Press, 1928).

Clarke, JA, 'Fichte's Independence Thesis' in G Gottlieb (ed), *Fichte's Foundations of Natural Right* (Cambridge, Cambridge University Press, 2016) 52–71.

Cohen, FS, 'Transcendental Nonsense and the Functional Approach' (1935) 35 *Columbia Law Review* 809–49.

——, 'Modern Ethics and the Law' reprinted in L Kramer Cohen (ed), *The Legal Conscience: Selected Papers of Felix S. Cohen* (New Haven, CT, Yale University Press, 1966) 17–32.

Cohen, JA, '"Rule of law" with Chinese characterisics: Evolution and manipulation' (2021) 19 *International Journal of Constitution Law* 1882–87.

Coleman, J, 'Negative and Positive Positivism' (1982) 11(1) *Journal of Legal Studies* 139–64.

Darwall, S, *The Second-Personal Standpoint: Morality, Respect, and Accountability* (Cambridge, MA, Harvard University Press, 2006).

——, 'Authority and Second-Personal Reasons for Acting' in S Darwall, *Morality, Authority, and Law: Essays in Second-Personal Ethics I* (Oxford, Oxford University Press, 2013) 135–50.

——, *Modern Moral Philosophy: From Grotius to Kant* (Cambridge, Cambridge University Press, 2023).

Davidson, D, 'On the Very Idea of a Conceptual Scheme' in D Davidson, *Inquiries into Truth and Interpretation* (Oxford, Oxford University Press 1984) 183–98.

Davis, M, *The Soul of the Greeks: An Inquiry* (Chicago, IL, University of Chicago Press, 2011).

Descartes, R, *Meditations on First Philosophy*, 2nd edn (trans J Cottingham, Cambridge, Cambridge University Press, 2007).

du Roy, O, 'The Golden Rule as the Law of Nature from Origen to Martin Luther' in J Neusner and B Chilton (eds), *The Golden Rule: The Ethics of Reciprocity in World Religions* (London, Continuum, 2008) 88–98.

Duke, G, 'Aristotle and Natural Law' (2020) 82 *Review of Politics* 1–23.

Duns Scotus, J, *Philosophical Writings* (trans A Wolter, Indianapolis, IN, Hackett, 1987).

——, *Selected Writings on Ethics* (trans T Williams, Oxford, Oxford University Press, 2017).

Dworkin, R, *Taking Rights Seriously*, 2nd edn (Cambridge, MA, Harvard University Press, 1978).

——, *A Matter of Principle* (Cambridge, MA, Harvard University Press, 1986).

——, *Law's Empire* (Cambridge, MA, Harvard University Press, 1986).

——, 'Objectivity and Truth: You'd Better Believe It' (1996) 25 *Philosophy and Public Affairs* 87–139.

——, *Justice in Robes* (Cambridge, MA, Harvard University Press, 2006).

——, *Justice for Hedgehogs* (Cambridge, MA, Harvard University Press, 2011).

Dyzenhaus, D, 'Hobbes' Constitutional Theory' in T Hobbes, *Leviathan* (ed I Shapiro, New Haven, CT, Yale University Press, 2010), 453–80.

Elster, J, *Nuts and Bolts for the Social Sciences* (Cambridge, Cambridge University Press, 1989).

Empiricus, Sextus, *Outlines of Skepticism* (ed J Annas and J Barnes, Cambridge, Cambridge University Press, 2000).

Ferrari, GRF, *City and Soul in Plato's Republic* (Chicago, IL, University of Chicago Press, 2003).

Fichte, IH, *Die Idee der Persönlichkeit und der individuellen Fortdauer*, 2nd edn (Leipzig, Dyk'sche Buchhandlung, 1855).

Fichte, JG, *Grundlage des Naturrechts nach Prinzipien der Wissenschaftslehre* (ed F Medicus, Hamburg, Meiner, 1979).

——, *Foundations of Natural Right According to the Principles of the* Wissenschaftslehre (trans M Baur, Cambridge, Cambridge University Press, 2000).

Finnis, J, *Natural Law and Natural Rights* (Oxford, Clarendon Press, 1980).

Fish, S, 'The Law Wishes to Have a Formal Existence' in S Fish, *There's No Such Thing as Free Speech* (New York, Oxford University Press, 1994) 141–79.

Foster, P, *Peirce and the Threat of Nominalism* (Cambridge, Cambridge University Press, 2011).

Fox-Decent, E, 'Hobbes' Relational Theory: Beneath Power and Consent' in D Dyzenhaus and T Poole (ed), *Hobbes and the Law* (Cambridge, Cambridge University Press, 2012) 118–44.

Frank, J, *Law and the Modern Mind* (New York, Brentano's, 1930).

Frankfurt, HG, *The Importance of What We Care About: Philosophical Essays* (Cambridge, Cambridge University Press, 1988).

Franks, PW, *All or Nothing: Systematicity, Transcendental Arguments, and Skepticism in German Idealism* (Cambridge, MA, Harvard University Press, 2005).

Freeman, AD, 'Legitimizing Racial Discrimination through Antidiscrimination Law' (1978) 62 *Minnesota Law Review* 1049–1119.

Fuller, LL, *The Morality of Law* (New Haven, CT, Yale University Press, 1969).

Gabel, P and Kennedy, D, 'Roll over Beethoven' (1984) 36 *Stanford Law Review* 1–55.

Gabriel, M, *Antike und moderne Skepsis zur Einführung* (Hamburg, Junius, 2008).

——, *Transcendental Ontology: Essays on German Idealism* (New York and London, Continuum, 2011).

Gamm, G, *Flucht aus der Kategorie: Die Positivierung des Unbestimmten als Ausgang der Moderne* (Frankfurt aM, Suhrkamp, 1994).

Gauthier, D, *Morals by Agreement* (Oxford, Clarendon Press, 1986).

——, *Moral Dealing: Contract, Ethics, and Reason* (Ithaca, NY, Cornell University Press, 1990).

George, R, *In Defense of Natural Law* (Oxford, Oxford University Press, 1999).

Gilligan, C, *In a Different Voice: Psychological Theory and Women's Development* (Cambridge, MA, Harvard University Press, 1982).

Goetz, S and Taliaferro, C, *A Brief History of the Soul* (Oxford, Wiley-Blackwell, 2011).

Grotius, H, *On the Law of War and Peace* (student edn, ed SC Neff, Cambridge, Cambridge University Press, 2012).

Guyer, P, *Knowledge, Reason, and Taste: Kant's Response to Hume* (Princeton, NJ, Princeton University Press, 2008).

Habermas, J, 'Erkenntnis und Interesse' in J Habermas, *Technik und Wissenschaft als 'Ideologie'* (Frankfurt aM, Suhrkamp, 1968) 146–68.

——, *Erkenntnis und Interesse*, 2nd edn (Frankfurt aM, Suhrkamp, 1973).

——, 'Legitimationsprobleme im modernen Staat' in J Habermas, *Zur Rekonstruktion des Historischen Materialismus* (Frankfurt aM, Suhrkamp, 1976) 271–303.

——, 'Was heißt Universalpragmatik?' in K-O Apel (ed), *Sprachpragmatik und Philosophie* (Frankfurt aM, Suhrkamp, 1976) 174–273.

——, *Theorie und Praxis: Sozialphilosophische Studien*, 2nd edn (Frankfurt aM, Suhrkamp, 1980).

——, *Theorie des kommunikativen Handelns*, vol 1: *Handlungsrationalität und gesellschaftliche Rationalisierung* (Frankfurt aM, Suhrkamp, 1981).

——, *Theorie des kommunikativen Handelns*, vol 2: *Zur Kritik der funktionalistischen Vernunft* (Frankfurt aM, Suhrkamp, 1981).

——, *Moralbewusstsein und kommunikatives Handeln* (Frankfurt aM, Suhrkamp, 1983).

——, 'Wahrheitstheorien' in J Habermas, *Vorstudien und Ergänzungen zur Theorie des kommunikativen Handelns* (Frankfurt aM, Suhrkamp, 1984) 127–86.

——, *Der philosophische Diskurs der Moderne: Zwölf Vorlesungen* (Frankfurt aM, Suhrkamp, 1985).

——, 'Handlungen, Sprechakte, sprachlich vermittelte Interaktionen und Lebenswelt' in J Habermas, *Nachmetaphysisches Denken: Philosophische Aufsätze* (Frankfurt aM, Suhrkamp 1988) 63–104.

——, *Faktizität und Geltung: Beiträge zur Diskurs-theorie des Rechts und des demokratischen Rechtsstaats* (Frankfurt aM, Suhrkamp, 1991).

——, *Wahrheit und Rechtfertigung: Philosophische Aufsätze* (Frankfurt aM, Suhrkamp, 1999).

——, 'Dialectical Idealism in Transition of Materialism: Schelling's Idea of a Contraction of God and its Consequences for the Philosophy of History' (trans N Midgley and J Norman) in J Norman and A Welchman (eds), *The New Schelling* (London, Continuum, 2004) 43–89.

——, *Nachmetaphysisches Denken: Aufsätze und Reden*, vol 2 (Berlin, Suhrkamp, 2012).

——, *Auch eine Geschichte der Philosophie*, vol 1: *Die okzidentale Konstellation von Glauben und Wissen* (Berlin, Suhrkamp, 2019).

——, *Auch eine Geschichte der Philosophie*, vol 2: *Vernünftige Freiheit. Spuren des Diskurses über Glauben und Wissen* (Berlin, Suhrkamp, 2019).

Hales, SD, *Relativism and the Foundations of Philosophy* (Cambridge, MA, MIT Press, 2006).

Halliday, PD, *Habeas Corpus: From England to Empire* (Cambridge, MA, Harvard University Press, 2010).

Halpin, A, *Rights and Law: Analysis and Theory* (Oxford, Hart Publishing, 1997).

Hamilton, A, Madison, J and Jay, J, *The Federalist* (ed C Sunstein, Cambridge, MA, Harvard University Press, 2009).

Hare, RM, *Moral Thinking: Its Levels, Method and its Point* (Oxford, Oxford University Press, 1981).

Harrison, R, 'The Equal Extent of Natural and Civil Law' in D Dyzenhaus and T Poole (eds), *Hobbes and the Law* (Cambridge, Cambridge University Press, 2012) 22–38.

Hart, HLA, 'Positivism and the Separation of Law and Morals' (1958) 71 *Harvard Law Review* 593–621.

——, *The Concept of Law* (Oxford, Clarendon Press, 1961; 2nd edn 1994).

Harvey, M, 'Grotius and Hobbes' (2006) 14 *British Journal of the History of Philosophy* 27–50.

Hausman, DM and MS McPherson, *Economic Analysis and Moral Philosophy* (Cambridge, Cambridge University Press, 1996).

Hegel, GWF, 'Über die wissenschaftlichen Behandlungsarten des Naturrechts, seine Stelle in der praktischen Philosophie und sein Verhältnis zu den positiven Rechtswissenschaften' in GWF Hegel, *Werke in zwanzig Bänden*, vol 2 (ed M Moldenhauer and KM Michel, Frankfurt aM, Suhrkamp, 1969–71).

——, *Enzyklopädie der philosophischen Wissenschaften im Grundrisse*, Part III: *Werke in zwanzig Bänden*, vol 10 (ed E Moldenhauer and KM Michel, Frankfurt aM, Suhrkamp 1969–71).

——, *Phänomenologie des Geistes* (ed H-F Wessels and H Clairmont, Hamburg, Meiner, 1988).

——, *Elements of the Philosophy of Right* (trans HB Nisbet, Cambridge, Cambridge University Press, 1991).

——, *System der Sittlichkeit [Critik des Fichteschen Naturrechts]* (ed HD Brandt, Hamburg, Meiner, 2002).

Heidegger, M, *Sein und Zeit*, 14th edn (Tübingen, Max Niemeyer, 1977).

Heidemann, DH, *Der Begriff des Skeptizismus: Seine systematischen Formen, die pyrrhonische Skepsis und Hegels Herausforderung* (Berlin & New York, de Gruyter, 2007).

Herzog, D, *Happy Slaves: A Critique of Consent Theory* (Chicago, IL, University of Chicago Press, 1989).

Hobbes, T, *Behemoth or The Long Parliament* (ed F Tönnies, reprint Chicago, IL, Chicago University Press, 1990).

——, *A Dialogue between a Philosopher and a Student of the Common Laws of England* (ed J Cropskey, Chicago, IL, University of Chicago Press, 1997).

——, *On the Citizen* (trans R Tuck and M Silverstone, Cambridge, Cambridge University Press, 1997).

——, *Leviathan* (ed I Shapiro, New Haven, CT, Yale University Press, 2010).

Hochstrasser, TJ, *Natural Law Theories in the Early Enlightenment* (Cambridge, Cambridge University Press, 2000).

Höffe, O, *Kants Kritik der reinen Vernunft: Die Grundlegung der modernen Philosophie* (Munich, Beck, 2003).

——, *Kants Kritik der praktischen Vernunft: Eine Philosophie der Freiheit* (Munich, Beck, 2012).

Hohfeld, WN, *Fundamental Legal Conceptions as Applied in Judicial Reasoning* (ed WW Cook, New Haven, CT, Yale University Press, 1964).

Holmes, OW, 'The Path of the Law' (1897) 10 *Harvard Law Review* 457–78.

Honnefelder, L, *Johannes Duns Scotus: Denker an der Schwelle vom mittelalterlichen zum neuzeitlichen Denken* (Paderborn, Schöningh, 2011).

Honneth, A, *Kampf um Anerkennung: Zur moralischen Grammatik sozialer Konflikte* (Frankfurt aM, Suhrkamp, 1992).

——, *Freedom's Right: The Social Foundations of Democratic Life* (Cambridge, Polity Press, 2014).

——, *Die Idee des Sozialismus: Versuch einer Aktualisierung* (Berlin, Suhrkamp, 2015).

Horn, C, *Nicht-Ideale Normativität: Ein neuer Blick auf Kants politische Philosophie* (Berlin, Suhrkamp, 2014).

Humboldt, W von, *The Limits of State Action* (ed J Borrow, Cambridge, Cambridge University Press, 1969).

Hume, D, *A Treatise of Human Nature* (ed EG Mossner, London, Penguin, 1969).

——, 'Of the Coalition of Parties' reprinted in *Political Writings* (ed SD Warner and DW Livingstone, Indianapolis, IN, Hackett Publishing, 1994) 142–49.

——, 'Of the Original Contract' in *Political Writings* (ed SD Warner and DW Livingstone, Indianapolis, IN, Hackett Publishing, 1994) 164–82.

——, 'Of the Origin of Government' in *Political Writings* (ed SD Warner and DW Livingstone, Indianapolis, IN, Hackett Publishing, 1994) 194–97.

——, 'Of the First Principles of Government' in *Political Essays* (ed K Haakonssen, Cambridge, Cambridge University Press, 2012) 16–19.

Hutchinson, AC, 'Of Kings and Dirty Rascals: The Struggle for Democracy' (1984) 9 *Queen's Law Journal* 273–92.

Inwood, B, Stoicism: *A Very Short Introduction* (Oxford, Oxford University Press 2018).

James, D, *Fichte's Social and Political Philosophy: Property and Virtue* (Cambridge, Cambridge University Press, 2011).

Jellinek, G, *System der subjektiven öffentlichen Rechte*, 2nd edn (Tübingen, Mohr, 1905).

Jeuland, E, *Theories of Legal Relations* (Cheltenham, Edward Elgar, 2023).

Jhering, R von, *Geist des römischen Rechts auf den verschiedenen Stufen seiner Entwicklung*, vol 1, 6th edn (Leipzig, Breitkopf und Härtel, 1907).

Johnson, R and Cureton, A, 'Kant's Moral Philosophy' in *Stanford Encyclopedia of Philosophy* at https://plato.stanford.edu/entries/kant-moral/.

Kalman, L, *Legal Realism at Yale: 1927–1960* (Chapel Hill, NC, North Carolina University Press, 1986).

Kant, I, *Die Metaphysik der Sitten, Werke in zwölf Bänden*, vol 8 (ed W Weischedel, Frankfurt aM, Suhrkamp, 1968).

——, 'On the Common Saying: That May be Correct in Theory, but It is does not Apply in Practice' in *Kant's Political Philosophy* (trans HB Nisbeth, Cambridge, Cambridge University Press, 1970) 61–92.

——, *Metaphysische Anfangsgründe der Rechtslehre* (ed B Ludwig, Hamburg, Meiner, 1986).

——, *Critique of Pure Reason* (trans P Guyer and A Wood, Cambridge, Cambridge University Press, 1998).

——, *Kritik der reinen Vernunft* (ed J Timmermann, Hamburg, Meiner 1998).

——, *Grundlegung zur Metaphysik der Sitten* (ed B Kraft and D Schönecker, Hamburg, Meiner, 1999).

——, *Kritik der praktischen Vernunft* (ed HD Brandt and H Klemme, Hamburg, Meiner, 2003).

——, 'Idea for a Universal History from a Cosmopolitan Perspective' in I Kant, *Toward Perpetual Peace and Other Writings on Politics, Peace, and History* (trans DL Colclasure, ed P Kleingeld, New Haven, CT, Yale University Press, 2006) 3–16.

Kelman, M, *A Guide to Critical Legal Studies* (Cambridge, MA, Harvard University Press, 1988).

Kelsen, H, *Pure Theory of Law* (trans M Knight, Berkeley, CA, University of California Press, 1967).

——, *Introduction to the Problems of Legal Theory* (trans B Litschewski Paulson and SL Paulson, Oxford, Clarendon Press, 1992).

Kennedy, D, 'Form and Substance in Private Law Adjudication' (1976) 89 *Harvard Law Review* 1685–1778.

——, 'The Effect of the Warranty of Habitability on Low Income Housing: "Milking" and Class Violence' (1987) 15 *Florida State University Law Review* 485–519.

Klare, KE, 'Judicial Deradicalization of the Wagner Act and the Origins of Modern Legal Consciousness, 1937–1941' (1978) 62 *Minnesota Law Review* 265–339.

Koller, P, 'Gesellschaftsauffassung und soziale Gerechtigkeit' in G Frankenberg (ed), *Auf der Suche nach der gerechten Gesellschaft* (Frankfurt aM, Fischer, 1994).

Komárek, J, 'Freedom and Power of European Constitutional Law Scholarship' (2021) 17 *European Constitutional Law Review* 422–41.

Korsgaard, CM, *Creating the Kingdom of Ends* (Cambridge, Cambridge University Press, 1996).

——, *The Sources of Normativity* (Cambridge, Cambridge University Press, 1996).

——, *The Constitution of Agency: Essays on Practical Reason and Moral Psychology* (Oxford, Oxford University Press, 2008).

——, *Self-Constitution: Agency, Identity, Integrity* (Oxford, Oxford University Press, 2009).

Kramer, M, 'On the Moral Status of the Rule of Law' (2004) 63 *Cambridge Law Journal* 65–97.

Kripke, SA, *Wittgenstein on Rules and Privat Language: An Elementary Exposition* (Cambridge, MA, Harvard University Press, 1982).

Lauterpacht, H, 'The Grotian Tradition in International Law' (1946) 23 *British Yearbook of International Law* 1–53.

Lewis, D, *Convention: A Philosophical Study* (Oxford, Basil Blackwell, 1968).

Lloyd, S, *Morality in the Philosophy of Thomas Hobbes* (Cambridge, Cambridge University Press, 2009).

Locke, J, *Two Treatises of Government* (ed P Laslett, Cambridge, Cambridge University Press, 1960).

Loughlin, M, 'The Political Jurisprudence of Thomas Hobbes' in M Loughlin, *Political Jurisprudence* (Oxford, Oxford University Press, 2017) 22–34.

Lukes, S, *Moral Relativism* (New York, Picador, 2008).

Machiavelli, N, *The Prince* (trans HC Mansfield, Cambridge, MA, Harvard University Press, 1985).

MacIntyre, A, *After Virtue*, 2nd edn (Notre Dame, IN, Notre Dame University Press, 1982).

Mackie, JL, *Ethics: Inventing Right and Wrong* (London, Penguin Books, 1990; 1st edn 1977).

Madison, J, 'Memorial and Remonstrance Against Religious Assessments' in J Madison, *Writings* (ed J Rakove, New York, Library of America, 1999) 29–36.

Mangabeira Unger, R, 'The Critical Legal Studies Movement' (1983) 96 *Harvard Law Review* 561–675.

——, *Passion: An Essay on Personality* (New York, Free Press, 1986).

——, *Social Theory: Its Situation and its Task* (Cambridge, Cambridge University Press, 1988).

——, *What Should Legal Analysis Become?* (London, Verso, 1996).

Mansfield, HC, *Machiavelli's Virtue* (Chicago, IL, Chicago University Press, 1996).

Marmor, A, *Social Conventions: From Language to Law* (Princeton, Princeton University Press, 2009).

——, *Philosophy of Law* (Princeton, NJ, Princeton University Press, 2011).

McCormick, JP, *Machiavellian Democracy* (Cambridge, Cambridge University Press, 2011).

McDowell, J, 'Virtue and Reason' in J McDowell, *Mind, Value, and Reality* (Cambridge, MA, Harvard University Press, 1998) 50–73.

McGrade, AS, 'Natural Law and Moral Omnipotence' in PV Spade (ed), *The Cambridge Companion to Ockham* (Cambridge, Cambridge University Press, 2006).

McGrath, SJ, *The Dark Ground of Spirit: Schelling and the Unconscious* (London, Routledge, 2012).

McMahon, C, *Reasonable Disagreement: A Theory of Political Morality* (Cambridge, Cambridge University Press, 2009).

——, *Reasonableness and Fairness: A Historical Theory* (Cambridge, Cambridge University Press, 2016).

Mead, GH, *Mind, Self, and Society from the Standpoint of a Social Behaviorist* (ed C Morris, Chicago, IL, Chicago University Press, 1934).

Meinwald, C, *Plato* (London, Routledge, 2016).

Melzer, AM, 'Rousseau's Moral Realism: Replacing Natural Law with the General Will' (1983) 77 *American Political Science Review* 633–51.

Menke, C, 'Liberalismus im Konflikt: Zwischen Gerechtigkeit und Freiheit' in M Brumlik and H Brunkhorst (eds). *Gemeinschaft und Gerechtigkeit* (Frankfurt aM, Fischer, 1993) 218–243.

——, *Tragödie im Sittlichen: Gerechtigkeit und Freiheit nach Hegel* (Frankfurt aM, Suhrkamp, 1996).

——, *Autonomie und Befreiung: Studien zu Hegel* (Berlin, Suhrkamp, 2019).

——, *Theorie der Befreiung* (Berlin, Suhrkamp, 2022).

Mercuro, N and SG Medema, *Economics and the Law: From Posner to Post-Modernism* (Princeton, NJ, Princeton University Press, 1997).

Messner, J, *Social Ethics: Natural Law in the Western World*, 2nd edn (trans JJ Doherty, St Louis, MO, B Herder Book Co, 1965).

——, *Das Naturrecht: Handbuch der Gesellschaftsethik, Staatsethik und Wirtschaftsethik*, 8th edn (Berlin, Duncker & Humblot 2018).

Mill, JS, *Considerations on Representative Government* (orig edn 1861, Buffalo, NY, Prometheus Books, 1991).

Miller, CB, 'Moral Relativism and Moral Psychology' in S Hales (ed), *Companion to Relativism* (Oxford, Wiley-Blackwell, 2011).

Miller, FD Jr, 'The Rule of Reason in Plato's Statesman and the American Federalist' (2007) 24 *Social Philosophy and Policy* 90–129.

——, 'The rule of reason' in M Deslauries and P Destreé (eds), *The Cambridge Companion to* Aristotle's *Politics* (Cambridge, Cambridge University Press, 2013) 38–66.

Misak, C, *The American Pragmatists* (Oxford, Oxford University Press, 2013).

Möhle, H, 'Scotus' Theory of Natural Law' in T Williams (ed), *The Cambridge Companion to Duns Scotus* (Cambridge, Cambridge University Press, 2003) 312–31.

Moyn, S, *The Last Utopia: Human Rights in History* (Cambridge, Mass., Harvard University Press, 2010).

Nagel, T, *The Possibility of Altruism* (Princeton, NJ, Princeton University Press, 1970).

——, *The View from Nowhere* (New York, Oxford University Press, 1986).

——, *What Does it All Mean? A Very Short Introduction to Philosophy* (New York, Oxford University Press, 1987).

——, *The Last Word* (New York, Oxford University Press, 1997).

Nedelsky, J, *Law's Relations: A Relational Theory of Self, Autonomy, and Law* (Oxford, Oxford University Press, 2013).

Nelson, E, *The Theology of Liberalism: Political Philosophy and the Justice of God* (Cambridge, MA, Harvard University Press, 2019).

Neuhouser, F, *Rousseau's Theodicy of Self-Love: Evil, Rationality and the Desire for Recognition* (Oxford, Oxford University Press, 2010).

——, *Rousseau's Critique of Inequality: Reconstructing the Second Discourse* (Cambridge, Cambridge University Press, 2014).

——, 'Fichte's Separation of Right from Morality' in G Gottlieb (ed), *Fichte's Foundation of Natural Right* (Cambridge, Cambridge University Press, 2016) 32–52.

Nietzsche, F, *Die fröhliche Wissenschaft*, 2nd edn (Leipzig, EW Fritsch, 1887).

——, *Unzeitgemäße Betrachtungen*, vol 2, 8th edn (Leipzig, CG Naumann, 1899).

Nozick, R, *Anarchy, State, and Utopia* (New York, Basic Books, 1974).

O'Neill, O, *Acting on Principle: An Essay on Kantian Ethics*, 2nd edn (Cambridge, Cambridge University Press, 2013).

Oakeshott, M, *On Human Conduct* (Oxford, Oxford University Press, 1975).

——, *Rationalism in politics and other essays* (Indianapolis, IN, Liberty Fund, 1991).

——, 'The Rule of Law' in M Oakeshott, *On History and Other Essays* (Indianapolis, IN, Liberty Fund, 1999) 129–79.

Oakley, F, 'Medieval Theories of Natural Law: William of Ockham and the Significance of the Voluntarist Tradition' (1961) *Natural Law Forum* 65–83.

——, *Natural Law, Laws of Nature, Natural Rights: Continuity and Discontinuity in the History of Ideas* (New York, Continuum, 2005).

Orwell, G, *Nineteen Eighty-Four* (London, Harcourt Brace and Co, 1949; London, Penguin Books, 1983).

——, *The Road to Wigan Pier* (London, Penguin Books, 1989).

Pappas, N, *The Routledge Guidebook to Plato's Republic*, 3rd edn (London, Routledge, 2013)

Parfit, D, *Reasons and Persons* (Oxford, Clarendon Press, 1986).

——, *On What Matters*, vol 1 (ed S Scheffler, Oxford, Oxford University Press, 2011).

Pauer-Studer, H, *Einführung in die Ethik*, 3rd edn (Vienna, Facultas, 2020).

Pauly, W, 'Georg Jellineks "System der subjektiven öffentlichen Rechte"' in SL Paulson and M Schulte (eds), *Georg Jellinek – Beiträge zu Leben und Werk* (Tübingen, Mohr, 2000) 227–44.

Pavlakos, G, 'Redrawing the Legal Relation' in JL Fabra-Zamora (ed), *Jurisprudence in a Globalized World* (Cheltenham, Edward Elgar, 2020) 174–94

Peirce, CS, 'What Pragmatism Is' in PP Wiener (ed), *Charles S Peirce: Selected Writings* (New York, Dover Publications, 1966) 180–202.

——, 'How to Make Our Ideas Clear (1878)' in N Houser and C Kloesel (eds), *The Essential Peirce: Selected Philosophical Writings*, vol 1 (Bloomington, IN, Indiana University Press 1992) 124–41.

——, 'The Fixation of Belief' in N Houser and C Kloesel (eds), *The Essential Peirce: Selected Philosophical Writings*, vol 1 (Bloomington, IN, Indiana University Press 1992) 109–23.

——, 'Harvard Lectures on Pragmatism (1903)' in The Peirce Edition Project, *The Essential Peirce: Selected Philosophical Writings*, vol 2 (Bloomington, IN, Indiana University Press, 1998) 133–256.

Pinkard, T, *Hegel's Phenomenology: The Sociality of Reason* (Cambridge, Cambridge University Press, 1994).

Pippin, R, *Hegel's Idealism: The Satisfactions of Self-Consciousness* (Cambridge, Cambridge University Press, 1989).

——, *Hegel's Practical Philosophy: Rational Agency as Ethical Life* (Cambridge, Cambridge University Press, 2008).

Placani, A, 'Joseph Raz's Service Conception and the Limits of Knowablity' (2021) 34 *Ratio Iuris* 207–23.

Plato, *The Dialogues of Plato*, vol 1 (trans RE Allen, New Haven, CT, Yale University Press, 1984).

——, *The Republic of Plato*, 2nd edn (trans A Bloom, New York, Basic Books, 1991).

——, *Statesman* (trans R Waterfield, Cambridge, Cambridge University Press, 1995).

——, *The Republic*, 2nd edn (trans D Lee, London, Penguin Books, 2007).

——, *The Last Days of Socrates: Euthyphro, Apology, Crito, Phaedo* (ed C Rowe, London, Penguin Books, 2010).

——, *Laws* (trans T Griffith, Cambridge, Cambridge University Press, 2016).

Pollman, T and Stinson, JM, *Legal Writing*, 4th edn (Waltham, MA, Aspen, 2023).

Poole, T, 'Hobbes on Law and Prerogative' in D Dyzenhaus and T Poole (eds), *Hobbes and the Law* (Cambridge, Cambridge University Press, 2012) 68–96.

Posner, RA, *Economic Analysis of Law*, 3rd edn (Boston, MA, Little Brown, 1986).

Pufendorf, S, *On the Duty of Man and Citizen According to Natural Law* (trans M Silverthorne, Cambridge, Cambridge University Press, 1991).

Putnam, H, *Reason, Truth and History* (Cambridge, Cambridge University Press, 1981).

Quint, PE, 'The Border Guard Trials and the East German Past — Seven Arguments' (2002) 48 *American Journal of Comparative Law* 541–72.

Radbruch, G, 'Statutory Lawlessness and Supra-statutory Law (1946)' (2006) 26 *Oxford Journal of Legal Studies* 1–11 (trans B Litschewski Paulson and SL Paulson).

Rawls, J, *A Theory of Justice* (Cambridge, MA, Harvard University Press, 1971).

——, *Political Liberalism* (New York, Columbia University Press, 1991).

——, *The Law of Peoples* (Cambridge, MA, Harvard University Press, 1999).

——, *Justice as Fairness: A Restatement* (ed E Kelly, Cambridge, MA, Harvard University Press, 2001).

Raz, J, *The Authority of Law: Essays on Law and Morality* (Oxford, Clarendon Press, 1979).

——, *The Concept of a Legal System: An Introduction to the Theory of the Legal System*, 2nd edn (Oxford, Clarendon Press, 1980).

——, *The Morality of Freedom* (Oxford, Oxford University Press, 1986).

——, *Practical Reason and Norms*, 2nd edn (Princeton, NJ, Princeton University Press, 1990).

——, 'Authority, Law, and Morality' in J Raz, *Ethics in the Public Domain: Essays in the Morality of Law and Politics* (rev edn, Oxford, Oxford University Press, 1995) 210–37.

——, 'The Obligation to Obey: Revision and Tradition' in J Raz, *Ethics in the Public Domain: Essays in the Morality of Law and Politics* (rev edn, Oxford, Oxford University Press, 1995) 341–55.

——, 'The Purity of the Pure Theory' in SL Paulson and BL Paulson (eds), *Normativity and Norms: Critical Perspectives on Kelsenian Themes* (Oxford, Clarendon Press, 1998) 237–252.

——, 'The Problem of Authority: Revisting the Service Conception' in J Raz, *Between Authority and Interpretation: On the Theory of Law and Practical Reason* (Oxford, Oxford University Press, 2009) 126–65.

——, 'Legal Positivism and the Sources of Law' in J Raz, *The Authority of Law*, 2nd edn (Oxford, Oxford University Press, 2009) 37–52.

——, *From Normativity to Responsibility* (Oxford, Oxford University Press, 2011).

Ridge, M, 'Reasons for Action: Agent-Neutral v Agent-Relative' in *Stanford Encyclopedia of Philosophy* at https://plato.stanford.edu/archives/spr2023/entries/reasons-agent/.

Riesenhuber, K (ed), *Privatrechtsgesellschaft* (Tübingen, Mohr, 2009).

Riker, W, *Liberalism against Populism: A Confrontation Between the Theory of Democracy and the Theory of Social Choice* (San Francisco, CA, Waveland Press, 1982).

Riley, P, *The General Will before Rousseau: The Transformation of the Divine into the Civic* (Princeton, NJ, Princeton University Press, 1986).

Ripstein, A, *Force and Freedom: Kant's Legal and Political Philosophy* (Cambridge, MA, Harvard University Press, 2009).

——, *Private Wrongs* (Cambridge, MA, Harvard University Press, 2016).

Ritter, J, '"Naturrecht" bei Aristoteles' in J Ritter, *Metaphysik und Politik: Studien zu Aristoteles und Hegel* (Frankfurt aM, Suhrkamp, 1969) 133–81.

Robertson, D, *The Judge as a Political Theorist: Contemporary Constitutional Review* (Princeton, NJ, Princeton University Press, 2010).

Rorty, R, *Contingency, Irony, and Solidarity* (Cambridge, Cambridge University Press, 1988).

——, *Pragmatism as Anti-Authoritarianism* (ed E Mendieta, Cambridge, MA, Harvard University Press, 2021).

Rousseau, J-J, *The Social Contract* (trans C Betts, Oxford, Oxford University Press, 1994).

——, *Major Political Writings* (trans JT Scott, Chicago, IL, Chicago University Press, 2012).

Ruger, TW et al, 'The Supreme Court Forecasting Project: Legal and Political Science Approaches to Predicting Supreme Court Decisionmaking' (2004) 104 *Columbia Law Review* 1150–1209.

Rundle, K, *Forms Liberate: Reclaiming the Jurisprudence of Lon L Fuller* (Oxford, Hart Publishing, 2012).

Salmond, W, *Jurisprudence, or the Theory of the Law*, 2nd edn (London, Steven and Haynes, 1907).

Savigny, CF von, *System des heutigen Römischen Rechts*, vol 1 (Berlin, Veit & Comp, 1840).

Savigny, KF von, *Vom Beruf unserer Zeit für Gesetzgebung und Rechtswissenschaft* (Heidelberg, Mohr und Zimmer, 1814).

Scanlon, TM, *What We Owe to Each Other* (Cambridge, MA, Harvard University Press, 1998).

——, *Being Realistic about Reasons* (Oxford, Oxford University Press, 2014).

Schedler, A, 'Democratic Reciprocity' (2021) 29 *Journal of Political Philosophy* 252–78.

Schelling, FWJ, *System des transzendentalen Idealismus* (ed W. Schulz, Hamburg, Meiner, 1957).

——, *Ages of the World* (trans J Norman, Ann Arbor, MI, University of Michigan Press, 2001).

Schmitt, C, *Über die drei Arten des Rechtswissenschaftlichen Denkens* (Hamburg, Hanseatische Verlagsanstalt, 1934).

——, *On the Three Types of Juristic Thought* (trans J Bendersky, Westport, CT, Praeger, 2004).

Schneewind, JB, *The Invention of Autonomy: A History of Modern Moral Philosophy* (Cambridge, Cambridge University Press, 2010).

Schofield, M, *Cicero: Political Philosophy* (Oxford, Oxford University Press, 2021).

——, 'Cicero and Plato' in JW Atkins and T Bénatouïl (eds), *The Cambridge Companion to Cicero's Philosophy* (Cambridge, Cambridge University Press, 2022) 88–102.

Schönrich, G, *Kategorien und transzendentale Argumentation: Kant und die Idee einer transzendentalen Semiotik* (Frankfurt aM, Suhrkamp, 1981).

Schopenhauer, A, *Die Welt als Wille und Vorstellung*, vol 1.1 (ed A Hübscher, Zürich, Diogenes, 1977).

Schriefl, A, *Stoische Philosophie: Eine Einführung* (Stuttgart, Reclam, 2023).

Schröder, J, 'Entwicklungstendenzen der juristischen Interpretationstheorie von 1500–1850' in J Schönert and F Vollhardt (eds), *Geschichte der Hermeneutik und die Methodik der textinterpretierenden Disziplinen* (Berlin, de Gryuter, 2005) 203–19.

Shaffer, G and Sandholtz, W (eds), *The Rule of Law under Pressure* (Cambridge, Cambridge University Press, 2025).

Shields, C and Pasnau, R, *The Philosophy of Aquinas*, 2nd edn (Oxford, Oxford University Press, 2016).

Shklar, JN, *After Utopia: The Decline of Political Faith* (ed S Moyn, Princeton, NJ, Princeton University Press, 2020).

Sibley, WM, 'The Rational Versus the Reasonable' (1953) 62 *Philosophical Review* 554–60.

Sidgwick, H, *The Method of Ethics*, 7th edn (Indianapolis, IN, Hackett Publishing, 1981).

——, *The Method of Ethics*, 7th edn (London, Hackett, 1987).

Simmonds, NE, *Law as a Moral Idea* (Oxford, Oxford University Press, 2007).

Simmonds, N and Neoh, J, *Central Issues in Jurisprudence*, 6th edn (London, Sweet & Maxwell, 2022).

Simmons, AJ, 'Authority' in D Estlund (ed), *The Oxford Handbook of Political Philosophy* (Oxford, Oxford University Press, 2012) 23–39.

Singer, JW, 'The Legal Rights Debate in Analytical Jurisprudence from Bentham to Hohfield' (1982) *Wisconsin Law Review* 975–1059.

——, 'The Player and the Cards: Nihilism and Legal Theory' (1984) 94 *Yale Law Journal* 1–70.

Singer, MG, *Generalization in Ethics: An Essay on the Logic of Ethics, with Rudiments of a System of Moral Philosophy* (New York, Alfred A Knopf, 1961).

Solumn, LB, 'On the Indeterminacy Crisis: Critiquing Critical Legal Dogma' (1987) 54 *University of Chicago Law Review* 462–503.

Somek, A, *Rechtssystem und Republik: Über die politische Funktion des systematischen Rechtsdenkens* (Vienna and New York, Springer, 1992).

——, 'Die Macht der juristischen Expertise: Rechtliches Wissen als Steuerungsmedium' in K Lerch (ed), *Sprache und Recht*, vol 3 (Berlin, de Gruyter 2005) 399–438.

——, 'Delegation and Authority: Authoritarian Liberalism Today' (2015) 21 *European Law Journal* 340–60.

——, *The Legal Relation: Legal Theory after Legal Positivism* (Cambridge, Cambridge University Press, 2017).

——, *Wissen des Rechts* (Tübingen, Mohr, 2018).

——, 'Ex facto ius oritur' in N Bersier-Ladavac, C Bezemek and F Schauer (eds), *The Normative Force of the Factual* (New York, Springer 2019) 121–34.

——, 'Legality and the Legal Relation' (2020) 33 *Ratio Iuris* 307–16.

——, 'Real Constitutional Law: A Revised Madisonian Perspective' in C Bezemek, M Potacs and A Somek (eds), *Vienna Lectures in Legal Philosophy*, vol 2 (Oxford, Hart Publishing 2020) 161–83.

——, *Knowing What the Law Is: Legal Theory in a New Key* (Oxford, Hart Publishing, 2021).

——, 'Über die Subjektivität des Rechts' (2021) 76 *Juristenzeitung* 1–7.

——, 'Herrschaft und Knechtschaft im Staatsrecht' in R Hofmann et al (eds), *Festschrift für Franz Merli* (Baden-Baden, Nomos, 2023) 851–63.

——, 'Parchment Barriers: The Constitution as Law' (2024) 20 *European Constitutional Law Review* 120–45.

Stick, J, 'Can Nihilism be Pragmatic?' (1986) 100 *Harvard Law Review* 332–401.

Straumann, B, *Roman Law in the State of Nature: The Classical Foundations of Hugo Grotius' Natural Law* (Cambridge, Cambridge University Press, 2015).

Strauss, L, *Natural Right and History* (Chicago, IL, University of Chicago Press, 1953).

Street, S, 'How to be a Relativist about Normativity' at www.academia.edu/19887937/How_to_Be_a_Relativist_About_Normativity.

——, 'In Defense of Future Tuesday Indifference: Ideally Coherent Eccentrics and the Contingency of What Matters' (2009) 19 *Philosophical Issues* 273–98.

——, 'Coming to Terms with Contingency: Humean Constructivism about Practical Reason' in J Leuman and Y Shemmer (eds), *Constructivism in Practical Philosophy* (Oxford, Oxford University Press, 2012) 40–59.

——, 'Objectivity and Truth: You'd Better Rethink It' in R Shafer-Landau (ed), *Oxford Studies in Metaethics: 11* (Oxford, Oxford University Press, 2016) 293–334.

——, 'Nothing "Really" Matters, but That's Not What Matters' in P Singer (ed), *Does Anything Really Matter? Essays on Parfit on Objectivity* (Oxford, Oxford University Press, 2017) 121–48.

Striker, G, 'The Role of oikeiôsis in Stoic Ethics' in G Striker, *Papers in Hellenistic Epistemology and Ethics* (Cambridge, Cambridge University Press, 1996) 281–97.

——, 'Aristotle's Ethics as Political Science' in G Striker, *From Aristotle to Cicero: Essays on Ancient Philosophy* (Oxford, Oxford University Press, 2022) 128–41.

——, 'Skepticism as a Kind of Philosophy' in G Striker, *From Aristotle to Cicero: Essays on Ancient Philosophy* (Oxford, Oxford University Press, 2022) 177–91.

——, 'Two Kinds of Deliberation' in G Striker, *From Aristotle to Cicero: Essays on Ancient Philosophy* (Oxford, Oxford University Press, 2022) 142–61.

Stroud, B, *The Significance of Philosophical Scepticism* (Oxford, Clarendon Press, 1984).

Suárez, F, *Treatise on Law and God the Lawgiver, in Selections from Three Works* (trans GL Williams et al, ed T Pink, Carmel, IN, Liberty Fund, 2015) 5–755.

Taylor, C, *Hegel* (Cambridge, Cambridge University Press, 1975).

——, *Philosophical Papers*, vol 1 (Cambridge, Cambridge University Press, 1985).

Thibaut, AFJ, *Theorie der logischen Auslegung des Römischen Rechts*, 2nd edn (Altona, Johann Friedrich Hammerich, 1806).

Thomasius, C, *Foundations of the Law of Nature and Nations (Selections)* in C Thomasius, *Institutes of Divine Jurisprudence* (trans T Ahnert, Indianapolis, IN, Liberty Fund, 2011).

Thompson, M, *Life and Action: Elementary Structures of Practice and Practical Thought* (Cambridge, MA, Harvard University Press, 2008).

Thomson, JJ, *The Realm of Rights* (Cambridge, MA, Harvard University Press, 1990).

Tuck, R, *Natural Rights Theories: Their Origin and Development* (Cambridge, Cambridge University Press, 1979).

Tuck, R, *Philosophy and Government 1572–1651* (Cambridge, Cambridge University Press, 1999).

Tuck, R, *The Rights of War and Peace: Political Thought and the International Order from Grotius to Kant* (Oxford, Oxford University Press, 1999).

Tushnet, M, 'Critical Legal Studies: A Political History' (1991) 100 *Yale Law Journal* 1515–40.

Vaihinger, H, *Die Philosophie des Als Ob: System der theoretischen, praktischen und religiösen Fiktionen der Menschheit auf Grund eines idealistischen Positivismus*, 9th edn (Leipzig, Felix Meiner, 1927).

Vander Waerdt, PA, 'Zeno's Republic and the Origins of Natural Law' in PA Vander Waerdt (ed), *The Socratic Movement* (Ithaca, NY, Cornell University Press, 1994).

Velleman, JD, *How We Get Along* (Cambridge, Cambridge University Press, 2009).

——, *The Possibility of Practical Reason*, 2nd edn (Ann Arbor, MI, Maize Books, 2015).

Vermeule, A, *The System of the Constitution* (Oxford, Oxford University Press, 2011).

——, The Constitution of Risk (Cambridge, Cambridge University Press, 2014).

——, *Common Good Constitutionalism: Recovering the Classical Legal Tradition* (Cambridge, Polity Press, 2022).

Vitoria, F de, *Political Writings* (trans A Pagden and J Lawrence, Cambridge, Cambridge University Press 1991).

Vogt, KM, 'Ancient Skepticism' in *Stanford Encyclopedia of Philosophy* at https://leibniz.stanford.edu/friends/members/preview/skepticism-ancient/.

——, *Law, Reason, and the Cosmic City* (Oxford, Oxford University Press, 2008).

——, *Belief and Truth: A Skeptic Reading of Plato* (Oxford, Oxford University Press, 2012).

——, *Skepsis und Lebenspraxis: Das pyrrhonische Leben ohne Meinungen*, 2nd edn (Freiburg, Karl Alber Verlag, 2015).

——, 'The Stoics on Virtue and Happiness' in C Bononich (ed), *The Cambridge Companion to Ancient Ethics* (Cambridge, Cambridge University Press, 2017) 183–99.

——, 'The Stoic Conception of Law' (2021) 38 *Polis: The Journal for Ancient Greek and Roman Political Thought* 557–72.

Vollrath, E, 'That All Governments Rest on Opinion' (1976) 43 *Social Research* 46–61.

von Bogdandy, A and Venzke, I, *In Whose Name? A Public Law Theory of International Adjudication* (Oxford, Oxford University Press, 2014).

von der Pfordten, D, *Rechtsethik*, 2nd edn (Munich, CH Beck, 2011).

Waldron, J, *Law and Disagreement* (Oxford, Oxford University Press, 1999).
Walzer, M, *Spheres of Justice: A Defense of Pluralism and Equality* (Oxford, Blackwell, 1989).
Ward, TM, 'A Most Mitigated Friar: Scotus on Natural Law and Divine Freedom' (2019) 93 *American Catholic Philosophical Quarterly* 385–409.
Weber, M, *Economy and Society*, vol 2 (trans E Fischoff et al, ed G Roth and C Wittich, Berkeley, CA, University of California Press, 1987).
——, *Economy and Society* (trans K Tribe, Cambridge, MA, Harvard University Press, 2019).
Weinrib, EJ, *The Idea of Private Law*, 2nd edn (Oxford, Oxford University Press, 2012).
——, 'Correlativity and Personality' in EJ Weinrib, *Corrective Justice* (Oxford, Oxford University Press, 2016) 9–37.
——, *Reciprocal Freedom: Private Law and Public Right* (Oxford, Oxford University Press, 2022).
West, C, *The American Evasion of Philosophy: A Genealogy of Pragmatism* (Madison, WI, University of Wisconsin Press, 1989).
Wieacker, F, *Privatrechtsgeschichte der Neuzeit: Unter besonderer Berücksichtigung der deutschen Entwicklung*, 2nd edn (Göttingen, Vandenhoek & Ruprecht, 1967).
Williams, T, 'John Duns Scotus' in *Stanford Encyclopedia of Philosophy* (2022) at https://plato.stanford.edu/entries/duns-scotus/ (pdf version).
Wimmer, A, *Rechtsverhältnisse im öffentlichen Recht: Ein Perspektivenwechsel* (Vienna, Verlag Österreich, 2019).
Wolf, U, *Aristoteles' 'Nikomachische Ethik'* (Darmstadt, Wissenschaftliche Buchgesellschaft, 2002).
Wolff, C, *Vernünftige Gedancken von der Menschen Tun und Lassen*, 7th edn (Halle, Rengerische Buchhandlung 1743).
Wolff, C, *Vernünftige Gedancken von Gott, der Welt und der Seele des Menschen*, 8th edn (Halle, Rengerische Buchhandlung, 1741).
Wood, AW, 'Deduction of the Summons and the Existence of Other Rational Beings' in G Gottlieb (ed), *Fichte's Foundation of Natural Right* (Cambridge, Cambridge University Press, 2016) 72–91.
Zizek, S, *The Indivisible Remainder: On Schelling and Related Matters* (London, Verso, 2007).

Index

www.ingramcontent.com/pod-product-compliance
Ingram Content Group UK Ltd.
Pitfield, Milton Keynes, MK11 3LW, UK
UKHW020245290926
15470UKWH00002B/741